GRANT AND TEMPERLEY'S
EUROPE IN THE NINETEENTH
AND TWENTIETH CENTURIES

Seventh Edition in two volumes

EUROPE IN THE
TWENTIETH CENTURY
1905 1970

Agatha Ramm

LONGMAN
London and New York

LONGMAN GROUP LIMITED
Longman House, Burnt Mill, Harlow
Essex CM20 2JE, England
Associated companies throughout the world

*Published.in the United States of America
by Longman Inc., New York*

First published (as Europe in the Nineteenth Century) 1927
Fourth edition (Europe in the Nineteenth and
Twentieth Centuries) 1952
Sixth edition 1971
First issued in paperback 1971
Seventh edition by Agatha Ramm (in two volumes) 1984
Second impression 1985
Third impression 1986

BRITISH LIBRARY CATALOGUING IN PUBLICATION DATA
Grant, Arthur James
  Grant and Temperley's Europe in the nineteenth and
  twentieth centuries.-7th ed. in 2 vols.
  Vol. 2: Europe in the twentieth century, 1905–1970
  1. Europe–Civilization–19th century
  2. Europe–Civilization–20th century
  I. Title   II. Temperley, H. N. V.
  II. Ramm, Agatha
  940.2   CB415

ISBN 0-582-49029-4

LIBRARY OF CONGRESS CATALOGING IN PUBLICATION DATA
Grant, A. J. (Arthur James), 1862–1948.
  Grant and Temperley's Europe in the nineteenth and
twentieth centuries.

  Rev. ed. of: Europe in the nineteenth and twentieth
centuries, 6th ed. 1971.
  Includes bibliographical references and index.
  Contents: v. 1. Europe in the nineteenth century,
1789–1905–v. 2. Europe in the twentieth century,
1905–1970.
  1. Europe–History–1789–1900. 2. Europe–
History–20th century. I. Temperley, Harold William
Vazelle, 1879–1939. II. Ramm, Agatha. III. Title.
IV. Title: Europe in the nineteenth and twentieth centuries.

D299.G7 1984   940.2'8   83–11986
ISBN 0-582-49029-4 (v. 2)

Set in 10/11 pt Linotron 202 Times
Produced by Longman Singapore Publishers (Pte) Ltd.
Printed in Singapore.

The first part in this
sequence is available as

EUROPE IN THE NINETEEN
1789–1905 ·

by *Agatha Ramm*

CONTENTS

Contents

Contents

Contents

LIST OF MAPS

PREFACE

Dame Lillian Penson, who prepared the sixth edition of this work, died on April 17, 1963, and it seems fitting that this new edition should begin by acknowledging the value of her work. I should like also to acknowledge my own debt to her, who set the pattern of my own teaching and research. She records in her note to the sixth edition the death of Harold Temperley in July 1939 and of A. J. Grant 'who was his elder by several years' in May 1948. She writes that she, 'who was closely associated with both the original authors in historical work, was therefore able to discuss with Professor Grant the revision which has now taken place.' I have had no similar advantage. I must ask the indulgence of those who knew the earlier book both for the temerity with which I have cut, altered and perhaps injured the original work and for the absence of any personal participation, except as an observer, in the events which I narrate in the new chapters of Volume Two. The reader of the old work often had a vivid sense of personal contact with political events through the writing of the original authors, especially that of Harold Temperley. Dame Lillian in her note recorded the wish of the original authors 'that there should be successive editions which should maintain some at least of these characteristics and at the same time take into account the differing outlook of a new era.' This is my justification for what I have tried to do.

Taking account of a new outlook indicated that I should diminish the English reference of the old book. It is impossible nowadays to write of the continent of Europe as if it were seen by a more politically mature country with her revolution in the past and her parliamentary system the model for all to follow, or as if it were seen by the immensely powerful country that Britain still was in 1939. Indeed, it is difficult nowadays to write so often of 'England.' I have not changed 'England' to 'the United Kingdom' to conform with modern usage, but I have preferred a consistent use of 'Britain.'

More important, I have tried to bring out clearly a theme latent in the old book: that is, the importance in the nineteenth century of parliamentary constitutions and the whole liberal movement which aimed at obtaining them. I have also tried to show that this essential theme is not only the rise and operation of liberalism, but also its decline and the beginning of its supersession, as a cause of historical change, by socialism. This I have tried to do by adding a good deal of material on domestic politics, on economic history and on political ideas in Italy, Germany, France and especially Russia. I have incorporated the results of modern writing on, for example, the union of Belgium and Holland, or rather their reunion, and its breakup in 1830; on the Italian Risorgimento, a word which is used nowadays for the movement of thought which preceded Italian unification and not of political unification itself; and on the German constitutions of 1867 and 1871. I have tried to leave untouched whatever was written on the Eastern Question and the Balkan countries which Harold Temperley knew so well. Volume Two, with two important exceptions, is much more my own composition than Volume One. Those who knew the old Grant and Temperley will even here, however, recognise the occasional untouched sentence, paragraph or page. The two exceptions in Volume Two are, first, the account of the Balkan Wars and, second, the account of the War of 1914–18 and of peacemaking after it, in which Professor Temperley was a participant. He wrote the authoritative *History of the Peace Conference*. As for the rest of Volume Two, the introduction and chapters 1 and 7 to 10 are nearly all mine, chapters 11 to 16 and the Conclusion wholly so. The reader will miss from these the slower pace and more reflective quality of the earlier writing.

In Volume One he will also miss two flights of fancy which are too characteristic of the old book to be altogether forgotten, though they no longer stand in the text. Polignac, the last Prime Minister of the Restored Monarchy in France, was described as 'this gingerbread conspirator.' The Confederation of German states, with scant justice either to states or animals, was likened to a hunting pack. 'It was like a number of animals formed into a hunting pack; the leader was Prussia, a huge grey wolf, at whose heels ran jackals, like Bavaria, Saxony, Württemburg and in whose train followed thirty-five smaller animals varying in size from large rats to small mice.' I hope I have preserved in both volumes the strongly personalised character of the narrative. I hope it is still history made by the decisions of known men and not by the action of anonymous forces. The earlier authors often thought it necessary to authenticate views or information which were new, when they wrote, with detailed references to their source in footnotes. When the views have become generally accepted or the information common knowledge, I have omitted the footnotes. When I thought authentication still useful, I have given references if possible to more recent books containing the same material.

I repeat, finally, two of the paragraphs which came towards the end of Dame Lillian's note. 'In the note to the fifth edition the authors referred to the personal experience of Professor Temperley in the British Imperial General Staff in the first World War and in the negotiations for peace. They acknowledged also the help given by a number of personal friends, some of whom are no longer available for consultation. In particular, acknowledgment was given for the criticisms made by Field-Marshal Lord Birdwood on the chapter relating to the War of 1914–18, and to Mr J. M. (later Lord) Keynes for help in dealing with the Reparation and Economic Section of the Treaty of Versailles. Sir Arnold Wilson had given them advice in connection with all matters upon the then recent history of the East; Mr L. S. Amery had commented upon the section relating to the reconstruction of democracy after the first World War and Major-General A. C. Temperley (the brother of one of the authors) had given advice upon the history of Disarmament and the later developments of the League of Nations.

'In the note to the fifth edition the debt of the authors was also acknowledged to Mr Raymond Postgate who had written part of the chapter which dealt with Marxism and with Russia.'

I think much of the debt to those named in this note may still stand, for, except that to which Raymond Postgate contributed, these chapters have been least altered in the whole work. Much, however, has been added on Marx, and the Russian section of that chapter rewritten as a separate chapter.

AGATHA RAMM

MARX AND BAKUNIN

There seems to be scarcely a chapter in this volume in which revolution is not either attempted or achieved. It begins with the Russian Revolution of 1905, which did not depose the autocracy. Among the opposition to the Russian autocracy there were already Marxists, and the first Soviet, or Council, of Workers' Deputies ever to be formed was elected during the strikes in St. Petersburg of October 1905. Marxist-Leninists brought Communist Russia, the Union of Soviet Socialist Republics, into being in 1917. Marxists and Socialists were the agents of revolution in Germany in 1918–19. Marxists, with the Anarchists, Syndicalists and Socialists, in 1936 attempted but failed to achieve revolution in Spain, and brought about instead civil war. They divided France, but were represented in her Government in 1936. They were persecuted in Fascist Italy and persecuted almost to extinction in the Third Reich of Germany. After the second World War, the western states took into public ownership some parts of production and distribution and instituted schemes of public support which equalised access to education at all levels, to health and to security and tended to equalise wealth. The ideas behind these measures were derived from Socialism. Meanwhile the whole of eastern Europe had fallen under Communist rule. Towards the end of the volume successive risings occurred among East Germans, Poles, Hungarians and Czechs. These were to some extent, at least, revolutions attempted within the Marxist-Leninist world itself.

Some discussion of the ideas of Marx and Engels as the founders of Communist doctrine, and of Bakunin as the founder of Anarchism (Syndicalism may be taken as Anarchism in a trade union context) would seem to be an appropriate introduction to this volume. In Volume One something was already said about the ideas of early French Socialists, from Baboeuf to Saint-Simon, from Fourier to Proudhon. These thinkers agreed only on one thing: that the arrangements men had made for living together in society had achieved injustice, inequality, and unfreedom. These negatives might be summed up in the greatest negative of all: poverty. So attention focused on property and its distribution, but without bringing a single comprehensive, acceptable system into being either to explain it or to cure it. Karl Marx (1818–83) and Friedrich Engels (1820–95) persuaded a great many that they had designed exactly this sort of system.

Marx was descended from a long line of Jewish Rabbis, but his own father was a lawyer. The family became Christian when he was six and he was brought up a Protestant, but early discarded all religion. Born in Trier, in the Rhineland, he was educated at Berlin University. There he studied Hegel's philosophy and came into contact with those who gave Hegel's ideas a Leftist interpretation. In 1842 he was appointed editor of the *Rheinische Zeitung* and came into such conflict with the censor that he had to leave Germany and go to Paris the next year. There he met Engels, and their lifelong collaboration began. Engels was a Prussian, son of a manufacturer of the firm of Ermen and Engels, which employed him in Manchester.

The two young men endeavoured to reconcile the Socialist theories of Weitling and Baboeuf, with which they were emotionally in sympathy, with the Hegelian philosophy which they intellectually supported. In so doing, in three years which they spent together in Brussels (1845–48), they constructed a philosophy of 'scientific Socialism' which was in due course nearly to extinguish all others. This they did by inverting Hegel's dialectic and applying it to economic and political history, renaming it Dialectical Materialism.

The Hegelian dialectic represented in its day a considerable advance in the knowledge of the human mind, and through it of the external world. As Hegel was an idealist philosopher (holding that ideas were real) these two amounted to much the same thing. We may explain the only part of his philosophy which interests us here in the following way. Perhaps the longest step made by a savage mind towards civilisation is when it fixes for itself categories. Distinction is the beginning of knowledge: when the savage begins to use and recognise the idea of the earth, say, or of justice, he is becoming a reasoning being. But these fixed ideas are of necessity exclusive. The earth is the earth; it is not the moon, it is not the forest, it is not that mountain. Justice is not injustice. As philosophy becomes more complicated it entangles itself by trying to define these. What is justice? What is truth? Before the ancient world broke up these questions became interminable and the practical man, like Pilate, stayed not for an answer. Hegel solved the problem by making a further step. Ideas were not rigid; they were flexible and changing, each containing within itself its opposite and implying it. Life implies death, justice injustice. One idea gives birth to another, which arises out of it though it is its opposite; from their conflict arises an amalgamation of the two, a synthesis of both into a new idea, containing elements of both though it itself is new. The first is called the Positive, the second the Negation, the last step the Negation of the Negation. Alternatively the process is described as Thesis-Antithesis-Synthesis.

What for Hegel was an explanation of the human condition in terms of ideas, or thought about experience, became in Marx's theory an explanation in terms of experience only. But Marx and Engels found, or considered they found, that the dialectic would still work, shifted to the material plane. They reasoned like this: Men must maintain life. They grow food and develop tools to help them to do so. Their work, their skill and their implements mix with the raw materials given by nature to make what Marx called productive forces. Another element entered into production when men co-operated together so as to produce more easily and efficiently. This element Marx called productive relations. Marx and Engels thought that the ultimate explanation of all human activity was to be found in the operation of productive forces and productive relations. Considered in relation to society, these things make 'the economic structure of society, the real foundation, on which rises a legal and political superstructure.' So Marx and Engels reached the conclusion that the mode of production of material life determines all social, political and intellectual activity. This is why their theory is called materialist. What, then, is meant by 'historical materialism'? Marx and Engels begin with primitive society, when the relations of production are those—or so they supposed—of co-operation. But at an early stage in the history of men certain members of their society gained control over the productive forces. The few came to live by the work of the many and the slave-owning system began; when some of the workers also held property this became the feudal system; when money was invented this became the capitalist system. In this Marx and Engels saw only two classes: the propertyless suppliers of labour and the capitalist exploiters of it. The material productive forces of society are now in conflict with the productive relations and the class conflict has arisen. From this they predict the social revolution, which will achieve both the classless society and the socialist system of organisation. But where in all this is the dialectic? Its influence is clear in the way related ideas form groups of three: productive forces relate to productive relations and both relate to society; feudalism, capitalism, the classless society. If one transposes the dialectic into this last group, then feudalism is the thesis, capitalism is its negation and the classless society the negation of capitalism, or the synthesis. Or, applied more strictly, the capitalist system (the thesis) implies the opposite, proletarian socialism (the antithesis), and from their conflict would result the classless society (the synthesis). We can understand, then that Marx's theory may stand without the dialectic, but that to apply the dialectic to it is to give it inevitability; to make it wholly convincing. Yet one difficulty Marx and Engels never overcame: to choose one variety of economic

3

organisation and to call it the thesis is to make an arbitrary choice.

They had, however, other means of reinforcing their reasoning. The Marxist economic theory, first expounded at length in *Das Kapital* (first volume published 1867; other volumes were posthumous), was important because it offered a theory of exploitation. An economic theory arose out of an attempt to answer questions such as why did one thing have one value and another thing another value? Was there behind actual values, or prices, something that could be called real value? Marx accepted an old theory: the labour theory of value. The one characteristic which all commodities have in common, allowing them to be accepted in exchange for others, or for money, is that labour has been used to produce them. Yet the employer did not pay for labour according to the actual number of hours a workman spent on producing something. He paid different prices for different kinds of labour or different prices to different persons. Marx overcame these difficulties by reasoning that the employer paid not for actual labour, but for potential labour, and that the price was determined by the average number of hours a worker needed to work to keep himself alive. Then, to overcome the difficulty of different kinds of labour, Marx asserted that it was possible to reduce all kinds of labour to something which he called 'simple average labour', averaging out, that is, skilled and unskilled work. Despite objections to which the theory (that the value of anything is determined by the amount of 'simple average labour' put into it) is open, Marx went on to the next step. This was to show that the price which a commodity in fact commanded allowed for another element, namely the profit of the employer. This was a truism of nineteenth-century economic thought. Marx's contribution was to call it 'surplus value' and to call it unjust. A man works, say, ten hours a day. In the first five, he does all the work that would be necessary to maintain himself and produces all the value he will receive in wages. The extra value he produces in the remaining five hours he does not get. It is stolen from him by his employer and represents the amount by which he is exploited. But the economic theory had another element which perhaps carries greater conviction. The employer retained the surplus value in the production of commodities. He used it, partly, to produce more and more of the commodity. So that under the capitalist system there were necessarily recurrent crises of over-production. The course of industrial history in the industrialised countries made this view plausible enough. For Marx and Engels and their followers it pointed to the conclusion that capitalism would eventually be overwhelmed as these crises became increasingly violent.

Marx and Engels further strengthened their position by offering a political theory. They went far beyond those in the nineteenth century who believed that the evils under which they suffered could be cured once they obtained political rights. Marxism diverged from all previous political theories in denying that the state existed, even potentially, for the good of those who belonged to it. It was by definition an organisation for the benefit of one part of the community only. But Marx and Engels were hostile to the state not only because it was organised in the interest of those who owned the means of production. They also believed it was incompatible with the classless society. In the latter government of persons will have ceased to exist. The exercise of authority by some over others will have become an archaism. 'Government of persons is replaced by the administration of things.' The demand for political rights was simply the way the bourgeoisie had won its own, earlier, revolution against those survivals of feudalism, the monarchies and the landed aristocracies.

But why should historical materialism, an economic theory and a political theory, even of the sort described, turn out to be a theory of revolution? Marx drew from the Hegelian system ideas which gave his predictions, not only the force of inevitability, but also the logic which inspired his followers to act to bring them about. Marx transported Hegel's theory of categories from the plane of ideas to that of experience. Hegel showed that ideas such as quality, quantity, causality, essence, existence, have a dialectical relationship to each other. Changes, for example, proceed by imperceptible quantitative mutation until a change of quality has taken place—as water at 100°C has changed into steam. Transposed on to the level of experience, this reasoning supports the opinion that social change proceeds gradually, or quantitatively, until a point is reached when, by a sudden leap, one system of social organisation replaces another and a qualitative change has taken place. Marx calls these leaps revolutions, and uses the Hegelian theory to show their inevitability.

There was, however, another line of reasoning which made the followers of Marx and Engels revolutionaries. They taught that the purpose of philosophy was not that it should enable a man to understand the human condition, but that it should show him how to change it. In other words, theory without action and action without theory were both inconceivable. This position was the more convincing in so far as it rested upon a theory of knowledge. Knowledge was not simply the product of someone's reception of the impact of the outside world upon him through his sensations. Rather it was the product of his active response to those sensations. Unless you did something in response to a sensation, you could not be said to have experienced it. All theory was to be tested by action and no action was to be taken without a correct dialectical analysis of the situation, conducted beforehand. The Marxist system, from the time when Marx and Engels first expounded it in November 1847 to the League of the Just, a predominantly German secret society, and then embodied it in the *Communist Manifesto* of 1848, was a dynamic theory constantly in the making. It defined itself by constantly discovering what it was not. Thus Marx was embroiled in a series of controversies: with Mazzini and with Bakunin, to name but two of his antagonists, even with himself. He said more than once in the seventies that he was no Marxist.

One of the most used arenas for this constant debate was the International Working Men's Association, the First International. It was founded in 1864 as a result of a meeting in St. Martin's Hall, Long Acre, London, called to protest against the atrocities committed during the repression of the Polish revolt of 1863. The members of the Socialist Parties in the different European countries belonged to it and after 1866 it held regular Congresses. By 1867 Marx was the dominating figure on the General Council in London, and both in the discussions there and in the large correspondence, official and unofficial, which he carried on with representatives of movements in other countries, he spread and clarified his ideas. Each Congress showed a further victory for him and an elimination of reactionary or of merely freakish proposals. His most notable victory was in 1869, when the Proudhonist programme was voted down in favour of a Socialist one by 54 to 4. By 1870 he could see large and powerful working-class movements, deeply influenced by his own ideas, in every European country, and imagined the world revolution very near. 'Things are moving,' he wrote to Engels, in September 1867. 'And in the next revolution, which is perhaps nearer than it appears, we (i.e. you and I) will have this powerful engine in our hands.'

Both Marx and Engels were throughout their lives rashly optimistic about the date of the revolution. They seemed to think that once they had discovered and explained the process which would lead to a victorious proletarian revolution, that process would forthwith begin. Each decade they expected victory, and were repeatedly disappointed. Two factors for which they had not allowed destroyed their immediate hopes, and behind these was the more important fact that capitalism was not yet, in Marxist language, 'a fetter upon production' but was showing itself capable of surprising expansion. The two immediate factors were the outbreak of the Franco German war, which set the French and German workers, the two chief hopes of the International, to shooting each other down, and the appearance of an organised opposition to Marx's direction within the International itself.

Among the recruits who joined in 1869 was a Russian refugee living in Switzerland, Michael Bakunin, who brought with him a group of personal adherents, with whom he constituted a branch in Geneva. He derived his principles from Proudhon, so far as he had constructive proposals, adding to them only atheism. But in his methods Bakunin was far different from his mentor. His political ideas were always vague, but they amounted to the affirmation, against the all-powerful state, of the value of the small social group. To live in social relations with other men was 'natural.' Bakunin taught that much must be destroyed to recover what was natural. In contrast to his ideas his instructions on organisation were precise and unchanging. Political action was forbidden; the state was an evil thing and must be destroyed. The oppressors and their agents were to be removed; half-converts were to be tied firmly to the chariot of the revolutionaries by every means available. Stolen letters, blackmail, threats, secret organisations within open organisation—all these were justifiable means, and the last indeed was his favourite method. 'Have you never thought,' he wrote to his chief French lieutenant, 'what is the principal cause of the power and vitality of the Jesuit order? Do you wish me to name it? Well, it is the complete effacement of private wills in collective organisation and action . . . I shall die and the worms will eat me, but I want our idea to triumph. I want not the more or less dramatic growth of my person, not of *a* power, but of *our* power, the power of our collectivity, in whose favour I am ready to abdicate my name and personality.' With a group of disciplined followers, who were on principle unscrupulous, Bakunin was soon able to set the International in an uproar. The Swiss federation was torn in half, the newly-founded Spanish and Italian movements came more under his influence than Marx's; and even the Belgian and North American sections began to lean towards Anarchism. Nor were the effects, except in Belgium, ephemeral. Italian anarchism remained very strong until Mussolini stamped out all working-class movements. In Spain anarchism was a great power in the twentieth century and strong on the Republican side during the Civil War of 1936–39.

Marx was as revolutionary in spirit as Bakunin, but his idea of the revolution was a mass movement of organised workers conscious of their purpose and not led like sheep. Armed raids by drilled conspirators, for whom the average worker was mere conspiracy-fodder, were in his view dangerous follies. The conflict between the two men became one of savage personal bitterness, and things were obviously moving to a climax when the Franco-German war broke out and the controversy was forcibly silenced.

The war was followed by the Paris Commune, whose history will be found elsewhere (see above, Volume One, pp. 289–91). The Commune, until the outbreak of the Russian Revolution in 1917, was the most venerated episode in Socialist history. Every March every Socialist journal brought out a special number to commemorate it, poets wrote their best (or at least their most well-meant) verses to celebrate it, annual delegations visited the famous Wall of Père Lachaise cemetery to lay red wreaths on the spot where the most famous massacre of its defenders took place. All this was not because it was a successful political experiment (it was not), but because it was supposed to be the first working-class Government and so con-

7

sidered to be the precursor of the revolution,. The legend of the Paris Commune had more consequences than the reality.

The International assembled in Congress the next year (1872) at The Hague. Bakunin did not attend, his spokesman being a Swiss delegate named Guillaume. Marx and Engels did. The proceedings were wholly occupied by the general quarrel between Socialists and Anarchists, and at the end the latter were expelled and the International split into two. Marx and Engels rejoiced too soon: the bloodletting of the Commune and the violence of the dissensions had in fact killed the International and their victory was empty. The Marxist section nominally existed until it was wound up in Philadelphia in 1876. The Anarchist section claimed a little longer life, though its effective power was broken in the unsuccessful Spanish Revolution of 1873. Separate sections survived. The Italian organisation remained strong; so too did the Russian. In France in 1890 and 1891 a series of systematic propagandas-by-deed (assassination of individual reactionaries) culminated in the murder of President Carnot. But this was the last effort of the Anarchists: the world had almost forgotten their existence until the Spanish Civil War brought the Spanish Anarchists back into importance, in 1936.

Marxism had more vitality. The Parties which had been founded, or adopted, by the International did not vanish when it disappeared. Nearly all of them survived, weak at first but steadily growing in importance. Until their death, Marx and Engels continually corresponded with them and encouraged them with advice, support and, on occasion, acid criticism. As we saw in Volume One, in nearly all European countries, except Turkey, a powerful Social Democratic Party appeared, securing if not the whole allegiance of the politically-interested working class, at least the support of a formidable minority. Only in Britain was this not true; the Social Democratic Federation (afterwards the British Socialist Party), despite the support of men such as William Morris, Tom Mann and H. M. Hyndman, remained to the end of its days (in 1919) a small sect. Workers preferred the Independent Labour Party and its Trade Union Movement.

The Socialist Parties of this period were of varying importance, some of very great weight indeed. Any observer who tabulated the results of the elections in European countries could not fail to notice one unvarying feature—the steady, if slow, growth of the Socialist vote. In town after town their numbers increased, and while other parties had fluctuations they alone (unless legal violence was used to suppress them) each time recorded a larger number of successes. One essential difference indeed passed almost unnoticed. The First International had been essentially international and revolutionary: in the Second International the Parties, despite assiduous repetition of

Marx's phrases, were essentially national, in that their character varied from country to country.

The German Party was the strongest Party on the theoretical level. The German Social Democratic Party, led by pupils of Marx, such as August Bebel, Wilhelm Liebknecht and Karl Kautsky, was also the richest and most successful Socialist Party. Eduard Bernstein denied three of Marx's characteristic predictions. He showed that the concentration of property was not happening; the number of property-owners was on the contrary increasing; the concentration of the means of production might be happening in industry but was not happening in agriculture; there were many checks on recurrent economic crises and they would not destroy the capitalist system. Marx had, therefore, been wrong in anticipating the collapse of capitalist society. Bernstein's Revisionism divided the Party but did not prevail. It had served to increase the power and vigour of the Party in formulating Socialist theory. The Danish Social Democrat Party led by Thorvald Stauning, the Swedish Social Democratic Party led by Hjalmar Branting, the Dutch Social Democrats led by P. J. Troelstra, the Austrian Social Democratic Party led by F. Adler, the Belgian Labour Party and the Norwegian Party were similarly without serious rivals, and the leaders were in every case men whom it was impossible not to recognise as politicians of high importance. In France an older revolutionary tradition raised obstacles to the dominance of the pure Marxists led by Jules Guesde. There were Blanquists and Reformists as well as Syndicalists. But when all the political groups were united by the tact, and under the leadership, of Jean Jaurès it was clear that Marxism was the predominant philosophy. In Italy Turati and Modigliani and in Spain Pablo Iglesias had to admit rivalry from the Syndicalists, revolutionary trade unionists who had refreshed Bakunin's practice with a dose of industrial unionism ultimately derived from Proudhon. They declared not only that the Marxist parties had ceased to be genuinely revolutionary, but that the nature of political campaigning made it sure that every Parliamentary Socialist Party would go the same way. Nevertheless, the Socialist Parties of Italy and Spain were indisputably the most important working-class organisations of their countries; the former had in 1914 a rich and splendidly organised co-operative organisation behind it, and the latter was the only Spanish Party which was an organised Party in the modern sense. In the Balkans turbulent political conditions prevented much constitutional success, but every country except Albania and Turkey had its Social Democratic Party, and among outstanding leaders were Christian Rakovsky the Rumanian, and Plato Drakoules the Greek, whose paper *Ho Rhizopastes* (*The Tearer-up-by-the-Roots*, less sensationally translated *The Radical*) was the most influential Labour newspaper published south of the Danube. In Russia the Social Democrats (SDs) had to meet serious rivalry from the Socialist Revolutionaries (SRs), successors to the Nihilists, who approved of individual terrorism as a reply to Tsarist methods. The Social Democrats were themselves divided into Mensheviks (minority) headed by Martov, and Bolsheviks (majority) headed by Lenin. But this division was at first regarded as of less importance than that between SR and SD. The personality of the unquestioned leader G. V. Plekhanov dominated both groups, and the busiest conciliator of all was a young Jew using the name of Leon Trotsky.

The outbreak of the war of 1914 shattered the Second International. The Socialist parties in all the belligerent countries, except Russia, called upon their supporters to rally to their national governments; the Second International might not have existed. A small neutral group, the 'Dutch-Scandinavian Committee' with Camille Huysmans, the Belgian Secretary of the International Bureau, made repeated but useless efforts to bring the parties together. In 1915 at Zimmerwald, in 1916 at Kienthal, and in 1917 at Stockholm steadily increasing minorities, who were discontented at this failure, met together to consider action to stop the war and start a Socialist revolution. Soon after the Armistice, at a meeting in Moscow in March 1919, they decided that the Second International was worthless, and started a Third International, the 'Comintern,' to replace it.

In its early years, working under the eye of Lenin, the Communist International secured the allegiance of every Socialist Revolutionary, Syndicalist and Blanquist as well as Marxist. It reverted, however, to the organisation of the First International, with a Praesidium to take the place of the General Council, and equally strict discipline for every member and Party. Each Party had to re-name itself 'The Communist Party of . . .'; some parties, with many years' honoured history behind them, much resented this, and even more doubted whether a band of Russian enthusiasts in Moscow possessed sufficient knowledge to direct them competently on the road to world revolution. The 'Twenty-One Points' which were drafted, partly by G. Zinoviev, who was president of the Third International from 1919 to 1926, included an insistence upon 'illegal work' which in itself outlawed (if need be) the parties which accepted it. Nevertheless the majority of the French Socialist Party, and powerful groups in the newly liberated Eastern European states joined the new organisation. In Scandinavia, Spain, the Netherlands and Britain the response was small, although for a while Labour supporters who declined to join it nevertheless maintained a benevolent attitude towards its propaganda.

Chapter 1

THE TROUBLED YEARS, 1905–12

Volume One of this book ended at the point where Europe was already divided into two camps. On one side was the Austro-German Alliance. On the other was the Franco-British Entente. Italy was attached to Austria-Hungary and Germany by the Triple Alliance and to Britain and France by common interests in the Mediterranean and North Africa, which she had safeguarded by agreements with them and assurances to them that the Triple Alliance would not mean war on Italy's part against either of them. The system remained to be completed by the Russo-British Entente. This did not come into existence until 1907.

Nothing could be done with Russia in 1905, for she was just emerging from revolution. Her defeat at the hands of Japan was the prelude to this revolution. She had been defeated militarily in the battle of Mukden (March 25, 1905) after a period of trench warfare which might, but did not, warn Europe what to expect in Flanders in 1914–18; navally in the battle of Tsushima (May 27, 1905); and diplomatically in the apparent uselessness of the alliance with France (1893) and in the harsh peace treaty, the Treaty of Portsmouth (September 5, 1905). But defeat in the Crimean War was just as decisive. It had been followed by reform and not revolution. The explanation why this time revolution forestalled reform is partly that the autocracy was both weaker and more rigid and partly that blind protest was now mixed with liberal and socialist ideas which gave a vision, in their different ways, of what they wished to achieve to those who demanded change. The revolution was, however, repressed before it was completed. The ultimate outcome, therefore, was in effect a further spate of reform. So that we are faced with a second question: why did the liberal Russia which emerged from the Revolution fail to survive. Before we turn to this second question we must make good the explanation we offered in answer to the first.

The autocracy ceased under the last Tsar, Nicholas II (acceded 1894), to command the whole range of matters that effective government now required it to do. Indeed, Nicholas II, though he knew much of foreign policy, knew little or nothing of other subjects. He saw everything in personal terms. His qualities of natural intelligence, charm and affection he applied to his family and immediate circle. Even for a landowner his range was circumscribed; for an autocratic ruler in the twentieth century it was narrow in the extreme. To govern Russia effectively now required a command of economics, an understanding of the educated, well-to-do but not landed, middle class, with its liberal ideas, some notion of urban working-class life with its social problems and the new doctrines of social democracy, and an acquaintance with peasant aspirations and the peasants' version of socialism. Abstract ideas were unpalatable to Nicholas II and he made no assessment of the importance of these things let alone had firsthand experience of them. His ordinary good abilities were insufficient. Since he had no notion of the importance of these things he could not appoint, as William I had appointed Bismarck, men who did understand their importance and could so identify themselves with the country as to be able to express its needs in their personalities and, in those terms, satisfy them. Nicholas II had three Ministers of the Interior within one year (1904–05). The first, Pleve, was assassinated; the second, Prince Svyatopolk-Mirski, recognised he was not up to the work and resigned; the third, Bulygin, was an official who did not even try to rise to the occasion. The Government allowed patent abuses and evils to persist, and still to persist, unremedied; the governed had greater opportunities, more education, a better understanding of how the state worked and how it should work than fifty years before. To the governed inefficiency, the burden of taxation, inequalities of wealth, were less and less acceptable; in the armed forces harsh discipline and no reward, not even victory, caused protest; in the countryside the poverty and land-hunger of a growing population caused attacks on the landlords; in the cities rising prices and falling wages caused strikes. On the side of the Government, persistent failure caused a weakening of all authority everywhere. Pressure from the gentry and liberal middle class was the first to make itself felt. In November 1904 a congress of Zemstva (elective Councils for local government in the countryside, see Volume One, pp. 301, 349) representatives demanded representative institutions at the centre in mild and generalised language. Nicholas temporised. After the congress was over the members continued their campaign with mounting impetus. The League of Liberation (Volume One, p. 348) adopted the eleven theses of the Zemstva movement as part of their programme too. Working-class protest followed. At the end of the month there was a one-day strike in Baku. Next, a strike at the Putilov works, outside St. Petersburg, was organised in protest against the dismissal of workers belonging to the trade union founded by a certain priest called Gapon. The strike spread to other works.

Gapon led a deputation from the strikers to petition the Tsar at the Winter Palace. The assembled strikers were fired upon by the troops. This was the massacre of Bloody Sunday, January 22, 1905. The result was a general strike in St. Petersburg and sympathetic strikes in some seven other cities. In February serious peasant riots began. They sometimes took the form of the burning of landlords' property, sometimes of the expulsion of the landlords. The Grand Duke Sergei, the Tsar's uncle, was assassinated. Bulygin promised an elective, consultative assembly for all Russia. Peasant riots and strikes continued to spread and minor trades were affected. In June 1905 the sailors of the *Potemkin* mutinied. Intellectuals of all shades of opinion now took a hand. There were further congresses of the members of the City Councils and the Zemstva, deputations to the Tsar and discussions of draft constitutions. During the summer riots and strikes quieted, but revived in September. There were mutinies among the troops returning from Manchuria and in October a great railway strike accompanied by a fresh general strike in St. Petersburg. The first Soviet of workers was formed in St. Petersburg that month; others followed. It was made up of members of the strike committees. It had 562 elected members, who appointed an executive committee. Its members were workers but also representatives from the Menshevik, Bolshevik and the Socialist Revolutionary Parties. Trotsky was one of the leaders. In December the police risked arresting them and the Soviet was dissolved by the troops. It had lasted fifty days. In Moscow, then Russia's second city, a general strike was now declared and there were for twelve days intermittent armed clashes between the police and the strikers, before the strikers were finally crushed by the troops.

The revolution, however, was really brought to an end by the October manifesto, as it was called, which granted Russia an elective parliament to be elected on a fairly wide franchise. At the same time Witte, whom we have seen modernising Russia in the nineties, was appointed Prime Minister. The first parliament, or Duma, sat for three months. In it the so-called progressive bloc had a majority. It was made up of the Cadets (a word made from the initial letters of the Russian for Constitutional Democrats) under Milyukov, Prince Lvov, of whom we shall hear again, and Peter Struve, of whom we have heard already in Volume One. They had 77 seats. Allied to them were the Octobrists under Guchkov. This group was prepared to let the autocracy continue on the basis of the manifesto and the limited consultative powers which it gave to the Duma. To its right were extreme conservatives; to its left the Socialist Revolutionaries and a few Social Democrats. The progressive bloc had the support of the leaders of the Universities and the professions. 'Their political success depended upon one of two conditions, if not both: either support from the autocracy to help to build orderly freedom from above, or the support of the socialist parties behind whom stood some of the peasantry and proletariat.'[1] Progressive reform failed because they never had either, let alone both, of these conditions, for long enough to do anything. They have been blamed for bringing on the crisis too soon. The Cadets and the Octobrists faced the Tsar with a demand for a Government which had the confidence of the country and appealed to the nation for support. The Tsar dismissed the Duma. The year 1905 had closed with the issue of a new electoral law restricting the franchise, and 1906 opened with the election of the second Duma. When it met the Cadets were seen to have lost their strength. The Octobrists had made the most gains. The Socialist Revolutionaries still had 34 seats. So even this Duma could show itself too independent for the Tsar to understand it. He dissolved it on June 16, 1907, and together with the dissolution edict issued a new electoral law which excluded the peasant electors and the Socialist Revolutionaries they voted for. The third Duma of 1907–12—it lasted its legal term—was totally unrepresentative. The Cadets lost heavily and had now only 54 seats; the Social Democrats had 17 seats and the Socialist Revolutionaries, now hidden under the name Trudovniks (Labourists), with 16 seats, just survived. The Octobrists were now the strongest party on the left (154 seats) but the parties of the right who had fought the elections with Government subsidies were strong too (127 seats). Nevertheless by the time of the fourth Duma, 1912–14, in which the Cadets (58 seats) played a useful role in contact both with the Government and the Socialists, Russia had a real parliamentary life: among a limited section of the population, it is true, and mostly the same classes who expressed themselves through the Zemstva and the City Councils. A more liberal régime obtained in relation to the Universities and the Press. Whether this liberal Russia would survive or not, depended upon reforms of a social and economic kind.

C. A. Stolypin was Prime Minister at the time of the second Duma. He was appointed in July 1906 and remained in office until he was shot in 1911. He was responsible for belated progress in dealing with the land question. There was important legislation in 1906 and 1910. Under the law of 1906 redemption payments (due to the state from emancipated serfs) were to cease from January 1, 1907, and the remaining inequalities between peasant and landowner were abolished. The act did much to create consolidated family farms; for it allowed the peasant to take his share of the land, farmed in common in the *obshchina*, into private ownership and to consolidate his strips into one compact farm. It allowed the *mir*, or community of peasants, to abandon the open-field system and to distribute all its land among its members. The act of 1910 was a codifying measure

---

[1] L. Schapiro, *The Origin of the Communist Autocracy* (2nd ed, 1977), p. 9.

which elaborated procedure for the breakup of the *obshchina* and stipulated certain cases where the cessation of farming in common might be automatic. Only the War of 1914–18 delayed its total disappearance. But, of course, poverty and land-hunger remained, though a prosperous class of peasantry was coming to the top.

In 1909 there was a second leap forward in Russian industrialisation. It continued into the period of prosperity that marked the pre-war years of 1912–14. Social reform, however, did not keep pace with the growing needs of the proletariat. Even in the good year of 1912 'the massacre' in the Lena goldfields (April 4) showed the persistence of social problems. Moreover, Russia's industrial structure was characterised by intense concentration. Powerful cartels and trusts widened the gulf between distant, anonymous employers and an equally anonymous labour force. Russia was, however, far from being an industrialised country even by the time of the Revolution of 1917. The proletariat of full industrialisation was created in the thirties after that Revolution had supposedly put it into power.

At the time of the fourth Duma Kokovtsov was Prime Minister. By now both Government and Duma were further over to the right. Social reform was out of the question. Only Russian finances, army and navy were reorganised and reformed and her railway network enlarged. Historians write of a Russian revival. Her foreign policy was assertive; her General Staff showed a growing confidence; by 1917 she was to have an army of 1,750,000 men and her finances were so healthy that she would not notice the cost of the increases. There was, however, an ominous revival of industrial discontent and strikes early in 1914. The War of 1914–18 used up the newly acquired strength of the country and liberal Russia foundered under the weight of its unsolved social problems.

Something more needs now to be said of Russian foreign policy in this period after the Japanese war. It was in striking contrast to her uncertain search for stability internally. She pursued a policy of forward driving, though it would be more exact to say that her diplomats in Persia and the Balkan states and her military agents in Tibet did so without much co-ordination from the centre. Serbia had undergone a change of dynasty in June 1903 when the last of the Obrenović was murdered and Peter Karageorgevič brought that dynasty back to power. She discarded the alliance with Austria-Hungary and repudiated the political and commercial vassalage to her which had existed since 1881. She went over to Russia. Bulgaria, which had also been hostile, was reconciled to Russia. She was now to build up a clientèle of Balkan states opposed both to Austria-Hungary and to Turkey. Rumania alone was pro-German and pro-Austrian for some time longer. Tentative approaches to Britain began soon after the conclusion of the Franco-British Declaration over Egypt and Morocco of April 1904 which, it will be recalled, marked, with another Declaration (on Madagascar) and a Convention (on New-foundland and West Africa), the beginning of the Franco-British Entente. Russia showed herself forward in assenting to the Khedive of Egypt's decree which consequential international arrangements, to be made over Egyptian finance, needed. In return she angled for British acceptance of the position she was building up in Tibet. This Britain gave in ambiguous and somewhat noncommittal terms. Britain was more interested in a Russian Declaration similar to the French, that she too would abstain from pressing for the British evacuation of Egypt. This Britain did not obtain. Nor did much come of talk about Manchuria. When approaches were renewed after the Revolution of 1905 they were put on a different and more hopeful basis. At the Persian (Iranian) capital of Teheran Britain and Russia had been rivals for influence and grants of concessions from the Shah for nearly thirty years. Sometimes rivalry had given place to a common policy or the suggestion of one. But rivalry was the dominant note, and there was always pressure upon Britain from the Government of India to keep in mind the importance of communications to India and naval supremacy in the Persian Gulf. When, in 1906, Britain made further approaches to Russia, she asked Russia to state her views about Persia. It was thought wise to put 'a ring fence' round the negotiations, that is, to avoid questions in which other European Powers might be concerned, and to take the questions—Persia, Afghanistan, Tibet—where there was Anglo-Russian disagreement, one by one. The British Ambassador in St. Petersburg, Sir Arthur Nicolson, to whose ideas this policy was largely due, managed the negotiations with skill and brought them to a conclusion in Conventions on Persia, Afghanistan and Tibet signed by Russia and Britain on August 31, 1907. They marked the inauguration of the Russo-British Entente. They were precipitated to a conclusion by Britain's showing that she no longer had a rigid view that the Straits of the Bosphorus and Dardanelles must be kept closed—a view which, as we have seen, had dominated her policy towards Russia and Turkey throughout the nineteenth century. As we shall see presently this was a matter which was to disturb Russia's relations with Austria-Hungary in the following year. One Convention with Russia divided Persia into three zones; the northern, containing the capital, Britain recognised as Russia's sphere of influence; the central zone both Powers were to leave free; and in the third zone, whose coast lay on the Persian Gulf, Russia recognised Britain's predominance. A separate document further safeguarded Britain's position in the Gulf. By two other Conventions Russia disclaimed any intention of interfering in Afghanistan and Britain any intention of altering the status quo there, and both Powers recognised the sovereignty of China over Tibet and affirmed their intention of maintaining its territorial integrity and not interfering in its internal affairs. It is noteworthy that there was no bargain between Britain and Russia, comparable to that over Egypt and Morocco between Britain and France. Persia stood by itself. The agreement was much more like a drawing of frontiers up to which each would tolerate forward action by the other. It is not, then, surprising that after the Conventions Russia turned away from the Middle East as from the Far East. Her policy concentrated upon Europe and the Balkan peninsula, that is to say, upon a zone dangerous to her relations with both Germany and Austria-Hungary.

For Russia's ally, France, the troubled years were 1906–10. There were strikes of the miners in the North in March and April 1906, demonstrations in Paris for the eight-hour working day in 1906 and for the six-day week in 1907, strikes of the electricians in March 1907, of workers in the food industries in April 1907 and also in 1907 a rebellion of the wine-growers. There was a strike of builders in 1908 and an attempt at a general strike in 1909. Clemenceau and Briand dealt with strikes by calling in strike-breakers and using the army to protect those at work. Postmen and schoolteachers, who were civil servants, could be dismissed if they intended to strike. Briand hit upon the drastic device of calling up strikers for their military service. Such measures brought the one part of France no nearer to understanding the other—proletarian—part. Since this part was still small no immediate damage was done, but distant consequences were more serious.

The General Election of 1906 brought the Radicals a substantial majority in the Chamber where they had 247 seats. To their left, Millerand and Viviani led a group of independent Socialists and to *their* left there was now a united Socialist Party, including both Guesde and Jaurès. The Socialists were strong, but the Radicals were stronger, so strong that they could govern, as they had not been able to do in the previous Chamber, without Socialist support. Georges Clemenceau (1841–1929) became Prime Minister with the clever and subtle Caillaux as his Finance Minister. Clemenceau had first come to the fore at the time of the Paris Commune, for he had then been Mayor of the 18th *arrondissement*. In the same year he became a member of the Chamber and for the next twenty years he made a reputation as the great puller-down of Ministries, which he never offered to replace by one of his own. In November 1906 he was at last in power. Expectations were high. Here was his chance to carry through the social programme to which he was committed. He had nearly three years of power, but he achieved nothing except the enactment of the six-day working week. The years were remembered for the oratorical duels between Clemenceau and Jaurès. It was an opportunity missed. Yet Clemenceau was to be Prime Minister in another critical period, 1917–20. Briand succeeded Clemenceau without much change.

The General Election of 1910 increased the Socialist representation by 20 seats, but otherwise made little change in the overall balance of parties. Yet the troubled years were over. There was a surprising number of Deputies, who had never sat in the Chamber before, and a complete change of mood. When Caillaux became Prime Minister in 1911, this serious mood was confirmed. He offered a programme of reform, 'lay, financial and social.' He fought to introduce an income tax into the tax structure, not changed since the Revolution of 1789. He fell in 1912 without having done anything except weather the Agadir crisis (to which we shall come at the end of this chapter). It was Poincaré who both succeeded in lengthening the period of military service and in introducing income tax. But that belongs to war preparations and the next chapter.

We last saw Germany under its Chancellor, Prince von Bülow (appointed October 1900), embarked on *Weltpolitik* and the building of a Battle Fleet. She was a powerful, dynamic economic unit but, like a battleship at large on the ocean, incapable of steering steadily along a single, chosen course. This may have been more appearance than reality; for Bülow had an unfortunate effect on foreign policy by his refusal to close options. He gave an appearance both of vacillation and over-reaching ambition. Contemporaries and subsequent historians blamed all the bad decisions in foreign policy upon the sinister influence of Holstein, a permanent official in the Foreign Office since Bismarck's first year as imperial Chancellor.[1] He was dismissed in 1906 and had been absent through illness at crucial periods in both 1904 and 1905. The responsibility properly belonged to Bülow, who was also, from 1897 until 1907, Reich Foreign Secretary as well as Chancellor (1900–09). But Holstein, as the repository of Bismarckian traditions and a permanent presence in the Office with a somewhat cautious and narrow view, was a convenient scapegoat for the failure, for example, of Germany's Moroccan policy in 1906.

We saw in Volume One how Germany opened a challenge to the Franco-British Entente by laying a claim to consideration, with the other signatories of the treaty of 1880, should France initiate any change in the status of Morocco. This led to a demonstration of Franco-British solidarity on the one hand and bilateral negotiations between Germany and France on the other. The latter arose out of a proposal by Germany for a European Conference on Morocco. The suggestion was made in Volume One that she would have done better to have worked for a bilateral agreement with France than to have allowed these negotiations to become simply a limitation of the agenda for the Conference. She clung to the Conference. This duly assembled at Algeciras in January 1906. Twelve states were represented. Two states, France and Germany, contended. The subjects of their contention were police and financial control in Morocco. In

---

[1] N. R. Rich, *Friedrich von Holstein* (1965), redresses some exaggerated views.

an undeveloped and disturbed area police control was likely to be the lever of power. The police were entrusted by the Conference to a Franco-Spanish personnel under a Swiss Inspector-General, so that the Conference was a victory for France. All that Germany gained was that she had established the theoretical principle that Morocco concerned all the European Powers equally: for a State Bank under the control of four Powers, France, Britain, Germany and Spain, was set up with equal opportunity for all nations. Otherwise the Conference was a demonstration of Germany's isolation. France was steadily supported throughout by Britain, Russia and Spain. President Theodore Roosevelt, representing the United States and making the first major incursion of the States into European diplomacy, effectively, but less openly, also supported France. Italy, bound by agreements with France of 1900 and 1902 (Volume One, p. 364), supported France. Germany and Austria-Hungary stood alone.

We saw in chapter 24 of Volume One how Germany was in the grip of social conflicts which were unable to work themselves out in the political arena. In the Reichstag, it is true, the political battle was fought out between parties which, except for the Centre Party, represented social classes. But the battle was one without victory. The outcome of battle in the Reichstag was frustration and not victory, with power for the victor, since Ministries were not set up nor pulled down by it. The Chancellor and the Secretaries of State (civil servants, not politicans) did not compose a Reich Ministry. The Chancellor had been made the only Reich Minister in 1871 in order to safeguard the powers of the Ministries of the separate states. Bülow fell in 1909 after a crisis that showed up both the diminished authority of the Emperor and the irresponsibility of the Chancellor. On October 28, 1908, there appeared in the London *Daily Telegraph* an article reporting the Emperor's language to an unnamed interviewer about Anglo-German relations. The text was submitted to Bülow by the Emperor, quite properly, before publication. Whether Bülow let it pass carelessly or deliberately, he should have stopped it. He could not exculpate himself before the Reichstag satisfactorily. There was an outcry against the so-called personal government of the Emperor, who then threatened to abdicate. He was brought round from a state of nervous collapse and for some years there were no more impromptu speeches nor public statements. Bülow's failure deepened. He was about to embark on a reform of Reich finance to make good the deficit caused by the expenditure on naval building. But his supporters in the Reichstag fell away: there was a coalition of the Liberal parties against him. The tax bill of 1909 failed to pass. In June he resigned. The agitation for constitutional reform, that is the establishment of a Reich Ministry responsible to the Reichstag, became serious. It was not to succeed until 1918 when Prince Max von Baden headed the first Reich Ministry. By then it was too late to save the Monarchy.

Bülow was succeeded by Bethmann Hollweg whom he himself had recommended. He was 'a man of intelligence, learning and the utmost integrity.' He was a man not unlike Caprivi, though Caprivi was a General and he an administrator (in the Prussian state service in the Ministry of the Interior, then Prussian Minister of the Interior and lastly Reich Secretary for Home Affairs). To both, loyalty, honour and devoted industry were the prime virtues. Bethmann Hollweg shouldered the responsibilities of his office as Bülow had not done, and restored to it some of its lost power. The strongest man in office continued, however, to be von Tirpitz. He made the *Reichsmarine-amt* into a propaganda office for the navy and the great Battle Fleet which he built under the navy laws of 1898, 1906 and 1908. W. von Schoen (1907), A. von Kiderlen-Wächter (1910) and G. von Jagow (1913) were in succession Secretaries of State for Foreign Affairs.

Of Austria-Hungary little needs to be added to what was said of her in chapter 24 of Volume One. There it was shown how the *Ausgleich* had ceased to provide internal stability. The Hungarians stood in the way of any chance of a trialist rearrangement to accommodate a developing Czechoslovak nation in an equal partnership or a quadripartite rearrangement to quiet, in addition, a growing Serbo-Croat or Yugoslav agitation. Neither of these possible rearrangements was ever seriously considered. In looking back the historian sees how Hungarian policy towards the nationalities prevented any forward-looking proposals for change from ever being made. But there was another obstacle to these. As the coherence of the Monarchy deteriorated, so did the rigidity of the ageing Emperor increase—he was 75 in 1905. This made overall reconstruction impossible. It also made Ministers, such as Aehrenthal, who took over foreign policy from Goluchowski in 1906 and was still in office when he died in 1912, or the Chief of Staff, Conrad von Hötzendorf, independent forces who could shape policy, within the competence of their offices, much as they wished. Thus Aehrenthal adopted a forward policy in the Balkan Peninsula and in 1909, during the crisis in Austro-Serb relations, which Aehrenthal had provoked, discussion between Conrad and Moltke, the Chief of the German General Staff, resulted in the incorporation of Austria-Hungary in the Schlieffen plan. This campaign plan, made by Moltke's predecessor in office, was for a lightning blow at Paris in the event of war with France. The German armies would go through neutral Belgium and Luxembourg, opening out near Paris to grip it in a pair of pincers: to gain total victory in six weeks. Other German forces would hold the French in Alsace. While the blow was delivered Russia would be held on Germany's other front and be defeated after her French ally. Under the arrangement of 1909, Austria-Hungary was assigned a rôle in this holding operation. War, when it came, it was assumed, would be a war in which Germany and Austria-Hungary stood united against France and Russia, equally united. Aehrenthal's foreign policy, to which we shall come presently, was to make such a war more rather than less likely. Meanwhile, though no change could happen, change was in the air. Francis Joseph's nephew, Francis Ferdinand, had come to the fore as the heir apparent. His part in government did not go beyond military duties, but he was already a centre of intrigue and one round which men were positioning themselves. He was credited with a variety of plans for reform. He had ideas, or perhaps dreams, but no plans—at least none fully thought through. That there would soon be change was certain. Its direction was one of the great uncertainties.

In January 1908 the harmony between Austria-Hungary and Russia over Balkan affairs was rudely disturbed. This was Aehrenthal's doing. The harmony had endured for a decade. In 1897 Austria-Hungary and Russia had agreed to maintain the status quo in the Balkan Peninsula, to abstain from intervention in the internal affairs of the Balkan states and to instruct their representatives to co-operate so that the states could not play off one Power against the other. This pledge was renewed by what was known as the Mürzsteg Punktation, signed by Austria-Hungary and Russia on October 2, 1903. Macedonia was the area of maximum disturbance in 1903. It was an area badly governed by the ageing Abdul Hamid of Turkey. Turkey-in-Europe seemed, indeed, to be breaking up at last when Macedonia revolted in 1903. Two other considerations had at that time made Austria-Hungary cautious. Goluchowski was convinced that Austria-Hungary was militarily and politically unfit for war and made more so by the beginning of the difficulties with Serbia already referred to (see above, p. 15) and in addition the massacres which followed the Macedonian rebellion had roused British humanitarian interests and some Government attention. Russia and Austria-Hungary finally gained the consent of the Powers to the establishment of an international gendarmerie in Macedonia. Germany, who was cultivating the friendship of Turkey, and mistrustful of Russia, declined to join the other Powers in controlling a zone of gendarmerie. Early in 1905 Britain attempted to set up international supervision of the collection of taxes in Macedonia. International control neither of police nor of taxation worked without friction, but resulted in much good to the inhabitants and kept Russia and Austria-Hungary together. In 1907 they stayed together to oppose a British attempt to increase the efficiency of the gendarmerie.

Austro-Russian agreement collapsed when Aehrenthal, the masterful new Foreign Minister of Austria-Hungary, suddenly announced in January 1908 that he meant to build a railway through the Sanjak of Novibazar, to connect with the Turkish terminus at Mitrovika. Vienna would thus be linked by direct railway with Salonika, and Montenegro more clearly than ever separated from Serbia. In fact the plan was crude to a degree and, because of its engineering difficulties, impracticable, but the spirit of aggression was evident. Isvolski, since 1906 Foreign Minister in Russia, made a counter-proposal of a railway from Rumania through Serbia and Montenegro to a point on the Adriatic coast of Albania. So a veiled Austro-Hungarian railway advance on Salonika was to be met by a veiled Russian advance through Serbia and Albania. Aehrenthal eventually accepted Isvolski's counter-proposal, but neither railway was ever built. Had either been, war between Austria-Hungary and Russia could hardly have failed to ensue; for rival railway schemes hid renewed competition for ascendancy. But the really serious matter was, as Isvolski complained, that Austria-Hungary had broken the agreement reached with Russia in 1897 and confirmed at Mürzsteg in 1903.

It was particularly unfortunate for the peace of Europe that Austria-Hungary's bold step forward came four months after the Anglo-Russian Conventions had been signed. When in June 1908 Edward VII paid a long-overdue visit to Nicholas II at Reval the demonstrations of Anglo-Russian cordiality excited German and Austro-Hungarian anxiety. Bülow was assured that the Anglo-Russian Conventions of August 1907 were not directed against German interests. But both Bülow and William II made speeches suggesting that Germany was encircled by hostile Powers and would have to defend herself. Their remarks were received with loud applause.

Just at this critical moment a revolution occurred in Turkey which had certainly been hastened by Turkish fear of an Anglo-Russian agreement to her disadvantage. But a secret Committee of Union and Progress (the Young Turks) had long been planning revolt among the officers of the Turkish army. Early in July 1908 Niazi Bey and Enver Bey put the plans into action and proclaimed a parliamentary constitution. The hitherto invincible tyrant, Abdul Hamid, collapsed with hardly a struggle and professed (as he had done once before) that he would become the mildest of constitutional kings. The able soldiers who had engineered the revolt were profuse in professions of liberalism. All Christian peoples—Greeks, Serbs and Bulgars—were to be free under the Turkish flag and to fraternise with Muslims. So monstrous and insupportable had been the tyranny of Abdul Hamid that for a time these professions were believed. Greek popes kissed Turkish dervishes, Serbs fraternised with Bulgars, and both walked in procession with Turks. The European Powers at once seized the opportunity to abandon all Macedonian reforms, on the pretext that the Young Turks were liberals and could manage their own affairs, but they were glad to be rid of a responsibility which only provoked quarrels among themselves. The Young Turks proved to be as ruthless and militarist as Abdul Hamid, and incomparably more efficient. Their professed liberalism proved to be a sham which they discarded when it suited them. Austria-Hungary's concern was lest Bosnia and Herzegovina should be invited to elect deputies to sit in the new Turkish parliament. This was likely since the Provinces, though occupied by her after 1878, were still under Turkish sovereignty. Both Provinces were anyhow in a state of agitation because the new hostility of Serbia to Austria-Hungary, noticed on p. 361 of Volume One (and above, p. 15), raised the hopes of the Croats for independence in a great Serbo-Croat state.

In April 1908, Isvolski had begun some negotiations of doubtful wisdom with Aehrenthal. At the end of July he made a definite proposal. He proposed, in short, that Austria-Hungary should annex Bosnia, Herzegovina and the Sanjak and support the opening of the Straits of the Bosphorus and Dardannelles to Russian warships. It will be recalled that the Straits had played a small part in the negotiation of the Anglo-Russian Conventions of 1907, but a part sufficient to encourage Isvolski to hope that Britain might agree to some re-arrangement. It is interesting that he should have made his firm proposal just after the Anglo-Russian meeting at Reval. In September the negotiations were carried further at a meeting between Isvolski and Aehrenthal at the castle of Buchlau, which Berchtold, then Austro-Hungarian Ambassador in St. Petersburg, had put at their disposal. Nothing was set down on paper but agreement was reached and subsequently recorded in different terms by the two men. Isvolski maintained later that he had recognised at Buchlau that, since both matters were regulated by the Treaty of Berlin, their agreement could not be implemented except by a European Conference. Aehrenthal denied this.

Aehrenthal, who was a bold and determined man, resolved to strike as soon as he could, and to make assurance doubly sure invited Prince Ferdinand of Bulgaria to Vienna in the first week of October. What was then agreed was soon obvious. On October 6 Ferdinand threw off the suzerainty of the Turkish Sultan and proclaimed himself King of an independent Bulgaria. Two days later, on October 7, Francis Joseph proclaimed the annexation of Bosnia and Herzegovina. At the same time Austria-Hungary withdrew her troops from the Sanjak. Germany and Italy had been warned in the summer, but preliminary consultations with Britain and France had not taken place, and even Isvolski was taken by surprise at the timing. He took his stand on a Conference and was supported by Britain and France. Grey, the British Foreign Secretary, maintained the sanctity of the Treaty of Berlin, asserted that its renegotiation could only take place in a Conference of its signatories and agreed with Isvolski on a possible agenda for it. The rule of the closure of the Straits was included but Grey made it plain that they should only be opened, if opened equally to all Powers and if Turkey agreed. The Conference agenda was presented to Austria-Hungary as a joint proposal from all three

Entente Powers. Aehrenthal, judging the situation with brutal realism, calculated that no Power would make war to maintain the Treaty of Berlin; and France, embroiled with Germany over Morocco (below, p. 32), would be weak over Bosnia. He, therefore, refused a Conference unless it was understood beforehand that it was only to sanction a *fait accompli*. Germany stood by Austria-Hungary.

The nub of the difficulty was not touched by these discussions. It was elsewhere: in Serbia. Serbia was outraged. As long as Austria-Hungary only occupied Bosnia and Herzegovina she could cherish the hope that the two million Serbs and Croats of the two Provinces might eventually be united with herself. They were now to be united with the five million Serbs and Croats under Austrian or Hungarian rule. Serbian nationalism seemed to be for ever frustrated. The agitation was extraordinary. Serbia and Montenegro demanded territorial compensation. Serbia ordered the mobilisation of her first reserve, 120,000 men, summoned her parliament which voted war credits and, in December, further war credits. Austria-Hungary strengthened her forces in Dalmatia and Bosnia. There might have been European war in 1909, supposing Austria-Hungary had made a punitive raid into Serbia or taken other military measures in answer to her frantic and chauvinist outbursts. Russia, going to the assistance of Serbia, would have become engaged with Austria-Hungary and the Austro-German Alliance would have become operative. On January 21, 1909, Germany had assured Austria-Hungary of support if she deemed it necessary to take steps against Serbia. There was a possibility of Russia's action, because Isvolski's policy of a bargain had been defeated. He was caught between the British and French insistence on no revision of the Treaty of Berlin except by European negotiation on one hand and, on the other, a new factor, an ebullition of Slavophilism in Russia and the insistence of the Prime Minister, Stolypin, and the Finance Minister, Kokovtsov, that a bargain over Bosnia and Herzegovina was a betrayal of the Slav cause. Though they also urged that Russia was not ready for war, she might have found it impossible to avoid going to the help of a Serbia overwhelmed by Austria-Hungary.

The position of Britain and France after the abandonment of the Conference was that they could recognise neither the annexation nor the independence of Bulgaria, except after an agreement of Austria-Hungary and of Bulgaria with Turkey. Turkey, as a means of inducing Austria-Hungary to make substantial compensation, had instituted a boycott of Austro-Hungarian merchandise. Germany was now counselling moderation. So agreement with Turkey was effected. Turkish diplomacy was extremely clever and Aehrenthal obtained agreement (February 26, ratified in April) only after he had undertaken to pay Turkey some £ 2.5 million (in the values of those days) in compensation for the crown lands the Sultan had lost in

Bosnia. The Bulgarian agreement was reached through the intervention of Russia. Isvolski had had an opportunity to take the lead again because Bulgaria was now a satellite to Russia. Turkey recognised the independence of Bulgaria—and other Powers followed suit—after she had agreed to pay Turkey some £5 million in compensation for the tribute due from Bulgaria and Eastern Roumelia. The money was found, not by Bulgaria, but by Russia who renounced the war indemnities still due to her from Turkey after defeat in the Russo-Turkish War of 1877–78. A Russo-Turkish agreement was signed accordingly on March 15 and a Bulgaro-Turkish on April 19.

Meanwhile Isvolski had made 'the great surrender' and persuaded Serbia and Montenegro to abandon their claims in the interest of European peace (February 27). Early in March Serbia put her case in the hands of the European Powers and disclaimed hostility to Austria-Hungary. Unfortunately this disclaimer coincided with Aehrenthal's opening of a new diplomatic offensive to gain recognition of the annexation by the Powers. He declared the Serbian note unsatisfactory and on March 15–16 there were ominous Austrian troop movements. It was Bülow's intervention which caused the whole commotion to evaporate. He put pressure on Austria-Hungary to satisfy Russia so that Russia could put further pressure on Belgrade. Eventually the annexation was recognised by all the Powers including Russia (who got no quid pro quo) by an exchange of notes of each individually with Austria-Hungary. Germany had persuaded Austria-Hungary to ask for this; and taken steps to ensure that she knew the answer would be favourable before she made the request (March 21). The war party in Serbia had received a great blow and under the stress the Crown Prince, who had put himself at its head, abdicated his claim to succeed his father (March 28). King Peter, wiser than most others, brought Serbia to admit to Austria-Hungary that her rights were not infringed by the annexation, to reduce her army to the level of September 1908, to abstain from further agitation and to promise to live with Austria-Hungary as a good neighbour. The relations of Austria-Hungary and Serbia were a factor of supreme importance for the future, second in importance only to the rebuff which, through Isvolski, Russia had received. It was to be the first of a series of rebuffs in her Balkan policy. A further rebuff, which seemed likely in June 1914, she would refuse to take. Indeed, the justification for treating these events at such length is that they foreshadowed, with one all-important difference, the events of June 1914. The difference was that Germany, after initial encouragement, restrained Austria-Hungary in 1909. She forced her forward in 1914.

During the Bosnian incident, Aehrenthal had caused fifty-three Serbs of Croatia to be put on trial in Zagreb for treason against the Monarchy, on the ground that they had conspired for unity with Serbia. They were convicted. But the trial had been so scandalously conducted that, on appeal, their sentences were quashed and a re-trial ordered. Then in December 1909 a libel action was brought by a number of Serbo-Croat politicians against the historian, Professor Friedjung, and the editor of the Vienna *Reichspost* for an anti-Serb article and pamphlet based on material supplied by the Foreign Office. The documents, like some of those used in the Zagreb trial, turned out to be forged. These trials served as an advertisement at once of Yugoslav (South Slav) unity and Hapsburg credulity and trickery. Even had it wished to, the Serbian Government could not now have stopped the Yugoslav propaganda inside Serbia or its spreading to Bosnia, Dalmatia and Hungarian Croatia. Nor could Austria-Hungary, except by a radical change of course, now stop the development of a movement of sympathy for the Slav cause in Britain, France and, to some extent, Italy. It was, of course, already strong in Russia.

Meanwhile Germany's constitutional, financial and social problems continued to be grave. The year 1910 saw the strengthening of the Left in Germany by the reunion of the three Left Liberal Parties in the *Fortschrittliche Volkspartei* (Progressive People's Party). It had political demands, which included the establishment of a Reich Ministry responsible to the Reichstag, and it had a long list of social demands, ranging from the establishment of labour exchanges and improved housing for workers to workers' participation in such things as factory inspection. It accepted a strong army but was anti-militarist. It was well organised with local associations of subscribing members, a party conference, a central executive and a strongly led Reichstag Fraktion. The most frightening display of strength on the left occurred when the Social Democrats reacted sharply to Bethmann Hollweg's proposals to reform the Prussian franchise in 1910. By dividing the electorate into three classes and providing that the small class of large taxpayers elected more members of the Prussian parliament than either of the others, the legislators of 1849 had arranged that the franchise permanently favoured the wealthy. Bethmann Hollweg merely proposed to enlarge the numbers of the top class. The Left wanted to abolish the three-class system altogether. The Social Democrats' response was frightening, less when they organised demonstrations of workingmen on a series of Sundays in February and May 1910, than when they discovered that by a massed general strike they could disrupt the whole operation of the state. There was no general strike, though much talk of it and a lurking fear that it would come. There was an unprecedented number of strikes in a variety of trades in 1910, a strike of the Ruhr miners in 1912 and of the Hamburg shipbuilding yards in 1913. Then in the General Election of January 1912 the Socialists joined the Progressive People's Party in a planned assault upon the Government parties and the united Left gained a majority in the Reichstag. A Socialist leader, Philipp Scheidemann, became Vice-President of the Reichstag, for with 110 seats the Socialists were the strongest single party.

The upper and middle classes in Germany could be deflected from their fears by imperialist activity, interest in which became more and more widespread. Imperialism did not necessarily imply overseas expansion, for it was connected with ideas derived from a misreading of Nietzsche, with social Darwinism and with generalised notions of racial superiority and so might imply continental aggression too. Something was said in chapter 24 of Volume One of the pressure groups which reinforced the tendency of the political parties to represent social and economic interests. The Pan German League, founded in 1890 in an ebullition of patriotism after the acquisition of Heligoland, was mentioned as an example. Among its members were men such as Max Weber, an early sociologist, who in an Inaugural Lecture at Freiburg University put the case in a powerful and persuasive way for Germany's aiming at world power and argued for the policy, begun two years later with the acquisition of Kiao-Chau. The Conservatives and the National Liberals were its main supporters. Its standing grew notably after 1912. It focused the intelligence and wealth of Germany upon the formulation of 'aims' in foreign policy, upon, that is, the direction of a forward drive which would keep the middle classes united with the upper classes against Social Democracy. Further to the left, among the National Liberals and Left Liberals, men such as Walther Rathenau and Friedrich Naumann pleaded for German economic and political ascendancy in Europe, for what was called *Mitteleuropa*. After the outbreak of the War of 1914–18 a parallel concept of *Mittelafrika*, that is the acquisition of a block of Central African territory to link all the German African coastal colonies, gained wide support. Among the Liberal Imperialists economic arguments for German expansion were most used, but they also urged that Germany should not be afraid of an imperialist policy for 'the imperial idea was the idea of the age.' For those interested in economic enterprise the question, how can we acquire territory for the German people, was the question of the age. The Hansa League, which organised business and trading interests, in 1912 called for 'a healthy—not a chauvinist—imperialism.' The League of German Industrialists, which organised business and manufacturing interests, with Gustav Stresemann, later to be Chancellor of the Weimar Republic, among its presidents, in 1913 hoped for a German-British association against the Slavs. The banks, heavy industry, export industries, the finished goods industries, all found appropriate arguments for German expansion or German ascendancy. Friedrich von Bernhardi, one of the leading military writers of this period, presented Germany with the alternatives of expansion or decline. He and Heinrich Class, President of the Pan German League, are said to have been the most extreme exponents of the doctrine of aggressive war as 'the renewal and purification of the German people.' At first the Social Democrats had seemed immune from imperialism. Yet after the Election of 1912, though they continued to protest against naval expenditure and the activities of the Navy League and the Pan German League, the trade union wing and the right wing of their party began to talk of the 'creative force' of the spirit of imperialism and to be in danger of falling under its spell.

Bethmann Hollweg's policy was not generally assertive. He spoke for the civilian Government of Germany that acted as a restraint upon the Emperor and his military advisers. Yet he did not always prevail; nor could he be out of sympathy with a forward policy, *if* and when it was successful. Above all he could not stop the building of the Baghdad Railway which antagonised Russia, since it was accompanied by the development of German ascendancy in Turkey, nor the building of the Battle Fleet which antagonised Britain. Germany had begun to be interested in Turkey as long ago as 1883 when General von der Goltz had been sent to train the Turkish army. The interest had not been encouraged by Bismarck, but continued. By the end of the nineties German salesmen were pushing their wares in Turkey, German financiers were investing their capital and German firms were supplying torpedoes, small arms, artillery, even bicycles. William II, with some flamboyance, twice visited Turkey, in 1889 and 1898. Meanwhile the Anatolian Railway Company, owned partly by French and partly by German capitalists, was promised in 1888 and 1893 that it would be given the concession for any prolongation of its railway system to Baghdad. It received a firm undertaking in 1899. At last an Imperial Decree actually granted the concession on March 18, 1902. Financial and administrative difficulties still prevented any start in building. On March 5, 1903, a revised Baghdad Railway Convention promised better results. The Turkish Government was to provide a share of the funds for the construction and to guarantee a return on their investment to the foreign investors of so much a kilometre. There were also favourable provisions for the security of the railway administration and for the land through which it was to go. British capitalists were invited to participate in the activities of the new Baghdad Railway Company. They were approached by German bankers and they in their turn approached the Foreign Office. But no encouragement was forthcoming from the British Government. In those circumstances the British capitalists shied away. By April 1903 it was clear that the Baghdad Railway would become more and more an exclusively German concern. By 1909 a stretch of railway had been built from Konia to Bulgurlu and preparations were being made for the next stretch to Aleppo. The convention of 1903 was re-negotiated and Turkey, to provide herself with increased revenue in order to ensure that her own financial participation was adequate, sought to raise her customs revenue. To do this she needed international sanction. A powerful lever was thus in the hands of the European Powers. It was at this point that Germany made an effort to appease the hostility of Russia. At Potsdam on November 4, 1910, a Russo-German agreement was signed. Germany recognised the Russian sphere of interest in northern Persia, as defined by the Anglo-Russian Convention of 1907, and undertook not to seek or support concessions for railways, roads, telegraphs or other means of communication in the area; Russia recognised the rights of the German concessionaires in the Baghdad Railway and undertook to withdraw all diplomatic opposition to the construction of the railway and the participation of foreign capitalists in the enterprise. But the concessionaires continued to be under strong pressure to put the line under international control. The British Foreign Office and Prime Minister were drawn into consultations. In 1911 Britain was induced to state her terms for the encouragement of British investment. It was not until 1914, on the eve of the War of 1914–18, that any settlement looked like being reached. Meanwhile the railway was not built. Germany continued to extend her influence in Turkey and Russia continued to watch her activities with increasing suspicion.

The naval rivalry between Britain and Germany was a sharper, less dragging cause of tension. For Britain, too, these were troubled years and the expenditure on armaments which the naval rivalry entailed was resented as it might not have been in a less troubled period. There is not space to say more here than that it was a period of social reforms, in themselves disturbing and costly, unprecedented expenditure and new taxation leading to the constitutional crisis of 1910–12. The question of Ireland was left unsettled, though that of the House of Lords was closed with the Parliament Act.

Germany's relations with Britain had been worsening since 1907. That year saw a second Peace Conference at The Hague, which lasted from June to October. A good deal of useful technical work was done at this Conference, but there was no advance whatever in the limitation of armaments. Towards the end of the Conference the British offered to keep naval armaments at their existing levels and promised to build no more ships, if other Powers agreed. This offer was not unlike that which was successful at the Washington Naval Conference of 1921. It shows the international tension and mutual suspicion that Germany opposed this project with vehemence and success. At the first Hague Conference she had equally opposed Russia's projects of military disarmament. Russia had wished to stop the race of armaments then, because her artillery was weaker: Britain wished to stop it now because her navy was stronger than the German. So the factors were complex and Germany's position a difficult one. But it seems that, while she could not have accepted both these offers, she might have accepted one of them. She was the only Power before 1914 that always and consistently refused all thought of limiting armaments. There was, indeed, more danger in accepting offers in 1907 than in 1899. For in 1899 Russia and Britain were bitter enemies and in 1907 they were negotiating an Entente. Indeed, in 1907 the assumption was widespread that a war between Britain and Germany was likely, or certain, in the future. Yet the Liberal Government in power in Britain was anxious to economise in naval expenditure and to repress jingoist and imperialist aspirations. A visit of William II to England in November 1907 did something to allay suspicion. He proved unexpectedly conciliatory and even offered to hand over to Britain that part of the proposed Baghdad Railway which was to end in the Persian Gulf. But Bülow finally vetoed the proposal and this was probably the last chance Germany had of keeping on really friendly terms with Britain.

In 1908 William II did as much harm to Anglo-German relations as he had done good in November 1907. He wrote a letter to the British First Lord of the Admiralty, the substance of which got into the papers and provoked much hostile criticism and a great demand for naval activity in Britain. During a visit of Edward VII to Germany tension was shown when the Under-Secretary in the British Foreign Office spoke to the Emperor of the dangers of naval competition and the Emperor replied that he would go to war rather than submit to dictation of his naval programme by a foreign Power. Edward VII's visit to Tsar Nicholas in June seemed like an answer to this. In August, King Edward met the Emperor Francis Joseph at Ischl and complained of the tension produced by the naval competition of Germany and, as Francis Joseph said, 'tried (without success) to detach me from the alliance with Germany.' At the end of October came the *Daily Telegraph* incident of which the domestic importance has already been noticed. In the interview which the paper recorded, the Emperor informed the British public that the majority of his people wanted war with them and that he alone stood between, and had, secretly and openly, been Britain's friend. This revelation provoked a loudly expressed suspicion both of Germany and of the Emperor in Britain.

The Admiralty learnt in the autumn of 1908 that the German naval programme of 1908–10 was being anticipated. In other words, by collecting materials and armament in advance and making other preparations, Germany had considerably shortened the time between laying down a hull and the ship's being ready for sea. Thus at the end of any building period she would have more Dreadnoughts than the British, who guided their own building by the German, had made allowance for.

In March 1909 the British Admiralty in defending the naval estimates revealed this to the House of Commons. The Government programme was considered inadequate and an agitation for eight Dreadnoughts to be laid down in 1909 began. It was crystallised in the popular slogan 'We want eight, and we won't wait.' After resisting the agitation for a time the British Government gave way to their public, and Germany was outdistanced in the race. Britain built eighteen Dreadnoughts between 1909 and 1911 and Germany, who made no further acceleration, nine. It is to the credit of Bethmann Hollweg that he instituted negotiations late in 1909, soon after taking office as Chancellor, for reducing the naval programmes, or rather for retarding them. He declared that he could not repeal the naval law, which laid down a programme only to be completed in 1918. But he could arrange that fewer capital ships should be laid down in the earlier years and the number be equivalently raised in the later. This suggestion did not come to much, but it was something. For the retardation of the shipbuilding for a few years would have meant a certain relaxation of tension though no ultimate reduction of costs. In return for this somewhat shadowy naval arrangement, Bethmann demanded a very definite political advantage. He asked Britain to pledge herself to an agreement that 'in the case of an attack made on either Power [Britain or Germany] by a third Power or group of Powers, the Power not attacked should stand aside.'

This neutrality proposal was repeated, in one form or another, in the next two years and again in 1912, and Germany always insisted that it should be accepted before any naval agreement was discussed. Its benefit to Germany was evident and substantial. If Russia or France (or both) attacked Germany, Britain would be neutral. But one Power (Japan) was bound to Britain by an alliance. Two others were bound by Ententes, and neither Russia nor France nor Japan was in the least likely to attack Britain. At the moment, so far as human probability went, Germany was the only Power ever likely to do so. The acceptance of the proposal, therefore, would have been, from the British standpoint, of no special advantage. It was, indeed, more than she had given either Russia or France.

The fundamental fact in the whole question of the 'neutrality formula' was that it would have been inconsistent with the assumptions underlying the Franco-British Entente; and this was reflected in the first reply made by Britain. She offered to give assurances, in July 1910, that nothing in her agreements with any other Power was directed against Germany and that she had no hostile intentions towards her. As a result of further negotiations Britain asserted that there was nothing exclusive in her Entente system, and that a similar method of settling difficulties might be embodied in an agreement with Germany. On the naval side Grey now offered an exchange of information. The German reply to this in May 1911 accepted it in principle, withdrew the retardation proposal but insisted on a general political agreement.[1] But at this moment a rash action on her part produced the crisis of Agadir: the second Moroccan crisis.

The root of the Morocco crisis of 1911 lay in Algeciras. Germany had been deeply wounded by the results of that Conference and showed it in 1908. A grave incident took place over German deserters from the French Foreign Legion sheltered by the German consul at Casablanca. Germany tried to bully France. Clemenceau happened to be Premier and refused to be intimidated and was supported by Britain and Russia, and the incident ended in arbitration at The Hague Tribunal, which was unfavourable to Germany (November 1908). As the Bosnian crisis was then to the fore and the Emperor was very unpopular because of his *Daily Telegraph* interview, Germany had no wish for further complications elsewhere. Accordingly she initiated *pourparlers* at the beginning of 1909, which resulted (February 8) in a Declaration being signed by France and Germany known as the 'Morocco Pact'. This practically assured to France special political influence in Morocco, while giving to Germany equal economic opportunities with France in that area. It seemed that a new order of things had begun, but after an annoying set of negotiations in which Germany was conciliatory, the two countries failed to reach any economic agreement either over the mines or railways of Morocco. By the end of 1910 Germany was thoroughly annoyed at the French inability to arrive at economic agreement, and by the beginning of 1911 she had real reasons for becoming alarmed at French political activity in Morocco.

The internal situation in Morocco was becoming impossible. The Sultan was overturned by his brother in 1908, and the usurper, though recognised by the Powers was not obeyed by many of his subjects. In 1910 his request for French officers to reorganise his army was refused, and he found himself unable to defend his capital (Fez) against rebellious tribesmen. He appealed to France for aid and in April 1911 she agreed to organise and despatch a Moorish, and if necessary a French, column to Fez to relieve the Sultan from anxiety. Even in March Kiderlen-Wächter had told the French that German public opinion would be excited by French operations in Morocco, which might appear to tear up the Act of Algeciras. When troops were actually sent in April both he and Bethmann saw the situation clearly enough. It was always easier to send troops into a disturbed area than to get them out again, and occupations by European Powers of backward territory, even if meant to be temporary and military, often become permanent and political. Spain agreed with Germany that the action of France endangered the Act of Algeciras, and with it the integrity of Morocco. Grey thought dif-

[1] E. L. Woodward, *Great Britain and the German Navy* (1935), chs X–XV deal with the negotiations of 1908 to 1911.

ferently, or at any rate protested that he was satisfied with the assurances of France, and meant to stand by her. France tactfully suggested the resumption of the Franco-German railway negotiations in June, but these were interrupted by an extraordinary step on the part of Germany.

On July 1, Germany informed the Powers who had signed the Algeciras Act that she had sent a German gunboat, the *Panther*, to the port of Agadir in southern Morocco, in order to protect German interests and subjects there. Germany explained that she considered the Act of Algeciras to be now dead, and could not look on while France and Spain seemed to be disregarding the Act. Kiderlen-Wächter was responsible for this Moroccan coup, but the Emperor and Chancellor had accepted his advice. Kiderlen's idea seems to have been a mere 'bluff.' He did not really mean to attempt to partition Morocco, but he thought it a good opportunity to get rid of the Algeciras Act, and to press France to cede Germany a slice of Congo territory in return for her abandoning political designs in Morocco. He thought he could do this by holding Agadir until France surrendered. Such was the gist of the memorandum he submitted to the Emperor and Chancellor.[1]

There were also domestic motives for Germany's action. A General Election was due in 1912. The Government wished to strengthen its support from the Right against the Social Democrats. A strong foreign policy was an appeal to the Right. Signs of Moroccan claims pleased the industrialists of the National Liberal party, interested in Morocco as a source of iron ore. But the act was unwise for several reasons. Grey was already known to be very sensitive about treaties, and here was another one openly torn up without Britain's being consulted or a Conference summoned. Next, to send a warship to dominate a port on the Atlantic was the best way to convince every Englishman that Germany was trying to secure a naval base at Agadir by violent means as she had done at Kiao-Chau. On July 4 Grey informed the German Ambassador that the action at Agadir created 'a new situation.' He seems to have expected information on the subject from Berlin, but Kiderlen chose to assume that this was unnecessary, and gave no assurances till July 23. During this period of three weeks there were important negotiations between Jules Cambon, the French Ambassador, and Kiderlen at Berlin. Kiderlen asked for a direct negotiation, thus excluding Britain and other signatories of Algeciras, and enabling him to demand compensation for retiring from Morocco, from France alone and in French territory (the French Congo). Cambon agreed to a negotiation *à deux*, but said he must keep friends and allies informed of the negotiation. Kiderlen then demanded practically all the French Congo, and his

---

[1] Fritz Fischer, *War of Illusions* (1975), pp. 72–3.

tone was so menacing that Britain and France began exchanging views as to the possibility of real danger. On the 21st Grey saw the German Ambassador and in plain language made clear to him that Britain thought Germany's demands for the Congo excessive and that her attitude at Agadir needed explanation, since she might even have hoisted her flag there. On the 23rd Germany gave the required assurances by telegraph. Had they been made earlier, these guarantees of good faith would have ended the crisis.

On July 21, and before the German reply had been received, Lloyd George, British Chancellor of the Exchequer, made a resounding entry into foreign politics. In a public speech at the Mansion House he stated that 'Britain should at all hazards maintain her place and her prestige amongst the Great Powers ... If ... peace could only be preserved . . . by allowing Britain to be treated . . . as if she were of no account in the Cabinet of Nations, then I say emphatically peace at that price would be a humiliation intolerable for a great country like ours to endure.' This statement was not suggested by Grey, but had his full approval and he subsequently defended it in public by saying that, if ever the time came when we could not make such a statement, 'we shall have ceased to exist, at all events as a great nation.' But it is one thing to make statements like this in private. Jules Cambon had used strong language to Kiderlen, but France had not openly protested. And it is quite another thing to make them in public. The sensation created was immense. The German public stated that Germany was flouted, menaced and defied. 'Stand firm, William!' called out the Berlin crowd to the Emperor, as they saw him riding down the Unter den Linden one day. But William could not stand firm. On July 24 and 25 the German Ambassador complained about the speech to Grey, but found him very determined. On the 26th and 27th he made a very courteous communication from Berlin which ended the difficulties between Britain and Germany.

But Britain rather than France had now become for Germany the main enemy. Moreover, the difficulties between France and Germany were not yet ended. The undercurrents of military preparations, though not of mobilisation, might have been detected in July in Germany, France, Britain and Belgium. But these were precautions, and in fact most diplomats knew, after the Mansion House speech, that Germany must yield or fight. She had not fought. Very tedious negotiations took place between Kiderlen and Cambon, and on August 20 the latter thought war possible. But the acuteness of the crisis became known to the public, there was a run on German banks in September, and the Emperor and Bethmann finally put the brake on Kiderlen. The consideration important to them was that the alliance with Austria-Hungary was not valid for a war with France only. In the second week of October an accord was reached, and the final agreement signed on November 4.

In substance France turned the interior of Morocco from an internationalised area to a French Sphere. Early in the next year the Sultan agreed to a French Protectorate and, except for Tangier and the Spanish zone, Morocco now became French. Germany retained only 'the open door' for trade. In compensation Germany obtained two large strips of French Congolese territory — running upwards from the German Cameroons, exactly as the horns of a bull spring from its head — and as it were transfixing the Belgian Congo with the two points. The aim was to give Germany direct access to the Belgian Congo, in order to put her in an advantageous position to secure a pre-emption on that territory. Pre-emption had been several times unavailingly mentioned by Germany. Germany had been defeated in the negotiation, and the extremely bitter debates in the Reichstag showed that the public realised the fact and put down the defeat to Britain. The British public was somewhat more moderate on hearing the news in November that the two nations had nearly been at war in July.

Agadir was an incident infinitely more serious than Algeciras and undoubtedly more critical than the Bosnian one. The Triple Entente had been defeated over Bosnia and Russia humiliated. But their defeat and humiliation were perhaps less public than that of the Triple Alliance, and of Germany in particular, at Agadir. This time Britain had appeared 'in shining armour' at a grave moment, to support her friend. An able publicist put his finger on the gravity of the new situation at once. He said that the bond of the Triple Entente is less close than that of the Triple Alliance, but for practical purposes Europe is divided by these two great combinations, and the tenseness of the situation makes crises inevitably recur. Russia and the Entente accepted defeat without war in the crisis of 1909. Germany accepted defeat without war in that of 1911; neither would accept defeat without war indefinitely. Both groups understood the danger, and both began to prepare. The Franco-British military conversations of 1905 (see Volume One, p. 377) had not been followed up after Algeciras. In July 1911 they were resumed and the mutual undertakings were recorded and signed. They included simultaneous mobilisation of a British expeditionary force of six divisions, to be landed at Le Havre, and of the French army. Britain had already been organising the expeditionary force; now arrangements were made with the Admiralty to transport it rapidly overseas. Preparations of all kinds for press censorship, for war legislation and the like were made. If a peace-loving country and its Government faced reality and made preparations like these, it is not surprising that military and naval activity developed elsewhere in a less liberal atmosphere. And the tensity of the situation was increased by military reorganisation everywhere and particularly by the designing and development of Russian strategic railways and of German strategic canals.

Russia and Italy used the crisis of Agadir to press demands on their respective Allies which they might otherwise have declined. Italy watched the crisis from June onwards with the full intention of obtaining Tripoli from Turkey while France, Germany and Britain were too occupied to prevent her. She had, indeed, previously obtained the consent of France, Germany and Austria-Hungary to her eventual occupation of Tripoli, but none of them approved of the moment she selected to execute her project. On September 26 Italy sent an ultimatum to Turkey and declared war three days later. Even as stated by herself Italy's reasons for war were pretexts. They were simply a cloak for a naked resolve to annex the territory. The war reflected little credit on Italy from any point of view, but she eventually annexed Tripoli (November 1911) and occupied the Dodecanese (April–May 1912)—twelve islands in the Aegean, of which Rhodes was the most important. When Serbia and her allies attacked Turkey, she brought the war to an end by the Treaty of Lausanne (October 1912).

Russia's action, while France and Britain were grappling with Germany, was less successful though even more discreditable. She intrigued so much in Persia, and showed so clearly her intention of annexing Teheran that Grey became extremely irate, and Paul Cambon, French Ambassador in London, advised Russia to abandon her designs unless she wished to end the Entente. Russia also returned to the old idea of opening the Dardanelles to Russian warships and made a formal demand to this effect at Constantinople in December 1911. Turkey was informed by both Britain and France that they did not support this demand, and accordingly refused Russia's request. But Turkey had become thoroughly suspicious of the Entente and was now more pro-German than ever.

In the beginning of 1912 the atmosphere between Russia and Britain had become so chilly that Germany made one more effort to break up the Triple Entente. William II asked 'his friend Lord Haldane' to pay an informal visit to Berlin. Haldane had hardly arrived when Winston Churchill (First Lord of the Admiralty since October 1911) offended Germany by a speech (February 9) in which he described her fleet as 'a luxury' and Britain's as 'a necessity.' But the reactions to this speech were probably not the cause of the failure of the overture. By now the risk theory had been rejected (see Volume One, p. 355). Germany believed herself at such a disadvantage in relation to Britain that she insisted on a 2:3 ratio. A supplementary Navy Law would be introduced later in 1912 to provide for this. The army too demanded increases—the biggest since 1893. The Treasury demanded a new tax to pay for these armaments. Haldane proposed the 'two keels to one standard', and said neutrality could not be reckoned on if Germany attacked France. Tirpitz tried to argue for a 10:16 keels' standard and communicated his *Novelle*, or naval programme, under the proposed supplementary law. Bethmann replied by the old neutrality proposal in the following form. 'If either of the high contracting parties becomes entangled in a war in which it cannot be said to be the aggressor, the other will at least observe towards the Power so entangled a benevolent neutrality, and use its utmost endeavour for the localisation of the conflict.' The British reply did not go even half-way to meet this view, and when Bethmann tried to secure what seemed to him an essential addition, Grey, in Bethmann's words, 'roundly refused' it. It is clear that Germany hoped to bind Britain to a formula separating her from the Entente, and that Haldane and Grey both saw this and refused to accede to the proposal. But, if Grey's suspicions were to some extent aroused by the neutrality proposal, a study of the *Novelle* increased them. At the end of July, Churchill indicated to the Commons that the new German programme meant an increase not only in ships and personnel, but also an unprecedented increase in the fighting efficiency of the forces available in peacetime.

British public opinion was being prepared for a further increase of the fleet in the North Sea and for the abandonment of the Mediterranean to France. Franco-British naval conversations took place in the summer and autumn. In October the third French Battle Squadron joined the other two in the Mediterranean. Britain left to France the defence of the Mediterranean against Austria-Hungary[1], and the British Squadron based on Malta was much reduced by the despatch of several ships to the North Sea. Britain in return practically assumed the defence of the Channel. These arrangements were formalised by an exchange of letters between Grey and the French Ambassador. Grey, in his letter of November 22, 1912, to Paul Cambon wrote: 'We have agreed that consultation between [naval and military] experts is not and ought not to be regarded as an engagement that commits either Government to action in a contingency that has not arisen and may never arise. The disposition, for instance, of the French and British fleets respectively at the present moment is not based upon an engagement to co-operate in war.' That might be so, but it rendered co-operation infinitely more probable. Moreover, he also agreed in his letter that in the event of either Britain or France suffering unprovoked aggression they should consult together and, if common action were necessary, the plans of the General Staffs should come into operation. The Entente thus became a defensive alliance. On August 2, 1914, when war between Germany and France was seen to be inevitable, Grey promised to protect the northern French coast from being bombarded by Germany. That was not war with Germany, but it was an action which rendered war with her

---

[1] It was not expected that the Italian fleet would side with Austria-Hungary and Germany.

extremely probable. When the North Sea and the Channel were defended solely by Britain, and the Mediterranean mainly by France, each Power felt obligations, when war broke out, towards the other. It was the 'moral obligation' to France that was adduced in the British Cabinet to justify the declaration of war on Germany on August 4. So November 1912 marked a decisive step towards war between Britain and Germany. The final failure to arrive at a naval understanding with her in the early part of 1912 caused Britain to concentrate her fleet in the North Sea and to rely on France to protect the Mediterranean. France was, in fact, though not in name, adding to British sea power. Germany, on the other hand, was compelling Britain to loosen her grip on the Mediterranean. The effect was to drive Britain away from Germany and to tighten the bond with France. In Germany the supplementary navy bill was passed in 1912 but the army bill was held back for the year on the Chancellor's insistence. It was brought forward again in 1913 and passed.

Chapter 2

THE TRUE PRE-WAR, 1912–14

No single event influenced the outbreak of war in 1914 more than the Balkan War of 1912. Other incidents, such as Algeciras, Bosnia or Agadir, disturbed the situation because they affected the Balance of Power in the future. But the overthrow of the Turk caused an immediate danger, for it affected the Balance of Power then and there. Serbia, Bulgaria, Greece and Rumania were revealed as conquering military states. The Turkish army—trained by Germany as a potential ally—was utterly beaten. Serbia added a million to her population, erased the humiliations of the Bosnian annexation, and triumphantly asserted her prestige in an outburst of Pan-Serb and Yugoslav enthusiasm, which swept Dalmatia and Bosnia like a prairie fire. Serbia, hitherto rebuffed and discredited, appeared armed, victorious and triumphant. As Italy had arisen from Piedmont so a united Yugoslavia was to arise from Serbia. The prestige gained by Greece and Rumania was only second to that of Serbia. All three states now looked forward to a time when each flag would cover all their kinsmen, whether to be freed from Austro-Hungarian or Turkish rule; a greater Greece, a greater Rumania, a greater Serbia. A perpetually increasing nationalist agitation in Austria-Hungary and Turkey, where such agitation was so dangerous, simultaneously arose.

The first in the new series of happenings was a movement by King Nicholas of Montenegro in the summer of 1911 to support the northern Albanians in an attempt to wrest independence from Turkey. Russia, Austria-Hungary and Italy joined together to restrain him, since they thought his aim was to gain a port on the coast and Albanian territory for Montenegro. The outcome, however, was that Serbia and Bulgaria, whom Russia had reconciled, chose this opportunity to attempt to realise their national ideals. Their plan was to attack the Turks while Russia and France held Germany in check. Austria-Hungary would be prevented from intervening by the furious Pan-Serb or Yugoslav propaganda which, despite her promise of 1909,

Serbia continued to conduct in the Dual Monarchy. To these three states a fourth was soon added; for in Greece a man of genius, Venizelos, had become Prime Minister. As early as August 1911 he had suggested to the Bulgars that a defensive alliance would ensure the safety of both Greece and Bulgaria and save the Christians of Macedonia whom the Young Turks were persecuting to extermination.

Serious Serbo-Bulgarian negotiations began in October 1911. A treaty was ultimately signed in March 1912, guaranteeing to each signatory its territory and independence and promising mutual support if one of the European Powers tried to annex or occupy any territory under Turkish rule. A secret addition arranged for common action against Turkey, subject to Russia's approval. A preliminary partition of territory to be conquered was sketched out and it was agreed that the so-called contested zone in Macedonia—the Monastir area, dear to Bulgaria—should be assigned according to the decision of the Tsar. In April 1912 a Serbo-Bulgarian military convention followed. As for the Greeks, they signed a defensive alliance with Bulgaria on May 29, 1912, and a military convention on October 5. Montenegro had been approached in August and joined the Serbo-Bulgarian-Greek League in September.

Sazonov, who had come to the Russian Foreign Office at the end of 1910, hoped to control Serbia and Bulgaria and warned them at an early stage that his Government would not approve action against Turkey. But Russia was divided. Sazonov wished for peace and even hoped at first to include Turkey in the Balkan League. The Slavophils in the Government wished to encourage Serbo-Bulgarian nationalist aspirations. Poincaré, the active French Premier, and the moving spirit in the Franco-Russian Alliance during the last year of peace, saw further than Sazonov. He told him when he was in St. Petersburg (August 9–16, 1912) that the League contained 'the germ of a war not only against Turkey but against Austria.' In October Sazonov accordingly joined Berchtold, who had become Foreign Minister on Aehrenthal's death in 1912, in warning the Balkan states against a rupture with Turkey and any attempt to change the status quo. The warning was presented in the name of all the European Powers on October 7. It was too late. The next day, October 8, Montenegro, disregarding altogether these menaces, declared war on Turkey, and set the Balkans aflame from one end to the other.

What followed is one of the miracles of history. There can be no doubt that the Powers believed that the Balkan League would be beaten. Both they and the Turks were speedily undeceived. On October 22 the Bulgars won a great victory over the Turks at Kirk-Kilisse; on the 26th the Serbs opened the way into Macedonia by a resounding victory at Kumanovo, which they followed up by a victory in front of Monastir, where their troops fought for a day breast-high in the water. The Greeks, who had been temporarily checked at Florina, found only fleeing Turks to contend with when they advanced again, and on November 8 they entered the coveted town of Salonika. This was really the end of the Turkish Empire in Macedonia. The British Prime Minister, H. H. Asquith, on November 9, in his speech at the Mansion House, brushed aside altogether the collective menace of the Powers to the Balkan League of only one month before. He said that they would recognise the new facts and consent to the territorial changes already won by blood and sacrifice.

The position of the Balkan League was, however, by no means so strong, nor were the Powers so weak, as they appeared to be. The Serbs had reached Durazzo on the seacoast of Albania, or had brought their steeds to water in the Adriatic, as King Nicholas of Montenegro poetically remarked. Austria-Hungary now threatened, in unmistakable terms of menace, that she would allow no Serbian annexation of Albanian ports; Italy supported her, and Sazonov reluctantly concurred. On December 3, 1912, an armistice was arranged between the Turks and the League, and it lasted till February 3, 1913. Three great Turkish fortresses still held out at the end of the year: Scutari in Albania against Serbs and Montenegrins; Janina in Epirus against the Greeks; Adrianople in Thrace against the Bulgars. The rest of European Turkey was in the hands of the Balkan League up to the lines of Tchataldja, which are but some thirty kilometres distant from Constantinople itself. There Bulgaria had penned in the biggest Turkish army, but had been informed by Sazonov that she would not be allowed to enter Constantinople.

France and Germany, for once, helped one another to keep the peace and to localise the conflict. In December Conrad certainly wanted to attack the Serbs, but the refusal of the aged Austrian Emperor to go to war was greatly strengthened by the attitude of Germany, which was extremely pacific. And Italy also assisted Germany to restrain her ally. Similarly Poincaré continued to restrain Sazonov, who could hardly avoid encouraging the Balkan League even when he professed to disapprove of their actions. Grey during this period at no time hesitated to throw his full weight into the scale of peace. Largely owing to his efforts, though heartily seconded by Poincaré and the German Emperor, the system of trying to settle matters by a European Conference was again adopted, and despite all difficulties, the method justified itself. A Conference of Ambassadors was at work in London from December 18, 1912 to August 11, 1913. It worked clumsily and disagreements made it difficult to put active pressure on the small and militarily triumphant League. But, though the Conference was at times hoodwinked and defied both by the Balkan League and by the Turks, it proved a good instrument for reconciling the Powers and a place where Britain and Germany co-operated.

On February 3 the League resumed hostilities against the Turks, and the danger of conflict between the Powers became very great. Austria and Hungary had mobilised troops to threaten Serbia and, in Galicia, to threaten Russia; Russia had mobilised in the Caucasus to threaten Turkey. On January 24, 1913, Enver Bey overthrew the relatively pacific Turkish Government at Constantinople, murdered the Turkish Commander-in-Chief and became a sort of military dictator. He promptly and contemptuously repudiated the arrangement for settlement made in December by the Ambassadors' Conference and resumed hostilities with the Balkan League. The results were at first disastrous to Turkey. The large island of Crete, which the Powers had so often denied to the Greeks, now surrendered quietly and hoisted the Greek flag. The Albanian city of Scutari fell to King Nicholas of Montenegro, and he refused to retire from it. But Austria-Hungary would not give way here, and, under her pressure, the Powers forced Nicholas to evacuate it by a naval demonstration (May 15, 1913). The great Epirot fortress of Janina fell before the Greeks, and Adrianople, the greatest prize of all, yielded to the combined efforts of the Serbian artillery and the Bulgar army. The situation was as follows: the Bulgars held Macedonia east of Salonika and all Thrace up to the Tchataldja lines, on which they made no impression. The Greeks held most of Epirus and southern Macedonia including Salonika. The Novibazar area and all Macedonia, hitherto unconquered, had passed into the hands of the Serbs. The crucial question really concerned the contested zone of Macedonia. This area, comprising Monastir and the heart of Macedonia, was the prize which Bulgaria had lost in 1878 and now trusted to regain. Unfortunately for her Serbia held it, and Serbia was not wholly satisfied with her share of the spoils. It is true that she had agreed that the contested zone was to be assigned according to the arbitration of the Tsar, but that was before she had conquered it. Force alone would make her or Bulgaria yield.

The Powers had already decided in principle that Albania should be independent, and, in this one instance, their show of force had taught Serbs and Montenegrins to evacuate territory. The Powers had also partially defined the boundaries of Albania to the north. They agreed on a northern boundary, which ran counter to all the dictates of common sense, and of which the result was further conflict between Serbs and Albanians. After the second Balkan War it was redefined by an international commission.

Albanian independence being settled, the Powers proceeded to cut off from Turkey all territory west of a line between Enos and Midia, thus confining her within a small corner of which the extremity was Constantinople. This area was ceded to the Balkan Allies *en bloc*, the island of Crete went to Greece alone, and the fate of other Turkish islands, such as Samothrace, and Lemnos, was left for the Powers to decide in the future. Their further assignments met with bitter opposition. Greece did very well in obtaining not only the great prize of Salonika, but a stretch of south Macedonia which included many Bulgars. Serbia got northern and (what was gall and wormwood to the Bulgars) central Macedonia. Bulgaria was to obtain Thrace and the Aegean coast. After much protest and pressure the Balkan League and Turkey signed this Treaty of London on May 30, 1913. They tore it up immediately afterwards.

The Bulgars were not prepared to surrender either Salonika to the Greeks or the contested Macedonian zone to the Serbs. But these two nations held the disputed areas, anticipated the Bulgar refusal, kept themselves ready, and formed an alliance. King Ferdinand of Bulgaria secretly ordered one of his armies to attack the Serbs in Macedonia and another to move on Salonika. The Bulgar attack at midnight on June 29, 1913, on the Serbs began the second Balkan War. The wrath of Serbs and of Greeks was thoroughly aroused against their treacherous ally. King Constantine, at the head of the Greek army, captured the Bulgars in Salonika and undertook a brilliant but reckless campaign up the valley of the Struma. He was extricated from a dangerous situation by the Serbs, who utterly routed the Bulgars at the Bregalnika. Within six weeks 50,000 of the allies were killed. Meanwhile two states, who were not members of the Balkan League, improved the situation by triumphing bloodlessly over the already helpless and defeated Bulgars. Enver Bey led a Turkish army by forced marches out from the lines of Tchataldja and speedily recovered Adrianople. The city, which had cost so many thousand Turkish and Bulgarian lives, was surrendered without a blow. Secondly, Rumania, which had viewed the division of the spoil with angry eyes, mobilised her army, invaded the absolutely helpless Bulgaria, seized important strategic points, and menaced Sofia. On August 10 the Bulgars signed the Treaty of Bucharest, with Serbia, Greece and Rumania. Bulgaria was forced to cede to Rumania the fortress of Silistria commanding the Danube and the southern part of the Dobrudja, which was ethnically Bulgarian. Montenegro received a large increase of territory to the east, taken from Serbia. The Serbs retained all north Macedonia and the contested zone (the Monastir area) which was certainly pro-Bulgar. The Greeks retained south Macedonia from Florina opposite Monastir up to the borders of western Thrace. They obtained the fine harbour of Kavalla, the only practicable opening for Bulgaria on the Aegean,[1] and the rich tobacco districts of the hinterland. Bulgaria, thus despoiled, still retained western Thrace with the poor roadstead of Dedeagatch as her sole Aegean harbour. The Serbs, Greeks and Rumanians had

---

[1] It is to the credit of Venizelos that he desired Bulgaria to have this port so that a Greco-Bulgar alliance might remain a possibility. He was overruled by King Constantine and the General Staff.

ignored the Powers over nearly everything except Albania. The Turks under Enver Bey equally despised the Treaty of London, and calmly retained Adrianople, which, according to the Powers' decision, should have become Bulgarian. The Greeks and the Turks equally refused to accept their decision as to the fate of islands like Lemnos and Samos, and technically continued to fight one another. The Powers stomached these affronts as best they could. They dared not resort to force, for that would have ranged Austria-Hungary and Germany on one side and France and Russia (if not Britain) on the other. Germany's policy, as in the first war, had been to restrain Austria-Hungary while France and Britain restrained Russia.

The actual gains in population meant something: Serbia added a million to its total, or about one hundred thousand fighting men to its army; Greece did about the same; and Rumania gained important strategic advantages. Even Bulgaria got some territory. The actual loss of territory and population by Turkey affected that strange Empire much less than it would have done a western state. Christian subjects were no loss, for they were not allowed to serve in the army, but the independence of Albania deprived Turkey of a fine recruiting ground for soldiers and administrators. The defeat in the field was a positive gain, for the Turks set to work to reorganise their army in earnest, and it proved its worth in the coming war. The recapture of Adrianople also awakened the national partriotism of the Turks, which was stimulated by the fact that their rule in Europe was now confined to areas ethnically Turkish.

As for results: what weighed with Austria-Hungary was that Serbia had more than doubled her territory and, as a magnet upon Serbs and Croats within the Dual Monarchy, was stronger than ever. She would not be indefinitely restrained from making war upon Serbia in the interest of her own survival. None of the interested states, whether defeated or triumphant, believed that the territorial decisions would be permanent. The victorious Serbs and Montenegrins knew they would have to fight Austria-Hungary. The defeated Bulgars made overtures for an alliance both with Austria-Hungary and with the Turks so as to be revenged on their former allies. The Greeks hovered uncertainly between the Entente and the Austro-German Alliance. All of them expected a new war very soon, and thought any treaties made in 1913 to be the merest 'scraps of paper.'

The attitude of Russia naturally became important after the two Balkan Wars. She controlled Serbia, was increasing her influence on Rumania, but Bulgaria, hitherto her chief client, had been defeated and was turning to Russia's possible enemies. Russia had been rebuffed in 1913 as in 1909. Would she stand yet another rebuff? Fortunately the fresh incident which occurred at the end of the year brought her a small victory. As early as April 1913 Turkey had appealed to Germany for a good German officer to reorganise her army, but it was agreed he should not be sent till the peace. Germany, as we have seen, was anxious to develop her influence in Turkey. She now wished in addition to build up Turkey in Asia. The Emperor and his military adviser decided in June to send General Liman von Sanders. In October agreement was reached with Turkey that he should have wider powers than von der Goltz (see above, p. 28) had had; should have a mission staff of forty-two officers; and should have the status of a commanding officer. His instructions from the Emperor spoke of Germanising the Turkish army and controlling Turkish foreign policy. His appointment provoked a serious diplomatic dispute between Germany and Russia. Russia, sensitive about the Straits, found cause for alarm in von Sanders's appointment to the command of an army corps stationed in Constantinople. Sazonov protested on November 17 and was backed up by Kokovtsov, now Russian Premier, and visiting Berlin. France and Britain gave general support, in Constantinople and Berlin, to the Russian position. They found difficulty in taking joint diplomatic action in Constantinople, partly because they were not clear how near to war Sazonov was prepared to go, but chiefly because a British Admiral was at Constantinople with a very similar naval mission to the proposed military one of von Sanders. He too had an executive command. Indeed, he was commander of the Turkish navy. In December Russia and France seemed near to war with Germany. But on the last day of the month Bethmann persuaded the Emperor and his military advisers to give way. Liman von Sanders became Inspector-General and a Turkish Field Marshal, but resigned his command over the first Turkish Army Corps in Constantinople.

The incident is instructive: it was clear that there were virtually two Governments in Germany, a military and a civil one. The power of the military one was at times greater than that of the civil, but the civil one could assert itself and prevail. The question for the future was whether this would always be so. Secondly the incident showed the importance of Britain. Germany was ready to go to the brink of war with France and Russia. The consideration that, the neutrality proposal having failed (see above, p. 31) and Britain acting as part of the Triple Entente, war with France and Russia meant a naval war with Britain, was decisive with Germany. Thirdly, the incident ended in a setback for the German imperialists. They were becoming increasingly vociferous and could look back on no really great successes, neither in the Far East nor in Morocco. How many setbacks would they tolerate?

Meanwhile Russia decided to drive forward with her assertive policy. There was an important Council meeting on February 21, 1914, which, on the basis of a memorandum drawn up by Sazonov, decided that the time had come to attempt to gain command of both Bosphorus and Dardanelles; that this command could only be secured by a European war and not by a localised conflict with Turkey; that for the moment a political atmosphere must be created favourable for 'operations leading up to the occupation of the Straits.' There is no doubt that this was a very serious decision, for the Tsar's views, according to the French Ambassador, were that 'to reopen the Straits, I would even use force.' But the essential prerequisite of any forward drive was to bring about a close agreement with Britain and on this Russia concentrated. In June 1914 legislation was enacted for the strengthening of the Black Sea Fleet by a building programme to be completed between 1917 and 1919.

Grey was not thinking of agreements with Russia or of using force anywhere. He still believed in a European Conference, for he thought that it had averted war in 1913 and saw that the inclusion of Germany in such an organisation was the surest road to peace. He persevered in a pacific attitude towards Germany. In fact, during the winter of 1913 and the first half of 1914 negotiations took place with Germany over the Portuguese colonies and also over the Baghdad railway, which resulted in a considerable measure of agreement. A full power for signing the Baghdad Treaty was actually sent off to London on July 22, 1914 by Germany.

For reasons too long to note here the Portuguese negotiation was dropped in March, but it is pathetic to note that on July 28, 1914, Germany was preparing to resume this negotiation. Thus, up to the very brink of war, Britain and Germany were pursuing a settlement of their own private difficulties. One unfortunate incident had occurred. When Grey accompanied George V on a state visit to Paris in April, pressure was put upon him to engage in naval conversations with Russia. France was asked and was ready to make a proposal which drew closer the ties of the Entente. Britain was at that time by no means on good terms with Russia and anxious to conciliate her. So the naval conversations took place. They became known and were reported in the press. On June 11, 1914, Grey, questioned in the Commons, replied in characteristic parliamentary style. 'The answer given,' he wrote in his memoirs, 'is absolutely true. The criticism to which it is open is, that it does not answer the question put to me. That is undeniable.' But, unfortunately, his answer was widely interpreted as a denial of all naval conversations whatsoever with Russia. This was bound to cause a bad impression; for the German Government had secret information not only of the British naval conversations with Russia in 1914, but also of the British military conversations with France authorised in 1912. It seems that Grey would have done better frankly to reveal the existence of both conversations to Germany. For he denied there were any secret agreements and yet tried to conceal the secret conversations. It is difficult to see how Germany could accept Grey's assurance, and, though we cannot help sympathising with this honourable man in his grave difficulties, his solution of them had unfortunate effects.

The real signs of the alteration to the Balance of Power made by the Balkan Wars are seen in their effect on the soldiers. A memorandum of December 1912, drawn up by Ludendorff for the German General Staff, contemplated war as the result. He was doubtful about Italy joining the Austro-German combination and fairly certain that Britain would side with France and Russia. He thought that it was necessary in case of war to take the offensive against France and violate Belgian neutrality, and to remain on the defensive on the Russian frontier. He insisted that it was necessary to vote large sums to increase Germany's military strength, and particularly to fortify the Russian frontier. It is interesting that he regarded the Triple Alliance as a 'defensive' combination and the Triple Entente as having 'marked offensive tendencies,' though this may be his way of putting things. On March 28, 1913, the money for this outlay came before the Reichstag for the vote, in the shape of a capital levy of fifty million pounds, and the news became public. It was of peculiar significance, for people saw that so great a financial demand could hardly be made again in peacetime. On the 29th it was announced that the German peace strength would be increased by 120,000 men.

Military developments were taking place, in the same period, elsewhere in Europe. The fruit of Haldane's reforms in the British Army now matured. About the same time arrangements were made in the Belgian Parliament for a considerable increase of the Belgian army. The French Government had already been planning a Bill for turning the military service from two years into three, and the German increases spurred on the French Government to carry this Bill in both Chamber and Senate by August. At the same time, France obtained an addition of strength by taking recruits at 20 instead of 21, and by extending the period of liability for military service from the age of 45 to 48 years. Here again the measure was ominous. France had no more to give either in men or in the period of military service. And when a country has no more to give, it becomes nervous or is likely to gamble on its last card. Russia also was not to be behindhand; during 1913 she increased her effectives by 135,000 and raised her period of service by three months. What was ominous about all this was that, at the moment, Germany was in the best military position, but that year by year her advantages would decrease; so the temptation to her military men to go to war was great. Russia expected to knock two days off the time required for mobilisation in 1914, to increase her network of strategic railways towards Germany's eastern frontier, and to be quite ready in 1917. At the end of 1912 Ludendorff had written that Russia was 'still very much behindhand with the reorganisation, equipment and arming of her forces, so that for the time being the Triple Alliance need not be afraid of an armed conflict even with her, in spite of her numerical superiority.' As, however, Russia 'will be stronger with every year that passes,' one can understand that Germany grew nervous as Russia's armaments increased.

Germany, or at least her General Staff, was nervous for another reason too. Ludendorff in his memorandum described Austria-Hungary as 'most threatened politically,' and says in a note that Moltke, Chief of General Staff, feared that she would take her own line and 'be swept along by overhasty measures which involved us without affecting our vital interests.' Ludendorff adds that Moltke had 'little confidence in our [German] diplomacy. He doubted whether it would adopt the right course at a critical moment.' We must bear these facts in mind in considering the motives which swayed William II, who considered himself a soldier and whose marginal notes of this period more than once exalted military at the expense of civilian judgments. On February 24, 1914, Moltke sent a long report to Jagow, the Foreign Secretary, on the development of the Russian army, and about the same time the Italian Chief of Staff was reported as feeling anxious about it, though he did not believe that Russia would make an aggressive war. A report from Germany's Ambassador at St. Petersburg stated that Sazonov was friendly but weak, and that other, and darker, forces in Russia were working against him. The Emperor annotated: 'In any case he neither can, will, nor wishes to alter anything. Russo-Prussian relations are once for all dead—we have become enemies.' There had been many war scares in Germany since 1870: a scare of war with France in 1875, 1887, 1905, and of war with Britain in July 1911. Now in the spring of 1914, after a movement to raise fresh tariff barriers against each other, there was a scare of war with Russia. It was set off by an article in the *Kölnische Zeitung* of March 4. The idea of a defensive war against the Slav menace was already much canvassed in Germany. Curiously enough William II at this time, and Francis Ferdinand about two months later at Konopischt, refused to be alarmed by Russia's military preparations at the moment. The latter indeed held that her internal unrest prevented any real danger from her. Moltke, however, was reported to be gloomy on June 1, and to have said, in reference to Franco-Russian preparations, 'We are ready, and the sooner the better for us.'[1]

The most serious feature, however, was Rumania's apparent defection from the Austro-German Alliance. Hitherto Rumania had been bound by a secret treaty which was known only to the King and a few leading Ministers, and it was likely that it would not be honoured by the Rumanian cabinet, parliament, or people. For there were three million Rumans in Hungary who were abominably oppressed by the Hungarian Government. Ludendorff had drawn attention to the military danger of Rumania's defection in December

---

[1] Cp. Fritz Fischer, *Griff nach der Weltmacht* (1961) translated *Germany's Aims in the First World War* (1967), pp. 33–37, on Moltke.

1912, and Conrad no longer doubted that she would default at the end of 1913. But the matter was not a simple one, for the Rumanian question affected the internal affairs of Hungary, as well as the foreign policy of Austria-Hungary. As long as the Hungarians oppressed Rumans in Hungary, the Rumanian Government outside Hungary would not be won back into the Austro-German fold. The Emperor William went to Vienna in March 1914 and found that both Berchtold and the Emperor Francis Joseph thought Rumania 'virtually lost.' A few days later William II spoke with Francis Ferdinand, the heir to the throne, who criticised Berchtold for want of openness and attacked the Hungarians for ill-treating their Ruman subjects. The situation had become worse on June 12–14 when William again visited Francis Ferdinand (as it proved for the last time) to admire the roses in his garden at Konopischt. In the interval between this and their former meeting the Ruman subjects of Hungary had scorned Tisza's overtures, and a serious bomb outrage had occurred at Debreczen. Francis Ferdinand expressed himself in very violent terms against the Hungarians and reiterated the need for conciliating the Rumans both within and outside Austria-Hungary. He also spoke of the need of a diplomatic alliance with Bulgaria, thus isolating Serbia and putting pressure on Rumania.

Serious as was the threat to Austria-Hungary, both internal and external, from the Rumanian danger, it could not compare with that from Serbia. The Government of that country had promised in 1909 to live in good neighbourly relations with Austria-Hungary and to repress hostile propaganda towards her. They were not anxious either in 1913 or 1914 for a new war, because they had much to gain by delay. Ammunition and rifles were deficient, their new territory needed consolidating, and Russia would not be ready for war until 1917. But the four millions of Serbian Serbs called to the eight million Serbo-Croats under the Hapsburgs. Even had the Serb Government desired to do so, they could hardly have suppressed the incessant propaganda and habitual intercourse between their own Serbs and those beyond the Danube and Drina. There was no press censorship in Serbia, the newspapers could say what they liked, and availed themselves liberally of their freedom. Pan-Serb agitation, which had been at blood-heat in 1908, was at boiling-point during 1913 and 1914. A feverish and furious agitation ran through Serbia, Bosnia, Dalmatia, Croatia. Hundreds of students dreamed of the days when Yugoslavia should be free and of how to die for her freedom. In 1910 a student sought to assassinate the Governor of Bosnia, and committed suicide before being captured. He exclaimed with his last breath, 'I leave it to Serbdom to avenge me.' This incident was glorified in a notorious pamphlet which had a wide sale. In 1912 a student demonstration at Zagreb ended in bloodshed, and the Ban, or Governor, of Croatia was twice within an ace of being murdered by students. In January 1913 two young Bosnians planned to murder their Governor, abandoning their attempt only at the last moment, and in August another Zagreb student made an attempt on another Ban. In March 1914 a new attempt at Zagreb was discovered, just in time to prevent the Ban and an Austrian Archduke from being assassinated. These attempts were due partly to propaganda, partly to criminal or terrorist organisations. But they were most of all due to the emotions aroused by the birth of new ideas. 'Thoughts burst forth, burning and irrepressible as lava. Do not demand of any new thought that it should be just to the thought that preceded it.' That would have seemed treason to the cause. The whole educational life of Croatia, Dalmatia, and Bosnia was a seething mass of discontent and smothered rebellion, and the students of independent Serbia inflamed the agitation.[1] These activities were so flagrant that they could not be concealed from the authorities. But they were infinitely more active inside Austria-Hungary than in Serbia.

Berchtold, the Foreign Minister of Austria-Hungary, and Tisza, the Hungarian Premier, were well aware of the agitation. They knew that it could not go on for ever, and were naturally inclined to think that it was more due to propaganda from outside than to unrest from within. But Istaván Tisza was, in his own way, a great man and wished to move cautiously. For he knew the difficulties and danger Hungary would encounter in war to be more serious than Berchtold dreamed of. But the defection of Rumania urged both men to action against Serbia, and during April and May 1914 they moved steadily in this direction. It was at this point that Conrad, as Chief of the General Staff, intervened with effect. Like the Sibyl he was perpetually offering the books of his wisdom which had hitherto always been repulsed. His views were summed up in his own epigram that war with Serbia would have been a safe game in 1909, that a similar war in 1913 was a game which still offered chances, that in 1914, though a desperate hazard, it must be undertaken as there was no alternative. The Serbs, he said, were led by irresponsible agitators, 'full of unquenchable hatred for us' and only amenable to force. In the winter of 1913 and the spring of 1914 he repeated this view over and over again to William II, to Moltke, the German Chief of Staff, to Berchtold, and to Francis Ferdinand. The last, while not apparently concurring in Conrad's views of an immediate attack on Serbia, agreed to a diplomatic offensive and recommended it to William II at Konopischt. Berchtold also agreed and understood that the point

[1] The only scientific description of these sinister activities is in R. W. Seton Watson's *Sarajevo* (1926), pp. 63–79. It should be read in conjunction with Hugh and Christopher Seton Watson, *The Making of a New Europe, R. W. Seton Watson and the Last Years of Austria-Hungary* (1981). But no one who saw Dalmatia, Bosnia or Croatia in 1912 or 1913, could doubt the prevalence of an extraordinary unrest.

of this offensive against Serbia was to bring Bulgaria into the Triple Alliance, and to inform Rumania of it. Serbia would thus be isolated, and Rumania might once more be won back. It was hoped ultimately to include Greece and Turkey in the new group. Russia would thus be effectively countered in the Balkans. After many revisions, Berchtold had at last, on June 24, finished a memorandum on the policy to be adopted, and was about to forward it to Germany for approval and support. But, while he was putting in the last touches, something occurred which converted him to Conrad's views at a blow. For on the afternoon of June 28 he and all the world learnt that a Bosnian Serb, who had just come from Belgrade, had assassinated Francis Ferdinand and his wife at the bridge of Sarajevo.

All those arrested after this event were subjects of Austria-Hungary. It is remarkable that the chief Austro-Hungarian investigator not only did not find any evidence of complicity of the Serbian Government in the assassination, but that he reported it as 'definitely improbable.' So the fact is that the Austro-Hungarian Government accused the Serbian Government of complicity in the plot, when all the evidence to hand showed that they were guiltless. To this extent, Austria-Hungary must bear the responsibility for war in 1914. From this point of view the Serb guilt is irrelevant and academic. It has not been proved that the Serbian Government had any share in the plot. Their interests seem to have been against any such reckless move. Moreover, they warned the Austro-Hungarian Government in general terms that an attempt might be made. It is a fact that two Serbian officers, one of them Chief of Military Intelligence, though strongly opposed to the civil Government, had knowledge of, and lent support to, the plot. Even so, the Austro-Hungarian accusation was not justified.

We have now to notice that nearly four weeks elapsed before Austria-Hungary made her accusation and presented her ultimatum to Serbia. June 28 to July 23 marks off the period within which peace might have been saved. The four weeks saw a struggle between Berchtold, the gambler, prepared to stake all, in fact the survival of Austria-Hungary, on a last desperate throw, and Tisza, wiser and cooler. Berchtold told Tisza that he meant to make the murder the occasion of a reckoning with Serbia. Tisza answered that a war of punishment on Serbia was impossible while Rumania was, at best, an uncertain quantity and, at worst, a likely enemy. What then caused Tisza to give way, as give way he did? Three things seem to have had a cumulative effect upon him: the attitude of Germany; the attitude of Francis Joseph, who at first supported him but by mid July had gone over to Berchtold's and Conrad's point of view; and finally the feeling in Hungary. But of these the attitude of Germany was the decisive influence. Berchtold told Tisza that Tschirschky, the German Ambassador in Vienna, had said that William II would stand behind any firm decision of Austria-Hungary. The German Government may have been misled and may have believed the Serbs guilty. It was fully aware that war with Serbia meant war with Russia. Next, but still within the first week after the assassination, Berchtold sent his *chef de cabinet*, Count Hoyos, who shared his views, to Berlin with a letter from Francis Joseph in which he told William II that Serbia, as a political factor in the Balkan Peninsula, must be eliminated. He did not refer to immediate war. Hoyos found everyone away in Berlin, but was eventually received by the Emperor at Potsdam. He returned to Vienna with an assurance of German support. He carried back a personal message from the Emperor for Francis Joseph approving an attack on Serbia and promising that, if it came to war with Russia, Germany would support Austria-Hungary. He was 'the living despatch.' But Hoyos was disavowed. A meeting of the Ministerial Council in Vienna on July 7 had been the scene of a conflict between Berchtold and Tisza, which Tisza won. Tschirschky went to Berlin to say that the proposals Hoyos had made were not official; Germany only confirmed her assurances of support. By the end of the second week Francis Joseph had come round to Berchtold's view. Tisza then agreed that there should be an ultimatum to Serbia, hoping that Serbia would yield to it. He held out for delay, while a diplomatic solution was attempted. On July 19 the ultimatum was drawn up. By then Germany had lost patience. She changed her tone and her communications became threatening. If Austria-Hungary did not take action against Serbia in the existing favourable situation, Germany would have to reconsider her position as Austria-Hungary's ally. Tisza was finally moved by this change of tone and he agreed to the ultimatum's going on July 23 with a time-limit of forty-eight hours. Tisza had also come to doubt whether he could any longer hold back Hungarian agitation, but Germany's incitement to war was the deciding factor.

So the ultimatum went to Serbia on July 23. But even at this last hour Austria-Hungary half hoped to localise the war. The crisis caught Poincaré, now President, and Viviani, Prime Minister of France, on an official visit to the Tsar in St. Petersburg. The presentation of the ultimatum was delayed an hour so that they should be at sea on their return journey, and, in these radio-less days, inaccessible, unable to concert immediate action with their ally. Serbia's reply, though conciliatory and judicious, was declared unsatisfactory and the Austrian diplomatic representative left Belgrade by a train arranged in advance, for Austria-Hungary intended war and insisted on unconditional acceptance of her demands. She declared war on Serbia on July 28 and shelled Belgrade next day.

There was now, however, hesitation on Germany's part. On July 26 the British fleet was prevented from dispersing after manoeuvres and was thus in effect mobilised. And some strong remarks, made by Grey, reached Berlin at 4.37 p.m. on the 27th, asking Germany to restrain Austria-Hungary from 'a foolhardy policy.' By 10 a.m. on the 28th William II had suggested a move on these lines to Bethmann, who sent off a wire that night. It reached Vienna at 4.30 a.m. on the 29th. Berchtold was asked to moderate his further demands on Serbia and to make a conciliatory approach to Russia. Grey also suggested mediation. Berchtold's action was inconclusive and unsatisfactory till midday on the 31st, when he took steps leading to war with Russia.

On the 28th in the evening Sazonov decided on a partial mobilisation of the Russian army, which the soldiers on July 29 persuaded him to make general. But at 9.30 p.m. the Tsar intervened and again made the mobilisation partial. Between 3 and 4 p.m. on the 30th Sazonov won over the Tsar to a general mobilisation, which was actually executed at 6 p.m. that night. There were two ways in which a mobilisation might be partial: one was to mobilise part of the force along the whole frontier; the other was to mobilise fully along part of the frontier. The latter was the Russian method and partial mobilisation meant a concentration on the south against Austria-Hungary, leaving the German part of the frontier uncovered. A general mobilisation was against Germany as well. A general mobilisation could not be quickly converted into a partial one.

It was the partial mobilisation ordered on July 29 which started the sequence of war declarations; for Moltke at 7.40 p.m. (when he knew of partial but not general Russian mobilisation) wired to Conrad at Vienna urging on him a general Austro-Hungarian mobilisation and stating that a German mobilisation would follow. Conrad took this at 10 a.m. on the 31st to Berchtold, who in a council decided on general mobilisation of Austria-Hungary at 11.30 a.m.

At exactly the same time on the 31st Germany received definite news of Russia's general mobilisation. At 1.45 p.m. she declared a state of emergency, the stage preceding mobilisation, and informed Vienna that mobilisation would follow. At midnight (31st July–1st August) an ultimatum went to Russia demanding the arrest of her mobilisation in twelve hours, and an ultimatum to France demanding her neutrality. Without waiting for an answer, Germany decreed general mobilisation at 5 p.m., and at 7 p.m. (6 p.m. German time) Germany declared war on Russia.

The part played by France was dictated partly by the obligations of her alliance and partly by an arrangement made by Viviani and Poincaré, who were visiting Russia and only left at 9.30 on July 23. This arrangement was for joint restraint on Austria-Hungary. But before any steps could be taken the Austro-Hungarian ultimatum had been delivered. Poincaré and Viviani reached Paris on the 29th and on that evening at a Cabinet meeting decided to stand by Russia. But their language to Russia was restraining and not provocative. Their military preliminaries were begun on the 25th, and on the 29th five army corps took up positions for defence on the frontier, though reservists were not summoned. On the 30th an important step was taken by drawing a cordon of ten kilometres round the French frontier, and withdrawing nearly all French troops behind it. In the military sense this was unimportant, but diplomatically it had excellent effects, especially on Britain. On July 31, anticipating the German declaration of war on Russia, the five French army corps were authorised to take all necessary steps to defend the frontier. On August 1 general mobilisation was decided, and actually decreed at 3.45 p.m., about an hour and a quarter before that of Germany. France was careful to explain that mobilisation was not war, but it does not seem to have been doubted that it would follow. The German ultimatum to France had been delivered at 7 a.m. on August 1. It demanded an answer in eighteen hours as to whether France would be neutral in a Russo-German War. This time limit was extended, for neither side was anxious to make the rupture, and each tried, by making use of petty frontier incidents, to put the other in the wrong. In result war was only declared by Germany on France at 6 p.m. on August 3. France made several appeals to Britain for assistance, but always, according to Grey, taking care not to appeal to any pledge of honour.

Britain's part in the outbreak of war is the last, and in one sense the most important, to be described. As told before, the fleet was prevented from demobilisation on the 26th, and on the same day a circular suggestion for a Conference was made by Grey. But this proposal reached Berlin at the same time as a report from Prince Henry of Prussia that George V thought Britain would be neutral, and this belief may have influenced events. The Conference suggestion was rejected by Germany. But a sharper tone from Britain on the 27th prompted her to suggest moderation to Austria-Hungary on the 29th. Unfortunately on that evening Bethmann made a bid for neutrality to the British Ambassador, offering in case of war to preserve the integrity of France (though not of her colonies) and hinting at a possible violation of Belgium's neutrality. Grey refused stiffly on the 30th, saying it would be a 'disgrace' to make this bargain, but suggesting once more the possibility of a Conference at the moment, and for the future, as a panacea for Europe's ills. In consequence of the hint about Belgium, Grey asked both France and Germany on the 31st for an assurance that each would respect the neutrality of Belgium so long as no other Power violated it. By 2.15 a.m. on the 1st France had given a definite assurance, while Germany gave an evasive answer by 3.30 a.m. Grey had already been pressed hard by France for support. He had also received on the 31st a strong private memorandum from Sir Eyre Crowe of the Foreign Office, advocating the maintenance of the Balance of Power, and the support of France on the ground that an 'honourable expectation has been raised,' which we could not repudiate 'without exposing our good name to grave criticism.' Grey admitted in his memoirs that if we had not decided 'at the critical moment to support France,' he himself would have had to resign.

By August 1 the period of indecision was coming to an end, for Germany had refused the Belgian pledge. But the Cabinet still refused to send the expeditionary force overseas or to defend the northern coasts of France against German attack. Grey informed Lichnowsky, the German Ambassador, on August 1, that he was disappointed at Germany's evasive reply as to Belgium. When asked 'whether, if Germany gave a promise not to violate Belgian neutrality, we would engage to remain neutral, I replied that I could not say that; our hands were still free, and we were considering what our attitude should be.' And he suggested that much would depend on public opinion.

On the morning of August 2 the Cabinet met again. It knew that Germany had declared war on Russia, and that German troops had entered the neutral territory of Luxembourg and were likely soon to enter that of Belgium. It had also received a promise of unconditional support from the Conservative Opposition. It was at this meeting that the argument for intervention turned on the British obligation to France. It accepted the moral obligation to France and at 2.20 p.m. Grey declared to the French Ambassador that if the German fleet came into the Channel or through the North Sea to undertake hostile operations against French coasts or shipping, the British fleet would give all the protection in its power. This was to be subject to the consent of Parliament. Grey pointed out to Cambon that this 'did not bind us to go to war with Germany unless the German fleet took the action indicated, but it did give a security to France that would enable her to settle the disposition of her own Mediterranean fleet.' It is here that we realise the importance of Churchill's remonstrance with Grey as to the very disposition of that Mediterranean fleet two years before (see Volume One, p. 377), and as to the consequences it might ultimately entail.

There was a Cabinet meeting on the morning of the 3rd, when it was already known that Belgium's neutrality was certain to be violated and that Belgium herself would fight. The Cabinet ordered mobilisation of the army and Grey went down to the Commons. His speech was a great success, and it was clear that the violation of Belgium, the point which he emphasised, would be supported by Parliament as a *casus belli*. Grey now knew what to do. At 9.30 a.m. on the 4th he demanded an immediate reply from Germany as to respecting Belgian neutrality. At 2 p.m., having been informed that Belgian territory had been violated, he instructed the British Ambassador at Berlin to demand 'a satisfactory reply' and to ask for his passports if he did not receive it by midnight. And so at midnight Britain entered into war.

Our materials from the beginning of this volume have been arranged so that they point to a conclusion in two parts. The first part is that the War of 1914–18 was the unavoidable outcome of the basic instability of two states, the Dual Monarchy and the Turkish Empire, the one likely to collapse into its national parts unless by some latent strength it battled its way to a settlement with the nationalities, the other already once—in 1912—defeated. The second part of the conclusion is that the War was the unavoidable outcome of the two armed camps and their rivalry in naval and military preparations and of the ascendancy in Germany and Austria-Hungary of military influences; in Germany, the more important partner, of the General Staff and the Navy Office, of Moltke, Tirpitz and William II, whom the civilians, such as Bethmann Hollweg, found it impossible to control. Some of what has been said may even suggest that war was looked forward to as in itself worth while. This attitude of mind is intelligible if it is remembered that the war which was expected was war as it had been in the past, on a relatively small scale, not world war, bringing civilians in large numbers into the armies and causing enormous casualties.

This whole conclusion deserves close scrutiny because there always exist causes of war, now latent, now operative. It is the task of Governments, Foreign Offices and diplomats to control them. A good example of a potential cause of war suppressed successfully for a long period was the German annexation of Alsace Lorraine in 1871. It could have caused a war of revenge, but it did not. The War of 1914–18 may have been caused in the last analysis by a failure of Governments, Foreign Offices and diplomats in their professional tasks. Indeed, Grey in his memoirs, *Twenty-Five Years*, blamed himself for exactly this failure, indicating that he should have made Germany understand that Britain would not be neutral and so held her back from putting the Schlieffen plan into operation. This may have been so, but there are three awkward facts which differentiate the situation of 1914 from earlier or later ones and suggest that three at least of the Governments had no will to control or suppress the causes of war.

The first fact is obvious but deserves restating. The crisis of July 1914 came in a series of crises. A tension was created that it would be a relief to break by going to war. The impression of Colonel House, the confidential adviser of the American President, Woodrow Wilson, on a peace mission to Europe in May 1914, was that the atmosphere was charged with electricity and that everything betokened a readiness to strike. The events that took place between February and June 1914 were symbols and signs of deeper and darker forces. The series of crises had generated ever deepening fear. During the five weeks before August 4 what everyone feared had at last come about. There was a kind of fatalism mixed with relief in June that deprived Governments, Foreign Offices and diplomats of the will to continue to try to save peace.

The second fact is that the Russian autocracy was using foreign and military policy as a way of controlling the internal situation in Russia. We have seen that the so-called Revolution of 1905 had not revolutionised Russia. A liberal, constitutional Russia had not displaced the old autocracy nor yet absorbed it. The autocracy had made an uneasy compromise with the parliamentary life of Russia and lived on. An adequate remedying of the disease of social discontent might have secured the safety of this compromise, but Stolypin's land reforms were no such adequate remedy. The Tsar and his Government adhered to the old ways of securing safety: sound finance, military and naval rearmament and an assertive foreign policy. But the assertive foreign policy had thrice failed: over the Straits at the time of the Bosnian annexation, when her client Bulgaria was defeated in the second Balkan War, and over the Straits a second time in the spring of 1914. The small success over Liman von Sanders masked the greater failure of her displacement as a dominant influence in Turkey by Germany. The Tsar and his Government in going to war in 1914, in going to the aid both of France and of the Slav cause, in taking on both Germany and Austria-Hungary, were striving for the safety of the régime. Victory might, if the matter were looked at in terms of power politics, redress the defeats of 1854–56 and 1904–05. Nothing else could.

The third fact was that hostility between Britain and Germany was fundamental—not a mere quarrel. In Germany even the Social Democrats in the Reichstag voted for the war credits and all accepted the Party Truce which the Emperor in a speech to the Reichstag proclaimed. They did so because the war was presented by Bethmann Hollweg and the Emperor as a defensive war against an aggressive Russia. The German public understood the war most easily in terms of the age-old struggle between Teuton and Slav. Somewhat better informed and more understanding Germans knew that what was at stake was Germany's claim to be a World Power, a claim commensurate with her energy and productive capacity. She had fulfilled her first colonial ambitions in taking her four African colonies, but there was no room for expansion in Africa except at the expense of another European Power. Later ambitions had been directed to China and the Pacific where she had obtained the Marshall Islands, Caroline Islands and Samoa. But she had been checked there too. Still later the North African coast of the Mediterranean had attracted her attention, but she had reached the limit in Morocco. Agadir could not be repeated. Her ambitions were now concentrated with some hope of development upon Turkey. She could not have worked for peace in 1914, by keeping out of Austro-Russian rivalry among the Balkan states, without her imperialism being frustrated even in this one last area. But even that is not the whole of the matter. Those in fact responsible for Germany's action, the naval and military advisers of the Emperor and Chancellor knew that she agreed to support Austria-Hungary, not only against Serbia, but also against Russia, because what was at stake was more than Germany's claim to be a World Power. What was at stake was Germany's ascendancy on the continent. Geographically placed as she was Germany could only be safe if she had freedom to manoeuvre, and she could only have this if she had ascendancy. She could only avoid encirclement, which was what the Emperor and others called checks to her freedom of movement, if she had ascendancy. Bismarck had understood this and how to obtain it. For one brief year, 1884–85, he obtained diplomatic ascendancy by an alliance system to which all the Powers, including France, were attached or related. Each Power needed Germany more than it needed any other Power. In 1914 Germany was in the opposite position and her security on the continent was at stake. She was divided from France by Alsace Lorraine, divided from Britain by the building of her Battle Fleet, divided from Russia by her Turkish policy. She had been building up this position piece by piece and the Schlieffen plan assumed that it existed, that the war on two fronts, the French and the Russian, could be faced and, indeed, could be won, after 1909, by concentrating on the west, while Austria-Hungary held Russia. It was a recipe for victory. War would give Germany ascendancy on the continent and renew her security. It was the ascendancy that would put France at risk and, through France, Britain.

On the British side of this hostility it should be noticed that the growing menace of Germany had been published abroad among all classes of the community, from the Foreign Office outwards. Historians write, with some exaggeration perhaps, of the anti-German party in the Foreign Office. This sense that Germany constituted a menace to British security was summed up in the vulgar war aim 'to hang the Kaiser.' Those better informed, Parliament, Whitehall and what was called the thinking public, generally knew that Britain was going to war for the things she believed safeguarded her security: the sanctity of treaties, the safety of small nations, the neutrality of Belgium. In the cabinet ideas were more precise. When the cabinet met on Sunday, August 2, the discussion centred on the moral obligation to France. Britain went to war because her survival depended on the survival of France: on France's power to balance the power of Germany. That Britain went to war only because Germany violated the neutrality of Belgium is untrue. That without the violation of Belgian neutrality Grey would have been unable to carry Parliament into war may be true. Britain went to war because her security would be destroyed if France was defeated. In these terms France had the least ground for war, but then France had the least choice. France was invaded.

Chapter 3

THE WAR, 1914–18

1914

Europe beheld a unique sight during the early days of the war. Huge columns of troops were on the move along its eastern, central, and western plains. They were moving in numbers so great as to resemble a migration of the peoples. Europe had armed on an unprecedented scale and her mobilised millions were already on their march to death. From Germany grey columns passed across the Rhine and streamed towards France. Blue French columns, with a few khaki-clad British ones, were straining to meet them in Belgium. A few grey German divisions could be seen on the borders of East Prussia. Long yellow columns were pressing to the northern frontiers of Austria-Hungary and watching anxiously for the green waves of advancing Russians. Far away to the south, huge yellow columns were swarming across the Bosnian border, to envelop the little army of Serbia. Six weeks sufficed to decide the fate of all these movements. The tiny Serb host had repulsed the Austro-Hungarians. The Russians had been flung back from East Prussia with enormous loss, but had routed the Austro-Hungarians and occupied most of Galicia. Paris was saved—and the blue-khaki columns had driven the grey ones before them from the Marne to the Aisne. Effects had been produced by one battle in the west, and by another in the east, which lasted till the end of the war. The green waves never again submerged East Prussia; the grey tide never again lapped the walls of Paris; until, coloured somewhat differently and with more devastating effect, it returned in a second World War.

The Russian offensive may come first. It was not so important as the German thrust in the west, but none the less weighty in ultimate result. The German plan was to make their thrust for Paris, and to leave a very small garrison in East Prussia, hoping that the Austro-Hungarians could make head against Russia for six weeks. After that

Paris would have fallen and German reinforcements could be sent eastwards. This plan had one defect, it left East Prussia naked and exposed to a daring thrust. If the Russians had overrun East Prussia and combined this success with a victory in Galicia, the results would have been startling. The Silesian coalfields and their immense industrial population would have been open, and the Austro-Hungarian flank would have been rolled up and destroyed. The German General Staff had considered these possibilities and decided to face the risks. They despised the Russian military machine for its slowness, inefficiency, and corruption.

The Russian Commander-in-Chief, the Grand Duke Nicholas, was perhaps the best choice Russia could have made. He had the advantage of rank, of energy, and of devotion to his profession. Moreover, unknown to Germany, he had in his pocket the war plans of Austria-Hungary, which had been betrayed to him by Slav officers in the service of Francis Joseph. He had another advantage—which neither he nor Germany expected. The first stages of the Russian mobilisation were passed with unexpected rapidity and the green masses were soon flooding not only Austrian Poland but East Prussia. For the Grand Duke had resolved to make a bold effort to influence the campaign in France. Originally the Russians had resolved to throw all their forces against Austria-Hungary, but the Grand Duke altered this plan in order to save Paris. He sent two large armies to envelop the German force in East Prussia. His plan might have succeeded had his choice of men been more fortunate. One commander, Samsonov, was bold to the point of rashness; the other, Rennenkampf, was cautious to the point of weakness. Had they been men like Ruzski or Brusilov the result would have been different. Victory was certain in Galicia where the Austro-Hungarian plan was known. It could have been secured in East Prussia by bold and resolute leadership.

East Prussia had a legendary horror of the Slav barbarians, and heard with terror the news of their invasion. Rennenkampf attacked the eastern border but made ground slowly, Samsonov pushed rapidly up from the south. The two commanders were divided by distance and did not act in unison, though each army was stronger than the whole German force. It was little wonder that the German commander lost his head and spoke of retreat. He was at once superseded and replaced by a retired general, drawn from obscurity in Hanover, and by a staff officer who had just won celebrity in France. Hindenburg and Ludendorff arrived on the scene too late to frame any plan of their own. But they found one drawn up by Colonel Hoffmann, who had studied the local conditions and taken the measure of the Russian commanders. He calculated that Samsonov was advancing too quickly and Rennenkampf too slowly, and that they were out of touch with one another. In that case each could be attacked separately, and destroyed by the German force which, though smaller, was more efficient than either. Any other course meant ruin or defeat, so Hindenburg and Ludendorff swallowed the plan whole, and applied it with the utmost vigour and resolution. They began by launching two-thirds of their whole force against Samsonov. Thousands of Russians were slain or captured in the marshes of Tannenberg, and Samsonov took his own life in the agony of defeat (August 26–29). Then Hindenburg turned eastwards against Rennenkampf – and drove him beyond the German border, slaughtering thousands in battles by the Masurian Lakes (September 6–12). In all something like a quarter of a million Russians were slain or captured. The Russians had none the less caused by their invasion the recall of two German Army Corps to Prussia at a critical moment during the advance on Paris (August 25–26). It is possible to hold that this diversion produced the German defeat on the Marne.[1]

The relief to Germany was immense. The slaughter of myriads of barbarians in these 'dim weird battles' amid marshes and lakes fired the Teutonic imagination. It was at Tannenberg in 1410 that the Teutonic Knights had been overthrown, and the Grand Duke Nicholas had boasted that the Slav sword, drawn there, had not rusted. On this twice famous field the verdict had now been reversed, and the Germans had been triumphant over the greatest odds. The names of Hindenburg and Ludendorff became linked, and this victory (which neither had devised) gave both immortal fame and led them ultimately to the highest positions of military command. Tannenberg became to the German what Salamis or Marathon were to the Greek, and Hindenburg became a living hero of legend.

The verdicts of the people are not always those of history, and even the defeat of Tannenberg was not necessarily decisive. The Russian troops were notoriously indifferent to losses, and had still a chance of overwhelming not only Galicia but East Prussia before the year ended. It took Russia only three weeks to pierce deep into Galicia. They had little superiority in numbers, but they had the priceless advantage of knowing the enemy's plans. By the end of August they had defeated the Austro-Hungarians in front of Lemberg and entered the town. In the early days of September they won a colossal victory in front of Grodek. Two-thirds of Galicia passed into their power, the great fortress of Przemysl was masked, and the Russian armies reached the passes of the Carpathians and approached the old royal Polish city of Cracow. Its capture would have been decisive, for it defends the gap which gives easy access at once to Silesia and to Austria. With Cracow in their grasp the Russians could have turned the whole German frontier line of

[1] B. H. Liddell Hart, *The Real War* (1930), p. 86.

defence by Posen and Thorn, and occupied Breslau and the Silesian coalfields.

Cracow was not saved by Austro-Hungarian or by German generals in Silesia but by Hindenburg. That commander had himself just had a narrow escape from defeat. He had crossed the border in pursuit of the flying Rennenkampf and in the eagerness of advance only just avoided falling into traps like those he had set for the Russians. He did avoid them however and eventually regained his own territory. In the early days of October he found that a unified direction had been arranged for the whole Austro-German line, and that he had the chief German command. He, or Ludendorff, had profited from experience. They had learnt that East Prussia was safe from invasion and that the Russian area east of it was dangerous for invaders. Looking at the front as a whole it was clear that there was only one way of saving Cracow. That was to threaten Warsaw, and he now attacked Warsaw at a moment when Austro-German power was increasing and Russian declining. The German reserves were arriving, along with ample supplies of munitions. The Russian mobilisation had been quicker than was anticipated, but the arrival of reinforcements and drafts was very slow. Curiously enough, the loss of Russian men had mattered little, but the loss of rifles and guns had mattered much. Russia could only produce munitions in small quantities and her supplies were already drying up. Her troops were feeling the strain of a continuous campaign in which they had not been relieved, they were imperfectly armed, and were undoubtedly outnumbered by the Austro-Germans during the late autumn of 1914 (not of course in actual ration strength, but in the number of men who could be efficiently armed).

In the second week of October Hindenburg moved on Warsaw with five converging attacks, extending from Thorn in the north to Cracow in the south. But his movements had been anticipated by the Grand Duke Nicholas, who had secretly withdrawn the Russian armies so that they formed an almost continuously straight line, stretching from the extreme end of East Prussia (with a bulge defending the capital of Warsaw) to a point on the Carpathians some forty miles east of Cracow. This time the German attacks were a complete failure and were easily flung back to the frontier. The Austro-Hungarians for a time had some success and temporarily relieved Przemysl. But by the end of October the whole attempt had proved a costly failure and the Russians were again close to the German frontier. Two Russian offensives followed – one against Silesia and the other once more against Cracow. Neither succeeded, but a second attack by Hindenburg on Warsaw was held up some forty miles west of the town. The campaign closed in December, with both sides fought to a standstill. It also closed—and finally—the chance of an early decision in the East. The German frontier was intact, Cracow was saved, Silesia defended, and the Carpathian barrier still held. The long green line stretching from East Prussia to the Carpathians was, in future, one for defence not for attack. The Russian 'steam-roller,' as it was called, was no longer effective for advance. Russia might be important in immobilising masses of German and Austro-Hungarian troops, but there was neither hope nor possibility of the 'Slav Colossus' achieving victory. It was the old story of Frederick the Great and the Russians, the battle of the athlete against the giant. The Titan was already severely punished, though his vast strength enabled him to prolong the struggle. The athlete was too agile to be knocked out, but still did not carry enough weight to knock out his opponent.

In the west, as in the east, deadlock was reached by the end of the year. The struggle in the west had been more dramatic, and the failure of the German offensive against Paris is much less easy to explain than the failure of the Russian attack on East Prussia. Russia's plans had miscarried because she lacked patience, energy, science, intelligence, power of organisation and all sorts of *matériel*. Germany had all these and many other qualities too. Foch said her army in 1914 was the best equipped and most formidable that ever took the field. Yet this stupendous exertion of military energy, this supreme effort of intelligence and will by a most gifted people, came to nought. The supreme objective—the capture of Paris—failed, and with that failure everything was lost. Indeed, looking at ultimates, it seems to have involved the destruction of the German military system and dynasty. Was the campaign then a gamble or miscalculation of chances? The stakes were so high that it was not worth playing unless Paris could be captured.

The German offensive plan against Paris had been perhaps more carefully studied than any military design in history. As we have seen, Schlieffen—then Chief of Staff—had finally evolved it in 1905, though it was not officially adopted until 1912. The French frontier —as left in 1871—offered formidable obstacles, unless the German advance violated the neutral areas of Belgium and Luxembourg. Northwards from Alsace stretched the Vosges and the Ardennes, a line of woods and hills which were militarily formidable. Art had supplemented nature by a second line of defence in the shape of a bristling row of fortresses from Belfort, Épinal, and Nancy to Toul and Verdun. In this restricted area, where the French frontier was to be breached by more mobile forces in 1940, the vast German masses had no room to deploy and would batter their heads against impregnable barriers. Belgium and Luxembourg offered ample space, while the French fortifications behind them were much less developed. Schlieffen left the ethics of violating neutral territory to statesmen and considered only the military problem. If they penetrated Belgium the vast armies of Germany could manœuvre on a wide circle, swinging round on the great German fortress of Metz as a pivot. Armies could be poured through Belgium and Luxembourg into north France and could then advance on Paris. The outermost army on the right was to pass Paris on the west (the side nearest to England) and to come round it from the south. The French armies would then be caught in a trap between Paris and the Vosges. They would either be immediately enveloped or driven across to the German armies in Alsace or over the frontier into Switzerland. Paris would fall and the war be at an end six weeks after it had begun. This was the Schlieffen plan, but when the younger Moltke became Chief of Staff he introduced serious modifications. He weakened the right or manœuvring wing and strengthened the left wing south of Metz. It was once thought that this change in itself explained the German failure. But the defects of the Schlieffen plan were fundamental. Schlieffen had planned the whole campaign up to final victory and assumed it could be carried through exactly, step by step, by central direction. He thought he could both foresee all the enemy's responses—they proved different from his expectations—and what would be the behaviour of the commanders of individual German armies—they too diverged from his expectations.[1]

The first clash was at the Belgian frontier fortress of Liège, which the Germans sought to seize by a *coup de main*. On August 5 the Belgian garrison, fighting with great gallantry, defeated the attempt. Altogether they delayed the advance of the first German Army by two, if not three, days, and this delay was of great importance. But no Belgian valour could stem the German tide. By August 20 Brussels, the capital, opened its gates. Most of the Belgian army retired into Antwerp, where it constituted a formidable threat to the flank of the advancing Germans. The invading force had been met by barricades, destroyed bridges and *francs-tireurs*. The Germans sternly repressed spontaneous resistance. 'Atrocities' introduced unprecedented bitterness: the destruction of Belgium became a war aim on one side and reparation in full on the other.

We must now leave the German hosts sweeping on through Belgium and Luxembourg to Paris and consider the French dispositions. General Joffre—the French Chief of Staff —was a soldier of strong nerves. But he had an army inferior both in numbers and in *matériel* to the German, and he had to guard every part of the frontier till he knew where the German blows would fall. The calculations of the French General Staff were at fault. They had rightly anticipated a German violation of Belgium and Luxembourg. But they had reckoned (and refused to be convinced until too late) that the line of advance would be east of the Meuse through Luxembourg and the

[1] G. Ritter, *The Sword and the Sceptre* (translated from the German, 1972), Vol. II, pp. 201–16.

Ardennes. They tried disastrous offensives in Lorraine and failed in their effort. They also hoped to get a British-French force up in time into Belgium to hold a line stretching south from Antwerp and Namur to Sedan. This was a good plan, but the Germans were too quick for it to be carried out. Joffre thereupon authorised a new plan. Namur was to be held as the apex of a triangle, with a western side ending at Mons and an eastern one stretching to Sedan. This manœuvre involved some danger, for it meant holding a sharp salient, but it had many advantages if Namur, the apex, could hold out for a fortnight. It was believed (though erroneously) that it could, and it was here that the Germans sprung on the Allies one of the first of their many military surprises. On August 21 they began to bombard Namur, and their immense guns caused its capitulation on the 25th. Its fall placed the allied troops, who were hurrying to their positions, in a situation of extreme peril. British troops had reached Mons on the 22nd and found the first German Army feeling round their left flank and threatening to encircle them. On the 23rd their neighbours the fifth French Army were flung back from Charleroi, and the fourth and third French Armies further eastward suffered still worse reverses, and fell back even more rapidly. The British, after a victorious rearguard action near Mons, followed the retreat of the fifth French Army on the 24th. The British won a small success against the first German Army at Le Cateau (26th) and the fifth French were victorious in a rearguard action at Guise (29th). The situation was, however, still grave; Amiens fell, and before the end of the month the British were cut off from the Channel ports and their supplies. Von Kluck's first German Army was sweeping on to Paris. Joffre, after seeing the failure of his original plan, was now at work on a new one. The second and first French Armies had resisted stoutly in front of Toul, Nancy, and Verdun. He therefore decided to hold on to this fortified area and swing back his exhausted armies in the west. The British, the fifth, fourth, and third French Armies were to retreat behind the Seine to prepare for an ultimate offensive. Meanwhile General Gallieni, with a newly organised army (the sixth), was to defend Paris. This plan involved certain dangers, for Paris was, or might be, isolated until the retreating troops could reorganise and advance to its aid. But it kept the armies (other than the sixth) united and intact.

The German advance had apparently been triumphant everywhere, yet the High Command was in difficulties. Wastages had told on the strength of the advancing armies. Two corps had been detached to watch Antwerp, and by a grave decision two more, as already related, had been hurriedly taken from the investing force of Namur and sent off to Russia (August 25–26). None the less the German Headquarters considered that the programme had been carried out, and Moltke issued orders accordingly on August 28. Von

Kluck with the first Army was ordered to circle round Paris and then to move southwards, Bülow with the second Army was to advance on Paris itself, and to keep in touch with the neighbouring third German Army. All this was according to plan, but not according to the ideas of Bülow. He had discovered one gap, which seemed to be widening, between von Kluck and himself, and another gap between himself and the third Army. The French repulse of his army at Guise had shaken his nerve. Without referring to Headquarters he implored the first and third Armies to close in to his support. Von Kluck agreed and closed rapidly in towards Bülow, hoping thus to catch the British or the fifth French Army. German Headquarters heard this news from von Kluck when it was too late to alter his movement. They approved it, though it entirely destroyed their plan. It would now be impossible for von Kluck to circle round Paris, or for Bülow to invest it. Von Kluck's extreme right wing was advancing so as to pass some thirty miles east of Paris. This blunder destroyed Germany's hope of victory, and gave France her opportunity.

Gallieni, who became Governor of Paris and commander of the sixth Army on August 26, had marked the advance from his watch-tower. By September 3 his anxiety was relieved. Von Kluck could not now attack Paris, and the capital could be in no immediate danger. The sixth French Army could therefore take part in the fighting. Gallieni considered that a sortie from Paris would be almost useless. But, as von Kluck's right flank was already exposed, he and his sixth Army could deal it a deadly blow if they fought in conjunction with the British and the French fifth Armies. It is a matter of dispute whether Gallieni himself devised the plan and forced it on Joffre, or whether Joffre took the initiative. Anyhow, Joffre assumed full responsibility on September 4, when he issued his famous General Order for resuming the offensive. 'The time for looking back is past. Every effort must be made to attack the enemy and hurl him back. Troops which find advance impossible must stand their ground and die rather than give way.' Joffre had realised that the supreme moment of decision had arrived.

On the same day the German High Command issued new orders. Von Kluck and Bülow were to defend the German flank, by forming a half circle facing west towards Paris and thus hold off the sixth French, the British, and the fifth French Armies. The third German Army was to attack in front. The fourth and fifth German Armies were to push past Verdun and take Nancy in the rear, thus separating the French Armies and placing them between two fires. The new German plan was a desperate attempt to pluck victory from defeat. Even now von Kluck did not obey orders and retire quickly behind the Marne. Hence when the sixth French Army attacked him on September 6 he was at a great disadvantage. On the 7th the British and the fifth French Armies joined in the attack. Von Kluck held the sixth French Army, but his forces were weakened at their points of contact with the British and the French fifth Armies. The gap in the German defences widened. Next to the fifth French Army, behind the marshes of Gond, a new French Army (the ninth) had been formed. It was weak in guns and men, but strong in its commander, General Foch. The German third Army hammered vigorously at his thin lines, and only Foch's extraordinary tenacity prevented a break-through. Further eastwards still the French lines held, though the fighting was extraordinarily severe, especially round Verdun, Nancy, and Toul. The war of movement, of manœuvres, and of decisive action therefore centred on the Marne and the marshes of Gond. But even on the 9th the Germans were not yet beaten in fight, and their defeat was due to the weakness of their own commanders rather than to the strength of the Allies.

The German High Command was still at Luxembourg, and, by reason of the immense distance, had in fact lost touch with the situation. By September 6 those 'central determining orders, which moulded the battle . . . two hundred miles away,' had ceased to mould it at all. Moltke finally delegated his authority as Chief of Staff to a certain Colonel Hentsch. He instructed him to motor to the Headquarters of each German Army and, if he judged a retreat necessary after local examination, to order it on his (Moltke's) authority as Chief of the Great German General Staff. This motoring delegate, a mere colonel, thus invested with supreme power was able to use it. On the 8th he visited the fifth, fourth, and third German Armies and satisfied himself that they could stand their ground. The question was whether the first and second Armies could still do so. Bülow, as he learned, had declined to retreat upon the 8th. But on the morning of the 9th Bülow heard that the fifth French Army was attacking him, and that Foch was holding his own beside the marshes of Gond. Bülow thereupon gave orders for the retreat of his own (the second) German Army. Some time on the morning of the 9th the motoring delegate arrived and found Bülow's orders for retreat being executed. Colonel Hentsch had to make the gravest decision of the war. He could still have ordered Bülow to stand firm, for von Kluck was now actually overlapping Gallieni's army. But he chose the line of least resistance, motored to von Kluck's headquarters, and used the authority of Moltke to force von Kluck to obey the order of retreat which he now gave. Von Kluck unwillingly agreed. About midday of September 9 the crisis was over. The German armies retired first to the Marne, and then to the Aisne, and Paris was saved.

The news of those orders and the fate of the great battle, which the German High Command had failed to control, came through to Luxembourg in the early afternoon of the 9th. The German Head-quarters were in a house

built for a large school and standing upon the public square opposite the post-office. . . . An order had been given at the front: the man upon whose responsibility it went—a man already broken with illness— rose and went out uncertainly, as though he were far older than his age, leaning upon the plain iron rail of the school staircase, as he painfully descended the steps. . . . He came in his full uniform, this general officer, who had accepted and ordered the retirement. He was a nobleman, superior in military talent to his fellows, even amid that great organization, which was the best designed for war in Europe. . . . He sat down publicly on the low stone wall that supported the railings, his head bending more and more forward, and staring on the ground. He bore a name with very different memories of cold triumph. It was Moltke.

A group of boys playing in the square ceased from play to gaze at the old boy, timidly approached the railings and stared at that poor, broken figure. They could know nothing of the traditions of the Prussian army, nor of how strange a sight they saw, but they felt its enormity. He, for his part, had forgotten what was around him—the place, the children; he stared at the ground, remembering as in a vivid dream his urgent appeal to his Emperor, his agony at defeat, his intelligence too great for his heart, and the knell still ringing there: 'The campaign has failed. . . . The campaign has failed.'[1]

In this strange fashion the great German design was foiled and the German armies turned back to the Aisne. There were still dangerous moments, there were still surprises in store for the Allies. In the first week of October the defences of Antwerp were smashed by the enormous guns of the Germans and the great fortress surrendered. But the Belgian Field-Army was successfully withdrawn and took its place in the Allied line. The Allies won the 'race to the sea,' protected the Channel ports, and ensured British communications by the heroic defence of Ypres. Both sides, exhausted by warfare, were digging themselves into entrenchments. France was defended for the first time by a continuous line of earth and iron stretching from the sea to the Vosges. A deadlock was established, which was not much disturbed till 1917, nor broken until 1918.

The year ended in the west as in the east with exhaustion and stagnation. But the failure of the German thrust at Paris is one of the mysteries of warfare as well as one of the problems of history. The Germans believed that, had they got to Paris, France would have been defeated and the war brought to an end, and in this view they were probably right. But the Germans also believed that the capture of Paris was a certainty, an assumption falsified by the event. Yet in some respects their military superiority was even greater than has usually been represented. The French General Staff miscalculated the direction of the German advance and the numbers of their divisions. They had an erroneous theory of the offensive, which rendered

[1] Hilaire Belloc, in *Scenes from Modern History*, ed. H. Temperley (1931), pp. 228–30.

their counters to the German advance a series of bloody and useless failures. Up to August 28 the German Command had fulfilled its programme to date, and success seemed within their grasp. Incidents like the detachment of two corps to East Prussia and of two more to Antwerp, or the resistance of Maubeuge, or the exhaustion of German troops are perhaps quite enough to explain the disaster. Yet the French had been decisively beaten at many points, and the Germans were still unbroken and victorious. The German failure began when von Kluck abandoned the original plan of marching round Paris, and struck south-east to join up the army of Bülow. This move enabled Gallieni and Joffre to launch a successful counter-offensive on the German flank. It is, of course, arguable that the gaps in the line were so serious that von Kluck was unable to act other-wise. But this assumption is doubtful. The German generals seem to have disregarded the High Command, when they did not agree with it. They did not seek to persuade it, but simply took action on their own. Thus von Kluck marched south-east at the request of Bülow on August 29 and Bülow gave orders for the retreat of his army on September 9, in each case without getting leave from the High Command. Indiscipline in the field was accompanied by a singular paralysis at Headquarters. The concentration of all power in the hands of Colonel Hentsch, who was sent as a travelling delegate by motor-car to settle the crisis on the spot, is an example of that palsy. Here was a colonel empowered to overrule generals and order retreats in the name and with the authority of a command which had already lost control of the situation. This display of impotence at the nerve centre explains much. The Emperor was, of course, quite unfit for supreme command, but the younger Moltke was also unsuited for it. His physical condition was poor, and his mental grasp appears to have been deficient. The Schlieffen plan required a right wing of overwhelming strength, the assumption being that (as events proved) French attacks on the centre in the Ardennes could easily be repelled. Moltke would not accept so bold a plan. Between 1905 and 1914 he added nine new divisions to the German Army, but placed only one on the right wing and eight on the left. If seven of these divisions had been given to the right they might have filled the gaps and deterred Bülow and von Kluck from upsetting the Headquarters' plan. He may, however, have achieved his political purpose of paci-fying the fears of Bavaria who largely supplied the forces of the left wing. In the last analysis failure lay in a variety of complex and contingent causes, such as the too great independence of local com-manders in the field, and the weakness of the High Command which first modified the Schlieffen plan and then withdrew units from the fight at the crisis. The fundamental defects of the Schlieffen plan itself have already been described. The fact is the great ability of the German generals has blinded us to some of their defects, both in staff-work and in command in the field. They had learned almost everything from books and from manœuvres, they had had practically no previous opportunity of real service in war. At any rate the Frenchmen knew better how to combine local initiative with firm direction from the centre.

The French General Staff had blundered badly in their appreciation of the German designs. But Joffre, like Foch, Mangin and Gallieni, had had experience of war and therefore a power of observing realities and profiting by mistakes. It is certain that Joffre did not consider himself beaten even on August 25, a day when the news of defeat came from every quarter, of the fall of Namur, of the hurried retreat of the British and of three French armies. On that day of ill omen Joffre conceived the idea of an eventual counter-offensive and arranged to re-form his armies behind the Seine. If it be true that Gallieni, and not he, was responsible for the decision for the counter-offensive, the lesson is none the less instructive. Gallieni did not first lead out his army from Paris against von Kluck and then inform Joffre of his action. He persuaded or forced the High Command to agree with him, and only moved after orders for a general advance had been issued. Even if they were due to an impulse from below, the orders of September 4 took the form of a command from above. Thus the counter-offensive of Joffre was a properly concerted movement, in which the subordinate commanders thoroughly supported one another and their chief. Gallieni, when hard pressed by von Kluck, consoled himself by the thought that the British were relieving him from the south; Foch, clinging desperately to the fringes of the Gond, reported the situation as 'excellent' and attacked, in the belief that pressure on his front must mean a German retreat before Gallieni and the British. It was in this manner that victory was snatched from defeat before Paris. These methods are a complete contrast to those by which von Kluck or von Bülow coerced or defied von Moltke.[1]

1915

It is best to look at the campaign of 1915 through the eyes of Falkenhayn. Moltke had faded out of sight as the German armies fell back

---

[1] The Schlieffen plan as such—as in all modern military operations—aimed at the destruction of the enemy's army in the field, but it was assumed that the fall of Paris would be the result of it. As regards Falkenhayn's plan for 1915, that given here is his own account, but the German official history declares he wanted to attack in the west but was overruled by the Emperor. His statements are questionable, though that quoted on p.75 is probably exact.

from Paris, and Falkenhayn took his place as Chief of the German Staff. He had to consider the whole problem of the war anew and to see what courses were open to Germany. Though the western thrust had failed Germany still had the initiative. Falkenhayn thought the situation extremely serious, but did not, in his heart, abandon the belief that German victory in the west could alone be decisive. He rejected the idea that he could get a decision there in 1915, as the Allies had a superiority in men and *matériel*. The situation in the east in his view demanded action. Turkey had joined Germany in the autumn of 1914, and Britain was preparing an expedition to force the Dardanelles and dictate peace at Constantinople. Falkenhayn counted on its failure if ammunition, guns, and German expert military advice reached the Turks. But a more formidable enemy was likely soon to be in the field. Italy had been Germany's ally, but at the beginning of the war had declared her neutrality. It was clear, however, even in the early months of 1915, that Italy would not long remain neutral and would soon attack Austria-Hungary. As soon as that event occurred large numbers of the Austro-Hungarian troops in Galicia would have to be diverted to the Italian front. This consideration was the decisive one with Falkenhayn. He was not in principle an Easterner, nor did he believe that any defeat of Russia would produce a real decision in the sense of ending the war. But he thought a vigorous attack would push back the Russian armies still further and render Austria-Hungary safe before she was attacked by Italy.

Before April ended Franco-British attacks took place in the west, and the first British landed at the Dardanelles. But Falkenhayn had made up his mind and was not be deterred. He had found an admirable leader in Mackensen and directed him to break through the Russian front—about 40 to 50 miles south-east of Cracow. On May 2 Mackensen's 'phalanx' pierced the Russian line between Gorlice and Gromnik. Its success could hardly have been greater and the Russians were completely routed. Falkenhayn exploited the success and diverted divisions from the west and from Hindenburg's part of the front for the purpose. Early in August Warsaw fell—and the Russians, despite furious struggles and counter-attacks, were pushed steadily backwards and expelled from Poland altogether. Their ammunition and rifles were so defective that they were hopelessly outclassed and the number of Russian prisoners taken was extremely large. By the end of September the Austro-German forces stood on a front stretching from the Bay of Riga in the north in an irregular line to the Bukovina and eastern Carpathians in the south. Falkenhayn had a much shorter line to defend, and had relieved Austria-Hungary. It was believed, though, as events proved, wrongly, that all fear of a future Russian offensive had been removed.

Serbia's gallant little army had flung back the Austro-Hungarians in utter rout in August and again in December 1914. It was dangerous to leave them unsubdued when Italy was beginning to batter at the western border of Austria-Hungary. In September Bulgaria, hitherto neutral, decided to join the Austro-Germans and signed a secret military convention with them. Mackensen was withdrawn from Russian Poland to command a united force of Austro-Germans against Serbia with Bulgaria operating on the flank. The Serb army, weakened by typhus, could offer little resistance, and finally made its escape through Albania after suffering the loss of more than half its effectives (November). Franco-British troops had entered Greek territory, but they were unable to protect Serbia, and had to content themselves with holding Salonika as a base. There for three years they remained.

The Franco-British campaign in the west, undertaken chiefly to relieve the pressure on Russia, was expensive and useless. The most serious efforts were in Champagne in September. On the Italian side the results were almost equally disappointing. Operating in the Isonzo country the Italians, though superior in numbers, were hampered by inexperience and a difficult terrain. They had achieved almost no result by the end of the year except that of attracting a large number of Austro-Hungarians from the eastern front.

It is impossible here to discuss why the Dardanelles expedition was decided upon. It is certain that the objective offered immense advantages if attained. If Constantinople fell and the Straits were opened, Russia would at once be relieved. Suffering cruelly from a German blockade she would be aided in the Black Sea by munitions, supplies and sea-power, while Russian grain and supplies would be available to the Allies. It is even possible that the glamour of obtaining Constantinople would have restored to the Russian Tsar all the prestige he had lost by his defeats. Rumania and Greece would have been compelled to join the Allies, Bulgaria would have been defeated and Serbia restored. But such an enterprise required fore-thought and preparation, which could not be improvised. It required, above everything, secrecy and celerity, and neither of these factors was present.

Early in November 1914 British cruisers had most foolishly bombarded the Dardanelles' forts. The expedition was resolved upon in January 1915, and another bombardment took place at the end of February. An attempt to force the Straits by warships alone failed in the third week of March, and it was then decided to effect a landing with troops. But when the military expedition arrived in April the Turks, thrice forewarned, were at last forearmed. The force, mainly British but with a French contingent under General Gouraud, effected landings both at the toe of the peninsula and at Anzac, but found it difficult to advance much beyond the beaches and nowhere held the crest line. When in August it attempted landings at Suvla it came nearer success, but still failed to achieve its purpose. It was a tragic failure and, though the British hung on with their usual tenacity, evacuation became inevitable when the heavy rains set in and swamped the trenches. The evacuation was carried out with almost no loss, owing to the masterly dispositions of General Birdwood.

On the whole it is probable that the risks of the Dardanelles expedition were too great to make success possible. Most of the troops were imperfectly trained, the maps were bad, and the experience of the past was not applied to the solution of the problem. Lord Kitchener's plan of landing in the vicinity of Alexandretta, though much less ambitious, was a more feasible project. It could not easily have been resisted by the Turks and it would have cut the connection between Constantinople on the one side and Jerusalem, Mecca, and Baghdad on the other.

The year 1915 closed in almost unbroken gloom for the Entente. Russia had been hopelessly defeated, Serbia and Montenegro had been annihilated, Bulgaria had joined the Austro-Germans, Italy had failed to win any real success, Britain had been beaten at the Dardanelles. Yet the prospect was not so bad as it seemed. Falkenhayn had succeeded in the east, but, as he well knew, the east was not the decisive front. The Italians, though still unsuccessful, were exercising a steady pressure on Austria-Hungary and absorbing the greater part of her energies. The French army was still intact in the west, the British army was steadily growing in strength and efficiency. British sea-power had already been effective in banishing the German commercial flag from the seas, and cooping the German navy up in the Kiel canal. All the German overseas colonies, except Tanganyika (Tanzania), had been conquered, and Tanganyika was certain to fall if the war went on. Above all, the British blockade of Germany was beginning to be felt, the strangulation coils were tightening. The effect of sea-power and the blockade was slow—but certain, provided the war was sufficiently prolonged.

1916–17

The year 1916 was intended by all parties to be a year of decision— and it was in the west that the decision was sought. Falkenhayn reported on the situation to the Emperor at the end of 1915.[1] His memorandum viewed Russia as incapable of an offensive, Serbia as shattered, Italy as contained by Austria-Hungary, Britain as the chief

[1] E. von Falkenhayn, *General Headquarters 1914–1916* (1919), pp. 209–18.

enemy from whom 'Germany can expect no mercy.' Britain was 'obviously staking everything on a war of exhaustion,' with blockade as her weapon. It was therefore necessary to 'show England patently that her venture has no prospects.' It was useless to attempt to attack Britain herself and she would not be convinced by ventures against Salonika, Suez, or Mesopotamia even if they were successful. 'England, which has known how to swallow the humiliations of Antwerp and Gallipoli, will survive defeats in those distant theatres also.' But it was necessary to prevent Britain using weapons in Europe. She had already used several, Russia, Italy, and France. Two of these had been stricken from her hand, or rendered impotent. It was not worth while to attack the British lines in the west, for that was at bottom a 'side-show.' But, if the French were defeated, Britain's 'best sword' would be knocked out of her hand, Germany's 'arch-enemy' would be deserted by her continental allies on the land, and might be coerced by a ruthless submarine campaign at sea. She might then be induced to make peace. Falkenhayn proposed to attack a limited sector of the French front at Verdun, to attract thither the best forces of France, and to 'bleed her to death.'

Here we see another great decision. The decision to aim at Verdun is as important, in its way, as Schlieffen's decision to pass through Belgium. It was equally a failure and is of peculiar interest because it is perhaps the last time that Germany had the free power of initiative. Her offensive in the case of Verdun was a matter of choice: all her subsequent operations were matters of necessity. It is probable that Falkenhayn adopted this plan from desire to economise his own men—and to save losses. He hoped that Verdun would prove a magnet of attraction and that Frenchmen would flock there from all parts of the front and be killed. But while it is true that many French divisions were badly damaged at Verdun, it was impossible to expect that a limited objective would put France out of action. Falkenhayn was not willing to take the risk of an offensive on the grand scale, and his more limited objective failed. It is true that the French were badly shaken, and lost more than the Germans. But what Falkenhayn had not realised was that the British army was no longer 'a side-show.' Its power was now to be felt in the main theatre of war. The French resistance at Verdun enabled the British to prepare their offensive in comparative safety. On July 1 a combined Franco-British offensive began on the Somme and raged with the utmost fury until October. In the month of September the British for the first time employed that valuable discovery of the war, the tank. Both the tank and the young British soldiers were in too experimental a stage to win decisive victories. But, none the less, the battle of the Somme was probably the greatest shock the Germans had hitherto received. It was fatal to Falkenhayn, who was compelled to hand over his authority as Chief of Staff to Hindenburg by the end of August. The

German attempt to reach a decision had completely failed. Not only had the French defended themselves at Verdun, but the astonished Falkenhayn beheld a British army equipped with abundant munitions and guns, and capable of contending on equal terms with the German. If the British had accomplished so much with an army imperfectly trained, what were they likely to do in 1917 with more experience and greater supplies? The emergence of Britain as a first-class military power struck the Germans with amazement and dismay. Britain no longer needed to use France as a sword on the Continent: she had her own, formidable in weight and sharpness.

One of the most important events of 1916 was the offensive of Brusilov in the east. Germany had considered the Russians to be passive and, though not actually defeated, incapable of resuming the offensive. For they had lost millions of dead, and were still poorly armed and insufficiently equipped. But the Russian soldier endured the cold and hardships of winter with stoicism—and moved forward to this last of his great offensives without enthusiasm but without fear. In March the Russians had attacked near the Baltic without much success. Urgent appeals from France and from Italy caused them to hurry on their great planned offensive and begin in the first days of June. Brusilov, who advanced in the south against Lutsk, may have meant no more than a reconnaissance in force. But he broke so easily through the weak ramparts of Austro-Hungarian resistance, that he decided on a grand offensive. He was followed by the armies on both flanks, and once more, but for the last time, the great Russian hosts broke through and drove the Austro-Hungarians in utter rout before them. Hindenburg promptly came to the rescue and by a series of brilliant counter-attacks checked the Russian advance and restored something like the old line in August. The Austro-Hungarians had lost half a million in prisoners and dead, the Russians even more. For internal reasons Russia was already breaking under the strain of warfare, but this last desperate offensive further exhausted the resources and man-power of Austria-Hungary. Her difficulties were increased by the fact that her attack on Italy from the Tyrol had failed, and that the Italians had definitely passed to the offensive in the Isonzo area, and won a number of successes. Last of all, Brusilov's offensive and the resistance of Verdun definitely decided Rumania to enter the fray. In August she declared war upon, and invaded, Austria-Hungary. Had she succeeeded, Transylvania and the cornlands of Hungary would have been overrun. Austria-Hungary could hardly have resisted such pressure and the end of the war would have been in sight.

Hindenburg and Ludendorff had been called to the High Command at a critical moment. They acted with promptitude and saved the situation then as so often later. Falkenhayn and Mackensen, than whom there could hardly have been better leaders, were despatched respectively to Hungary and Bulgaria to organise the offensive against Rumania. These two masters of warfare showed Rumania what Samsonov and Rennenkampf could have done in East Prussia, if they had acted in perfect time with one another. Mackensen pushed up the Dobrudja with a German-Bulgar force, and thereby stopped the Rumanian attack on Transylvania. Falkenhayn, who had been watching his opportunity, broke through the mountain passes of Rumania's northern front in mid-November, and struck for Bucharest. Mackensen with admirable judgment crossed the Danube and attacked the Rumanian capital from the south. The two German leaders met in Bucharest. It was a real victory. The Rumanians were henceforth confined to Moldavia, Austria-Hungary was not only relieved from all danger on this front, but Russia had now to send troops to garrison Moldavia and to defend a longer line of front. Above all, the vast resources of Wallachia in corn and oil were now wholly at the disposal of the Germans and undoubtedly helped them to prolong the war. They certainly counteracted the worst effects of the collapse of the German economy in 1917.

The year 1916 thus closed with a gleam of triumph for Germany. But there can be no doubt that she had had the worst of the fighting. She had failed at Verdun and suffered defeats on the Somme. Austria-Hungary had been routed on the Russian front and beaten on the Isonzo. It was a poor compensation to have conquered half of Rumania.

Meanwhile the German navy had failed to achieve any of the purposes for which it had been built. It neither kept the sea routes open for Germany, nor deterred the British from battle. The only great naval battle of the war had been fought off Jutland (May 31). The Germans had claimed a victory and that Britannia no longer ruled the waves. No one believed them. The result was indeed indecisive and in the crisis Jellicoe had played for safety. He may have been wise, for he was the only commander whose operations could have lost both a battle and the war in a few hours. The British public showed no anxiety at the news, and the effect was equivalent to a victory. The stranglehold of the blockade increased in rigour, and the main German fleet never again sought battle on the high seas. The British command of the sea was wholly unshaken. Indeed the German resort to a ruthless submarine campaign was actually a confession that they could fight Britain under the sea but not above it.

There were indeed no illusions at Berlin and Vienna. Falkenhayn and Conrad—the respective Chiefs of Staff—had been removed from their posts, the privations of the peoples were alarming their rulers, and the actions on the Somme had confronted them with the new menace of Britain as a formidable military power in the west. This appears to have completed their dismay and the civilian rulers decided to speak of peace. William had indeed promised his soldiers that they should have it 'before the leaves fall.' Many of them had found peace by the waters of the Somme or in the marshes of Pinsk while the leaves drifted down on them. Consequently the German Government published its willingness to make peace in the last days of December. They had great advantages if they had negotiated on the basis of *uti possidetis*. They had captured and still held four enemy capitals, Belgrade, Cetinje, Brussels, and Bucharest. They occupied Belgium and north France, Serbia, Montenegro, Wallachia, all Poland and much other Russian territory. These were strong bargaining counters to trade against their lost colonies, a strip of Austro-Hungarian territory, the Turkish port of Basra. Peace was, however, wrecked by the German militarists who insisted on the retention of strategic advantages in Belgium and north France. Nothing shows the determination of Britain and France better than the fact that they put forward as their conditions of peace demands which would have involved the break-up of Austria-Hungary and the expulsion of the Turks from Constantinople. These demands could not have been—and were hardly meant to be—accepted by Germany. So the war went on—and Germany was driven into her greatest blunder.

To Germany, however, the situation appeared so desperate that she forced into the war the only neutral power strong enough to resent her dictation. Wilson had won his re-election as President because the American public thought him less bellicose than his opponent and more likely to keep them out of the war. At the end of 1916 he had formally approached both belligerents with a view to peace. Within four months after his effort America was at war with Germany. The situation was peculiar. Britain had begun by blockading the German coasts and the pressure became worse and worse. She held on like a bull-dog and every now and then tightened her grip and approached nearer to the throat of her rival. It was a situation like that between Napoleon and Britain. The struggle was so intense that neither side would suffer neutrals gladly. Germany had cowed all those on the Continent, and she now decided to cow the United States by the use of the submarine weapon. The United States had always believed in the rights of neutrals and in what they called the 'Freedom of the Seas.' They had had sharp passages with the British. But the Franco-British market absorbed endless supplies of Americans munitions. British naval commanders, if they confiscated property, did not sink defenceless travellers. Since 1915 German submarines had at times sunk neutral ships and, as in the case of the *Lusitania*, American passengers in British ships. From 1916 onwards the United States had shown signs of restlessness and had made Germany promise (May 4, 1916) to restrict her submarine activities. On January 31, 1917 the German Government informed the United States that the Entente Powers by 'brutal methods' compelled Germany to resume freedom of action (i.e. to break the promise). 'Under these circumstances Germany will meet the illegal measures of her enemies by forcibly preventing after February 1, 1917, in a zone around Great Britain, France, Italy, and in the Eastern Mediterranean, all navigation, that of neutrals included, from and to England and from and to France, etc. All ships met within that zone will be sunk.' No great neutral nation could accept such provocation. Diplomatic relations were severed at once. And in April the United States declared that 'a state of war' existed with Germany.

In this gravest of all decisions taken during the war on the German side, Hindenburg and Ludendorff accepted the naval view that the introduction of an absolutely 'ruthless' submarine campaign would destroy Britain's supplies and end the war. It was believed that six or at most twelve months of such warfare would starve Britain out.[1] This calculation explains why the Germans attempted no offensive in the west in 1917, and viewed the entry of the United States into the war with indifference. They thought that all would be finished in Europe before America could intervene.[2]

Viewed at this distance the German calculation seems absurd. The entry into the war on the side of the Entente of a great nation with almost unlimited supplies, wealth, and population seems absolutely decisive. But it took in truth a very long time before America's resources and energy told. America's soldiers had to be armed almost entirely with French and British rifles, big guns and fighting aeroplanes till the end of 1918. They took long in coming over and were not always fully trained. But they had youth and unbounded confidence and thus more than compensated for the loss of Russia. In two respects their aid was absolutely decisive, in their almost limitless supplies of money and of men. The most dangerous crisis of the war was during the German offensive of 1918. At that grave moment American troops were already in small numbers in the trenches, and the supply of munitions was practically unlimited. Britain lost nearly a thousand guns, but they were all replaced from reserve stores in three weeks! And the reason was this. British money had financed the Allies and pegged the American exchange up till America's entry into the war. From that date a series of expedients could have maintained the credit of Britain for a time, but ultimately there would

---

[1] Ludendorff, *My War Memories*, vol. I, pp. 315–17, says the Chief of Naval Staff put it at six months—at the critical Council of January 9, 1917, and that he himself thought it safe to put it at twelve months. As will be seen by reference to p. 75, Falkenhayn had contemplated a submarine campaign in the future.

[2] Their calculations were ludicrously false. Thus they reckoned a million American troops would require five million tons of shipping, and that this amount could not be spared. In fact, three million troops were transported to Europe. See Ludendorff, *My War Memories*, vol. I, p. 316. The chief American contribution after entry into war was not so much munitions as the raw material of munitions, which was worked up in Britain and France.

have been a collapse of credit and therefore a slowing up of the supplies of food and munitions from America. That 'slow-up' would have been very evident in March 1918, and during the next five months, when they were most needed, they would have been most lacking. Without the aid of America's men and money the Entente could not have been victorious and might have been defeated.

Ludendorff's plan in 1917 seems to have been simply to wait until the submarines had brought Britain to her knees. Britain and France were prepared to attack with vigour in the west before the strain was felt, and Ludendorff sprang a clever surprise on them by retreating from a large part of his front. He fell back to the famous 'Hindenburg line'—and left the Entente to push their offensive over a desolate area. Nivelle, who had replaced Joffre as generalissimo, engaged in a costly offensive which resulted in the failure of the troops and his own disgrace and retirement (end of April). What was worse, a most serious mutiny broke out among the French soldiers, disheartened by pacificism, by losses, and by blundering leadership. The danger was very real, a further French offensive was impossible, and the Germans might discover the truth and attack them. Pétain, the hero of Verdun, was put in command at the front and succeeded in the most difficult of all tasks, in reorganising and reinspiring the sullen, discontented, and mutinous troops. He was blamed for over-severity to mutineers and for caution in the face of the foe. But Pétain accomplished the seemingly impossible and in the end nursed his froward children to victory. He was not the equal of Foch as a commander, but he deserves honour for not having 'despaired of the Republic' when her own children forgot her. It was this that was remembered when, in his old age, he was called to power after the defeat of France in 1940.

The British offensive had begun before the French and was planned in combination with it. But in May the French offensive came to an abrupt stop, and Haig, who knew the reasons of cessation only too well, determined to continue a resolute offensive as long as his men could endure it. He thought it the only way of distracting the attention of the Germans. All through the spring, the summer, and the autumn the British army hammered remorselessly and tirelessly at the Germans. Ludendorff compared the British advance to that of a 'mad bull', and at times it was as blind as it was furious. This *via dolorosa* ended at last in November in the swamps and blood of Passchendaele. The German lines had been thrown back but not pierced; the French army had been saved by the sacrifice of the British—for the best part of that gallant army lay in the mud of Flanders.

On the eastern front everything went wrong except at Salonika, Baghdad, and Jerusalem. Under Entente pressure King Constantine of Greece abdicated in favour of his second son. Venizelos, returned to power, at last brought Greece into the field against Germany and enabled the Allies to prepare for an offensive against Bulgaria. In March the British forces avenged the capitulation of Kut, drove the Turks before them in defeat, entered Baghdad, and occupied nearly all Mesopotamia. In Palestine Allenby showed himself superior to Falkenhayn, who commanded the Turks. He seized the port of Jaffa, and gave Jerusalem as a Christmas present to the delighted British public. These successes, though small and in outlying theatres, were significant. They were all in areas where the Entente had previously been defeated, and they all secured important strategic advantages, from which the spectacular victories of the next year were achieved.

Elsewhere there was unrelieved disaster. The Russian Revolution occurred in March, the Tsar was deposed and the Monarchy overthrown. For a time the Russian front held, but the Revolution had completely demoralised the troops. Even Kerensky, who was pro-Entente, said that Russia was worn out and could not remain in the war after the end of the year. The end came even quicker. The army was demoralised and leaderless. It had been defeated in August, and thereafter it rapidly dissolved. The Bolsheviks overthrew Kerensky in October and made an armistice with Germany before the end of the year. Rumania, which had fought gallantly and defeated Mackensen himself, was compelled by the defection of her ally to accept a peace on most humiliating terms. It was hard on her, for her resistance at Marišesti was as heroic as that of the French at Verdun.

It had been supposed that Italy's successes on the Isonzo in 1916 would be improved in 1917, and that Austria-Hungary would be finally overthrown. In fact, Italy avoided complete disaster only by the narrowest margin. In September the Austro-Hungarian command thought the situation so desperate that they resolved on an offensive as the only possible chance of restoring the jaded morale of their troops. Ludendorff showed the coolest daring when appealed to for aid and lent them his only reserve, a force of six German divisions. These were however enough, for they were led by Otto von Below. That great commander found a weak point in the Italian defences, used the German divisions as the spear-head, broke through with ease and drove the vast Italian forces before him in complete and headlong rout. The precipitation of their flight actually saved the Italians. The victors had not expected such success and had no time to organise the pursuit. The Italians tried to stand on the Tagliamento, but finally had to fall back to the line of the Piave. There the Germans were held up. The line was shorter and easier to defend, and the Italians were heartened by the arrival of reinforcements from France. These French and British veterans were 'men who knew how to die,' and they were led by fearless commanders. Italy reorganised her shattered forces and found an Italian Pétain in General Diaz. None the less Caporetto had been a shattering disaster, and the weakness of Italy continued to be a grave

81

preoccupation for the Entente during most of 1918. It was well that at this time both Britain and France were regenerated.

At the beginning of 1917 a strong government was just assuming power under Lloyd George in Britain. She had opened careers to the talents in a way impossible in hide-bound Germany or aristocratic Austria-Hungary. Lloyd George, the new Premier, had been brought up on a village green; the Chief of Staff had served for years as a trooper; the First Lord of the Admiralty on the railways. General Smuts, the only member of the Cabinet who came from a Dominion, had been fighting against Britain fifteen years before. British energies were enormously developed; British munitions were supplying all the Allies. France was cursed with a succession of ministers so weak as to be unable to prevent anti-war propaganda from spreading to the troops, and causing mutiny at the front. In the last days of 1917 these very disasters worked their own remedy. Politics had become worse and worse, but finally the fall of one feeble minister after another enabled Clemenceau ('The Tiger') to become head of the French Cabinet. The pacificists were at once assailed, Caillaux was convicted of treason, Sarrail, the dubious generalissimo at Salonika, recalled. A new spirit of resolution ran through France under a leader as patriotic and fearless as Danton. 'Je fais la guerre,' said the indomitable old man. 'I shall fight in front of Paris, I shall fight within Paris, I shall fight behind Paris.' 'No surrender' was at last the motto, and France feared the enemy within no longer.

1918

Ludendorff's thoughts, as he planned his campaign for 1918, ran somewhat as follows: 'The manhood of Germany has been bleeding to death these four years and the strain cannot go on beyond a fifth. We are stinted not only in men but in everything—horses, goods, chemicals, metals, rubber. Austria-Hungary is in still worse need and is visibly perishing. Our ruthless submarine campaign has failed. Limitless supplies and overwhelming masses of men exist in America, and our submarines cannot prevent them from being brought to Europe in ever-increasing quantities. But we still have a chance of victory. Russia is at last out of the war, and the whole forces of Germany can be turned against France. Nearly forty divisions and four hundred thousand men can reinforce the western front. With these we have at last a superiority of force which will last for about four months. We will strike for victory at the point of junction of the Franco-British forces, separate their armies and win the war. Once we have done this, no American reinforcements can affect the issue.' Ludendorff told the Emperor that it was 'the greatest military task that has ever been imposed upon an army.' But his military brain could not conceive of any half-measures or of peace. 'It must,' he said, 'be victory or defeat.' He showed that the fate of the Hohenzollern dynasty and of Germany hung upon the event, by formally announcing that 'His Imperial Majesty the Kaiser' was in command of the offensive. There was a saying that 'William II was the only monarch in Europe who could not lead back a defeated army to his capital.' Ludendorff was to prove that the saying was true.

The Allies in the west had made some efforts to meet a German offensive by unifying their military policy. A supreme War Council had been created, which was intended to co-ordinate effort. Its chief advantage was that its first French member was Foch. They studied the situation and finally worked out a plan for controlling the reserves at the front. But neither Haig on the British sector, nor Pétain on the French, was willing to submit to an international committee dictating their use of reserves from the rear. Their objects were indeed different; Pétain had to defend Paris, Haig the Channel ports. Neither could think in terms of unity nor look far beyond his own needs. But if one man assumed control of the whole front, he would dispose of the reserves not according to French or British needs or prejudices, but as the general situation required. A few weeks after the establishment of the supreme command, Haig was protesting that Foch was neglecting British interests, Pétain that he was neglecting French ones. Could anything have more completely justified both Foch and the supreme command? Yet it was not until March 26 that he was appointed to 'co-ordinate movements' on the whole front. It was even longer before he was given the reality as well as the title of Supreme Command. By that time the Germans were in sight of Amiens.

The junction between two allied armies is always a weak point in their defences, and Haig's difficulties had been increased by having recently been forced to take over fifteen miles of the French lines at a time when his own forces were being reduced to supply men for Salonika and Palestine. He was more correct than the Supreme War Council in fixing both the date and the locality of the German offensive. But it so happened that he had placed his least experienced army commander with the smallest forces in the most important sector—that adjoining the French, and that no real reserves were immediately available. Pétain, on the other hand, was expecting a blow far away on the French front east of Rheims and his strategic reserve was not near enough to give immediate aid to the British.

On March 21 Ludendorff attacked on a forty-three mile front, between Arras and La Fére. On the Somme the fifth British army was simply swept away and the Germans were soon within twenty miles of Amiens. But Ludendorff's main blow had been aimed at

Arras, where he calculated on breaking through and then rolling up the British and forcing them towards the coast. Here the third army under Byng—the most dogged of British commanders—offered a successful resistance and drove back the victor of Caporetto with loss from Arras on the 28th. Ludendorff thereupon stopped von Below's attack in this area and drove his forces onwards against Amiens. But this time he was too late. French reinforcements had aided the beaten British, and Foch had assumed command. His first public utterance was: 'The Boche is stopped. . . . I can guarantee Amiens.'

Foch was a remarkable character. He had been eminent as a professor of military science, and had produced a theory of the offensive which the French army had adopted. But his practical application of it had discredited him in 1916. He was also objectionable to Republicans as a Catholic, and he had been for a time in retirement. Enforced leisure and his work on the Supreme War Council had helped him to view the war from behind the lines. He was accompanied everywhere by Weygand, a little bird-like man who never brought papers to a conference and carried the whole organisation of the army in his head. The staff methods of Weygand and his chief were difficult to penetrate, and caused amazement to the British. Foch had no popular gift of inspiring the troops, and was never loved as was 'Père Joffre' by the French or 'The old Plum' (Plumer) by the British. But he possessed a cold power like the elder Moltke, and, like Wellington, felt sure of beating the enemy as soon as he was called to command. In his view Ludendorff's methods were 'buffalo strategy.' He stuck one horn in at one place, and the other at a second without real calculation or thought. It would not be possible to beat this blindly goring animal at once. He must wait till the German buffalo had exhausted its strength, and until the Entente had recovered theirs. Till then no sentiment and no popular pressure must be allowed to interfere with his plans. He intended, for instance, to make the British army resist until the last gasp, and to send them no reinforcements until their line was absolutely breaking. By being niggardly of assistance he would accumulate reserves. By sacrificing a part he would preserve the whole. Even if he had understood and explained his methods better they could hardly have been popular. He was acting the part of a matador in the bull-ring, who renders no aid to his assistants even when they are injured or tossed into the air by the bull. They risk their limbs as they worry the bull, but the matador risks his life as he gives the death-blow. To succeed his nerves must be cool, his strength unexhausted, and his hand sure.

Ludendorff disengaged his left horn from in front of Amiens, and stuck in the right one between Béthune and Ypres (April 9). The defenders of this front, mainly British, slowly retired and the Germans were soon on the Lys. Haig issued his famous order: 'Every position must be held to the last man. . . . With our backs to the wall and believing in the justice of our cause, each one of us must fight on to the end.' Haig's words—so different from his usual taciturnity—marked the crisis. This was on April 12, and the offensive lasted a fortnight longer. But even on the 14th Foch considered the battle as *finie*. He ultimately sent French reinforcements, but only allowed them to be used with the utmost sparingness. The Germans managed to capture Kemmel hill from a French division, but broke off their offensive before April ended.

Ludendorff had made two huge bulges in the British line—one upon the Lys and the other near Amiens. But he had not broken it. He decided, therefore, to attack the French in the Soissons-Rheims area; he would attract sufficient Allied reserves there by sticking one horn in west of Rheims, and the other east of it. He would then return to the British positions in Flanders and finally break through. On May 27—and for four days longer—the Germans burst over the Chemin des Dames and drove the French and some British troops before them. A huge gap appeared some forty miles broad, and twenty-five miles at its deepest point. There were over 60,000 prisoners. For the first time the German Crown Prince commanded an army which was successful, and for the second time the Germans reached the Marne. Ludendorff now decided to stick his left horn in east of Rheims. After that had again attracted reserves, he would begin his final offensive against the British. But east of Rheims was General Gouraud, who had learned from Pétain the principle of an elastic defence and how to hold the front lines with a mere screen of troops. On July 15 the blow fell, but it was parried with little loss of men to the French and little gain of ground to the Germans. Before Ludendorff had recovered from this surprise, Foch struck his first offensive blow.

The huge bulge in the French line, like the two bulges in the British, was not all to the advantage of the Germans. They had had to hold a longer line shaped like a deep half-circle, which could be attacked on both flanks. Just below Soissons, Foch found his opportunity and began his offensive. The leader was Mangin—the Hotspur of the French armies—a man absolutely impervious to losses, and with an extraordinary capacity for getting the most out of his men. Mangin struck at the neck of the bulge, hoping to catch the Germans before they could retreat. He did not succeed, but the Germans fell hurriedly back, pressed from all sides of the half-circle. There were 30,000 enemy prisoners, a third of what Germany took before Amiens, a half of what she took on the Chemin des Dames. But it was an authentic victory, and like a gleam of sunshine dispersed the gloom that had settled on the Allies. To experts in such warfare it meant much. Foch was not a man to pass to the offensive at all in half-hearted fashion. He meant to strike hard and to go on striking.

Ludendorff was still dreaming of breaking the British front, and was not going to be disturbed even by a big local reverse on the Marne. On August 2 he actually ordered preparations to be made for one offensive near Amiens, and a second in Flanders. Neither materialised, for on August 8, to the German amazement, Haig struck hard in front of Amiens. The material results were not astounding, though a fair amount of ground and 20,000 prisoners were gained. But the moral effect was immense. August 8 was called by Ludendorff himself 'the black day of the German army.' The twice-defeated British had suddenly passed to the offensive, disorganised Ludendorff's plans, and broken his spirit. Ludendorff saw all his schemes crumble. He could no longer attack, and the enemy obviously could. The situation had worked out in terms of mathematics. For four months the Germans had held a slight numerical superiority over the Allies. That period had ended—America's millions were pouring in, and the German reserves had ceased to fill up the gaps. The longer the allied offensive went on, the more certain was the ruin of Germany. Foch feared that Ludendorff had grasped the lesson, and would retreat, while there was time, to shorter and more defensible lines in the rear. But Ludendorff would not confess to defeat, and refused to retire until too late.

Foch himself, though always yearning for the offensive, had not expected a decision till 1919. His aim had at first been to free lateral railways and to secure better positions for the Allies. But Foch learned from Haig's victory of August 8 something that Ludendorff did not. Haig considered it a proof that the German morale was affected, and that further attacks would succeed. With iron tenacity of character, he now pressed Foch along a path which he was already inclined to tread. Foch had noted that Haig's converging attacks produced the effect of a surprise on a small scale, and that the system could be used for offensives on a grand scale. Foch agreed to strike home, but even now expected no more than to inflict heavy loss on the retreating Germans. The British and French commanders had, however, to win over General Pershing, the American commander. He had scattered American forces all over the front to help the Allies. He was now determined to unite them and to fight with an American army, and he had strong views as to what his objectives should be. Ultimately, however, a series of grand offensives was planned on the following lines for September. The British had the hardest task, they had the mass of the German army facing them and the strongest defences. Haig was to strike at the Hindenburg line and drive the Germans back. As soon as his offensive developed, King Albert and the Belgians were to attack in the region of Ypres. While the bulk of the German forces were thus held in Flanders, the French under Mangin were to strike up from Soissons. The American objectives were twofold. They were first to hammer out the salient of St. Mihiel, near Verdun. When that was accomplished, they, with

French support, were to attack in the Meuse-Argonne area and press forward to Sedan, thus cutting the Germans' line of communications. A last French army, under General Castelnau, was held in reserve to attack in the Ardennes, that area in which the French offensives of 1914 had failed so disastrously and in which they now meant to finish the war. Foch calculated that Ludendorff's reserves were exhausted, and that his armies, thus held fast to all parts of the front, must give way at some points, and that a general German retreat must in any case result. He proposed to produce the effects of surprise tactically by the use of tanks, and strategically by a series of offensives arranged in a timed and harmonious fashion. And during September the blows of Foch fell in relentless succession.

On September 28 Ludendorff was sitting in his headquarters at the Hôtel Britannique at Spa. The news was everywhere bad. The Americans had straightened out the St. Mihiel salient, and were attacking with the French in the Argonne. The Belgians were attacking in their own territory, the British had just broken the Hindenburg line. The German prisoners numbered a quarter of a million in the Allied offensives of three months. They were speaking, too, of internal revolution in Germany. Yet Ludendorff was still unconvinced by the news from the home front and from the west. What finished him was the news which reached him from the east. As he spoke of the Bulgarian disaster before two officers, he gradually got worked to a frenzy and fell down in a fit. 'Foam appeared on his lips and in a slow, gliding motion, the heavy body of a giant fallen for Germany fell athwart the room.'[1] When he recovered he gave orders to conceal the fact of his seizure and to sue for peace. His decision was accepted on the 29th.[2] In the weeks that followed he recovered his nerve and made attempts to stop the peace-making that he had himself begun. But the forces once set in motion could not be arrested, and peace once asked for came certainly and soon. The final impulse to it came, as has been seen, from the east.

Far away on the Salonika front was a tall, bare hill, which commands so wide a view that the Macedonians say 'you can see from it all the kingdoms of the world.' Up that hill, late in June 1918, rode and scrambled a group of Entente officers. They consulted a plan and maps, and studied the horizon long with their glasses. Before they rode away the commander had adopted the proposed plan, and the

---

[1] *Rhenische Westfaelische Zeitung*, September 28, 1928, on the evidence of an eye-witness.

[2] The story of Ludendorff's fit on the 28th (not the 29th) has been denied, but not convincingly. It is true that he did not receive the news of the Bulgarian Armistice till early on the 30th. But he knew Bulgaria's surrender was inevitable on the afternoon of the 28th, and this was the cause of his decision to make peace on the 29th. See Ludendorff, *My War Memories*, vol. II. p. 721.

decision made him a marshal of France and the victor in the most successful of Allied offensives. The plan was that of a Serb general, Mišić, but Franchet-d'Espérey was bold enough to take the great risk of throwing his army against immense mountain walls, relying on the effect of a surprise attack on the centre. On September 15 the offensive began, it was all over in a fortnight, and on September 29 Bulgaria surrendered, and was out of the war. That meant the collapse of the whole eastern front and of Austria-Hungary, and the news of this surrender broke the heart and will of Ludendorff, and caused him to sue for peace.

Germany sent out her first peace note to President Wilson on October 3. Her cause was already hopeless. By a strategic masterpiece, similar to that of Salonika, Allenby captured and destroyed the entire Turkish army in Palestine and entered Damascus on October 1. Turkey signed an armistice before the end of the month. By that time the Italians had driven the Austro-Hungarians before them in complete rout at Vittorio Veneto. Early in November the British had passed all the German lines and reached open country in north France. The Americans had got to the French frontier at Sedan; the French reserve army was threatening Lorraine. Foch himself still did not regard the war as finished in the west. He thought it might last even five months longer. Germany's armies had been defeated but even yet her front was not broken. What was broken was the nerve and will-power of her High Command. It was that which hastened the end. The armistice at the eleventh hour of the eleventh day of the eleventh month of 1918 merely registered the fact of Ludendorff's decision to sue for peace at the end of September.

The final defeat of Hindenburg and Ludendorff on the western front in 1918 provoked surprise after their previous victories in Russia, in Rumania, in Italy, and in France. It is true that their material difficulties were great. They had no tanks, they lacked all sorts of supplies, from rubber and leather to chemicals and fats. Yet they succeeded in three great offensives, and in each case sprang tactical surprises on the Allies. Yet after each of his great offensives in 1918 Ludendorff hesitated. He had expected to break through in March and, having failed, turned to the Lys, where success was less easy. He succeeded at the Chemin des Dames beyond his hopes, but failed to appreciate the effect of Foch's counter-stroke. He displayed always the tactics of a master-fencer but, as Foch said, the strategy of a 'buffalo.' It is at least interesting that Hindenburg when advised in the east by Hoffmann and Ludendorff was masterly in both tactics and strategy. When advised by Ludendorff alone in 1918 in the west he excelled only in tactics. In any case the German offensives of 1918 so nearly succeeeded that they are their own justification. Nor was their strategy so much at fault as their disregard of Napoleon's maxim that you must draw up plans in case of defeat as well as to secure victory. What they lacked was an alternative plan once their offensives had failed. Here as elsewhere Hindenburg cannot avoid responsibility. Nor would he desire to do so, for, during the crises of 1918, and apparently at all times, he showed a greatness of character to which his subordinates never attained.

Some, if not all, of the deeper causes of German defeat are now evident. Lack of man-power was the first. The well of German manhood had run dry, as had the British and the French, but American man-power was an almost inexhaustible fountain. Military defeat was, however, only one side of the enormous reverse inflicted upon Germany. It was moral, political and, above all, naval. British sea-power worked by blockade and by hunger. The effect of this attrition finally coincided with, and greatly intensified, the military reverse. While the Allied offensives lessened the material power of Germany, insufficient food, defective equipment, and tales of the anguish at home sapped the soldiers' morale. Breaking-point had been reached because of the strain imposed by the navy at the time of the armistice negotiations. The German Government were so convinced of this fact that they would have accepted any armistice terms which the Allies had chosen to offer. Even the gallant German soldier was showing signs of indiscipline and demoralisation, and the German people were already in revolt. They were prepared to sacrifice Emperor, dynasty, army, glory, everything for peace and food, and so were their Allies. Neither Bulgaria, Austria-Hungary nor Turkey had the hope, the desire or the power to resist longer. The mills of God, or of the devil, had ground slowly, but they had ground small and fine, at last.

During this war America played the old part history assigned to Britain in Europe. She decided the issue by throwing her weight against the strongest Continental Power. Britain had failed to decide the issue herself in spite of the fact that she excelled all her previous efforts in European wars. From the first she not only dominated the seas, but departed from her traditions by raising an army equivalent to a Continental one which she ultimately based on conscription. Yet, none the less, she failed to decide the issue. It is improbable that Britain would herself have been beaten and starved out, for she carried three million Americans to France during the strain of the submarine campaign in transports which could have been used for food. But the war might well have ended in defeat for France and a stalemate between Germany and Britain, if the United States had not intervened with her boundless resources. Philip II, Louis XIV, and Napoleon were baffled or destroyed when help came from over the Channel. Germany was not beaten in 1918 until help had come from over the Atlantic. That is the greatest testimony to her power and her valour.

Chapter 4

THE PARIS CONFERENCE AND THE TREATY WITH GERMANY, 1919

On the afternoon of June 28, 1919, the fountains in the gardens of Versailles were playing in their famous cascades for the first time since the war had begun. Immense crowds were there, but they had not come to see the fountains. They were looking at four men who had left the palace and walked down past the *tapis vert* to gaze for a few minutes at the jets bursting forth from the largest fountain. As they returned, the crowds pressed so closely upon them that gendarmes and soldiers came to their aid. These four men had just signed an instrument which they imagined would give permanent peace to the world. That was a delusion, yet none the less the men were worth looking at. They had enjoyed more power over wider areas than any man then living on the earth. They had governed the world since the Armistice, and they had just laid the German Empire in the dust in the very place in which it had arisen in glory.

The 'Big Four,' as they were called, were Orlando,[1] Lloyd George, Clemenceau and Wilson. The peace and world settlement were theirs; their characters and their power had moulded them. Orlando had the face of a disillusioned idealist, worn, thoughtful and sad. He had an impossible task at the Conference, for Italy's part in the war had been real but her people's demands were large. Faced with stronger colleagues, and distracted by party politics at home, he found himself unable to gain his ends and was compelled to give way to events. The fate of everybody was really in the hands of a triumvirate, each of whom was, in Shakespeare's phrase, 'a third part of the world.' Of the three Wilson appeared to be the most commanding. His tall stature, his long Puritan head and firm jaw, suggested something at once narrow, resolute and formidable. He was one who could break but could not bend. His stiffness was indeed his bane as well as his merit. It provoked ridicule, it led alike to wrong decisions

---

[1] Orlando was not present on June 28, but Sonnino deputised for him and walked down to the fountains.

and unwise concessions. A magnificent orator, he had no legal pre-cision of mind, and no sort of readiness in debate. In detail and in discussion he was unequal to Lloyd George or Clemenceau. Yet even they confessed to the weight of his character. The ablest Belgian statesman revealed the truth when he said that Clemenceau and Lloyd George were both men he understood, but that Wilson was beyond him. Wilson sometimes exercised a power (*une puissance*) which could be neither understood nor resisted. It is true that he gave way in some points, but also there were things in the Treaty which he alone could have won.

Clemenceau was a complete contrast to Wilson. Short instead of tall, plump instead of spare, walking slowly through age and the wound he received during the Conference, he seemed old and tran-quil. The serene expression of his face in repose, with his brown eyes and white hair, made him look like some grave Oriental sage. The aspect belied him, for his temperament could be volcanic. On one occasion he found too many expert advisers in the room and curtly ordered them to leave. Their last look was of him with his face suf-fused with fury, his moustache bristling like that of a tiger, demand-ing explanations of Pichon, his Foreign Minister, who literally cowered before him. At times he could be coarsely satirical and cyni-cal, at others he showed a literary and artistic insight. But he knew when and where to indulge his moods. While he treated the smaller Powers and even Italy with such indifference as to provoke violent protests, he well understood that neither Britain nor the United States could be so handled. He understood Englishmen and Amer-icans far better than most Frenchmen. His belief in France was noble and sincere, but she was the only thing in which he believed. It is certain that he laughed in secret at the 'fourteen commandments' of Wilson. It is hardly doubtful that he wished for a peace based on force, and on force only; but he knew—as other Frenchmen did not—that he could not obtain that. He had judged the limits of Brit-ish and American concession, and was strong and wise enough to restrain his extremists. Moreover in debate he had a readiness and even a tact and delicacy which were at times invaluable.

The part of Lloyd George has not always been fairly described. The terms of peace (which he and his advisers drafted at a week-end party) are sufficient to show his real views and to prove that he pos-sessed the instincts of a statesman.[1] He had no thought of exacting impossible amounts of reparation from Germany. 'Was it sensible,' he said later, 'to treat her as a cow from which to extract milk and beef at the same time?' But he was hampered by the ferocious demands of the British public, by the cries of 'hanging the Kaiser'

[1] See H. W. V. Temperley, *A History of the Peace Conference of Paris* (1924), Vol. VI. pp. 544 *ff*.

and 'squeezing Germany till the pips squeak.' At the most crucial moment of the peace negotiations Lloyd George was confronted by a telegram from 370 Members of Parliament demanding that he should make Germany pay. Of course he had to capitulate, and he replied that he would keep his pledge (April 9). What else could he do? If it was possible to produce an arrangement such people would accept, it was not likely to be permanent or wise. It is probably true to say that, in so far as Lloyd George had a bad influence on the Treaty, it was because he faithfully reflected these forces.

If these were the difficulties created for Lloyd George at home, they were equally great abroad. He had to reconcile two colleagues, one of whom wanted a peace to be based almost wholly on force, and the other a peace based almost wholly on idealism. Lloyd George had to adjust the two points of view, and the task was inconceivably difficult. It meant self-effacement on his part, sacrifice of his pledges, of his consistency, sometimes even of his dignity. Yet he succeeded in many instances. There are points, as will be shown, in which he is liable to severe criticism. But this fact should not exclude the services which his inconceivable adroitness and flexibility rendered to the common cause. It cannot be said that he neglected any purely British interests. The charge that will lie against him in history is that he neglected nobler and more universal interests.

The old world of Europe disappeared during the war. It went down fighting, but it went down. Consumed in the furnace of war, Europe had become a mass of molten metal, and had to be reshaped anew. The old political conceptions had many of them disappeared before the Peace Conference met. Hereditary military dynasties had ceased to exist in Russia and Germany, in Austria-Hungary, in Turkey. Constitutional kings had been deposed in Greece and Bulgaria. The Balance of Power, that fundamental concept of European diplomacy, was called by President Wilson 'the great game, now for ever discredited.' Men spoke now of a League of Nations. The limitation of armaments and the destruction of militarism were everywhere declared to be the aim. But the old forces, though weakened, were still there, and Clemenceau embodied these.

The basis of the Peace Treaty was not, as has sometimes been asserted, the armistice, but the pre-armistice negotiations. These resulted from Germany's suing for peace by the note issued, at Ludendorff's demand, on October 3, 1918. The note was addressed to President Wilson and asked for peace on the basis of the Fourteen Points set out in his Message to Congress of January 18, 1918. A correspondence ensued. In ultimate result the Allies made an offer on November 5, 1918, accepting this basis provided that Germany first evacuated occupied Belgium and France and stopped the submarine campaign. The Allies excluded Point 2, 'the Freedom of the Seas,' from discussion, and added a definition of loss and damage to the terms in Wilson's speeches. Germany signified her consent to this whole offer of November 5 by approaching Foch and signing an armistice which was intended to be purely military and naval in character (November 11, 1918), though one clause in it refers to Finance and Reparations (Art. XIX), but this is probably only an expansion of the loss and damage clause of the November 5 offer. It contained provisions for the surrender of the German navy and other war *matériel*.

The Peace Conference opened in January 1919 at Paris, with Clemenceau as President. The first great principle of the Peace Treaty was to found a League of Nations, in accordance with the last of the Fourteen Points. It was here that Wilson scored his greatest success. Clemenceau hardly owed even lip-service to the League. Lloyd George, though not unfriendly, thought it in 1919, and indeed until long after, secondary to other issues. Neither certainly desired to have the League and the Peace Treaty so tied up that one could not work without the other. This was exactly what Wilson intended. Lloyd George and Clemenceau moved for a Commission to discuss it. Wilson, to the surprise of all, put himself on the Commission. It was therefore impossible to adjourn or ignore the Commission's report. When it was presented Wilson got it accepted, and the Covenant of the League was solemnly adopted. But even towards the end of March opposition revived, and attempts were made by Clemenceau and Lloyd George to separate the Covenant from the Treaty. Wilson this time showed his teeth, the two statesmen of the old world gave way, and the Covenant became part of the Treaty. Wilson seems to have reasoned thus:

> Europe is exhausted with war and excited by popular clamour. These facts make it impossible to make a good treaty. But, if the League once passes into law as the Covenant, it can be used as a means of revising the objectionable clauses of the Treaty itself. As racial hatreds die down, the power of the League will assert itself, wrongs will be healed and remedies applied. It matters little if some of the Treaty is bad, so long as the League is good. The one is temporary, the other permanent, the lesser instrument will ultimately be absorbed in the greater.

There can be little doubt that this reasoning was sound, and had America remained in the League its conclusions might well have been justified by time. There is no doubt that, but for Wilson, the League would either never have existed at all or have had little practical importance.

Connected with the League was the establishment of the great mandatory system. This was a system enjoined on the Powers who undertook to govern the German colonies and the Turkish areas which were now at the disposal of the conquerors. Instead of annexing them, the Allies worked out a system by which the Power taking over any of these so-called mandated areas was bound to conduct the government in the interests of the governed, as 'the well-being and development of such peoples form a sacred trust of civilization.'[1] 'Securities for the performance of this trust' were embodied in the Covenant, and took the form of requiring each mandatory Power to submit an annual report, and of constituting a permanent Mandates' Commission. The latter received the annual report, and could inquire into the working of each mandate and demand publicity in any case that seemed necessary. The system was not perfect, but was infinitely preferable to mere annexation, and it was again largely due to Wilson. The principle of trusteeship was later to be taken up by Roosevelt and applied after the War of 1939–45.

The League organisation was to consist of a Council of the Great Powers, including representatives of minor states, and an Assembly including all members of the League. Ultimately, provision was also made for the constitution of a Court of International Justice. Thus the international executive, legislature and judiciary were constituted. Securities for the future permanent existence of international organs for the control and regulation and revision of the Treaty were thereby provided. The whole was an immense advance on the achievement of any international conference in the past. Akin to it was the creation of the International Labour Office, with its Labour Parliament of Governments, employers and workmen.

With the Covenant in his pocket Wilson paid a flying visit to America (February 14), not returning until March 14. This month was a fateful one, as it showed exactly the position of the Allies to America. Wilson returned to find a new situation. Clemenceau and Lloyd George had no objection to Wilson and his international covenant or mandatory system as such; but their chief concern was that their own national interests should not be imperilled by his idealism.

From the point of view of military security, and this is the first of all national interests, Britain was in a very favourable position. The whole fleet of Germany had been surrendered and was soon to be at the bottom of the sea, and with that surrender the chief cause of Anglo-German enmity disappeared. Nor was there likely to be any dispute about the colonies which caused serious difficulties. Lloyd George could therefore view the European situation with tranquillity. Not so France. The German army had not surrendered *en masse*, nor had it yet been effectively disarmed. Thrice in a hundred years forces from Germany had passed over the Rhine, twice they had entered Paris, and the third time they had entirely devastated northern France. No Frenchman could contemplate a fourth attempt

---

[1] See Article 22 of the Covenant. For the League generally, see F. P. Walters, *A History of the League of Nations* (1952), 2 vols. A useful short treatment is G. Scott, *The Rise and Fall of the League of Nations* (1973).

without horror. Foch proposed a drastic solution: the permanent disarmament of Germany and the creation of a client Rhine Republic (really dependent upon France), which would interpose a demilitarised area between Germany and France for the next fifty years or more. Foch urged this plan with bitterness and intensity, but Clemenceau refused to put it forward. Wilson and Lloyd George were determined that the German area west of the Rhine should not be subject to France, and Clemenceau admitted their opposition. A compromise was agreed upon, a compromise which in the long run was to prove unworkable. The German area west of the Rhine was to be entirely demilitarised for ever. But in 1936 Hitler sent German troops into this demilitarised area, occupying and fortifying it. France and Britain accepted the fact and deplored only that it was done without preliminary negotiation. The Saar basin was to be held by an Inter-Allied force and administered by the League of Nations for fifteen years. At the end of that time a plebiscite was to decide whether the inhabitants wished to belong to France or Germany. The plebiscite, held in 1935, was for Germany. There was not much doubt as to how it would go, as only one per cent of the Saar inhabitants was non-German.

As regards the other points of the frontier, the areas of Eupen, Moresnet and Malmédy were ceded by Germany to Belgium, though a show was made of consulting the wishes of the inhabitants. According to Wilson's eighth point, 'the wrong done to France by Prussia in 1871 in the matter of Alsace-Lorraine, which has unsettled the peace of the world for nearly fifty years, should be righted in order that peace may once more be made secure in the interests of all.' Alsace-Lorraine was accordingly to be ceded outright to the French by Germany. In these provinces France acquired nearly two million subjects and three-quarters of the German iron production.

Thus was the western frontier settled. The north was soon settled, also by a plebiscite which returned the North Schleswig area to Denmark. The eastern frontier offered much greater difficulties. By Point 13, Poland was to be allowed access to the sea, constituted as independent and guaranteed by international covenant. Now Poland must have a frontier, and the Polish and German elements were inextricably mingled on the whole frontier from Danzig to Upper Silesia. It was no more possible to distinguish them than to draw a line between colours in a piece of shot silk. No solution could be exact. East Prussia (the area of Hindenburg's victories and the home of the Prussian junker) projected into Polish territory. Danzig, a German town surrounded by Polish villages, stood sentry over the Vistula, the river which carried the commerce, and therefore the life-blood, of Poland. A Polish corridor was carried from the south separating East Prussia from Germany and ending in Danzig. As the result of an ingenious and fateful proposal made by Lloyd George, Danzig was put under the control of the League of Nations, Poland remaining responsible for her foreign relations. A large area—West Prussia and Posen, containing many Prussians—was assigned *en bloc* to the new Polish state. Ultimately it was arranged to decide the fate of three other areas by plebiscite. Those of Allenstein and Marienwerder voted for, and were returned to, Germany. In Upper Silesia, an area rich in coal, the plebiscite took longer, and its results were fiercely disputed. It was not until 1921 that a dividing line was finally drawn—it was drawn by experts appointed by the League of Nations—and each side contended that it would work out unfairly for itself. As a result of these decisions Poland acquired a considerable number of Germans as well as Poles, and part of the mineral wealth in Upper Silesia. In result, much bitterness naturally remained. It may be said roughly that the Germans accepted, at least for a time, the western frontier, with the demilitarised area of the Rhine, and the return of Alsace-Lorraine to France; but from the beginning they steadily refused to accept the idea that their eastern frontier was a final settlement. The German's hatred of the Pole was even deeper than his hatred of the Frenchman, and the prospect of rich districts and large German populations remaining permanently Polish was hateful to Germany. The situation on this frontier was one of the dangers of Europe.

In addition to Poland, Czechoslovakia was erected into an independent state. This vigorous young state of Czechs and Slovaks took over from the old Austria the areas of Bohemia abutting on Germany. It was only in Bavaria, therefore, that Germany touched Austria. And as an additional security, it was provided that there should be no political union between Austria and Germany without the consent of the Council of the League of Nations. The protection to France on Germany's eastern frontier was therefore the constitution of two new independent states (Poland and Czechoslovakia), which promptly allied themselves with France. Germany was deprived of something like two million subjects and a great source of wealth in the shape of coal. In addition, Austria was separated from Hungary and reduced to a state of some eight million. She was surrounded everywhere by hostile states. The one exception was Germany, and with Germany she was forbidden to unite, though this did not prevent her annexation in 1938.

The securities so far required to render Germany less dangerous in future were either territorial, by readjusting the frontier, or economic, by reducing her wealth. In addition on her flanks states were created (Poland and Czechoslovakia) or strengthened (Belgium and Luxembourg which were deneutralised). It might be thought that these precautions, which strongly resemble those applied to France in the settlement of 1815, would have been enough. But the lesson of the war and of the enormous and increasing power of Germany had been thoroughly learnt by the French at least. Their plan was a drastic one. It was to abolish Germany for ever as a military power by limiting her army practically to a police force. Lloyd George added the interesting innovation of a voluntary long-period service army. The existing forces were to be demobilised and conscription abolished in Germany. Instead soldiers were to serve for twelve years—and the total number was to be limited to 100,000 men. In this way no large numbers of recruits could ever be trained and, as the years went on, very few would have any experience of military service. The existing armaments were to be destroyed, and the production of munitions to be strictly limited in future. As an additional precaution, the German Staff was to be strictly limited in numbers and powers. The aim was to prevent the production of war materials, to limit effective forces, to defamiliarise Germany with militarism, and to prevent the brain (i.e. the General Staff) of the army from functioning in future. This system was also to be applied to the navy, which was limited to 6 battleships, 6 light cruisers, 12 destroyers, and 12 torpedo boats. Germany was forbidden to include military or naval air forces in her armament. The system was applied, *similia similibus*, to Austria, Hungary, Bulgaria and Turkey. It was an ingenious system—and only Turkey refused to have it forced upon her.

The first defect in the German disarmament was that the limitation of the army to 100,000 was too low a figure for Germany. It was four times less than what the British General Staff recommended. In result Germany and the others were tempted, or compelled, first to evade, and finally to repudiate, these clauses. All these four countries had, in less than twenty years, as many men trained or armed as they liked. These military, naval and air clauses were introduced into the German Treaty with the statement that they were enforced on Germany and her allies, 'in order to render possible the initiation of a general limitation of the armaments of all nations.' Germany (and Austria and Bulgaria and Hungary) complied with the demands, but awaited in vain any effective 'general limitation of the armaments of all nations.' Germany and the other states, in the result, rejected the clauses openly in 1936. In the end the feverish competition in armament production was resumed on a greater scale than that which led to the War of 1914.

Great severity was shown in the case of German rights and interests outside Germany. All German state property in her former colonies was confiscated, and all her trading privileges and rights in countries such as Morocco, China, Siam (Thailand), Equatorial Africa, were abrogated. It was therefore made extremely difficult for her to trade outside Europe. Kiao-Chau and German rights in Shantung province went on lease and the Marshall Isles on mandate to Japan. All her other colonies were assigned to mandatories: to France, part of the Cameroons; to Britain, the rest of the Cameroons,

Togoland and part of Tanganyika (Tanzania); to Belgium, Ruanda-Urundi (part of Tanganyika); to South Africa, German South-West Africa (Namibia); to Australia, German New Guinea; to New Zealand, Samoa. She also received very stern treatment as regards control of her ports, waterways and railways wherever they had an international character. The Rhine, for instance, by an extreme application of the doctrine of international rivers, was governed by an international board on which Germany was in a hopeless minority; Great Britain and Italy together had, actually, as many representatives on the Rhine Commission as Germany herself. The Kiel Canal, more justifiably, was neutralised and demilitarised. Both the internationalisation of the Rhine and the neutralisation of the Kiel Canal were later repudiated by Germany. These provisions, taken in conjunction with those relating to enemy property and debts, were of extreme severity. Indeed, those relating to private property, which enabled individual property to be confiscated in Allied countries as a set-off against national reparation debts, were revolutionary in character. They were clearly most dangerous as a precedent for future treaties, and are a good illustration of how hard it is for experts pursuing a formula, to do justice to a defeated enemy.

The heated atmosphere of the Peace Conference led more than anything else to the Penal Clauses. These provided for the extradition from Holland of the German ex-Emperor, and for his trial by a special tribunal 'for a supreme offence against international morality and the sanctity of treaties.' They also provided for Germany's surrender to the Allies, for trial by special tribunal, of certain German persons who had violated the laws and customs of war, or had been guilty of criminal acts against Allied nationals. In the end these clauses proved unworkable. The Dutch refused to give up the ex-Emperor, on the very justifiable ground that it was against international law for the Allies to demand the surrender of a political refugee from a neutral state. A vast list of war criminals was drawn up, but it proved impossible to extradite them from Germany in view of the ugly temper of the German people. A few of them were tried and punished by German tribunals. When the President of the German Republic was elected in 1925, the French thought of declaring the election annulled by the Treaty, since the successful candidate was a war criminal. They eventually desisted, and were wise to do so—for the name of the old war criminal and the new President was Hindenburg.

The last and most important section of the Treaty to be mentioned here was concerned with reparation. Passions ran high. France, with her devastated areas and desolated cities, clamoured for the amplest indemnities. She held, too, that the exaction of huge sums from Germany was a kind of *revanche* for the indemnity of 1871. And there was further a desire to cripple and injure Germany by fines and amercements. French hatred of Germany was so fierce, her demands so impassioned, that no moderation could be expected from her. Lloyd George was unfortunately in nearly the same position. The war-time Coalition won the Election of 1918 in Britain on the cry of 'making Germany pay to the last farthing.' This cry conflicted with the legal basis of the Treaty, but Lloyd George never denied that he advocated it. Unfortunately there were different opinions as to how many farthings Germany possessed. Before Lloyd George left for Paris a committee of British financiers, headed by the Australian premier, William Hughes, produced what was known as the 'business man's estimate'. They reckoned that Germany could pay twenty-four thousand million pounds![1] The sum was ridiculous. No one at the Peace Conference seriously suggested more than a third of that sum as possible, few believed that more than a fifth of it could be exacted. Keynes, the best British financial adviser, suggested two thousand million, in a lump sum, as the most that could be got out of Germany. This was only one-twelfth of the 'business man's estimate,' which had been popularly acclaimed in Britain. Lloyd George might well ask in private (as he frequently did), 'What is a poor politician to do?' It was no use asserting too openly that 'the business men' were drunk with passion and their 'estimate' moonshine. For the politician who did that would quickly lose his job. Even as it was he came near doing so. The telegram of 370 members of Parliament demanding that Lloyd George should make Germany pay to the utmost was a danger-signal. It was a threat he could not openly disregard, and it hampered all his subsequent policy. The most extraordinary part of the whole affair is that the 'business men' never demanded an inventory of Germany's assets nor a calculation on a business basis. It was always an estimate based on passion and on prejudice, which eschewed contact with realities.

One chance, and one chance only, remained. President Wilson had said very nobly, 'America wanted nothing for herself' in reparations or money. But on his voyage to Paris he had said very naively that he was 'not much interested in the economic subjects' to be discussed at Paris. That was just the tragedy. There is little on the subject in Wilson's speeches and addresses, which formed the legal basis of the Treaty. He himself was interested in enabling republics to be erected in Germany, Poland and Czechoslovakia, and drawing their frontiers for them. But the economics of Europe—and indeed of the war in Europe—were hard for him to understand, and still harder for him to settle. Keynes proposed a plan for cancelling Inter-Allied debts, but this was too bold for America. But the question of reparation was different. Some of Wilson's advisers prepared a business estimate of German assets. When that was rejected and a total of

---

[1] See the document in Lloyd George, *The Truth about Reparations and War-Debts* (1932), pp. 12–13.

five thousand million was proposed, Lloyd George showed complete frankness. 'Lloyd George admitted that this was all that could reasonably be expected, but objected that [British and French] public opinion would not accept it.'[1] This stand destroyed all idea of getting a lump sum out of Germany. The settlement ultimately adopted left the sum which Germany was to pay undefined. A Reparation Commission was formed and endowed with very large powers of control to determine Germany's capacity to pay. The British and French public were satisfied, assuming that Germany would be made to pay enormous sums. The aim of Lloyd George (and doubtless also of President Wilson) was just the opposite. It was to get that sum down to reasonable limits, when the Reparation Commission sat in an atmosphere free from passion and in which it was safe to tell the public the truth. Also, if the United States had remained on the Reparation Commission, it is clear that its decisions and its conclusions would have been very different. The Treaty, even as it was, appeared to demand something like eight thousand million pounds[2] But it was certainly the intention of Lloyd George and Wilson greatly to reduce this sum.

In connection with reparation, however, a most unfortunate incident occurred. Lloyd George and the French had at first tried to make Germany 'pay the whole cost of the war.' This principle was knocked on the head by President Wilson, who declared, and rightly, that it was inconsistent with the legal basis of the Treaty. This basis was not that Germany should pay the whole cost, or even an indemnity; she had simply agreed to pay compensation 'for all damage done to the civilian population of the Allies and their property by the aggression of Germany by land, by sea, and from the air.' Now this definition would only have produced about three thousand millions from Germany. Moreover, it would have been enormously to the advantage of France as against Britain. Lloyd George therefore desired to find a basis by which more could be demanded, and a bigger share of reparation obtained for Britain. He found it in pensions to widows and orphans of persons killed in the war and in separation allowances during the war—a category which could not possibly be covered by the definition of loss and damage given. France agreed to this proposal, which meant adding some five thousand million pounds to the original three thousand million. But President Wilson had to be convinced—and it took much time. It was argued that pensions could not possibly be included in the loss and damage definition; it was argued much less reasonably that it could. Smuts submitted an argument that it was legal and logical. Wilson finally astonished everyone by saying: 'Logic! Logic! I don't give a

---

[1] R. S. Baker, *Woodrow Wilson and World Settlement* (1923), vol. II, p. 377.

[2] J. M. Keynes, *The Economic Consequences of the Peace* (1919), p. 207.

damn for logic. I am going to include pensions!'[1] So pensions were included. There can be very little doubt that this decision was wrong. It is also hardly possible to deny that, if so, it was a breach of faith by the Allies of an international engagement with Germany of a sacred character. But it is not likely that Wilson included it because he did not realise the legal or logical objections to doing so.

In this fashion the Treaty was completed and the Germans were asked to sign. By a very grave breach of international courtesy and usage, the German delegates were not allowed to discuss the Treaty in private with the Allies. They were restricted entirely to written intercourse. The result, curiously enough, worked out entirely to the Allied disadvantage. Had there been discussion in committee there would have been full explanations at close quarters of the whole meaning of the Treaty. There would also certainly have been modifications of some clauses. As it was, the Germans could not find out the true meaning of everything. They therefore misinterpreted Article 231, which begins the reparation section of the Treaty, as charging them with war-guilt. It was, in fact, merely a technical verdict of guilty against Germany, in order to justify the exaction of money from her. But the Germans always interpreted it as fixing the guilt of the war upon Germany in the practical and moral sense. And this interpretation was repeated so often that even the Allies, or at least the Allied press and public, came to believe it. It is perhaps the most impressive demonstration ever given that the denial of courtesy and a fair hearing even to a foe brings severe penalties with it.

By a sort of symbolic retribution carefully planned and designed by the French, the signature of the Peace Treaty took place at Versailles, in the Galerie des Glaces. This was doubly memorable. It was the hall where Louis Quatorze set up his motto, *nec pluribus impar*, which he decorated with the painted trophies of his victories, in which he received and humiliated the Doge of Genoa, in which he proclaimed his grandson King of Spain. In that same room William I, King of Prussia, had been proclaimed German Emperor by the warriors and princes of Germany, fresh from their triumph over France. And in the room where imperial Germany had recorded her victory, republican Germany was to record her defeat.

Here is the account of an eye-witness on June 28, 1919:

> To-day I saw the Germans sign. The entrance to the Galerie des Glaces was up two lines of stairs, guarded by a line of troopers, with blue uniforms, steel breast-plates, and helmets with long horse-hair plumes, making a splendid appearance. . . . At three p.m. there was suddenly a tense interval and silence, and, preceded by four armed officers, the Germans appeared. One pale, bowed, with glasses like a student

[1] E. M. House and C. Seymour, *What really happened at Paris* (1921), p. 272.

(Müller); the next head erect and hair like an artist's (Bell).
Immediately after, I suppose by design, the cuirassiers all suddenly
sheathed their swords . . . a symbolic and conscious act. The
atmosphere of hate was terrible. They advanced and sat down on the
fourth side of the square, near the table of rose and almond-wood, on
which lay the Treaty. In a minute or two Clemenceau got up, and
speaking in a sharp, clear, musical voice, like a succession of strokes on
a gong, said: 'We are in complete agreement. I have the honour to ask
messieurs the German plenipotentiaries to sign.' At this point the
Germans got up and bowed low. They were asked to sit down again
and the speech was translated. After this they came forward and signed
slowly amid a tense hush.

Then came Wilson (and his plenipotentiaries), Lloyd George, who
smiled broadly as he finished, the Colonial Premiers, and the
Maharajah of Bikaner, looking magnificent in a pale khaki turban.
After that Clemenceau, with Pichon and Tardieu behind him. Then
Sonnino, on the last day of his reign, and then the plenipotentiaries of
Minor States. As Paderewski, with his tawny mane and stage-bow,
signed, the guns began to boom outside.

The ceremony ended soon, the Germans were carefully escorted out,
and Clemenceau came down the hall slowly, beaming, shaking hands. As
he went out the old man reached me his hand, or rather the hand covered
as always in a grey glove. 'Felicitations,' said I. 'Mille remerciments,'
said he . . . A great moment, but I fear a peace without victory, just as we
had a victory without peace.

Chapter 5

NATION-MAKING IN THE NEW EUROPE

CENTRAL EUROPE

The history of the war and the peace is overhung with dark clouds of delusion. It is assumed that the war was a purposeless agony, the peace treaties a series of penal measures and amercements. These half-truths obscure the real facts. For, whatever may be thought of the German Treaty, it developed international organisation to a point unknown before in human history. Whatever may be thought of the treaties with Austria, with Hungary, with Bulgaria, they satisfied national aspirations to an extent unprecedented in eastern and central Europe. These treaties enabled two nations—Rumania and Yugoslavia—to become great states and to reunite themselves to their long-severed kinsmen. It brought two others to life, Czechoslovakia and Poland, after centuries of extinction. Four others, Estonia, Latvia, Finland and Lithuania, recovered their freedom. These achievements seem likely to be memorable in history. And, if they are, importance will attach to the treaties which made them possible.

Popular delusions abound with regard to the treaties with Austria, Hungary, Bulgaria and Turkey. It was contended, for instance, that the Entente Powers were legally bound to apply the Wilsonian principles to these treaties and to other countries as well as to Germany. To Germany the pledge was admitted. An offer was made on November 5, 1918, which Germany accepted by signing the armistice, and this offer was a promise to make peace on the basis of Wilson's speeches from January 8, 1918 onwards (the Fourteen Points). Bulgaria signed an armistice on September 29, Turkey on October 30, and Austria-Hungary on November 3. Their terms all differed from the German, for each of these countries sued for peace after admittedly overwhelming defeat, and received it on the basis of unconditional surrender. Consequently the Entente Powers in no way made a contract (as they did by their offer of November 5 to the

Germans) to apply Wilson's principles to these countries. Any such pledge was implicit and moral, not explicit and legal.

It will be best to take Austria-Hungary first. The last act of the old Common Monarchy was to sign an armistice on November 3, 1918. Immediately afterwards Austria parted from Hungary and the two became separate and independent states. Hungary then, on November 13, 1918, signed a separate military convention with the Entente Powers. Ultimately Austria signed one Peace Treaty (St. Germain, September 10, 1919) and Hungary another (Trianon, June 4, 1920), and peace negotiations with each were entirely separate. The population of Austria as distinct from Hungary was over 26 millions. The Treaty of St. Germain reduced Austria to a third of her old population. She surrendered seven and a half million Slavs in Galicia to the new Poland, and over a million other non-Germans. She gave up also nearly four million Germans, of whom three and a half million went to Czechoslovakia. Austria's new boundaries confined her to Upper and Lower Austria, Carinthia and Styria and the Tyrol, with a population of about eight millions odd, nearly all of pure German race. The once proud Austria, which had ruled over fifteen different races, was reduced to less than half of her former size, and lost a third of her purely German population. She became miserably poor and dragged out a pathetic existence from this time until she was annexed by Germany in 1938. She was again separated in 1945.

Poland, on the principle of self-determination, had received the Slav populations of Ruthenes and Poles from Austria. But why was it necessary for Czechoslovakia to take three and a half million Germans from Austria? The reason was that some of these Germans were separated by Czech territory from Austria and had formerly faced imperial Germany, while others were inextricably mingled with Czechs. If Czechoslovakia had a right to exist at all, she could only do so as a polyglot and multi-racial state. To be viable at all, she must include all sorts of races and stretch her tentacles far. As finally constituted there were over six million Czechs, nearly two million Slovaks, three and a half million Germans and not quite a million Magyars. This was the only instance at the Peace Conference in which any state was deliberately formed on a multi-national basis. In other cases alien races were reluctantly admitted, not deliberately chosen as the basis of a state.

In history the Czechs had once been a nation, and it was held that they had a right to be so again. Their ability and organising capacity, like their hatred for the German, was great. Moreover, it was evident that, in so polyglot a state, the ruling race would not attempt to coerce, or if it attempted, would not succeed in coercing, the alien races. On the whole, Czechoslovakia justified these hopes. Under two great teachers, Masaryk, their first President, and Beneš, his successor, she showed a largeness of international outlook and a tolerance towards her subject races which was unique in central and in east Europe. Certainly the Poles treated their Ruthenians (who were Slavs) much worse than the Czechs treated their Germans (who were Teutons).

Austria in one sense had more to suffer from Italy than from Czechoslovakia. For, though she lost much less to Italy, the Hapsburg monarchy had been an eternal enemy, the tyrannical power reigning in Lombardy and Venetia and denying Italians their freedom. Such memories are not easily forgotten, and in 1866, when Austria finally abandoned Venetia to Italy, she retained the Trentino. The fact that the southern part of the Tyrol was inhabited by Italians provoked Italian patriots, who gave it the name of *Italia irredenta*. But there was another provocation too. The Austrians had taken great care to retain spurs and tongues of mountains running down into the Italian plains. The territory thus retained projected like a bastion into Italy, protecting Austria from all assault and facilitating attack on Italy from this area. The Italians succeeded at the Peace Conference in exactly turning the tables on Austria. They pushed the Italian frontier right up to the Brenner Pass, not only thereby annexing a quarter of a million Germans, but giving Italy an offensive advantage against Austria in the case of war. It was wholly needless to give her this power or to hand over so many Germans to her keeping. Two other frontiers were proposed which would have given her adequate defence, without sinning so much against racial ethics. But the fear of a revived Austria, the ghost of a dead past, prevailed.

The line thus conceded to Italy in the Tyrol was part of the price Italy demanded for siding with the Entente. The secret Treaty of London, April 26, 1915, promised territory in Istria, which meant ceding half a million Yugoslavs to Italy, and half of Dalmatia as well. Britain and France were agreed to cede Istria, but they tried hard to avoid ceding half Dalmatia as well. President Wilson, who was not bound by a secret treaty, stubbornly resisted. The Italian case was a bad one, for they wanted the port of Fiume as well, and the port of Fiume had not been included in the Treaty of London. Hence if they got half Dalmatia they would not get Fiume. If they got Fiume they would have no claim to half Dalmatia. Wilson took a strong stand against their having Fiume, and was supported by Britain and France. But the whole matter was not settled at the Peace Conference. It was ultimately decided by direct negotiations between Italy and the Yugoslavs. In the end Italy got Fiume and one or two islands in the Adriatic and the town of Zara in Dalmatia, surrendering all the rest. Italy eventually included within her borders half a million Yugoslavs, in addition to the quarter of a million Germans in the Tyrol. It was not a good settlement, but it was better than none. If you are trying to absorb parts of other races, it is best to place them behind strong barriers, which will make it difficult for their brethren to free them. Italy had effectively done this. The quarter of a million Germans in the Tyrol and the half million Yugoslavs in Istria and the Julian Alps were separated from their kinsmen by enormous mountains, so the prisoners were behind walls which were strong, and Italy held the key.

As a result of the war the old kingdom of Serbia grew into the new state of Yugoslavia. During the war the Serb army under the Regent (later King Alexander) had suffered intensely and performed miracles of valour. They had their reward, and trebled the size of their country. To the old kingdom of Serbia were now added Montenegro, Dalmatia, Bosnia and Slovenia. The old kingdom of four million swelled to thirteen, partly at the expense of Austria, but mostly at the expense of Hungary. The inhabitants of the new kingdom were nearly all Yugoslavs—of similar blood and speech to the Serbs.[1] Twelve out of the thirteen million in the new kingdom were Yugoslavs. There had never in the past been a kingdom uniting all Yugoslavs, and this made its formation difficult. There were differences of religion and history, and old barriers of prejudice. The quarrels in parliament and the disputes between the different parties or races finally became so bitter that King Alexander abolished the constitution of 1921, and governed as dictator. In 1931 he sought to set up a modified form of representative government, of which the success was moderate. Alexander was murdered at Marseilles in 1934 after having untiringly pursued the Yugoslav ideal. A Regency under Prince Paul followed and was still in office when war came again to the Balkan Peninsula. He was the victim of the German invasion in 1941.

Rumania, like Yugoslavia, derived enormous accessions of wealth and population from the war at the expense of Hungary. She was particularly fortunate, because she was late in entering the war and had to make peace at the end of 1917. She again took up arms very late in 1918. Her statesmen at the Peace Conference showed considerable truculence, and, in defiance of the Great Powers, sent their soldiers into Budapest in August 1919, and terrorised and looted it to their hearts' content. By the subsequent treaty with Hungary Rumania obtained enormous advantages. The whole of Transylvania, rich in forests and ores, fell into her hands; so did the great city of Temesvár and a large slice of the fertile cornland of Hungary. In addition Rumania regained the Bukovina from Austria, and the great province of Bessarabia from Russia. She more than doubled her old territory and population, obtaining over eight million new subjects, of whom more than half were Rumanians. The Rumanian kingdom,

---

[1] The Slovenes speak a different dialect, but Croat and Serb are the same language.

thus strengthened and reorganised, was not, however, an ideal state. Historical differences were very great, Bucharest was not well situated to be the capital, the government was intolerant and corrupt, and the lot of the subject peoples was hard. In one direction alone Rumania was far-sighted. Despite opposition from her landowning class of nobles, she insisted on a forced distribution of land to peasants. She did this not only in the conquered lands but in old Rumania also.

We are now in a position to estimate what the Treaty of Trianon (June 4, 1920) really did to the kingdom of Hungary. It cut off the Slovaks and some Magyars from her in the north and gave them to Czechoslovakia. It severed Rumanians and Magyars, Slovenes and Croats from her and gave them to Rumania and to Yugoslavia in the south. It left her with a population of seven and a half million, of whom over six million were Magyars. She therefore lost about three million Magyars in all. Czechoslovakia, Rumania and Yugoslavia thus took from Hungary not only subjects of their own race, but three million Magyars in addition; about half a million went to Yugoslavia, one million to Czechoslovakia and a million and a half to Rumania. It must however be remembered that Hungary before the war had over half its subjects aliens, and the populations of Czechoslovakia, Rumania and Yugoslavia were distributed a great deal more according to racial unity than was the case in any of these regions in 1914.

This is not the only argument to show that in central and east Europe at least the carving up and redistribution of races was, on the whole, to the good. Pre-war Hungary had been ruled by a narrow, aristocratic Magyar caste, able and courageous, but hostile to all non-Magyar elements in the state. After an interval of revolution and the Communist régime of Bela Kun (March to August 1919) these tendencies reasserted themselves. The rule of the Regent Horthy was supported by a reorganised Magyar aristocracy, with a tight hand on democracy and no disposition to make land easy for the peasant to acquire. This was the real difference between Hungary and the countries which surrounded it. In that part of the world the war was a war for free land for the peasant. The Entente fought for the peasant, Hungary for the landowner. Rumania, reactionary and corrupt as she was, recognised this truth and compelled even her nobles to distribute land to the peasants on a generous scale. In Czechoslovakia land was freely assigned to the peasant by the new Government. The Serbs have never had any aristocracy since the Turks destroyed it. The Serbs applied their old policy freely and readily to the whole of Yugoslavia, and distributed land to peasants in fair shares, taking care that it should be inalienable. Without the Austrian and Hungarian treaties these experiments could not have been made. To the objective eye there can be no doubt that Hungary, with its chivalric virtues, represented a vanishing past, and that the new states represented the future. Whatever may be said of treaty-making in the west, the new forces, created by the Treaties of east and central Europe, were stronger than the old and more in touch with modern life.

THE BALTIC, POLAND AND RUSSIA

Four states of the Baltic coast had a most prominent share in the war, and were, as a result of the peace, all of them enabled to realise their national aspirations. These states were Finland, Estonia, Latvia and Lithuania. They had always in the past been the battleground between Swedes, Russians, Poles and Germans. After the war they were for twenty years free and able to live their own lives. Finland was the most mature of these countries as regards national status and evolution. Since Russia wrested her from Sweden in 1809 Finland's position always approached that of independence. For a time she actually attained it during the Russian Revolution of 1905; and, even when Russia resumed control, her separate position remained. She sent no members to the Duma and paid a tax in lieu of military service. A foolish and violent attempt was made to russianise Finland, but this broke down as soon as war began. In 1917 the Russian Revolution brought her complete autonomy. Finland was for a time in danger both from her own reactionaries and from the Communists in neighbouring Russia. It was, in fact, hard to say whether White or Red influences were more dangerous to her. Ultimately peace was made with Soviet Russia in 1920, and from this time until 1939 Finland pursued her own national development untouched from without.

Estonia and Latvia may be taken together. There are differences between them. The Esths, like the Finns, are Ugrian and primitive in race, while the Letts are a Slav people. None the less both in servitude and in freedom the two states have had a common history. In the Middle Ages they were both subjected to German landlords (the 'Baltic barons') and reduced to the condition of mere serfs. Russia conquered both countries at the beginning of the eighteenth century. As the Russian Government did not like Germans it did something to raise the condition of the serfs as against their masters. At last in 1861 it emancipated all the serfs. In this way a new era for both countries began. Education was pushed forward, and national aspirations gradually took shape. The Esths soon became one of the best educated races in Europe. They were almost wholly homogeneous in race, and they were particularly active in expelling German influences in higher education. The Letts were not far behind them, and both were prepared for independence when the war began. Latvia was a theatre of war from the start, but in 1918 the Germans finally occupied Estonia as well. During the years 1919–20 both countries had to struggle against Germans on the one side and Russians on the other, Both were ultimately successful, and were admitted as independent states into the League of Nations in 1921.

The same year witnessed the resurrection of Lithuania. That state was neither so homogeneous as the others, nor were its inhabitants so tough in fibre, nor were they trained so much to the sea. In Finland at Helsinki, in Estonia at Reval, in Latvia at Riga, the capital was a port. Lithuania's capital was Vilna, in the interior, and it was threatened by Poland. During the war Germany had found it politic to allow the Lithuanians a considerable amount of freedom as a counterpoise to the Poles. After the armistice she was in a dangerous position, though she received friendly aid from Estonia and Latvia in 1918. During 1919 she gradually disencumbered herself of Germany, only to meet with fresh threats to her independence from Poles and Russians. The former, not the latter, proved the more serious menace. The Poles, remembering the old mediaeval connection of Lithuania and Poland, fought desperately to preserve it. When that hope failed they decided at least to secure control of Vilna. They sent a Polish general, Zeligowski, to seize it. He did so and held it in the name of Poland and undoubtedly at the instigation of the Polish Government.[1] The Great Powers had recognised the independence of Lithuania in 1922. But they proved entirely unable to shake the Polish grasp on Vilna and finally acquiesced in its retention by Poland in 1923. Thus Lithuania, though deprived of its capital by Polish agency, recovered its independence.

All these four Baltic states may be described as states whose national independence existed 'on sufferance.' They were plainly not strong enough, either individually or collectively, to stand out against the attack of an armed Great Power. The Poles or the Russians might equally be a danger to them. Their independence in fact was governed by the ability of Poland and Russia to counterbalance one another.

Lying outside and beyond modern Austria and Hungary, and the newer or enlarged states of eastern Europe and the four Baltic states, the two Powers of Poland and Russia were of fundamental importance. Behind them there stood a long history of opposition. In the past Poland represented Catholicism and Latin culture, Russia Byzantinism and Orthodoxy. Poland thought Russians barbarous and, finding no defensible frontier between the countries, invaded and dominated and colonised many parts of Russia. She gradually

---

[1] This instigation was denied at the time, but was subsequently admitted by Pilsudski himself.

grew stronger and pushed the Russians out. Finally in the eighteenth century Poland became weak, was partitioned by three Powers and destroyed. But nations do not die readily, much less a nation so gifted and brilliant and patriotic as the Poles. Poland had once been a great nation. She determined to be so again. As the three partitioning Powers, Russia, Germany and Austria-Hungary, suffered defeat in the war, they relaxed their grasp on Poland. The Poles seized their opportunity and were already a nation again before the war ended. The Peace Conference, in recognising Poland's independence, merely acknowledged a fact. But difficulties arose at once about drawing her frontiers. The German frontier was not easily settled, but was the least of the difficulties. It was soon found that in East Galicia three million Ruthenians had no desire to belong to the Poles. It was also found that Lithuania wished to be independent. The Poles knew what they wanted, and the Great Powers gradually wearied of the struggle. They obtained East Galicia and, by very questionable means, also got possession of Vilna, the capital of Lithuania.

Poland thus obtained territories to the west and the south, but what was to be her boundary to the east? The boundary in the past had never been the ethnic frontier, and the Poles may perhaps be excused for wanting to keep Russia at as great a distance as possible from Warsaw. From 1917 onwards the Communist Government of Russia had announced a policy of war against capitalists and the bourgeoisie and their intention of releasing the proletariat in bourgeois countries from the state of degrading servitude under which they laboured. The bourgeoisie in countries other than Poland received this news with calmness, as they were not directly affected by these threats. Poland, however, was near and therefore became excited. A conflict between her and Russia was inevitable, as soon as the Communists had destroyed opposition in Russia itself. For the Poles represented the armed patriotic bourgeoisie—the Russians the proletariat. Having overthrown its own bourgeoisie, Soviet Russia moved on the Poles. The Powers made some futile attempts to intervene, but neither side was disposed to listen to their demands. Foch, however, sent his *alter ego*, General Weygand, to act as military adviser to the Poles, and this one very small Frenchman was a reinforcement more valuable than thousands of soldiers. Pilsudski—the head of the Polish state—wisely took his advice. Poland seemed in extreme danger. For the Soviet army was commanded by the famous ex-Tsarist General, Brusilov, and was within a few miles of Warsaw. Then Pilsudski suddenly made a desperate counter-offensive. It was entirely successful (August 10, 1920). The victorious Poles pursued the fleeing Russians over three hundred miles. Finally, an armistice (October 12, 1920) and peace treaty (March 1921) were signed at Riga. This established the Polish-Russian boundary on the Disna-Minsk-Ostrog line.

The Powers had studied ethnic data at Paris and produced a boundary for Poland which represented the eastern limit of purely Polish territory. This was known as the 'Curzon line' which is roughly the present Polish frontier. But the boundaries of 1920 were settled by the sword, and by Poland's own sword. By the treaty with Russia at Riga she acquired a population and territory about double that recommended by the 'Curzon line.' There were some twenty-seven millions in all, White Russians and Ruthenians and Lithuanians being the alien elements. In the year 1935 Poland lost Piłsudski, her strange, brilliant but sage dictator; his successors were not his equals in prestige or in actual power. But Poland continued the policy of friendship with Germany, inaugurated by Piłsudski in 1933, until the Nazi-Soviet pact and the development of Hitler's offensive against Europe brought about a spectacular change. Poland suffered a fresh partition in 1939–40, was once more destroyed and in 1945 rose again. She is now a Communist State and part of the eastern bloc. It is well to remember the long history of Polish misfortune and resurgence and the peculiar strength of her national traditions.

Chapter 6

WORLD SETTLEMENT AND NATION-MAKING IN THE NEAR, MIDDLE AND FAR EAST

If the nineteenth century was the age which produced nations in Europe, the twentieth produced them in Asia. The phenomenon is most remarkable. Nation states appeared indeed in different forms in the various countries: in Japan which early in the century became recognised as a Great Power; in China where freedom from the West was followed all too rapidly by other threats to independence; in India and Persia; in Turkey and throughout the Arab world. The phrases of nationalism and self-determination were everywhere. The new nation states were admitted to the Peace Conference after the War of 1914–18, and this lent an enormous impulse to these movements. For the first time every one of the nations here mentioned met the nations of the West in an International Conference on equal terms. The Peace Treaties affected all three parts of the East directly, but principally the Near and Middle East.

The settlements under the Turkish Treaty fell into three parts: first, settlements in Europe, mainly in Thrace, which affected Greeks, Turks and Bulgars; second, the internationalisation of the Straits and Constantinople, which concerned Turkey, Britain, France and Italy; third, the problems of Asia Minor, Iraq, Palestine, Syria and Arabia, which concerned Greeks, Turks, Armenians, Arabs and Jews, and raised the problem of nation-making in the East in an acute form.

For many centuries the Bulgars have been established in Bulgaria proper, Macedonia and Thrace. In the south they have conflicted with the Greeks, in the east with the Turks, and in both cases with extreme bitterness. But at the Peace Conference Bulgars and Turks appeared as defeated and as detested enemies. Greece was radiant and victorious. But it was only for the moment. Venizelos, the great man of Greece, had but recently returned to power and his position was insecure. His territorial demands were needed to popularise him in Greece and were against his better judgment. Bulgaria was forced to give strategic advantages on the frontier to Yugoslavia. She was compelled to cede western Thrace to Greece and was thus cut off from all access to the Aegean. In addition Venizelos secured Adrianople and eastern Thrace from Turkey by the Treaty signed at Sèvres on August 10, 1920. He thus brought Greece within a few miles of Constantinople, a prize he one day hoped to gain for her. The actual settlement proposed for Constantinople and the Straits from the Dardanelles to the Sea of Marmora was that they should be internationalised and neutralised (demilitarised). It was also proposed that the United States should take the mandate, as also for Armenia. This hope flickered out in September 1919, and thereafter both areas were assigned to Turkey, but the Straits remained neutralised.

Even the gains won by Greece were not enough for Venizelos, and he aspired to a Greek dominion in Asia Minor based on the sea. Ever since the days of Troy Greeks had been active as settlers and traders on the west coast of Asia Minor which was called Ionia. Greek troops had been in occupation of Smyrna since May 1919, and in and around this province Venizelos designed to establish a permanent Greek dominion. He found there something like half a million Greeks or Ionians and doubtless hoped to attract more. This concession was embodied in the peace with Turkey signed at Sèvres.

Sèvres is the French factory for the most delicate china ware, as the wits did not fail to notice when the treaty was signed there. Ominous signs appeared from the first. The United States, Yugoslavia, and the Arab King of the Hedjaz refused to sign at all. Turkey signed under protest. The Turkish army in Asia Minor began to look dangerous. There was no one to execute the treaty. Venizelos, with a British loan, undertook to do so. The Greeks easily defeated the Turks and captured Brusa, their old Asiatic capital. Very soon afterwards, however, Venizelos fell from power in Greece and fled the country. The ex-King Constantine returned from exile to Greece in triumph. The fall of her greatest statesman deprived Greece of the favour of the Allies and of her last chance of Asiatic dominion. The china-shop of Sèvres was entered and smashed by a bull. The bull was Mustafa Kemal Pasha, known later as Kemal Atatürk.

Mustafa Kemal appeared at this time to be simply a brutal and fearless soldier, but he stood for a principle and had all patriotic Turks behind him. The wretched Sultan and his minsters lived at Constantinople beneath the guns of the British fleet and had been forced to sign the Sèvres Treaty. But the humiliations of Turkey, above all the presence of the detested Greeks at Smyrna, had roused the best or worst feelings of patriotic Turks. Anatolia was their home and in its highlands they could defy the Allies. Mustafa Kemal, who had distinguished himself at the Dardanelles, openly revolted and stirred up the army. In 1920 he had been defeated in the first round by Venizelos and driven into the interior. But early in 1921 he held a National Assembly at Angora (now Ankara) and drew up what is called the 'Angora Pact'. It demanded complete independence for the Sultan and Constantinople, and the union under Turkish sovereignty of all parts of the Ottoman Empire 'inhabited by an Ottoman Moslem' majority. In reality the manifesto amounted to a refusal to accept the Sèvres Treaty, and to an announcement that Mustafa Kemal and his soldiers would reconquer by force any part of Turkey that they could. One can hardly blame them for this attitude, especially in view of the fact that they had a fierce national patriotism behind them.

It was King Constantine, now restored to his throne, who decided the fate of the Greek Empire in Asia. Venizelos had shown no desire to venture much beyond the coast in attacking the Turks, and had even disapproved of going as far as Brusa. Constantine decided that it was necessary to attack the evil at its centre. He would penetrate to Ankara, the Kemalist capital, and dictate peace in the highlands of Asia Minor. It was a good scheme if it could be done. He was himself a general of repute, but his project was declared impossible by the best military experts, among whom were Sir Henry Wilson and Foch. But in the interests of his dynasty Constantine decided to make the attempt, backed by the moral support and financial aid of Lloyd George. The French troops in Cilicia had intimated that they would not attack the Kemalist Turks and would perhaps send them supplies and arms.

Mustafa Kemal was confident as to the situation. He said 'that the Greeks might beat him, but that he did not mean to be rounded up. He would retire to regions where the Greeks could not get at him and would continue the war until the Greeks gave in.'[1] In 1921 the great Greek offensive began. It was pushed with the utmost gallantry over difficult country by devoted efforts. But no valour could penetrate to the stony and waterless plateau around Ankara. The Greek offensive died away before it reached there, and the Greek army was left clinging to a precarious front stretched vertically down the map of Asia Minor. No permanent frontier had ever run along the line the Greeks now held. The coasts have been dominated or protected by sea-power, but Ankara, or some such city, has always commanded the interior. The Greeks could not go forward and dared not go back, and the end was inevitable. In August 1922 Mustafa Kemal suddenly descended from his hills in great force. He broke the thin and wavering Greek line at several points, and drove their dispirited troops in utter rout before him. It was a complete and colossal disaster. In September Smyrna itself fell and was given to the flames. It was the end not only of Greek dominion but of Greek residence in Asia. For

[1] C à C. Repington, *After the War* (1922), p. 360.

ultimately Mustafa Kemal expelled not only every Greek soldier but every Greek inhabitant.

Mustafa Kemal led his victorious troops onwards to the Straits, where they found sectors held by British, French and Italian troops. British troops still garrisoned Constantinople and British warships were in the Sea of Marmora. French and Italian troops hurriedly withdrew, but the British troops stood firm. Lloyd George stated that he would defend the 'freedom of the Straits', and prevent the Kemalist troops from crossing into Europe. His gesture was not so bold as it sounds, for he had already intimated to Mustafa Kemal that eastern Thrace could be returned to Turkey. Still it produced an armistice (October 11, 1922) and after nearly a year resulted in the Treaty of Lausanne (July 24, 1923).

Turkey regained Adrianople, from Greece she got back eastern (but not western) Thrace. The Greeks were entirely expelled from Asia Minor whether as a government or as individuals. The neutralised zone round the Straits was much reduced in size, but preserved in essentials It was still possible for them to be rushed quickly from the Mediterranean by French, British or Italian war vessels Mustafa Kemal, triumphant in his military success, refused to submit to any limitation of his armaments. Turkey was therefore the only ex-enemy Power not restricted in the manufacture or use of her armaments or in the number of her troops. This treaty was humiliating to the Great Powers of Europe, and simply registered the fact that, in everything except demilitarising the Straits, Mustafa Kemal was strong enough to defy them. And, in order that he might continue to defy them, he shifted his capital from the now vulnerable Constantinople to the impregnable hill fastness of Ankara.

Mustafa Kemal set a most striking example in Turkey after 1923. He was a man of great courage and determination. In the face of local opposition, he introduced wide-sweeping reforms, dealing with every aspect of the life of the people. His achievements include the complete overhaul of the administration, the introduction and enforcement of new legal codes, the improvement of communications, finances and agricultural and industrial methods, the emancipation of women, the Europeanisation of dress, and in writing the introduction of the Latin letters. A law of 1934 compelling all Turks to adopt a surname resulted in his own change of name to Atatürk (the father of the Turks). Perhaps the most daring and symbolic of his reforms was the abandonment of Constantinople (renamed Istanbul) as capital and the building of the new capital at Ankara. Atatürk was certainly ruthless in his suppression of all opposition, particularly in the early days of his régime His methods were undoubtedly those of a dictator, but they were necessary if the chaos of centuries was to be reduced to order. Atatürk himself declared in 1932:. 'let the people leave politics alone for the present. Let them interest themselves in agriculture and commerce. For ten or fifteen years more I must rule. After that perhaps I may be able to let them speak openly.'[1] He died in November 1938, before this work was fully accomplished.

Yet, from a state which, in the nineteenth century, had been regarded as an intruder in Europe, Atatürk built up a Turkish state which gave to its citizens—men and women—greater freedom and security than any of their forefathers had enjoyed, and transformed Turkey into an independent sovereign state, free from foreign interference for the first time for almost two centuries.

The tragedy of Armenia was the saddest of all the countless horrors associated with the War of 1914–18. History is not a censor of morals. Yet it is the duty of the historian to draw attention to any exceptional event or departure from ordinary standards, and both were found in Armenia during the War of 1914–18. Unfortunately there is no doubt where the responsibility lies. On the Turks of this period of vigorous Young Turkish nationalism lies the blame for massacres and cruelties such as authentic witnesses had never before related. The Armenian tragedy is a page of history which the Turks dyed purple with innocent blood.

The sum total of massacred persons will never be known. But it can hardly be wrong to reckon that something like six hundred thousand perished out of twelve hundred thousand deported. Of the survivors a good many were forcibly converted to Islam. But these terrible events did not end the tragedy and it is still more appalling to record that the Turks found yet further means of wreaking their vengeance. The Russians captured Erzerum in 1916, but their army melted away with the revolution of 1917. Gradually the Turks recovered not only their own part of Armenia, but entered Batum, Kars, and even Erivan. Enver was gone, but Mustafa Kemal and his successors 'did not their work negligently'. Their progress was marked by a trail of blood. Even in Cilicia those Armenians who were left were massacred. At Sassun and Bitlis the Turks completed their destruction. Even Erivan itself, the heart and capital of Armenia, had to pay its tax of blood. At least a hundred thousand more were added to the death roll. During the war the Armenians had raised troops for the Entente Powers and Britain had promised them a national home after the war. The Treaty of Sèvres safeguarded the Republic of Erivan.

The Armenians were abandoned by the world in spite of the Treaty of Sèvres. After the armistice British troops for a time kept order in Transcaucasia; when these retired the Republics of Georgia, Erivan, and Azerbaijan struggled vainly against the Turks but also unfortunately among themselves. Finally Soviet Russia established

[1] H. C. Armstrong, *Grey Wolf* (1932). p. 329.

control of the area and signed an agreement with the Turks (March 16, 1921). By this Turkey surrendered Batum and Kars and therefore a good two-thirds of Armenia. All Armenia that was left, the Republic of Erivan, was absorbed into the Soviet system of Client Republics. This was the true settlement of Armenia. The settlement of the Treaty of Sèvres, recognising the Republic of Erivan, and the wide boundaries subsequently given to it under President Wilson's arbitration, were entirely disregarded when Mustafa Kemal signed the Treaty of Lausanne in 1923. The Powers of Europe, by acquiescing in the omission of all mention of Armenia, recognised the Soviet-Kemal agreement of March 1921.

The Soviet Client Republic of Erivan flourished. Canals were dug, copper was produced, and experiments in cotton-growing and textiles were developed. The remnants of the Armenian race, though not much over a million, showed once again inexhaustible elasticity and vitality. They were strengthened by refugees and immigrants from without. Indeed, if we are to believe their own and the Russian statistics, nature came to their aid. The rate of population growth increased faster than is recorded in any other instance in history.

It is a relief to turn from the sickening tragedy of Armenia, where the Turks massacred helpless victims to whom friendly nations could bring no aid in the confusion during and after the war, to Arabia which took arms against its oppressor and won freedom by the help of other nations.

Syria, Palestine, Iraq and Arabia had always been the home of the Arabs, a gifted and passionate people. The Arab had always hated and despised the Turk. Even a desert Arab can quote poetry, and Turkish culture owed everything to Arab art, architecture and literature. Each tribe had a tradition of hatred of the Turk or of victory over him. Each one had stories and legends of how they had cut off patrols or pashas' heads. They had sometimes even defeated a Turkish army, but it was a very different matter to overthrow Turkish rule altogether. The Arabs were brave, but they were scattered and quarrelsome like the Highland clans of Scotland. It was difficult to organise or unite them or keep them together for a common object. They had a national object—the resurrection of the Arab race, but they wanted a religious sanction and a leader. They found both in the person of an old man at Mecca.

The only office the Turks had allowed to become hereditary was that of Grand Sherif or Governor of Mecca. This Holy City was the birthplace of the Prophet, and the Sherif belonged to his tribe, and was thus of the purest and noblest Arab descent. Hussein, the Grand Sherif in 1914, had a lineage much older than that of the Sultan. Arabs had often questioned the Sultan's right to be Caliph (or successor of the Prophet): was that title not due to Hussein? When the war opened the British began by repulsing the Turks from the Suez

117

Canal and seizing Basra, the port of Sinbad the Sailor. The time seemed to have come. Hussein might dream a true Arab's dream of driving the Turks back into Anatolia and of sending Arab horsemen to water their steeds in the old Arab city of Damascus. Hussein was spurred on by his two sons, Abdulla, an administrator, and Feisal, a man with a great moral influence over the desert sheikhs. 'He won over and inflamed new tribes', said T. E. Lawrence. At length Hussein took his courage in his hands and in July 1915 sent a secret letter to the British at Cairo. He offered to revolt and to free the whole Arab race from the Persian Gulf to Mosul, from the Red Sea to Beirut and Damascus. He asked Britain to aid him in this grandiose plan.

The British had long known the Arab hatred of the Turk, and even played with the idea of using the Grand Sherif.[1] The correspondence with Hussein was not published by the British Government until March 1939 though its gist was widely known. The British Government intended to reserve by implication the question of Arab independence in Syria and Palestine. Hussein claimed that they did not do so. Their language was not clear, but the British certainly encouraged him to revolt. They promised him money, arms, supplies, aeroplanes, instructors and, in extreme need, British troops. A small group of men studied the question and devised the plans: Hogarth an old scholar, Lawrence a young one, Storrs the Oriental Secretary of the British High Commissioner, and Admiral Wemyss. Lawrence, the youngest of them, carried out the design, became the friend of Feisal (a son of Hussein), the Hero of the Arabs, and a prince of Mecca. Hussein was encouraged by British promises and soon proved that he was in earnest. He did not intend to risk anything and chose his own time to revolt. But the time that he chose was in itself a service to the British, and when he drew the sword he used it. In April 1916 the world was amazed to learn that three thousand British and six thousand Indian troops had surrendered to the Turks at Kut. But in June that event was eclipsed in importance for both Turks and Arabs by the astonishing news that Hussein had revolted in the Hedjaz, had announced himself as the true Caliph, and declared for the freedom of the whole Arab race. The effect in the Hedjaz, Akaba and Medina was immense. There, men saw the prospect of freedom for themselves and of vengeance on the Turk. In Iraq and Syria British gold and steel were the main influences.

In March 1917 the British avenged the defeat of Kut and entered Baghdad in triumph, and by the autumn of 1918 they had destroyed the last Turkish army and captured Mosul and all Iraq. They had not

---

[1] Public Record Office, F. O. 78/1514. From Sir H. L. Bulwer to Lord John Russell. No 847 of December 12, 1860. This shows that the project of using the Grand Sherif to counteract French influence in Egypt was discussed and vetoed by Lord John Russell as far back as 1860.

had much aid from Arab rebels; the Pan-Arab crusade had not disposed the local inhabitants to be friendly and to reveal the military secrets of the Turks. In the Palestine-Syrian area Arab resistance counted for a good deal. Arab spies were everywhere, Arab contingents, raised and drilled by the British, did good work against the Turks. Allenby learned their value when he captured Jerusalem in 1917. When he won his 'crowning mercy' at Megiddo in the autumn of 1918, he sent Lawrence and Feisal to act as a flying right wing east of Jordan. They won the race, and on October 1 the wild Arab horsemen galloped into Damascus a few hours ahead of the Australians. The first chief rode on a liver-coloured stallion, the finest Arab steed in the army. This knight of the desert had the privilege of entering first, because he had fought in over fifty battles against the Turks. That night Lawrence sat alone in the city and heard the muezzins call the faithful to prayer. 'One, with a ringing voice of speical sweetness, cried into my windows from a near mosque... "...God alone is great: there is no god—but God."...and softly added: "And He is very good to us this day, O people of Damascus." ' It was six centuries since the Arabs of that city had enjoyed a 'night of perfect freedom.'

Some opportunists had proclaimed Feisal 'King of all the Arabs' before he arrived at Damascus. Waves of Pan-Arab nationalism swept rapidly over all parts of the Middle East. They conflicted soon enough with the ambitions of two great European Powers. With the independence of Arabia proper no one wanted to interfere. But Britain had conquered Iraq and Mosul, Palestine and Syria. Since the days of Louis Quatorze France had coveted Damascus and Beirut and now received what Britain had conquered in Syria. Even Mustafa Kemal only slightly modified the Treaty of Sèvres in relation to French territory. By the Sèvres line (1920) the Franco-Turkish frontier ran from a point north-west of Alexandretta until it reached the British area of Mosul. By the Lausanne Treaty (1923) Mustafa Kemal pushed the French line a little further south. By 1920 France had expelled Feisal from Damascus since he had attempted to found an Arab kingdom there. Syria, including Damascus, Aleppo, Beirut, was finally constituted a French mandated area. Further south Britain occupied Palestine, constituted as a mandated area, but with the special mission of making it the national home for the Zionist Jews, and reconciling the Arab inhabitants (who were in a great majority) to the process. Transjordania was organised as a state under British protection, with Abdulla, another son of King Hussein, as ruler. The

[1] T. E. Lawrence, *Revolt in the Desert* (1927),pp. 434–5. He had added in the original. 'While my fancy, in the overwhelming pause, showed me my loneliness and lack of reason in their movement: since only for me, of all the hearers, was the event sorrowful and the phrases meaningless.' See R. Graves, *Lawrence and the Arabs* (1927),p. 381. Yet nearly half the population of Syria was non-Arab and much non-Muslim.

settlement in these countries was neither satisfactory nor permanent. Disturbances followed in Damascus and the Lebanon; and in Palestine the reconciliation of Arab and Jew proved well-nigh impossible. The story of partition and war between Arab and Jew will be found in the concluding chapter.

In Iraq the situation was more satisfactory. When Feisal lost his Syrian kingdom the British obligingly found him another in Iraq. An Arab of Mecca was not entirely suited to Baghdad, but Iraq grew in power and in wealth under his rule and that of his successor, King Ghazi. It ceased to be a mandated territory in October 1932.

The Arabs began by throwing off the yoke of the Turk, they ended by throwing off that of King Hussein. In 1915 the British Government, after making their compact with Hussein, found it convenient to make another with a second Arabian chief. His name was Ibn Saud and he ruled over the Wahhabis, an obscure inland tribe. No one thought that he would drive Hussein from Mecca in a decade. But his warriors were as devout, as fearless and as formidable as the Ironsides. In Ibn Saud they had found an Arabian Cromwell, and they now went forth to conquer. While Hussein fought the Turks with British aid, Ibn Saud fought the tribes of the interior with his own resources. In 1924 he had finished his task and decided to advance on Mecca, where King Hussein dwelt in fancied security. Since the abolition of the Sultanate he had claimed the title of Caliph, and worn the black mantle of the office. It availed him little when Ibn Saud led his puritan warriors against the Holy City. Resistance was hopeless and Hussein fled in despair. Ibn Saud entered Mecca six months after Hussein had proclaimed himself Caliph and for the first time for centuries brought Arabia beneath the sway of one man. The destiny of Ibn Saud was strange, but not so strange as that of Hussein. At the word of that old man of Mecca Arabia's horsemen set out on their thousand-mile ride to Damascus. One of his sons who rode with them gained a principality beyond Jordan, another son a kingdom (Iraq) by the Tigris. The father himself became a king in the Holy City which his ancestors had ruled for seven centuries. Then he became Caliph for six months, only to be driven from Mecca by a conquering puritan from the desert. The Holy City has already forgotten him, and Hussein, the last of the Caliphs, found a refuge and, in 1931, a grave in Jerusalem.

This brief survey will have made clear that the catchwords of self-determination and nationalism in their extreme form spread like fire in the East, and gave new ideals to old or dead nations. In each case there was an intense national pride and a desire to remove alien influences altogether. An evolution somewhat similar to the Turkish, though on a smaller scale, has been seen in Persia (Iran). The previous history of Persia is of some interest. For she had a reforming and constitutional movement in 1907, which promised well. It was checked partly by reactionary influences but largely by Russian interference from the north. As we have seen, Persia had been divided into British, Russian and neutral spheres in 1907. Russia's interference ended with the war, but after it Britain made an effort to secure political control over Persia by the Anglo-Iranian Agreement (August 9, 1919). This arrangement was upset by the refusal of the revived Iranian Parliament to accept it. The Russians then intervened and appeared to be threatening to conquer the country. But early in 1921 they not only withdrew their troops, but abandoned every attempt at influence in Iran altogether. They retired from all concessions, abandoned public works, harbours, railways and roads in which they had any interest or influence. The Iranians were greatly encouraged by this attitude and proceeded in 1921 to remove all British supervisory influences. British advisers, civil and military, were promptly dismissed and every possible trace of foreign influence eradicated. The power behind this movement was again a successful soldier, Reza Khan. He ultimately deposed the feeble ruler and became himself Shah in 1925. Iran had long been a prey to feudal anarchy and brigandage in the provinces, which Reza Shah's military efficiency at length subdued. The modern enemy of the brigand and the rebel is the road and the aeroplane, and Reza Shah used both with effect. He ruthlessly executed or imprisoned brigands and feudal chiefs. He made good roads and modernised the government, the army, the education and even the dress of his subjects. He did much for Iran in the sixteen years of his rule. Behind him as behind Mustafa Kemal was the idea of expelling the foreigner and equipping his countrymen with weapons and improvements sufficient to resist the influences of the West.

The same influences and tendencies were to be seen, though working more subtly, in the development of China and Japan between the Wars. Through the return of its students from abroad and the influences of western education, China became permeated with liberal and democratic ideas. These worked in the main as a disorganising force, dissolving the old fabric of empire without substituting anything durable in its place. Brigand-generals terrorised some areas till Chiang Kai-shek and the Nanking government achieved relative stability. The hatred of the foreigner became less conspicuous, and it was from their own kinsmen rather than from Europeans that they had most to fear. This was all the more disastrous because of the opportunity it gave to Japan.

The problem cannot be said to have arisen from the war, but it was immensely affected by it. During the eighteen-seventies Japan accomplished the work of six centuries in as many years. Great revolutions, abolishing the old institutions of Japan, and throwing her open to western progress, were carried out with amazing ease and almost without bloodshed. In the nineties Japan was victorious over China, in the first decade of the twentieth century over Russia. Her victories were won by a constitution and a ruling class resembling the Prussian, with militarism, efficiency and bureaucracy for their watchwords. The alliance with Great Britain tended for a time to assimilate Japanese diplomacy to European standards. During the war, however, Japan had no need to pay attention to such influences; she extorted various concessions from China, in particular the celebrated twenty-one demands of 1915. Then, in 1919, some of these concessions were revoked, though she obtained the province of Shantung on lease from China as a result of the German Treaty. European and American diplomacy was again brought to bear, and in 1922, as a result of pressure from the Washington Conference (see below, page 176) Japan signed a treaty with China providing for the Japanese evacuation of Kiao-Chau and Shantung (4 February 1922). After that date, however, trouble in China increased and Japan sent into Manchuria and even to Shanghai great military forces. The meaning of these movements is apparent. Japan had shaken off European tutelage. She looked to the Asiatic mainland as a sphere of economic expansion. Canada, the United States, and Australia ring round the Pacific. They declared for white settlement only and protected their respective continents from Japanese immigrants. Japan had lost the restraining influence of her alliance, which Britain herself terminated in 1921. There were no longer outside influences to temper her policy.

Although in the late nineteenth century Japan equipped herself with the machinery of constitutional government, it was a very superficial structure. The Constitution of 1889 established a legislature of two Houses and other trappings of constitutional government: but the Constitution, having been granted by the Emperor, could not be amended, since the Emperor remained infallible. There was in fact no clear break with the past, and the government preserved its autocratic character behind a thin veil of liberal political institutions.

By the end of the 1914–18 War, Japan was fully launched upon her career as a member of modern industrial society. She was ready to set herself up as the political and economic leader of eastern Asia. It was this desire for hegemony that led Japan to attempt to subordinate China to the status of a vassal, first in the economic and later in the political sphere. Japan had developed enormously in the industtrial field, and she was anxious that China should not rival her, but should provide a market for her goods. It was China's resistance to this absorption by Japan which provoked the Sino-Japanese War which broke out in 1937 and eventually merged into world war.

Chapter 7

REVOLUTION IN RUSSIA AND THE U.S.S.R. UNDER STALIN

In Russia defeat in 1905 at the hands of Japan was followed by a revolution which failed to end the autocracy; defeat at the hands of Germany in 1916 was followed by a revolution which not only overthrew the autocracy, but in the end overthrew the existing social and economic structure as well. The defeat was perhaps less at the hands of Germany, though she had checked the Brusilov offensive, Russia's last, in 1916, than at the hands of her own leaders. Their economic planning for the war had been minimal; so that by the end of 1916 the army was beginning to run short of essential supplies and the cities to run out of food. Their psychological control of the country was negligible; so that a sense of defeat needed no military disaster to create it. It existed in the rumours that the Emperor, Nicholas II, and the circle round Rasputin (a man of peasant origin who had gained the Emperor's and Empress's confidence by his ability to relieve their son, suffering from haemophilia) were betraying the country and was not alleviated when Rasputin was assassinated by Prince Yussupov in the presence of other courtiers (December 30, 1916). The sense of defeat existed because there was a vacuum where the autocracy once, under Nicholas I, had commanded and given coherence to an easily disintegrated country. The liberal Ministry had too little independent authority to fill the vacuum. In Volume One much already was said of the opposition groups ready to overthrow the liberal régime which in the dozen years of its existence had struck no deep roots. Now was their opportunity.

In Petrograd—the name adopted in 1914 to avoid the German-sounding St. Petersburg—there were bread riots on February 23, 1917 or, to use the more convenient modern style, March 8, and strikes, riots and street demonstrations of housewives on March 10. On that day Nicholas II, acting from his military headquarters, dissolved the Duma. A standing committee, consisting of Cadets and Octobrists (see above, page 13) and others of the moderate Left, constituted itself and remained in session. On March 12, as a demonstration of opposition to the dissolution of the Duma, the army in the city rallied to this committee. This was the beginning of the so-called February Revolution because an alternative authority to the autocracy had thus offered itself. Moreover, on this same day, delegates from several strike committees formed a workers' council, or soviet. It soon became the Soviet of Workers' and Peasants' Deputies. and then the Workers' and Soldiers' Soviet of Petrograd. When it stayed firm a third possible authority had appeared. This was important because the beginning of the train of events which was to lead to the ultimate outcome was a struggle for power between the committee of the Duma and this Soviet. But first the former, after hesitating openly to challenge the autocracy, at last took courage and made itself into the Provisional Government. Prince Lvov was Prime Minister, Milyukov was Foreign Minister, both Cadets, and Guchkov from the Octobrists was War Minister. Kerensky, a Trudovnik (see above, page 14) and a member of the Workers' and Soldiers' Soviet, was included as Minister for Justice. He should have been the link between Socialists and Liberals, but he proved to be a Socialist instrument to undermine the Liberals and replace them by his own dictatorship, exercised in the name of the Soviet. But that was some two months ahead. In mid March troops controlled the city in the name of the Provisional Government and the police disappeared from the streets. It persuaded the Tsar, without difficulty, to abdicate. He chose to do so in favour of Prince Michael, his brother. When Michael refused to act, Russia virtually became a republic, though the Provisional Government postponed a decision on the form of the state for a Constituent Assembly to make. Russia was ultimately proclaimed a Republic in September before that body met.

Some five weeks after the February Revolution, on April 16, Vladimir Ulyanov (Lenin) arrived in Petrograd in the famous sealed train which the Germans allowed through from Switzerland. Lenin combined 'a variety of qualities, enormous scholarship, the passionate temperament of the revolutionary, tactical genius and great administrative ability.' He published the April theses, so called, soon after his arrival. They explained to the revolutionary workers what they were doing. He told them that they were engaged in bringing the socialist revolution out of the democratic revolution, which had given power to the bourgeoisie, whereas their, socialist, revolution would bring the workers to power and make a state without standing army, police or bureaucracy. By showing them that they were furthering an inevitable sequence of events he seemed to give them confidence and a fresh impetus. Lenin was, moreover, the strength of the Bolshevik Party which, since 1912, had been a party distinct from the Mensheviks and no longer merely the left wing of a divided Social Democratic Party. He gave to this Party an organisation and discipline so tight that its executive knew its instructions would be carried out to the letter. The Mensheviks, equally a proletarian party, but one drawing its strength from the trade unionists, had the prestige of great names, such as Plekhanov and Martov, the founders of the Social Democratic Workers' Party, as already related, but not this monolithic structure. The Socialist Revolutionaries, it will be recalled, were not Marxists but belonged to the Populist tradition among Russian revolutionaries. They were the mouthpiece of the peasants and had the advantage of very wide support. The situation was becoming more and more complex because behind the struggle between the Provisional Government and the Soviet for predominance was a struggle of the Bolsheviks (since March 25 under the leadership of Kamenev, Stalin and Molotov) against the Mensheviks and Socialist Revolutionaries. The prize would be the control of the Revolution. In the struggle for predominance the Soviet had gained the first advantage by issuing its order no.1 which bade the soldiers to take orders from it alone, to obey no directions contrary to its orders and, above all, to resist any attempt of the officers to disarm them. It removed at the same time most of the marks of military discipline and initiated the election of officers. Nevertheless Milyukov told Britain and France that Russia would honour her obligations and Guchkov carried on the war. But it was a hopeless effort. On May 16 Milyukov and Guchkov resigned. This was the end of the first stage of the Revolution: a setback for the Provisional Government.

From May 16 to July 15 was the second stage of the Liberal Revolution when the Provisional Government was under pressure from the Socialists, in their turn under pressure from the Bolsheviks, now under Lenin's leadership. Lenin had established his authority by reuniting the Social Democratic Workers' Party, whose Congress was in session from May 7–12, behind himself. His goal, however, was power for the Bolsheviks and for them alone. Meanwhile, Kerensky had become Minister for War and allayed any suspicions that the Provisional Government would continue the bourgeois war. But the settling of this question only exposed the dangerous land question. It dominated this stage of the Revolution. Hitherto confined to Petrograd, Moscow and some other cities and industrial centres, the Revolution now spread to the countryside. Partly spontaneously, partly under the direction of the Socialist Revolutionaries, the peasants attacked the landowners and seized the land. The Provisional Government postponed the settlement of this question, too, for the Constituent Assembly. But this policy was impossible and, on July 15, it brought about the fall of the Provisional Government.

From July 16 to September 12—the third stage—a new Government under Kerensky ruled. General Kornilov now attempted a counter-revolution and was widely supported by the liberal bourgeoisie, frightened by the forces it had released. Kornilov's aim was not to restore the autocracy, but to set up a military dictatorship in order to control the anarchy into which the country was falling and to keep the Bolsheviks from power. By September 10 he was defeated by Kerensky's Government aided by the Bolsheviks. Lenin had by now made the Bolsheviks so strong that they were on the point of winning control of the Revolution. This he had done after establishing his moral authority over the Social Democratic Workers' Party Congress in May, by creating 'in each district, sub-district and factory an organisation "capable of acting as one man" and bound to the Central Committee' of the party by strong ties and supplementing these by recruiting Red Guards. He was obeying the precepts formulated in his own writing. Meanwhile on June 22 the First All-Russian Congress of Soviets had met. Under its influence, but not under its direction, there was a fresh wave of demonstrations in mid July. In April Lenin's slogan had been 'all power to the Soviets,' but he now used the Bolshevik Party machine to check these demonstrations: his slogan now was 'all power to the Party.' It was a superb tactical move, which put him and the Bolsheviks in a good position to assist Kerensky against Kornilov and to begin preparations for the final take-over. On August 8 the Bolshevik Party Congress had met and witnessed a further strengthening of Lenin's authority.

The fourth stage of the Revolution lasted from September 12 to November 7. It was the period of Kerensky's personal rule and the preparation by the Petrograd Soviet for its take-over of power. When the Bolsheviks arrested the members of Kerensky's Government— the last Provisional Government—on November 7 they effected the so called October Revolution (by the then Russian style of date). In name the Soviet took power. In fact the Bolshevik Party, as Lenin had organised it during the summer, took power. That is to say, an autocractic alternative to the Tsarist autocracy took power. Arbitrary illegality was present in the Communist autocracy from the beginning. A minority imposed its rule in the conviction that it alone possessed the truth and that this gave it the right to rule and to use violence against its enemies. Trotsky organised the armed forces which made the coup, but it was Lenin's careful preparation during the summer of local committees in districts and factories and his recruitment of the Red Guards which enabled the results of the coup to survive. Trotsky put the Soviet in power but the Bolshevik Central Committee and the local committees it commanded enabled it to maintain its power. The Bolshevik Military Revolutionary Committee seized power on November 6 and arrested Kerensky and his colleagues on November 7, after Lenin had defeated those among the Bolsheviks (Zinoviev and Kamenev) who argued that the time was not ripe. The Second All-Russian Congress of Soviets met on November 7 and succeeded Kerensky's Government as the governing power, giving the armed insurrection a kind of legality.

Lenin's next step was to achieve Bolshevik control over the Congress of Soviets. This was the fifth and last stage of the Revolution. He had an initial advantage for some 300 out of the 650 delegates were Bolsheviks. The remainder were Mensheviks or Socialist Revolutionaries. Some of the latter were ready to support the Bolsheviks, thus increasing Lenin's advantage. When Lenin refused to set up a Praesidium from all three Parties some of the Socialist Revolutionaries withdrew, further increasing his advantage. The rest were disarmed when, under Lenin's leadership, the Congress passed a land decree (November 8). It was a complicated measure, in detail, the work of the Socialist Revolutionaries. 'It abolished private ownership forever and redistributed the land for the peasants' use in accordance with a formula designed to secure an adequate standard for all.' Lenin had jettisoned the Bolshevik land policy, which aimed at collective, not family, farms, in order to outwit the Socialist Revolutionary opposition. The Congress next set up a Central Executive Committee in which the Mensheviks were not represented and the Socialist Revolutionaries were a minority of 29 to the Bolshevik 67. Finally the Congress set up a Government: the Council of People's Commissars. It was exclusively Bolshevik and headed by Lenin.

At this point, and unexpectedly, the Bolsheviks had to meet the demand of the Trade Union of Railway Workers for a coalition government and their protest against the dominance of a single party. The railway men were in a strong position because they could cut off assistance to the Moscow rising as well as Petrograd's food supply. There was also protest at the suppression of the Liberal press. Lenin, Trotsky and their allies kept the Bolshevik Party firm against both protests and within a week had defeated both.

On November 25 elections to the Constituent Assembly, in view since March, at last took place. The Socialist Revolutionaries won an outstanding victory, polling 15 million votes against the Bolsheviks' 10 million. The Bolsheviks were as much committed as the Liberals to the Constituent Assembly as the ultimate authority to legalise all necessary change. But after the elections had gone against them they could not allow it to meet. It in fact assembled on January 18, 1918, and was dismissed by the action of the Red Guards the same day. Neither the courage nor the illegality of this defiance of the popular will can be denied.

The Bolsheviks consolidated their position with further socialist measures. The Congress of Soviets decreed on November 27 that industrial production should be under the workers' supervision. Gradually this came to mean, when it meant anything, the supervision of Bolshevik Party officials. The trade unions were for some time autonomous, but eventually they too were brought under Party control. The State Bank had been seized by an armed detachment on November 20 and on December 27 the Congress of Soviets nationalised all private banks and amalgamated them with the State Bank into the Peoples' Bank of the Russian Republic. By February 1918 all shareholders had been expropriated and foreign debts repudiated. Like the trade unions the Bank was originally autonomous, but like them it too came to be run by officials of the Bolshevik Party. Moreover the Department of State which ran the Bank was manned by appointees of the Party.

The need to bring the war to an end was most urgent. This business, too, Lenin managed with superb tactical skill so as to strengthen the position of the Bolsheviks. Practically there was no alternative to peace, for the army had disintegrated and, after less than a fortnight of negotiation, an armistice had been signed on December 15. It was not, however, only the practical situation which concerned Lenin. In order to retain their dominance the Bolsheviks needed to show that peace was also in conformity with theory and justified by it. The difficulty was that the Bolsheviks were committed to peace without annexations and without indemnities: the German peace terms, had they not been invalidated by the victory of Britain and France at the end of the year, would have deprived Russia of all her western provinces, including the Ukraine as well as Lithuania, Latvia, Estonia and Poland. On January 20, 1918, Lenin published his *Theses on Peace*. They shaped the new Bolshevik position: everything must give way to creating a situation favourable to the ultimate Revolutionary War. Within this general position Lenin changed his tactical arguments three times in order to keep control of the Central Executive Committee and the Congress of Soviets to which it was responsible. In the period when Trotsky, the negotiator, on Lenin's instructions, was using delaying tactics to get better terms, Lenin was using the argument that to keep the peasants from returning to the land, clearly their resolve, since the army, largely made up of peasants, was dissolving, would militate against the ultimate Revolutionary War and their part in it. When Germany renewed the invasion in February 1918, Lenin used the argument that to renew resistance would militate against the Revolutionary War—by uniting Russia in the patriotism of the old ruling classes, the Cadets, the Octobrists and non-Bolshevik Socialists. After the signature of the Treaty of Brest-Litovsk (March 3, 1918) Lenin had to meet widespread dissatisfaction and a demand for renewal of the war. The Left Socialist Revolutionaries, hitherto embarrassing allies, were responsible for the assassination of the German Ambassador (July 6, 1918) which set off a series of risings both in Moscow and Petrograd as part of a campaign to renew the war. There was even opposition from some Bolsheviks. Lenin now used the argument effectively of Party solidarity. Indeed, the Party to mark its assertion of solidarity changed its name to the Russian Communist Party (March 1918). Lenin also gained practical advantages: the Left Socialist Revolutionary press was suppressed, their leaders arrested and brought before a Revolutionary Tribunal. The suppression of opposition gave Lenin the opportunity to bring three characteristic Communist instruments of social control into full working order by mid 1918: the press censorship with press tribunals, manned by Party members and empowered to suppress any journal spreading falsehood dangerous to the people, all over the country; revolutionary tribunals to administer summary justice—the first had appeared already in December 1917; and the Cheka or secret police already using 'administrative arrest', or detention without trial, to silence opposition.

Victory in the civil war finally consolidated the Communist power. This began in May 1918 and was not over until March 1921. There were many and diverse groups arrayed against the Communists. The mass of the Socialist Revolutionaries fought against them for a Constituent Assembly and a multi-party society. There were the Czech Legionaries. The makers of Czechoslovakia had obtained permission to recruit an army among prisoners of war in Russia. By the end of 1917 the Legion numbered 45,000 men and was under a French commander ready to make its way via Vladivostok to the front in France against Germany. In May they rebelled against a Communist attempt to disarm them. There was every variety of Tsarist supporter. White Russians, under able commanders such as Denikin, Kolchak, Wrangel and Yudenic, assailed the Republic from all sides. They received advisers, tanks, aeroplanes, and munitions from Britain and France and their allies. Simultaneously the Allies cut off Communist Russia by blockade from war and civilian supplies, even from medical supplies. It seemed impossible that the Soviet Republic could survive. There were many contributory causes of the Communist victory. Areas where the several opposition groups gained control were isolated, the one from the other. To the Socialist Revolutionaries and Anarchists military and autocratic discipline was an alien habit. Two causes of victory were more important. Trotsky devoted his colossal energies, great abilities and fine administrative sense to rebuilding the Red Army with complete single-mindedness. This was the first important cause of victory. The second was the support of the peasants. When it seemed that defeat of the Communists might mean victory for generals who would take from them the land the Communists had given them, any inclination the peasants may have had to support the other side died away. In November 1918 the Council of Workers' and Peasants' Defence was set up. It included Trotsky as Chairman of the Revolutionary War Council, the Commissars for Food, for Supply and for Communications, and Stalin from the Central Executive Committee. It mobilised peasant action behind the Red Army. In 1921 there was one final flare-up in the Kronstadt Mutiny. Several thousands of sailors and civilians were involved in the revolt. It was not an insurrection in support of Tsarism, but against Communist dictatorial methods. It lasted from February 28 to March 18 and after it was crushed, the reprisals involved hundreds. It was the last out-burst of slaughter before the Stalin terror.

Despite war, terror and famine the structure of the Soviet state took shape during 1918–21. During 1918 anti-Communist Parties, except for the Mensheviks and Mensheviks disguised as non-party men, were squeezed out of the local soviets which existed in towns, villages and factories up and down Russia. Terror and manipulation exercised at elections were the methods used by local Party members for this purpose. At the centre, the Congress of Soviets became less and less important. The Central Executive Committee which it elected, intended to be the body to which the Government or Council of Peoples' Commissars was responsible, had lost all importance. The Praesidium of the Congress of Soviets gained what other bodies had lost. By 1920 all legislation was done either by the Praesidium or by the Council of Peoples' Commissars. Their composition was virtually identical. The local soviets also became less and less important. They lost power to their executive committees which were virtually officials controlled from the centre. The soviets were state institutions. Parallel to them were a set of Party institutions. They experienced the same centralising process. Party Congresses were still annual assemblies. But the Central Committee of the Party (19 members and 12 candidate members in 1921) was the all-important institution, though it had to take account of Congress opinion. The Politburo, which had existed since 1917, was reorganised in 1919 as a sub-committee of the Central Committee of the Party. It consisted in that year of five men (Lenin, Trotsky, Stalin, Kamenev and Bukharin) and took decisions which could not wait for a meeting of the much larger Central Committee. In 1919 also the Party Congress set up a Secretariat to the Central Committee, appointing at first one man, but next year three men. It was of key importance and acquired an increasingly large body to service it. In 1919, too, the Party Congress set up the Orgburo to be responsible together with the Secretariat for all appointments (such as those of Party Commissars assigned to work beside all specialists, non-party men and non-workers, in all sorts of bodies including the army) and for moving Party members from one assignment to another. The composition of the Orgburo (five men in 1919, later seven) overlapped with that of the Politburo. These two bodies together, with the General Secretary, who was Stalin after 1922, were the power house of the régime.

Centralisation was to some extent the outcome of practical needs, however much it may have served the interest of Communist autocracy. This can be illustrated from the army, from industrial production and the trade unions. In order to bring the army back to life Trotsky had to use former officers and NCOs. They were introduced as specialists and, to ensure their loyalty, Party Commissars were set to work beside them. Workers' control of industry in so far as it was implemented under the decree of November 1917 led to the collapse of production and communications. To revive them the railways were centralised under the Commissar for Communications and specialists were introduced into industrial enterprises who brought them back to one-man management as a temporary measure. There were said to be more than 6 million members of trade unions in 1920. If the workers really ruled the state, trade unions were unnecessary. If the members were loyal Communists the Party members intruded into them were also unnecessary. But practical needs meant that both were retained. Both were justified on the ground that they were temporary expedients.

The system of the Soviets and the machinery of government which developed from them was finally embodied in a written constitution, adopted in 1936. It defined the U.S.S.R. as a federal state formed on the basis of the voluntary union of the eleven Soviet Socialist Republics, equal in rights. The first section of the constitution is devoted entirely to the economic organisation of the Russian 'socialist state of workers and peasants.' It is important, therefore, to understand something of the economic development of Communist Russia from the period of War Communism to the New Economic Policy of 1921 and finally to the period of forced collectivisation and five-year plans after 1929.

From 1918 to 1921, that is during the period of War Communism, there was no question of the orderly imposition of reform. Instead there was nothing but improvisation under pressure. There was pressure from the war and the civil war; there was pressure from spontaneous, local initiative; there was the pressure of happenings caused by plain inexperience. The seizure of property for the people was general and indiscriminate. What was done with property once seized varied, being subject both to the difficulties of carrying central orders out locally and to the vagaries of individual behaviour. Thus land allocation after the land decree in thousands of villages produced neither systematic collectivisation nor a system of family farms but, the hiring of labour being forbidden, some sort of mixture of joint cultivation and exclusive rights. In the factories the application of the decree on workers' supervision generally served to destroy the old ownership and management, but could not reconstruct methods of exploiting raw materials, production or distribution and the factory discipline necessary to operate them. It was a period of extreme Communism: no wages, no private trade, and free rations of food. If such organisation as existed was improvised, absence of organisation was in part deliberate purpose. It was the Marxist-Leninist 'leap into Socialism' when the opportunity of universal destruction gave it a chance. So that Communist teaching and the needs of the situation interacted.

Reconstruction had to come and to come from the top. On

December 15, 1917, the Supreme Council of National Economy (VSNK or Vesenkha) had been set up. Its task was to elaborate general norms and the plan for regulating the economy in all its aspects. It developed several departments for controlling particular industries or sectors of the economy and a hierarchy of regional and local bodies through which it worked. The plan was an economic strategy devised for the whole country on the basis of local knowledge and it was applied locally. It is the chief characteristic of the Soviet economy. In the period of War Communism, Vesenkha had not begun to plan and it could not make itself obeyed. It tried, for example, to prohibit expropriation without authorisation from itself and failed. It was without the power to command, which it later acquired. But something had to be done if only to get food to the cities. So the system of food procurements became the second distinguishing mark of the Soviet economy. Deliveries of food by the peasants became compulsory and detachments of armed men enforced what was virtual confiscation, for there was nothing to buy with any money paid for the deliveries. The practice promoted the despoiling of the rich, or more efficient, by the poor as well as the economic power of the central planning authority. In June 1918 the method of requisitioning grain and other supplies was systematised. In industry the decree on nationalisation also put power into the hands of Vesenkha. It enforced the ban on private trade and private manufacture. It allocated nearly all stocks of raw materials and nearly all output for a variety of purposes, at this date mainly war purposes. Central oversight, if not control, of production is the third characteristic of the Soviet economy. At this period there was complete disorder while free rations and free work was the rule, when there was anything to ration or anything to work at, and terror and arbitrariness were the only means the state Commissars had to make themselves obeyed in the urgent situations of the fighting. Food production fell; foreign trade disappeared; industrial commodities were not being made; an illegal economy flourished beside the Communist ideal. The final result was collapse in 1920 and famine in 1921 and millions died.

The succeeding period when Lenin organised the new economic policy, or NEP, followed the end of civil and external war and lasted from 1921 to 1926. It was a period of reconstruction based on a partial restoration of a market economy with some computation of costs and gains, a restoration of money-wages and an end to the arbitrary requisitioning of grain and other food. Requisitioning was replaced by a tax in kind as a means of directing surplus production to the towns and giving the peasant at least a fixed and foreseeable obligation. During this period industrial enterprises were organised in a wide variety of ways. They ranged from state owned and run concerns to small privately owned workshops, which were again legal. The state retained complete control of banking, foreign trade and large-scale industry. After March 1921 private trade was again legal and the demand for it was so great that it grew and swept away in its train other restrictions on free economic activity. In the countryside there was a widespread return to privately worked and owned farms. The state paid a price, though a low one, for food procurements beyond the fixed obligation. Food production went up and food rationing was ended in November 1921. The rouble was devalued and stabilised; the budget was balanced. It was a mixed economy, partly controlled and partly free. It was marked by two characteristic figures: the Nepmen, so called, or profiteers who flourished under the new system, and the agents of Vesenkha. This latter body increasingly filled the role designed for it and became more and more powerful.

One unforeseen result of Lenin's change of economic policy was the destruction of the Mensheviks. They, in their readiness to believe that Russia was experiencing not the socialist but the bourgeois democratic revolution of Marx's analysis, had long advocated the restoration of private enterprise in order to get the Russian economy working after the war. Lenin's change of policy might have been their opportunity to step into power. If Lenin's overriding aim was to retain monopoly of power for the Communists, he had no alternative but to destroy them. During the first three months of 1921, while the NEP was being implemented, some three thousand were arrested. Their leaders were imprisoned, others went into exile or concealed their identities and their organisation was broken. By 1922 the U.S.S.R. was a one-party state. Lenin shared fully in the decisions of 1922, but in that year he suffered the stroke which deprived him of movement and coherent speech. In 1924 he died. Bukharin, Zinoviev and Stalin now constituted a leading triumvirate. In 1925 Stalin, the Party Secretary, the unobtrusive Georgian, had become the most important among the leaders. The rise of Stalin was the rise of national Communism, or Socialism in one country. It had originally been Party doctrine that a Socialist state could not be achieved until Revolution had converted the whole world. Trotsky continued to hold this view. He is associated with the internationalism of Communism. But he was not expelled from the Party until 1927 and not exiled from the U.S.S.R. until February 1929. Stalin's régime should be dated, then, from that year.

The years 1926–29 were transition years, important because they highlighted great unsolved problems. Two of these were of special importance; the problem of capital and the problem of the peasant. The U.S.S.R. was still industrially undeveloped; full industrialisation needed a vast capital accumulation; no incentive to the production of capital in the short term was so effective as private enterprise. Yet the NEP and the legalisation of private enterprise had neither produced the required capital nor been without its own crises. The crisis of 1923, for example, resulted from industrial commodity prices being three times higher, relative to agricultural prices, than they were before the war, so that there were critical shortages and distortions before a sound relationship was achieved. How then was capital to be built up? Secondly, the U.S.S.R. was still an overwhelmingly peasant country and the peasant way of life engendered of itself capitalism and private property. How was the peasant to be converted into a wage-earning member of a collectivised, large-scale agriculture run as a food-producing industry? The greatest problem of all resulted from the conclusion that the NEP had failed to solve these problems. The economy then could not be left to direct itself by its own internal forces derived from the free interaction of supply and demand. If so then a directed economy must be set up. If a directed economy was set up, in what direction should it go and if that direction was against the grain of the wood then how, except by dictation and terror, could the people be forced to go in the prescribed direction?

In short, the NEP was squeezed out gradually between 1926 and 1929. It had to go, for there was no compromise possible between a free economy and a completely controlled or command economy. If the control was going to aim at industrialisation instead of the production of things people wanted, clothing, furniture, housing, luxuries, what are called consumer goods, then capital investment would have to be directed over the whole area, not just one part, of production. Secondly, if agriculture was to come second and industry first, as the fields for capital investment by the state, this again ran so sharply counter to the direction in which the economy would go if it were uncontrolled, that it could only be done by complete control. Finally, the state was committed to low prices. Its price policy both for industrial products and for grain was to keep prices so low, when there were no commodities available to satisfy demand, that it was impossible to prevent a free market from being a very profitable place to sell and the only place to buy many things in demand. Again absolute, complete control, backed by the use of force, would be needed to keep such a market from coming into existence. Speculation after 1930 became a crime.

Moreover, Stalin had a political motive for wiping out private trade and the hiring of labour by private individuals—both again illegal in 1930—in short, for the command economy and above all for the destruction of the peasants, the class which was the very seat of private enterprise. Stalin was identified with 'the stern imperative of conformity, centralised authority, the suppression of uncontrolled initiative.' It was his style, the source of his dogma. His way to power lay along that road. Any milder policy was the victory of a set of men other than himself.

So we come to the five-year plans. These were the instrument of the command economy. Article 107 had been added to the criminal code in 1926. It indicated 'imprisonment for up to three years with total or partial confiscation of property for those guilty of evil-intentioned increases in the prices of commodities through purchase, hoarding or non-placement on the market.' It was used by Stalin for the enforcement of economic control and was eventually the legal basis of terror. The first five-year plan was for 1929–34. The institution which brought it into being was known as Gosplan and it worked in close contact with Vesenkha. VSNK established centralised control over the whole economy, gradually by an accumulation of simple administrative decisions. It was used to direct the economy towards heavy capital expenditure, towards the development of heavy industry and an adequate return on investment only in the distant future. The targets set by the plan far exceeded what was possible. It combined, moreover, a set of incompatibles; increases in both investment and consumption; increases in both industrial and agricultural production; the substantial reduction of both costs and prices. The very impossibility of the plan gave both opportunity to whip up a kind of frenetic enthusiasm for approaching the targets and a sort of justification for arbitrary terrorist action to enforce it.

Next, forced collectivisation destroyed the peasants. Stalin's attack on the peasants was initiated by his speech at the fifteenth Party Congress in December 1927. The way out of the contradiction between capital investment in industry and dependence on the peasant, with his capitalist and individualist lifestyle, for grain, for its work-force, for the army and for export, said Stalin, was to turn the small and scattered peasant farms into large united farms based on the cultivation of the land in common, to go over to collective cultivation using higher techniques. So wealthier peasants, who were able to farm independently, were taxed more heavily; the state grain procurement system was streamlined to favour collective farming; the informal associations, known as Toz, where cultivation was joint but livestock, implements and tools were individually owned and the land to some extent individually controlled, were encouraged. Next year, 1928, state procurements in both industrial crops and grain were disastrously low. Stalin experimented with force. A task force of officials and police was sent to the Urals and West Siberia, where the harvest had been good, with orders to close free markets, expropriate private traders and, using article 107, to prosecute peasants, who held back the grain demanded, as criminals. They also stimulated attacks on the kulaks or wealthy peasants, but it was a name that could be given to anyone better off or more efficient than his neighbour. Between 1929 and 1934 force was ruthlessly applied. The atmosphere was hectic and false as the workers reached after the impossible targets of the five-year plan and officials falsified statistics to encourage the effort and prove its success. The agencies for enforcing collectivisation were the state grain procurement machinery, the local officials and Party members. By a decree of July 1929 the machinery was adjusted so that it could impose the penalty of expropriation for individuals—even imprisonment—and the uniting of farms into collectives when villages failed to supply the quotas demanded. Local officials instructed to bring about 100, 80 or 60 per cent collectivisation in a particular region, with no instruction which of the many varieties of collective to impose, generally took the shortest course and aimed at the full kolkhoz. A decree of February 1930 systematised the attacks on the kulaks which had already begun. Concentration camps for the wealthiest, deportations to Siberia for others and wholesale starvation for the rest was the rule. The kulaks having been liquidated in 1930, the attack shifted to the middle peasants, who were treated in the same way. In 1932 the peasants, demoralised and hungry, could be found guilty of pilfering on socialised fields or the railways and were exposed to 'the maximum means of social defence' which meant shooting. Only the famine of 1933 gave some pause to untempered cruelty. But the villages were emptied; the work-force in industry increased; the land collectivised. Some figures will best show what happened. On June 1, 1929, the total number of peasants who were members of collectives was under 1 million. In 1934 71 per cent of peasant households and 87 per cent of cultivated land belonged to collectives. Another calculation is the following: given Russia's rate of population growth—3 million a year—and a population of under 160 million in 1929, it should have been well over 180 million in 1939. It was in fact 170 million. But the deaths one can deduce from that calculation include lives sacrificed to carry out the second five-year plan (for 1934–39), lives lost in the army purges of 1936–37 and in the police terror of 1937–38.[1]

In the three years before the War of 1939–45 persecution inspired by political rather than economic motives began. In August 1936 Zinoviev and Kamenev, who had formed with Stalin the triumvirate which had governed Russia after Kamenev had displaced Bukharin were tried, condemned and executed, on charges of having organised terrorist groups for the assassination of Stalin, Voroshilov and other outstanding opponents of Trotsky. Early the following year a great purge of the Red Army was carried out. In June 1937 Marshal Tukhachevksy and seven other generals were tried in secret, sentenced to death and shot, whilst thousands of Red Army officers were removed. The trials were hailed by enemies of Communism as an indication of the breakdown of the Soviet system and as proof of the weakness of the Soviet Army. Others, however, considered that the purpose of these purges was to suppress a certain reorientation of Soviet foreign policy, allegedly supported by these generals and for-

[1] A. Nove, *An Economic History of the U.S.S.R.* (1969), pp. 174 and 180. The account of economic development in this chapter is mainly based on this book.

mer leaders. It was an orientation towards Germany and away from France, and it is perhaps significant that a similar purge of German officers suspected of favouring co-operation with the U.S.S.R. took place early in 1938. One important result of the trials was to make the French military authorities very reluctant to embark on talks for closer co-operation of the French and Soviet armies—a Franco-Soviet alliance had existed since 1935—and, notwithstanding the efforts made by Soviet military chiefs, the General Staff talks did not take place.

The strength of the Soviet Union was at this time arousing a good deal of controversy outside Russia, for there was little reliable information from which an independent and objective judgment could be formed. It was almost impossible to tell whether the existing régime was so unpopular that recourse had to be had to extreme and terroristic methods during a time of peace, or whether the rulers had so lost balance as to strike wildly at any semblance of opposition. It is clear that very drastic measures were certainly taken against those who, in other countries, might have been accepted as honest critics of the régime.

The achievements of the U.S.S.R. in twenty years were considerable. These achievements were not attained without great hardships on the part of the people of Russia, but the ruthless exploitation of human material, without regard to life, loss or damage, did in fact produce remarkable developments. By the threat or reality of starvation or death, the Russian peasant was compelled to re-shape his agriculture on new and modern lines. All economics, all politics, all society was moulded to a series of plans. Vast industrial enterprises and whole new cities were created. In the cities the poor received what was doubtless better treatment than they were wont to receive, as far as housing, education, wages and hours of labour were concerned. Science was developed to an extraordinary degree, especially industrial and agricultural science, physics and mechanics. The almost boundless natural resources of Russia were tapped. River, field and mine were used to increase the wealth and self-sufficiency of the new Soviet State. Materially, the Soviet experiment was successful, and from the chaotic, famine-stricken land of 1919–21 there grew a country economically almost self-sufficient from the point of view of food supplies and of the major industries necessary for war.

Chapter 8

THE GERMAN REVOLUTION
AND THE WEIMAR REPUBLIC

Revolution in Germany originated in the country's pre-war divisions. In August 1914 these had suddenly disappeared. The nation united to defend itself against Russia. Whether it remained united would depend on what it thought it was fighting for. War aims thus became the test of leadership. The Emperor retreated into the background until October 1918. Leadership was Bethmann Hollweg's responsibility until he fell in July 1917, and then that of the Army Command, which usurped power from the civilians and whose instruments succeeding Chancellors, Georg Michaelis and Georg von Hertling, were. Both Bethmann Hollweg and the Army Command failed the test. The old divisions reappeared. First the extreme Left of the Socialists, then the Socialists and the proletarian masses, then the liberal classes, made demands that were unsatisfied. They were not united among themselves, however, so that there was really no alternative leadership. When the Socialist leaders took power, they did not make a socialist revolution. They co-operated with the liberals and with the Catholic Centre Party to lead Germany in a reformed version of her old self. This was the Weimar Republic. The revolution of 1918–19, therefore, stopped half-way. The Weimar Republic fell in 1933 when there was again a revolutionary situation. But power was captured then not by revolutionary Communists but by Adolf Hitler and his National Socialist Workers' Party.

The German offensives made it impossible to preserve the notion of the war as a defensive one much beyond August 1914. Already when the Reichstag voted the second war credits in December 1914, Karl Liebknecht, of whom we shall hear more, registered the first contrary vote. But Bethmann Hollweg equivocated. To retain in the united nation the Right and the nationalists and, indeed, most of the middle and working class, he allowed, perhaps encouraged, an ever-widening vision of annexations. To retain the Socialists and to keep touch with a more moderate and realist policy, he disclaimed annexations, restrained, until 1917, the U-boat war, avoided commitment and, in 1916, referred in his speeches to the possibility of a negotiated peace and the dependence of its terms upon the military situation.

Nevertheless, it is important to grasp just how large a programme of annexations the claim for securities against a renewal of encirclement involved. These in their extreme form were as follows: from France, Belfort (the Alsatian fortress not annexed in 1871) and the iron-bearing districts of Longwy and Briey, perhaps the coast from Dunkirk to Boulogne; from Belgium, the Flanders coastline and Liège; Luxembourg; from Russia, Estonia, Latvia, Lithuania, Poland and the Ukraine (the whole of what the Treaty of Brest-Litovsk gave to her); in Africa, after the restitution of her colonies, some extension including the Belgian Congo or part of it. In addition, she would claim trade treaties which would ensure the economic dependence upon her of Belgium and France and the achievement of *Mitteleuropa*—a customs union that would begin with Germany and Austria-Hungary and include eventually France, Belgium, Holland, the Scandinavian countries, even Italy. It is not clear how seriously one should take this vision, nor even just how much it meant to Bethmann Hollweg. Certain it is that equivocation about war aims undermined Bethmann Hollweg's leadership. Moreover, the shock of defeat, when it came, was greater in proportion to the grandeur of the annexationist vision and, indeed, was increased by the sudden prospect of the war in the west being transferred to German soil, hitherto immune.

A second result of 'annexationism', even in a moderate form, was that, despite all Bethmann Hollweg's equivocation, it alienated the Socialists and, by 1917, other sections of Reichstag opinion. The Socialist vote in the Reichstag was important because with 110 seats they were the largest single Party. In 1915, 30 Socialists abstained and Liebknecht was joined by a colleague in a contrary vote when the budget, which included the war credits, was passed. In December 1915, 20 Socialists voted against the fifth war credits and 22 abstained. By then the Socialists had begun their agitation for a peace without annexations and without indemnities. In this the extreme Left among them was strengthened by International Socialism, sufficiently active even during the war to convene meetings at Zimmerwald in 1915 and Kienthal in 1916 of Socialists from all the belligerent countries, at which this slogan was elaborated. Though the Socialist Party (SPD) would have nothing to do with Zimmerwald or Kienthal, the effect of the international stand was to strengthen a division among them, already beginning on other grounds. The division was eventually threefold. The extreme Left, after January 1, 1916, known as the Spartacists (the leader of slave insurgents in ancient Rome was called Spartacus) led by Karl Liebknecht and Rosa Luxemburg, rejected the Party Truce proclaimed on August 4, 1914, and were ready to use illegal means to promote the Revolution. They were wholly anti-war, anti-parliamentarian and ready to receive money and support, after 1917, from Soviet Russia. Liebknecht and Rosa Luxemburg were feared and respected above other Socialists; he, because of his courage and integrity, she, because of her intellectual ruthlessness. On December 30, 1918, the Spartacist League reconstituted itself as the German Communist Party. Before that, another section had split off from the SPD. This last division was formalised at a Party Congress at Gotha in April 1917. The division had thus extended beyond the Reichstag deputies and became a national one. The minority, which split off, adopted the name Independent Socialist Party of Germany (USPD) and included Kautsky, Bernstein, Haase, Dittmann and Ledebour. They organised their own Party machine in the constituencies and in the summer of 1917, the peak of national discontent, claimed a membership of 120,000, only 80,000 less than that claimed by the SPD. They stood for the restoration of Belgium, the breakup of Austria-Hungary and the restoration of an independent Poland. They allied with the Spartacists for the purpose of the peace agitation, but only for that. Though they stood on the razor-edge during the last year of the War between treason and legality, they were reformist and not anti-parliamentarian. The Majority Socialists under Scheidemann and Ebert could only have recourse to ambiguities in order to tolerate the police methods of the Government, which the USPD denounced. Nevertheless, their agitation for a peace without annexations and without indemnities was so far successful that it attracted support from a cross-section of the country by 1917. This was shown when the Reichstag passed the Peace Resolution, after which Bethmann Hollweg resigned, on July 19, 1917; for it was moved by Erzberger, the leader of the Catholic Centre Party, or rather at this date of its left wing, and was supported by the Progressive Peoples' Party and some National Liberals. It called for a negotiated peace without annexations or indemnities.

The third effect of the failure of leadership over war aims was only obvious after Bethmann Hollweg fell. It became impossible to control the distress and discontent consequent upon economic collapse, the more so because it was accompanied by a political movement arising from a revival of the pre-war protest against the Prussian franchise and the absence of a Reich Ministry responsible to the Reichstag (see above, p.19). Economic collapse came in 1917–18 partly as the result of the blockade which confined Germany to her own resources or those of conquered territory for her food supply, and partly because her highly cartelised and centralised economy was not resilient and could not be adapted under pressure as quickly as one organised in small businesses. Urban hunger, peasant hoarding, the Black Market, pilfering and profiteering created social hostilities and individual despair. Reduction of rations, shortages of coal, textiles and leather meant that work capacity and morale were running out as well. Germany was saved temporarily by Rumanian resources, but a wave of industrial strikes in Berlin, Magdeburg, Halle, Brunswick, Leipzig and a strike of metal workers in Berlin in January 1918 foreshadowed the situation of 1918–19. The call for constitutional reform had not been satisfied by Bethmann Hollweg, who equivocated on this subject too. The Prussian three-class franchise remained; the Reich Secretaries of State were not replaced by a Reich Ministry. The Army Command was responsible for the choice of Michaelis as Chancellor. It now had everything its own way in domestic policy and was not interested in constitutional reform. Michaelis, an official from the Prussian food administration, could only temporise. Hertling, too old at seventy-five—he was a Bavarian elder statesman— to struggle successfully against the Army Command could only stall on the constitutional question too. The next event was the collapse of the Army Command. This event of September 28, 1918, has already been described and no more need be said except that it was Hertling who received Ludendorff's demand for an immediate armistice. But Hertling resigned. The Reichstag for the first and last time grasped its latent power. The Emperor appointed the liberally inclined Prince Max of the royal house of Baden, because he had the Reichstag's confidence. He had been brought forward by the Left Liberals in the Reichstag. The Reichstag majority and the Army Command were now really rivals for power. Prince Max chose a Ministry, not from civil servants, but from the Reichstag majority: two Secretaries of State from the Centre Party, two from the Left Liberals and one from the Socialists. They retained their seats in the Reichstag. Legislation was now introduced and passed to make the necessary constitutional changes. The widening of the franchise in Prussia and the appointment of a Reich Ministry were the first part of the German revolution. These changes were completed when the Emperor dismissed Ludendorff and appointed General Gröner in his place. The Army Command now lost its ascendancy though, as we shall see, not its capacity to play a significant part in the events which followed.

The next thing to do was to persuade the Emperor to abdicate and to bring about the abdication of the Kings of Saxony, Bavaria and Württemberg and of other German rulers. All these abdications were brought about separately and not correlated. The abdication of the Emperor was, however, connected, on one side with the armistice negotiations, since the Allies had made it a condition of the armistice, and, on the other side, with spontaneous insurrections of sailors, soldiers and workers, backed to some extent by the USPD and the Spartacists, since these threatened a breakdown of public order which it was essential to maintain for the sake of the armistice. One notices the absence of any single ruthless figure, such as Lenin in Russia, who could make events happen as he intended they should happen.

Proclamation of the Republic (1918)

In Germany different interests interacted to bring about the final outcome. The Reichstag had been adjourned on October 26, so that it did not influence this part of the revolution. Since the beginning of October Prince Max had been trying to bring the Emperor to offer abdication. But the Emperor, at the military headquarters at Spa, with his back to the wall, fought for his crown and dynasty believing he had the support of the nation. The month's delay strengthened the position of the Socialists, because Prince Max thought that reliance on them was the only way to keep order. Their position was further strengthened by the events which took place between November 7 and 8 in Saxony, Württemberg and Bavaria where Socialist Governments were installed when the Kings abdicated. Kurt Eisner headed an extreme revolutionary Government in Bavaria, but otherwise moderation was the rule. The position of the Socialists was so strong that by the time the Emperor's abdication came through to Berlin on November 9, it was to Friedrich Ebert, their leader, that Prince Max handed over power. When the Emperor's message came through, Prince Max published his intention to resign on the formation of a Regency and to recommend Ebert to the Regents as his successor. Thus Ebert took power in a legal way. That no Regency was appointed was neither Max's nor Ebert's fault. Events overtook them. A great meeting had assembled in front of the Reichstag and there Scheidemann proclaimed the Republic. He had acted independently, but what he had done could not be undone. Ebert's Government signed the Armistice on November 11.

It was impossible to gauge the strength of the revolutionary impulse at work among sailors, soldiers and workers. The sailors at Kiel had mutinied rather than put to sea in a last desperate effort on October 28. Though many of the sailors belonged to the USPD and seemed to be attempting a Socialist revolution, they were reconciled to the Government by Noske, an SPD member of the Reichstag sent to pacify them and eventually made Governor of Kiel. But, on the other hand, their movement had spread and the great ports of Hamburg, Bremen and Cuxhaven were in the hands of Workers' and Sailors' Councils on November 8. Something similar was happening in Berlin. The streets from mid morning on November 9 were filled with crowds marching to demonstrate at the centre. Neither SPD nor USPD nor Spartacists nor revolutionary shop stewards planned or controlled what was going on. But Workers' and Soldiers' Councils had been elected and on the following day a mass meeting, said to have been attended by some three thousand of their members, assembled and elected an Executive Committee. It was this Committee on which SPD, USPD and Spartacists were represented, which spoke for the revolution from below. Though no one could foresee this, when it accepted Ebert's Government its action was virtually over. Its importance lay in its giving Ebert another set of credentials. It remained to be seen whether the link with the past through Prince Max or the link with the revolution from below, would prove the stronger. Meanwhile the situation remained ambiguous. On one hand, Ebert's Government called itself the Council of Peoples' Commissars and was composed of three from the SPD (Ebert as Chairman, Scheidemann and Landsberg) and three from the USPD (Haase, Dittmann and Barth). (The exclusion of other Parties also linked it to the revolution from below.) On the other hand, at the side of the Commissars were liberal men such as Solf, and later Brockdorff-Rantzau, in charge of Foreign Affairs, Scheuch, Schiffer and Preuss in other Ministries. None of them was Socialist and they preserved continuity with the past. A movement forward to, for example, the dictatorship of the proletariat was indeed excluded, for Ebert and the Socialists had committed themselves to the summoning of a Constituent Assembly and meant to keep their promise. Not only that: Ebert had already on the evening of November 10 formed an alliance with General Gröner, Ludendorff's successor. Ebert would have the support of the army to keep order (Gröner sent ten divisions to Berlin in December) and, so it turned out, to keep the Communist Revolution at bay. Gröner would have the support of the Socialists and the Workers' and Soldiers' Councils to keep discipline in the army during demobilisation.

Two meetings from all Germany now took place. They cleared away many uncertainties and allowed the Government at last to gauge the strength of revolutionary pressure. The first assembled the Prime Ministers from all the German states on November 25. It came out clearly for the Constituent Assembly, though it was ready to postpone the elections, persuaded by the plausible argument that the prisoners of war had still to return. The second assembled representatives from the Workers' and Soldiers' Councils from all Germany on December 16–21. Its discussions showed three things: that most Germans wished to live in a parliamentary state; that they wished for a greater degree of demilitarisation than even the armistice exacted; and that though there was widespread support for a socialist programme of industrial nationalisation, the restoration of the economy was their aim, not further revolution. It too came out for the Constituent Assembly and agreed that elections should take place on January 16. This decision was the final check to the revolution.

The remaining uncertainty was what would the USPD and, above all, the Spartacists now do. The Spartacists, despairing of revolution, might at least provoke civil war. And that was exactly what they seemed to be doing. There were three incidents in December, including one when soldiers fired upon a crowd of Spartacist workmen in a working-class suburb of Berlin, which they used for their purpose. The USPD had rallied to the support of the Spartacists when the Congress of Workers' and Soldiers' Councils, before it dispersed, elected a Central Committee of twenty-seven men to replace the Executive Committee elected by the Berlin Workers' and Soldiers' Council in November, because it contained no one from the USPD. At the end of December Germany suddenly polarised between the parties of order on one side and the USPD with the Spartacists on the other. There were demonstrating soldiers and sailors in Berlin. Order seemed to break down. So came the second part of the revolution or the Spartacist rising. It was preceded by the conference at which the Spartacists changed their name to Communists, remarkable for the force and ruthlessness of Rosa Luxemburg's address. The Berlin rising of January 3–9, 1919, was an attempt to seize power for the proletariat, but it had no chance of success. Noske had been appointed by the Ebert Government to find the armed power with which to quell it. It was not difficult. Already on January 4 he had at his disposal the first of the Freikorps. These were volunteers, fully equipped and well disciplined, mostly regular officers and NCOs, but others as well, for they numbered, it was said, some 4000. They were assembled on the outskirts of Berlin and began the systematic reconquest of the city on the night of January 10–11. They probably had the sympathy of most Germans. But there were atrocities, which included the brutal murder of Karl Liebknecht and Rosa Luxemburg on the evening of January 15. Wilhelm Pieck, the future President of the German Democratic Republic, escaped on this occasion.

The revolution was now over. The Peoples' Commissars unobtrusively changed their name to Ministers and the elections for the Constituent Assembly took place. The 421 members met on February 6, 1919, at Weimar, both to be secluded from the revolutionary capital of Berlin and to associate the new Republic with Germany's past cultural centre. The two Socialist Parties had between them 185 seats (22 USPD), the Centre 91, the Democrats (successor to the Progressive Peoples' Party) 75. These parties were to constitute the Weimar coalition. With 7 members unattached to any of the main parties, only 63 seats were left to be shared among the parties of the Right: the DVP or People's Party of Gustav Stresemann and the DNVP or German National People's Party. It was the resurgence of the old Reichstag Germany.

The Weimar Republic was not a Socialist, but a liberal democracy. The Socialists did not stand by their commitment to nationalise industry. In 1918 they had entered a situation; they had not made it; they were a party in Government and their first duty was to govern, to restore confidence to industrialists afraid of expropriation. To have nationalised industries in 1918–20 would have loaded the state with debt. Although as early as November 18 a commission had been appointed to enquire which industries were ripe for nationalisation, its recommendations were ignored and the arguments of the Minister of Finance for postponement adopted. The constitution, drafted by Hugo Preuss, the Minister for the Interior, a Liberal, enacted by the Constituent Assembly and effective from August 14, 1919, contained a section on the economy. It formulated the principle of social justice, but guaranteed the economic freedom of the individual. It gave power to the Reich to take economic enterprises by legal enactment into the possession of the community, but did not prescribe that it should do so.

The state was to have the oversight of the economy, not its direction. Nor did the Socialists incorporate into German life the Workers' and Soldiers' Councils, so active in November and December 1918. During 1919 they disappeared. The constitution referred in general terms (Article 165) to district and Reich Workers' Councils, providing that they should represent all interests engaged in production, but no attempt was made to implement the article. The eight-hour working day and unemployment relief, enacted by proclamation on November 12, 1918, were the workers' only concrete economic gains. In the years of economic crisis the first was not much observed. The constitution aroused the greatest optimism among liberals. The whole was governed by a single sentence which based it upon the will of the people to renew its Reich in freedom and justice. The Reich was a Republic made up of the several German states. The Republic's President was elected by all the German people. In fact the Constituent Assembly appointed Ebert the first President. The Reichstag was elected by universal, equal, direct and secret suffrage and had sovereign legislative power, overriding the power of the state parliaments. The Reichsrat representing the states was a co-ordinating body, assenting to the legislative proposals of the Reich Ministry before they were put before the Reichstag.

Much attention is paid to the weaknesses of the Weimar Republic because it lasted only fourteen years. There were certainly provisions in the constitution which could be abused. The safeguards for the power of the people were many: proportional representation, popular initiative in legislation (hedged about to prevent frivolous proposals) and provision for referenda. The single-member constituency was replaced by elections on the basis of party lists, which could give over-great importance to the party organisation. Indeed, all these provisions multiplied politics. If Imperial Germany had had too much government and too little politics, the Weimar Republic had too much politics and too little government. The President, elected for seven years, had a powerful position which he could abuse. He appointed (and could dismiss) the Chancellor, the head of the Government, who then made his Ministry, which had to have the confidence of the Reichstag. The President's choice of Chancellor played an important part in the events of 1930–33. The President had the power to dissolve the Reichstag, so that he could appeal to the electorate over the heads of the Reich Ministry and against it. This too was a power which could be abused. Finally he had emergency powers which allowed him to dispense with the Reichstag altogether. This too was to play an important part in the events of 1930–33.

Constitutional forms are, however, probably less important than the will to make a constitution work. This will was weak. The Weimar Republic had no positive friends and too many enemies. The Socialists virtually deserted it. They lost seats in the General Election of June 1920, falling to 102 (the USPD, always in opposition, gained). They were not part of the governing coalition between 1920 and 1922. After Kurt Eisner's assassination (February 21, 1919) and a brief Communist interlude, a Government without SPD participation was installed in Bavaria (May 1920). Only in Prussia did a Socialist Government survive. Otto Braun, Carl Severing and Albert Grzesinski, however, showed the difficulty Socialists in government experienced in implementing a policy shaped in opposition, especially when they had to work through a civil service and local government agents opposed to socialist measures. The Liberal Parties, that is the Democrats (DDP), successors to the Progressive People's Party, and the People's Party (DVP), successors to the National Liberals, should have been the Republic's source of strength. But the DDP had lost heavily in the General Election, only retaining 39 seats. Moreover, the Liberal Parties were middle-class parties and, as we shall see, the middle classes were seriously disabled by the economic crisis and their loss of wealth. Positive action on behalf of the Republic was scarcely in their power. Moreover, what they wanted—in Thomas Mann's phrase—was 'impartiality, order, propriety,' not decision by debate. The civil service, which included the judiciary, was either hostile or failed to understand the importance of active goodwill. The constitution safeguarded the position of civil servants. They had been appointed under the monarchy and were either monarchists or only nominally loyal to the new Republic. The judiciary was so hostile that some have written of a state of war between it and the people at this time. A more subtle and slowly working cause of hostility was that a stronghold of monarchical and nationalist feeling survived in the schools. Nor were the Churches actively friendly to the Republic. It is true that the Catholic Centre Party was part of the governing coalition, but the Roman Catholic Church was not fully behind the Centre Party. It distrusted the SPD and wanted a policy for the schools that the Republic was not going to provide. The three Protestant Churches, Lutheran, Calvinist (Reformed) and United, detested the Socialists and mistrusted a Republic so dependent on the Centre Party. But there was a more interesting obstacle to their accommodation to the new régime. Historically they were state churches closely associated with the Prince of each state. They would have found it easier to fit into the Republic had each been a single

German Church, historically separate from the states.

A third weakness was the persistence of violence with which the Republic had no Republican army to deal. Matthias Erzberger, the Centre Party member of the Reichstag, who negotiated the armistice terms with Foch and persuaded the Reichstag to accept the peace terms in June 1919, in 1921 paid with his life for his patriotism. Walther Rathenau, Minister of Reconstruction and then Foreign Minister, paid the same debt in 1922. The Kapp *putsch* in Berlin in 1920 and the attempt of the NSDAP (the Nazis) in Munich in 1923 were suppressed by recourse to the Freikorps. For the Government to be thus dependent on volunteer armed force was for it to throw the Republic into the arms of the Nationalist Parties on the Right who were neither liberal-democratic nor Republican.

It should, however, be said that though the Weimar Republic failed after fourteen years it is entitled to a larger place in men's memories than the twelve years of the Third Reich. It is unlikely to be given it, for destruction and terror are more memorable than unrealised hopes and cultural achievement. The cultural achievement was in architecture and design, associated with Walter Gropius and the Bauhaus, in drama, associated with Bertolt Brecht and a host of producers and actors as well as playwrights, in literature, where one thinks of the novels of Thomas Mann, in painting and in film. It was a flowering period of much that had begun under Imperial Germany.

The history of the Weimar Republic falls into three periods. The crisis of 1923 was the turning-point in the first period. The Government struggled against financial collapse. It was a battle at home to save the currency. It was a battle abroad to save something for Germany from reparations under the Treaty of Versailles. The Government was almost equally engaged against the activities of the Nationalist Parties, who were involved in an attempt to reconstruct surreptitiously the army. In 1923 there was sudden, rapid and unprecedented inflation. It was caused partly by the financial policies of all the German Governments since 1914. The War was financed by borrowing. Moreover, in August 1914, the restriction placed upon the printing of notes, beyond the sum covered by the gold reserves of the banks, was removed and the organisation of Loan Banks, to afford credit on securities which did not qualify as securities under existing regulations, was provided for. The mark already by 1918 had declined to about half its value in gold. When the resumption of international trade after the war made this obvious, there was a general loss of confidence in the mark and this in turn caused further depreciation. But at this stage Germany had large gold reserves and could have stabilised her currency had she adopted a different financial policy from that of constantly increasing the money supply. The second cause of inflation was the magnitude of the financial and economic burdens imposed upon Germany in the years following the armistice. The total amount of reparation due would not be certain until the Reparation Commission reported, but meanwhile some payments were to be made between August 1919 and May 1, 1921. In the spring of 1920, because of strikes and the Kapp *putsch*, Germany fell behind in the delivery of that part of what was due which had to be paid in commodities. An attempt was made at revision, but produced an impossible arrangement in January 1921 for an annual payment during the next forty-two years and a payment of 26 per cent of the proceeds of German exports. After the Reparation Commission reported in April 1921, Germany was informed that the total sum was 132 billion gold marks. The use of the unit of the gold mark made the figure quite unreal. The notification demanded not only acceptance of this figure, but payment of a billion gold marks within twenty-five days. Germany paid. But the Government, on the advice of the Reichsbank, paid by selling newly printed paper currency on the foreign currency exchanges. As a result the mark fell during 1921 from 60 to the American dollar to 310. By October Chancellor Wirth with Rathenau's assistance had gained a revision of the arrangements, which at least lessened the amount to be paid in money and increased that to be paid in commodities. Cuno, a Director of the Hamburg-American Steamship Line, was then made Chancellor in the hope that his place in the business world would enable him to contrive means for Germany to pay. But she fell into further arrears. The Reparation Commission at the end of 1922 declared Germany in default. On January 12, 1923, French and Belgian troops carried out the threat that had been used as a sanction to induce Germany to pay: they marched into the Ruhr Basin. The occupation of the Ruhr Basin was answered by passive resistance. This stop in production was the third and precipitating cause of the inflation crisis.

Inflation lasted at its worst from March to November 1923.[1] The quality of the experience is best indicated by giving the fact that men and women wage-earners were paid twice a day and allowed free time during the day to spend their earnings on what there was to buy. Even before the worst, butter on the breakfast table might cost by the evening what a house would have cost in the morning. Notes and postage stamps were simply overprinted with noughts.

The results of inflation were enormous profits for the few who knew how to manipulate credit—for the borrowers, debts were wiped out. It caused moderate difficulties for the wage-earners, greater difficulties for civil servants and professional people who relied on fees and salaries; complete ruin for those dependent on income from invested capital. In other words, the classes who normally give stability to a régime by their progressive conservatism or moderate liberalism were henceforward unlikely or unable to do so.

[1] The table in Gordon Craig, *Germany 1866–1945* (1978), p. 450, gives exact figures.

Small businessmen, shopkeepers and self-employed artisans were almost as badly hit as the professional classes. The farmers and land-owners had a better chance of keeping income and expenditure level. The crisis, therefore, exacerbated the hostility between the urban and rural communities created by the war. A hectic, irresponsible, cynical mood beset Germany in the mid twenties and discouraged a thought-ful, confident approach to social and political problems. The year 1923 closed with the revelation of General von Seeckt's plan to resurrect the German army with Soviet aid.

By 1924 inflation was over. A new Chancellor, Gustav Strese-mann, before his Government fell in November 1923, had made the arrangements which enabled production to start again in the Ruhr Basin and with Hjalmar Schacht's assistance and that of his Finance Minister, Hans Luther, had taken the steps which stabilised the cur-rency on the basis of a new mark: the Rentenmark, first issued in November 1923. The Rentenmark was secured on the land and was for domestic use only. It was replaced by a Reichsmark, based on gold, and so usable in international trade, in 1924. The Dawes Plan of 1924 adjusted Germany's reparation payments to her advantage, in the same year. The second period of the Weimar Republic thus began in stability. But the Germans were now in a strange mood. They had never been a people politically self-conscious or articulate, and they had no power of improvisation and not enought practical instinct to meet their difficulties half-way. They drifted gradually into a condition in which they were ready to surrender everything into the hands of a single individual. The first sign of this tendency was the movement which ended in the election of Hindenburg, the hero of the battle of Tannenberg, as President on Ebert's death in 1925. This was a significant move towards the Right. No one thought that Hindenburg was a Socialist; he was known to be a monarchist and the most striking representative of the old upper class. At the same time he was a true soldier and, as he had taken the oath to the con-stitution, it was believed that he would observe it. Meanwhile from 1924 under a succession of Chancellors (Hans Luther, Wilhelm Marx and Hermann Müller) Gustav Stresemann, until his death on Octo-ber 3, 1929, was Foreign Minister.

The second period was essentially the period of Stresemann and stability. Stresemann understood foreign policy as the key to the preservation of stability. It was also the field in which his particular talents would bring rewards. He was objective, patient and concili-atory. He conducted foreign policy as a well co-ordinated whole. He co-operated with the west and confirmed Germany's alliance with Russia in the east. The three men, Austen Chamberlain, Aristide Briand and Gustav Stresemann, understood each other in the west. The Rapallo Treaty of 1922 with Russia had given Germany her ally in the east. Stresemann began with a proposal to Britain for an inter-national guarantee of west European frontiers. It was timely; for

Chamberlain, having been obstructive to proposals over security from the League of Nations, was anxious to show himself generous and Briand had just replaced the hard-liner, Poincaré, in France. The year 1925 ended, then, with the conference of Locarno and the Locarno Treaties, initialled in October and signed in London on December 1, 1925. By these Treaties the states bordering on the Rhine abjured the use of force in their relations with one another and, together with Britain and Italy, mutually guaranteed their existing frontiers. In addition Germany and France signed the Rhineland Pact by which Germany reaffirmed her acceptance of the demilitarised zone in the Rhineland. Next, Germany was promised admission to the League of Nations with a permanent seat on its Council. Britain and France failed to impose the condition they wished for: Germany's acceptance of her eastern frontier as permanent. All they obtained was Germany's signature of arbitration Treaties with Poland and Czechoslovakia. Germany obtained the condition she had wished for: exemption, since she was disarmed, from the obligation under Article 16 of the League Covenant to take, eventually, military measures against any member of the League who broke its obligations. In the end, Germany's entry into the League did not take place, as intended, in March 1926, because her claim to a permanent seat on the Council was countered by other states' claims to the same privilege. In the interval when these were being considered, Stresemann turned east. Already the agreement with France over the demilitarised zone had been regarded as having an eastern meaning: it would balance France's alliance with Poland. Now Stresemann signed the Treaty of Berlin (April 24, 1926) with Soviet Russia. Thus he resumed the policy begun at Rapallo. The Treaty obliged each to remain neutral if the other were attacked and to consult together in time of crisis. Britain and France were now ready for further concessions. Chamberlain thought he was 'battling with Soviet Russia for the soul of Germany.' In December 1926 the occupation forces, of which Germany paid the costs, were cut to 60,000 men and the Military Control Commission withdrawn. By August 1928 Stresemann had persuaded the French to consider an early evacuation of the Rhineland and to agree to a fresh review of reparations. The outcome was the conference at The Hague presided over by an American banker, O. D. Young, from which came the Young Plan of 1929, as well as a promise from Briand to evacuate the Rhineland by June 30, 1930. Germany had been admitted to the League in September 1926.

The balance-sheet for Stresemann was not bad. On the credit side: Germany had been freed from most of the restrictions placed on her sovereignty by the Treaty of Versailles; she had been accepted as one among the Great Powers. On the debit side: she had not regained military parity with the other European Powers; she had not regulated her relations with Austria; she had not rectified her eastern frontier. Perhaps, too, Stresemann had simply postponed internal problems. They could not all be solved by being exported. The primacy of foreign policy can never be absolute.

During the third period of the history of the Weimar Republic, from 1929 to 1933, internal affairs resumed first place. Heinrich Brüning, Franz von Papen and Kurt von Schleicher were in turn Chancellor. They presided over the struggle of the Republic against a new enemy, whose strength was neither obvious nor capable of being beaten by the ordinary political methods of persuasion and manoeuvre. The followers of Hitler were the new enemy. Adolf Hitler (1889–1945) was an Austrian-born demagogue. He had served as a non-commissioned officer in the German army. He was never penniless unless by his own distaste for steady employment; and his parents had sent him to good schools. He organised a political following after the war and with it attempted a *putsch* in the unsettled conditions of Munich in 1923. Failure brought him imprisonment and time to write *Mein Kampf.* His serious political career began on his release. His strength lay in the streets and taverns, in the demonstrations and violence of the National Socialist Workers' Party (NSDAP). His accession to power is less well understood by tabulating causes than by following the chronological succession of events; for it was the outcome of an accumulation of decisions all trending one way.

The failure of the Socialists persisted. The SPD now had a reformist programme drafted at Heidelberg in 1925. The membership had diversified. Managers and clerks in industry, civil servants, schoolteachers, intellectuals, professional men, businessmen and housewives accounted for 40 per cent of the party. It was wealthy, with 200 newspapers and trade union support. But its intentions were out of phase with its rhetoric. It no longer intended revolution, but it preserved revolutionary slogans; it no longer intended nationalisation, but it preserved the doctrine. It flourished in the cities and industrial centres, but it left the countryside and small towns to the Nationalist Parties, the DNVP and the NSDAP. It retained its older members but left the young to join the Communists or the NSDAP. Socialists were in several Governments, but they tended to be short-lived Governments and the SPD gave no lasting strength to any Government.

The failure of the Liberal Democrats (DDP) also persisted. Their representation in the Reichstag continued to fall. In December 1924 they gained only 32 seats; in May 1928, only 25. They were less well represented now than the Communist Party, who had won 45 and 54 seats in those elections. Their ideas, which seemed abstract and impractical to the electorate, made them into an élitist party of strong individuals, yet they no longer had the interesting and gifted leaders that Left Liberals had once had. They tended to take unpopular and unintelligible positions in the Reichstag debates. They moved away from the Socialists towards the Right.

As for the DVP, Stresemann was disappointed with his party. The DVP had become more clearly than ever the party of the businessman and industrialist, the party of wealth and education. Ten DVP members of the Reichstag had 77 Company directorships between them. It was less and less liberal; for it assumed that the authoritarian methods which were sometimes good for industry were good for the nation. The DNVP (the German National People's Party) was openly nationalist. Its main objective was the revision of the Treaty of Versailles, but after the Kapp *putsch* it abandoned formal opposition to parliamentary democracy and Karl Helfferich, until his death in 1924, held it to parliamentary loyalty. After 1928 it fell under Hugenberg's influence. He had been associated with the Pan German League and, during the War, with the extreme nationalists of the *Vaterlandspartei*. He led it away from the Republic into alliance with the NSDAP and Hitler. For Hitler it was an alliance with wealth and the landowners.

The Centre Party alone remained stable. It gave strength to every Government. But its later leaders did not have the parliamentary skill of Wirth, Marx or Müller. Upon it must fall some responsibility for what happened between 1930 and 1933. Because of its strength, when the Müller Government fell in March 1930 Hindenburg appointed Brüning, the leader of the Centre Party in the Reichstag though not of the whole Party, Chancellor. Brüning was an extremely able man though his political skill fell short of his intellectual ability, for he was slow in assessing men's motives. At least, it seemed that Hindenburg had appointed Brüning because his party was so strong. Appearances were deceptive. Hindenburg and Brüning's Government, like those Governments which followed it, were being manipulated from behind. The military element had reappeared in politics. It is easy to understand why Hindenburg should have listened to its persuasion. Brüning's appointment was not due only to the political strength of his party, but also to Kurt von Schleicher, head of the political section of the Defence Ministry, and behind him stood General Gröner, Ebert's ally of 1918–20. It was they who had suggested Brüning to Hindenburg.

Brüning's Government was a younger and more vigorously led one than its predecessors. This gave ground for hope. The depression of 1929 and the economic crash of 1930 soon had results which changed hope to despair. Mounting unemployment—the 3 million of March 1930 had become 5.5 million by March 1931—constant bloodshed in street battles against Communists, deliberately provoked by the brown-shirted toughs of the NSDAP, were seen as the consequences. Brüning adopted a deflationary policy of higher taxation and cuts in public expenditure. He failed to take the SPD or trade unions into his confidence and he persuaded Hindenburg to enact the financial programme by using his constitutional emergency powers to govern by decree (July 1930). He then dissolved the Reichstag. In the General Election which followed, the NSDAP did unexpectedly well. It was never to gain a Reichstag majority, but it now won 107 seats as against its 12 in 1928. The Liberal Parties virtually disappeared, they were so reduced: the DDP to 20 seats and the DVP to 30. The Communists won 77, the SPD, now again the strongest single party, won 143 seats. The Centre Party at 68 had 6 more seats than in 1928 and Brüning carried on for nearly two years longer.

The NSDAP was a different party from the one that had failed in 1923. For one thing, it now had martyrs as well as uniforms, flags and songs, its characteristic salutation and its swastika badge. For another thing, its leader as a political animal had matured. Hitler had a gift for capturing his politics from his public. He knew what people wanted to be told and when to tell it them; he had an unequalled understanding of propaganda, that is the constant repetition of the simplest, exaggerated statement of half-truths. He had already exploited this gift in *Mein Kampf* of 1924 and his second book of 1928. He was completely ruthless and understood the attraction as well as terror of violence. He also exploited young people's need for comradeship, sacrifice and an ideal to live by. But he drew his support from a very wide range of social groups. Men of independent means, salaried employees, farmers and even wage-earners—though these last not in proportion to their percentage of the total population. The backbone of his party was, however, the middle and lower-middle class.

During his last two years, Brüning, like Stresemann, sought a solution of internal problems by way of foreign policy. To restrain the rising nationalism at home he introduced a new clamour abroad into efforts to scale down reparation payments and achieve military parity. This alienated Britain and France and failed to achieve its purpose. The climax came in 1931 with his announcement of an Austro-German Customs Union. Britain and France promptly invoked the ban of the Versailles Treaty on Austro-German union and Brüning suffered a bad rebuff. His failure in foreign policy coupled with his failure to control disorder lost him his authority in the country. Hindenburg refused him any further use of the President's power to rule by decree. In May 1932 he resigned.

General Schleicher then engineered the appointment of von Papen. He too was designed to be an instrument. He never established the authority in the Reichstag or country that Brüning had had, although Britain and France granted to him the revision of the Young Plan which they had refused to Brüning. Nor was he consistent. He first banned the paramilitary organisations of the NSDAP (the SA or Sturmabteilungen and the SS or Schutzstaffeln) and then permitted them. He dissolved the separate Government of Prussia in July 1932 by decree on the ground that it had failed to maintain public order. This meant a strengthening of the Reich which took over the considerable resources of the largest German state and no longer had to tolerate a rival to its own authority. But it was the Third Reich and not the Weimar Republic which profited. By now the NSDAP had won electoral successes in the parliaments of all the states except Bavaria, and at the General Election of July 1932 which followed Papen's dissolution of the Reichstag in one more effort to get a Government majority, the NSDAP gained 230 seats. (The total number of Reichstag seats in this year was 608.) There was, as a result, a question of bringing Hitler and his party into the Government. He refused except on his own terms. Hindenburg administered a widely published rebuke. Hitler in revenge forced a fresh dissolution of the Reichstag and fresh elections. But he had overshot the mark. In the General Election of November 1932 he lost 34 seats. The struggle with von Papen continued for one more round. He devised a scheme for constitutional reform to be decreed by the President. To Schleicher this was folly. Schleicher persuaded Hindenburg to refuse and to appoint himself as Chancellor. This was in November 1932. Within a month he too had failed to control either the country or the Reichstag. In January 1933 Hindenburg appointed Hitler to the Chancellorship. Hitler to that extent came to power by legal means.

Hindenburg, according to his lights, was a good President, at least until extreme old age rendered him helpless in the hands of his advisers. Like most soldiers he was a good judge of a man, but a bad judge of a political tendency. Moreover, the constitutional position of President was difficult: like that of the Prince-President Napoleon in France in 1849, one in which it was hard to observe the constitution and yet maintain efficiency and order. The fact that Hindenburg was President had alone ensured continuity of government. He remained sphinx-like and impassive while a succession of embarrassed and transient Ministries passed like shadows before him. At last he saw a man whom he had once rejected, who seemed a little less unreal than the others. He chose him for his Chancellor and speedily found his prediction a true one. It turned out to be a tragedy that the man he had chosen was Adolf Hitler.

Chapter 9

THE RISE AND CONSOLIDATION OF FASCIST ITALY

The making of United Italy had been a political achievement. The Risorgimento which preceded it had been a movement of minds in which all had shared, each according to the range of his experience. Until unification was complete it had been possible to keep an open mind about what the relationship exactly was between the Risorgimento and unification. By 1876 it was clear that it was not a simple one of fulfilment. That year was a turning-point in Italian history, because the generation associated with the Risorgimento and unification withdrew from the stage. The Papal *non expedit* (1874), a declaration that it was not expedient for Catholics to offer themselves as parliamentary candidates or even to vote in parliamentary elections, underlined, even though it was not fully observed, the withdrawal of the old political families. There was, moreover, distress and discontent, prompted by heavy taxation (the grist tax was called the tax on hunger) and the passivity of the Governments which followed Cavour's death. The King summoned Agostino Depretis to form a reforming Ministry from the Left. He was to reform administration, balance the budget, lower taxation, get rid of the grist tax and, above all, establish schools and lessen illiteracy. Depretis, who with Cairoli and Mancini dominated the decade 1876–87, did none of these things. His resources were too small. Nevertheless economically and socially his was a good period. The Governments of the Left had a favourable attitude to business interests and there was an industrial spurt into economic growth. But the good period was over by 1887. In that year the Government introduced a protective tariff. Special protection was given to iron and steel, though Italy was without the raw materials for heavy industry, so that this may not have been sound policy. A duty on imported wheat protected the interests of the landowners. An alliance developed between industrialists and landowners that was not altogether to Italy's advantage. There was anyhow a recession after 1887.

Though it has been the subject of much controversy, it is now gen-

155

erally accepted that the true beginning of Italy's industrial revolution was some ten years later, during the era of Giolitti rather than Depretis. Between 1896 and 1914 Italy's industrial production doubled and industrial investment trebled. The great industrial area in the triangle between Genoa, Turin and Milan was firmly established. Italy made her reputation for fine skill and ingenuity in engineering and the manufacture of motor cars, bicycles, sewing machines and rubber tyres was her speciality. Shipbuilding and heavy industry rapidly expanded. The disparity between the wealth of the north and the poverty of the south continued. Some of the difficulty of dealing with it arose from the false assumption that Italy constituted a single economy. On the contrary, there was throughout the period before Fascist Italy no single national market. Italy constituted two economies, not one. The problem of the land (some redistribution was overdue in order that peasants might own their land), the problem of excessive emigration, even to some extent the problem of colonial ambitions, were all problems of the south.

To return to the main theme: the period of Depretis was also a good period in foreign policy. Italy consolidated her friendship with Austria-Hungary in spite of her claims on Austrian territory (*Italia irredenta*), and extended it to Germany, making the Triple Alliance in 1882 and renewing it thereafter every five years. She established good relations with Britain making the Mediterranean Agreements with her in 1887. She reconciled herself to France and she acquired her first colonies in Eritrea and Somaliland.

Between the periods of Depretis and Giolitti came that of Crispi. He came to power first in 1887. As an old follower of Garibaldi he might have given prestige to the monarchy and rallied to it those disappointed with the fruits of the Risorgimento. He was cast in a more heroic mould than his predecessors, but he had a full share of faults. He was harsh, unscrupulous and impulsive. After almost two years out of office, he returned to power in 1893 with a vision of an imperialist Italy. Hitherto, Italy had pursued her imperialist ambitions by subsidising companies and leaving them to develop the settlements. Crispi conceived a grandiose dream of giving King Humbert a new crown. In his first ministry he had obtained Britain's consent to expansion in Ethiopia, and he now pushed this policy still further. A forward colonial policy would give Italy a vast African Empire and distract her thoughts from internal affairs. But his ill-advised interference with the men on the spot, his demands by telegraph for 'an authentic victory', his reproaches stung General Baratieri into action. He went forward with 20,000 men against 80,000 Ethiopians. The Emperor Menelek came out from church to head his army and on March 1, 1896, the Italians were defeated at Adowa. Over 6000 of them were killed or captured. This defeat ended Italy's dream of conquering Ethiopia and it drove Crispi finally from power.

The low state of Italian morale is shown by the fact that no efforts, either of King or of Army, could induce the parliament to vote the money for a new colonial campaign. On that point the people, as well as the parliament, were agreed.

The year 1898 was marked by serious bread riots in Milan and elsewhere, and by severe repression of socialistic movements. It is perhaps significant that these events took place when the King and the Ministers were uttering platitudes to celebrate the jubilee of the constitution, and when thirty provinces were placed under military

spended between 1898 and
ntury of the constitution, it
worth continuing. Troubled
strations, and King Humbert
ragedy, however, tended to
a reaction in its favour. The
fact that it was not deeply
rulers were strangers to two-
ss was evident and the new
ple increased the prestige of
ve than his father. He took
istry in 1901, which showed
and did something effective
bination.

the time from 1901 to 1914
social unrest, however, con-
en San Giuliano was Foreign
pursued. In 1911 Italy picked
with her, seizing Tripoli and
e Aegean. Strangely enough
barren Turkish province was
ient, holding out to them a
oman Empire overseas. The
e in 1913.

beral Italy declined; for the
ct descent from the Risorgi-
1914–18, it was beginning to
d; that far from fulfilling the
surrection) United Italy had
oups who felt this disillusion-
for disenchantment. The first
zzini and his followers, who

had seen in the resurrection of Italian greatness hope for all Europe, even for all mankind, had made their peace with United Italy, but had not seen in the circumscribed politics of the eighteen-seventies any realisation of their generous hopes. Nor did the next generation see, in the correct observance of the Constitution of 1848, the careful adherence to parliamentary forms and the all-too-rapid succession of Ministries, any of the dynamic growth which they had been led to expect from national renewal. The slight widening of the franchise in 1882 was no compensation for the general failure of the Left Governments to abolish the grist tax or to deal with illiteracy. The complete failure of Crispi and the collapse of parliamentary government in 1898 turned the idealists to Socialism, though on the whole to Socialism of a revisionist kind. The first two Socialist deputies were elected in 1882 but by 1900 there were 32 in parliament. Under Turati's leadership they played a full part in parliamentary life. Giolitti's period continued hodden grey in colour as far as domestic politics were concerned.

The second group disappointed with the effects of the Risorgimento comprised the descendants of the moderate leaders of 1848–49 and 1859–60. The Right, as we have seen, withdrew from politics and had been reinforced in its withdrawal by its Catholic loyalty. In 1882, however, Depretis, who was of the school of Machiavelli, made a pact with Minghetti, the old leader of the Right. There is ground for believing that the old families gradually returned to public life, if not to parliament, taking positions of responsibility in the civil service or as Prefects. But though loyal to the state they were opposed to the Governments in power. The Catholic Church continued hostile to the liberal state and continued to command the loyalty of the old families and the peasants. Moreover, it developed a social policy and attached the working class by Catholic trade unions. By the end of Giolitti's time the *non expedit* no longer held and a Catholic electoral union operated in the General Election of 1913. The Catholic position in politics developed, like the Socialist, in a direction that drew men away from the liberal state. It was part of a rebellion against Giolitti and the Giolittian system.

The third group disappointed with the results of the Risorgimento was interested in a social revolution. For the peasant, and especially the peasant in the south, the Risorgimento had meant a hope of satisfying land-hunger and relieving poverty. But under United Italy no redistribution of the land had taken place. The peasant constituted the great excluded class of United Italy. For those critics who divided Italy into 'legal' Italy and 'real' Italy, the peasants and the workingmen were the 'real' country. Antonio Gramsci, the Communist leader who died in 1937 after years of imprisonment by Mussolini, was the chief source of the theory of *la rivoluzione mancata*, the revolution that failed to happen. He had, of course, a political purpose and developed his theory as a way of appealing to the peasants among whom the Communists were weak. There was historical truth in it none the less. He argued that the bourgeoisie had not, as they had in France at the time of the Great Revolution, allied with the peasants. Then, they had carried out a redistribution of Church and *émigré* land to the advantage of the peasants. United Italy had betrayed the Risorgimento. The bourgeoisie which had joined with the landowners to make United Italy had made it at the expense of the peasants. The expected social revolution had not happened.

The first of the substantive reasons for dissatisfaction with the political system of liberal Italy was the degrading trafficking and corrupt bargaining that dominated parliament. Liberal Italy was a true parliamentary state. Parliament, not the King, determined the composition of Ministries, that is to say, no Ministry could govern without a parliamentary majority. But all Ministries were coalition Ministries. Ministerial office circulated among a small group of men of whom each, or so it appeared, must have his turn of power. By the end of Giolitti's period Italy was a liberal democracy, for universal manhood suffrage had been established in 1911. But the system went back to a period when the political nation was much smaller. It is, indeed, customary to trace it back to Cavour's *connubio* or alliance with the Right, in the Piedmontese Parliament in 1852. Depretis's pact with Minghetti in 1882 followed that precedent. The system whereby Ministries were transformed, rather than replaced, was known as *trasformismo*. It was said that bargaining and trafficking prevented an alternation of power between a party in office and a party which offered an alternative Government. There was much moral aversion from *trasformismo* and a growing disrespect for a parliament which tolerated it. This did not help parliament to resist the Fascist attack.

The second substantive reason for dissatisfaction with the political system of liberal Italy was that parliamentary weakness was reflected in national politics. There were no well organised or even clearly defined political parties. There was thus no means of canalising political debate. This was not surprising when the political nation was small, but it set up political habits as a substitute for genuine debate which were not appropriate to the larger political nation of the Giolittian period. When so much of the population was poor, illiterate and bound to the long daily work-routine in order to survive, a narrow franchise was not altogether out of place. But it had the effect of preserving rather than breaking down political indifference. Political indifference allowed another practice to grow up from which, too, there was much moral aversion. This was clientèlism, *caciquismo*. Each Deputy had his clients, his following of friends in Rome through whom he could get things done, that is, could obtain advantages for his locality. He had not been elected to support a party or a body of opinions in parliament, but to gain favours for his neighbours at home. It was a practice which also weakened parliament's power to resist the Fascist attack. Indeed, the political clientèle made the Fascist bands of friends seem a not altogether unfamiliar phenomenon.

The origins of fascism lay in the interventionist crisis of 1915. In

May 1915 *fasci di azione rivoluzionaria* (groups for revolutionary action, the first squads) were formed by nationalist and revolutionary agitators for Italian intervention in the War. Three features distinguished it from all other political movements in Italy. It was violent. Its adherents had no scruples in resorting to violence and were completely ruthless in using force to gain their ends: indeed, they admired violence as virile. Violence was, however, sporadic, unpredictable and lawless; for they preferred the fiat or decree of the leader that had to be obeyed to any rules or laws and a style of behaviour to any code. The second feature of the movement was that it was irrational and addressed itself to the creation of emotion rather than conviction. If it was true that the movement modernised politics to make them suitable to an age of mass action, it was because its adherents depended upon an understanding of crowd psychology and their power to stir up loyalty, and hate, devotion and anger. They depended less than any previous politicians upon personal contact and arguments directed to the individual mind by the spoken or written word. Mass media, apart from the cinema, did not, of course, exist in the twenties. The third feature was the leader: at the top the Duce, lower down the *ras* or *federale*. Fascists claimed to belong to a movement, not to a party. The founding rally on March 23, 1919, neither founded a party nor adopted a political programme. Party organisation came later (1920–21) and fascist doctrine later still (after 1929). The Fascists were kept together by a personal leader. Many of the squads had their origin in groups of kinsmen and friends and they seemed to spring to life spontaneously and disappear as mysteriously. The provincial *ras* or *federale* owed his power to no formal assignment, but to his personality, his ability to terrorise, manipulate, or spellbind. Coupled with personal ascendancy was hierarchy. The ras had village or commune bosses (*federali*) below him and the Duce above him. Nevertheless Mussolini had to manoeuvre with great skill to preserve a relationship with the various sections of his followers so that his decree would, in fact, be immediately obeyed.

Benito Mussolini was born in the Province of Romagna in 1883, the son of a blacksmith and a schoolmistress. Already in his boyhood he refused to be bound by any rules. His contempt for morality and religion began then and was lifelong. He identified himself with his father's 'populist. anarchic socialism.' As a young man he was 'an intellectual without the wealth to sustain the career of an intellectual.' At thirty he became the editor of the socialist newspaper *Avanti*. But his Socialism was adulterated with many other ideas. From Nietzsche he culled the doctrine of the superman as popularly misinterpreted. (The Nietzschean superman won his victories over himself and not over other men.) From Georges Sorel, the syndicalist, he culled a scorn for the cowardice and peace-loving complacency of the middle class; from Wilfredo Pareto, the sociologist, ideas about the prime importance of the community or group; from Max Stirner, the anarchist, ideas about the relationship between the individual and the group. During the War of 1914–18 he founded his own newspaper, *Popolo d'Italia*, and used it to make his political return after the War. The interventionist crisis had convinced him that the Socialist Party had reached a dead end. His return to politics was in the nationalist cause.

Most people think of the poet Gabriele d'Annunzio as the typical Italian nationalist of this period and his romantic, but hopeless, seizure of Fiume on September 12, 1919, as typical of their mentality. But there were other leaders such as Enrico Corradini, who founded the Associazione Nazionalista with its weekly journal *L'Idea Nazionale*. Already in 1913 five nationalists, headed by Luigi Federzoni, had been elected to the Italian parliament. Moreover, there were some half-dozen societies, many of them old and not originally political, such as the Dante Society of Rome or the Navy League, which acted as channels for currents of nationalist thought. Nationalism, then, at the time of the War and just afterwards was an inchoate but not insignificant movement. In May 1915 it welled up into demonstrations for entry into the War on the side of the Entente Powers. These were not demonstrations of sympathy, but of ambition. Italy wanted *Italia irredenta* from Austria-Hungary. They were interventionist: Italian national honour demanded that she should intervene and not be left out of great events. Those who might have opposed or controlled the agitation were strangely passive. The Socialists and democratic Left seemed to be paralysed. Giolitti had resigned in March 1914 in one of the parliamentary manoeuvres characteristic of the system; San Giuliano had died in October 1914. Salandra, the Prime Minister, proved incapable of quieting the rising dissatisfaction with neutrality and out of hostility to Giolitti was even courting the nationalists' favour. Giolitti, when he realised the seriousness of the interventionist agitation, came back to Rome. The parliamentary majority fell away from the Government and could, it has been thought, have been rallied by Giolitti to the policy of neutrality. But Giolitti, too, became passive. He declined to form a Government and would not take responsibility for keeping Italy out of the War. So Sonnino, the new Foreign Minister, negotiated the Treaty of London (April 26, 1915) and Italy joined the Entente Powers. The triumph of the nationalists was already a triumph for the politics of unreason, since Italy was ill-prepared to win a war which most Italians had not wanted.

The war effort proved profoundly dissatisfying. It allowed Fascists to affirm that it was an unfinished episode which their movement was gloriously to conclude. The defeat of Caporetto was remembered and not the victory of Vittorio Veneto (see above, pp. 81, 88). A Fascist victory must in good time avenge the defeat. Finally, the war disastrously impaired the authority of the Government and the Liberal

Parties from which it was drawn. Successive Governments had failed to organise Italy for victory, had failed to prevent or quell the Turin riots of August 1917 and in the end had failed to bring home from the Peace Conference Italy's due reward. Italy gained Istria, Trieste, the Trentino and part of the Tyrol, but not Dalmatia nor colonies. Giolitti returned to office in June 1920, but even he failed to restore the authority of the Government, which had sunk still further during the so-called Red Year of 1919–20. With the onset of post-war unemployment, strikes and riots, involving the extreme Left and a Communist minority, culminated in the occupation of the factories in September 1920. They were answered with the violent retaliation of the Fascist squads—the *fasci di combattimento* (combat groups) had been formed in 1919. The Government looked helplessly on. November 1920 was a turning-point. The occupation of the factories having failed, there was a marked turn to the Right away from Liberal Italy. During the winter of 1920–21 the Fascist movement expanded dramatically.

It drew its support from five principal sources. Many of the leaders of the Fascist squads were young army officers. Excited by the effort and comradeship of war, disappointed by its results, they saw in the leadership of squads both a prolonging of the War and the means of discovering a satisfying national identity. With them should be grouped non-commissioned officers and other demobilised soldiers, who shared this attitude and were confronted, in addition, with the difficulty of recovering or finding civil employment. The Fascists attracted the ablest and most energetic of the ex-servicemen. Secondly, they attracted the workmen for whom Socialism was too remote and doctrinaire and to whom the strikes and riots of the past year had brought no gains. But the mass support for the Fascist movement was lower middle class and not proletarian. The workingmen on the whole stayed loyal to Socialism and to the trade unions, Catholic and Socialist. The third group, then, comprised employees or self-employed men, shopkeepers, and people at the lower levels of the teaching and legal professions. They looked, paradoxically, to the Fascist squads for the protection against violence and attacks on property which the Government no longer seemed able to supply. A fourth source of support was found among the wealthy industrialists. A few of them from the beginning looked to the Fascists to protect them against the Communists whom they feared. In 1919 Mussolini, as proprietor of the *Popolo d'Italia*, was given large contributions by Milan businessmen. Finally, the Fascists seemed able to attract the young Bohemian intellectuals, those who called themselves the intellectual proletariat. Marinetti and the Futurists were their most articulate spokesmen.

After the inaugurating rally of March 1919, the Fascists acquired a skeleton organisation. An elected Directorate of five men, a Secretary and annual Congresses were the marks of organisation, but it did not develop, because there were always two possibilities in front of the Fascists and they never chose one to the exclusion of the other. One possibility was development as a normal party within the normal political framework. The advantage of pursuing this possibility was that, with the decline of the Liberal Parties, there seemed to be a position waiting to be filled in the middle between the two great mass parties by a third mass party. On its Left would be the Socialists, on its Right the Popolari, the great Catholic Party under the priest, Don Sturzo. In the middle it would have the decisive influence, allying Right or Left as suited it. The other possibility was to develop further the technique of violence, to shed all democratic forms, to become increasingly militarist—the military element had so far been confined to Mussolini's office bodyguard—and more insistent upon the leadership principle. The advantage of development in this direction was that the power of armed force would give the movement virtual autonomy. Corresponding to these two possibilities were two dominant kinds of Fascist. The city Fascists, mostly students and ex-combatants, and their *fasci di combattimento*, put on a new basis in 1920, hoped for the abandonment of violence and a future of normal politics. Their capital might be said to be Bologna, where Dino Grandi was the leader. They were to develop into the moderates of the Party. The Fascists of the Provinces, mostly peasants and rural workers attracted by promises of land reform and protection against the Socialists, were not democratically inclined and favoured violence. Their capital might be said to be Ferrara, where Italo Balbo was the leader. They were to develop into the militants of the Party. In 1921 both possibilities were simultaneously pursued. The Fascists joined the *Bloco Nazionale*, an electoral coalition of Liberal, Democratic and Rightist Parties. Their candidates looked like normal election candidates for the General Election of 1921. In July 1921, Mussolini made the Pact of Pacification with the Socialists and came out in favour of turning the movement into a party. On the other side, the Fascists organised the collusion of civil and military authorities in their recruitment, organisation and intimidation of voters. They founded the Fascist militia, bound by an oath of loyalty to Mussolini (October 1922) and they organised the syndicates or unions of employers and employed. Confindustria and the Confederation of Agriculture came to be wealthy and powerful and were sources of Fascist party power outside the framework of the state. (After 1925 they were of course incorporated in the fascist state and replaced the banned trade unions.)

After the Election there was a prolonged political crisis. While the bourgeoisie lost confidence in the state, the parliamentary leaders gave less and less ground for confidence in it. First Bonomi, then Facta, failed in efforts to form a broad Ministry of national pacification. Every move against the Fascists was foiled by their cleverer tactics. When, for example, there was a move to suppress the squads, Mussolini decreed that all members of the Party should be members of the *fasci*, so that the squads could not be suppressed without suppressing the Party as well. No liberal or democratic Government could suppress a political party.

The unresolved political crisis made the power vacuum in which the march on Rome took place. The march on Rome (October 27–28, 1922) imposed upon the King a Fascist Ministry headed by Mussolini. He made a Ministry on October 30 containing representatives of the Popolari, Democratic, Liberal and Nationalist Parties. He had come to power by legal, constitutional means; for the march on Rome was a colossal 'bluff'. What needs explanation is the King's decision. He had at his disposal the regular army—12,000 men under General Pugliesi—which could have effectively defended the city against the fascist mobs mostly coming up from Naples by train, had he decided to use it. Victor Emmanuel, however, was not temperamentally given to open confrontations; he wished to avoid bloodshed; there is some evidence that General Diaz advised him to accept Mussolini on military grounds. But the lesson of the prolonged political crisis probably weighed most with him. Though militarily he might fight it out, political success might still elude him; for the events since the Election of November 1921 had shown him that the Liberals had virtually abdicated power, and where else was he to look?

There was as yet no question of dictatorship. The parliamentary state had been rescued by a national movement. The anniversary of the armistice on November 11, 1922, was used to demonstrate national unity. Parliamentary forms were fully observed when the Chamber voted Mussolini full powers for financial and administrative reform. By the end of the year d'Annunzio's armed legionaries had been disbanded, two Communist leaders, Bordiga and Gramsci, had been arrested and the Communist Party driven underground. The parliamentary state began to look less secure.

Mussolini's dictatorship was a personal dictatorship. His first step in establishing it was to form a set of party institutions parallel to the apparatus of the state. The militia, already mentioned, was parallel to the army. The Fascist Grand Council, set up at the end of 1922, was parallel to the Government. The *federali* were parallel to the Prefects and organs of local government. These institutions gave him a party power-base which he could use against the state. But the final outcome was not a party dictatorship. This was because, by using one wing of the party against the other, Mussolini always retained some freedom over against the party. He has been shown to have allied with the moderates when the militants threatened to control him and with the militants when the moderates came on top. These were the tactics behind the scenes. We must turn to the events which succeeded each other on the political stage.

In April 1923 Mussolini broke with the Popolari, still keeping Liberals and Nationalists in his Government. He could afford to shed that alliance because the support of the Catholic Church was assured by the advantages he offered it. Fascist educational policy restored religious teaching in the primary schools. Mussolini's break with the Popolari indicated that he was prepared to govern without a parliamentary majority; for the resignation of the two Popolari Ministers from his Government meant that their party went into opposition. He was able to put a bill for changing the electoral law through the Chamber, though he no longer possessed a formal majority. The bill was incidentally a defeat for the Fascist militants in the ever-changing tactics he pursued to preserve his personal freedom. It was put through the Chamber by the combined votes of those (the Socialists) who hoped it would show up the fundamental hostility of the Fascists to parliamentary forms and of those (the Liberals) who hoped after its passage that the Fascists would be reasonable and those (some of the Popolari) who hesitated to oppose because the Pope had repudiated Sturzo and the politics of the party he had led. It was called the Acerbo Law — after an under-secretary. It marked a long step towards dictatorship because it allowed the Government to nominate two-thirds of the Chamber. In the General Election which followed in January-February 1924 the Socialists and Popolari suffered. The Fascists gained, but the Chamber of 1924 was a falsification rather than an expression of the popular will.

The next event was the murder on June 10, 1924, of Matteotti. Giacomo Matteotti, the Secretary of the Socialist Party and leader of the Socialists in the Chamber, was a man notable for his courage, integrity and steadfastness. He was immovable in the face of Fascist blandishments. Matteotti had to be killed for two reasons; he was the unconquerable element in the parliamentary opposition; he had an unpredictable effect on the struggle between the two wings of the Fascist Party and Mussolini's manoeuvres between them. He had made a speech on May 30 which showed up the unreality of the moderate Fascists'moves for a reformist, tolerant fascism. He was too dangerous for Mussolini, who was held responsible for the murder, to allow him to survive. An important feature of the Matteotti crisis was the secession from parliament of the greater part of the opposition. The Aventine seceders, as they were called, refused to stay to be abused and even physically assaulted by Fascist Deputies. Secession was, of course, not the way to defeat Fascism.

For a week after the murder Mussolini was extremely vulnerable. The Fascist militia was mobilised. But it was touch and go until Mussolini was received by the King on June 17. The rest of 1924 saw Mussolini preoccupied by a complicated set of manoeuvres within the Party as he strengthened himself first against the militants, then the moderates. By January 1925 he was sufficiently strong as head of the Government and sufficiently free within the Party to take the decisive step. On January 3, 1925, he proclaimed his personal responsibility for crime and terrorism. 'I alone assume the political, moral and historical responsibility for what has happened.' This was Mussolini's break with the Liberal, parliamentary state, the political beginning of his dictatorship. In October 1925 the Socialist Party was suppressed. On October 3, 1926, all opposition Parties were suppressed. The rule of the one-party state had begun.

About 1925 the term totalitarian, which was invented in Italy, became current. It was used to describe a régime in which all public institutions as well as the machinery of Government became imbued with the assumptions and manners of the single, mass Fascist Party. Totalitarian does not refer to the power of the state. It has been pointed out that the old word 'authoritarian' would have described the all-powerful state and a new word would not have been needed. The Fascists were obliged to retain the existing civil servants at their posts, because the Party could not provide enough qualified men to replace them, however much talk there was of a new kind of administration by groups of experts. The civil servants, on the other hand, wanted to stay in the posts on which they depended for their income. There was really no alternative to a slow impregnation with the assumptions and manners of the Fascists. The process had gone far enough by 1925 for Mussolini to risk the law of May 18 which allowed the dismissal of officials who showed 'incompatibility with the general directives' of the Government. By then no clean sweep was necessary. At the same time an oath of loyalty to the régime was imposed. Local government was more quickly coloured with Fascism. Where the Prefects submitted to Fascist control, as they early and widely did, the local *ras or federale* took over. He sustained his power by force, intimidation, financial levies, patronage, the cultivation of friends in Rome, the making of a personal clientèle, even by a mere natural ascendancy. In the villages or communes the local, lesser *federali* aped the *ras*. By 1925 all local elections had been stopped, the power of the Prefect under the Minister of the Interior was absolute. After 1925 the Prefects, like other civil servants, were purged of noted non-Fascists and their powers were increased. It was obvious to all now that local government bore the Fascist imprint. By 1925 the freedom of the press had disappeared. Strict control was only persistently exerted from that year. The decree had been issued in 1924. Its administration was in the hands of the Prefects. They could warn any editor guilty of publishing 'false or tendentious news' or damaging 'the credit of the nation at home or abroad' and other offences depending on interpretation. The Prefect might dismiss any editor warned twice within a year. The press now too bore only the Fascist imprint. The freedom of the judiciary disappeared the following year. The Law on Public Security of November 1926 instituted the penalty of political exile from one's home or an instruction to live in a prescribed place for political opinions disliked by the régime, reintroduced the death penalty, and enacted a number of provisions which left the individual with no appeal against the state and no right that he could legally defend against it. The police, though kept under the Ministry of the Interior and its officials, took on the Fascist manners and largely absorbed the repressive functions once exercised by the Fascist squads. Prevention rather than persecution was the motto, but after 1926 Italy was nevertheless a police state because of the prevailing Fascist assumption that the individual had no rights against them as the agents of the state. What was total was the Fascist demand on the individual.

'Totalitarian' then did not mean that the state was subordinate to the Party. Mussolini saw to that. As the Fascist assumptions and manners came to infect all the institutions of Italy, the independent power of the Party declined. This is not the place to describe the several internal crises through which it passed between 1923 and 1925.[1] Suffice it to say that they were caused by the perennial struggle between the moderates and the militants, that Mussolini exploited them, if he did not cause them, to strengthen his personal power, and that the Party ended up in 1926, monolithic in structure, centralised, hierarchical and run by its officials. After the Party Statute of October 1926, there were no more elections. The General Secretary nominated the *federali* and the *federali* nominated the local Party secretaries. At the top was the Directorate and General Secretary with his secretariat, next, the Fascist Grand Council and, then, the Party Congress. There was no question now of the dynamic of permanent revolution: the Party had been tamed. Grand Council meetings assembled only to be harangued by Mussolini. The Congresses became staged occasions for Mussolini to vaunt the glories of his régime and the new Roman Empire he was bent on resurrecting by his foreign policy. But to control the formalised bureaucratic Party Mussolini needed the Crown. For the power to inspire the Crown he needed fine achievements: the colonisation of Tripoli, the conquest of Ethiopia and intervention in the Spanish Civil War. When achievements failed him, he boasted of his glorious intentions. He inflated the strength of his army, navy and air force. In the end he seems to have believed his own false figures or those with which sycophantic officials supplied him. By the time of his intervention in the War of 1939–45 he had lost all contact with reality. The story of these ventures must be told in the next and a later chapter.

Something may, however, appropriately be said here of another

---

[1] Adrian Lyttelton, *The Seizure of Power. Fascism 1919–1929* (1973) is authoritative on this subject.

167

side of Fascist rule. In 1929 Italy elected an all-Fascist parliament. There was much rejoicing, though it is difficult to believe that the quarter of a million Germans in the Tyrol or the three hundred thousand Slavs on the Adriatic willingly returned as their representatives, members of a party which denied them the elementary rights both of language and of nationality. Yet the rejoicing was a sign that the Fascist state felt secure and assured of its power. It had outgrown its opportunist origins. It began, therefore, to develop a philosophy of its own. This was the philosophy of the corporate state. The idea which governed it was that all interests should be represented in institutions which would control production, employment, social welfare and labour relations. By the mid thirties a structure of such institutions existed. Every Italian citizen belonged to a workers' and employers' syndicate or a professional society according to his occupation. There were some 160 of these. Above them were 22 corporations, 16 representing employers and workers together in one particular branch of production, 6 representing the professions. At the top of the structure was a National Council of Corporations, supposed to be a deliberative assembly, and a Ministry of Corporations. In theory this structure was to evolve into an 'economic democracy'. In fact the Ministry of Corporations was a powerful directing body for the application of economic decrees and the institutions below it, instruments for regimenting the working class.

Another result of the new self-assurance of the Fascist state was that it achieved a settlement with the Catholic Church. This exhibited not only the diplomatic skill of Mussolini, but a victory which every other ruler of united Italy had failed to secure. He reconciled the Quirinal with the Vatican, the Italian nation with the Pope, and thus healed a festering and gaping wound in the body politic. On February 11, 1929, a solemn Concordat was signed between the Pope's representatives and Mussolini. Cavour, with all his ability, had failed to propose an acceptable settlement with the Pope and inaugurated a treatment of the Church which shocked even liberal Catholics. His successors exaggerated his methods and their treatment of monastic orders and of the Church was drastic and oppressive. The Pope retaliated by disavowing and condemning their acts, by asserting his undiminished rights to the Patrimony of St. Peter, and by retiring into the Vatican and becoming a prisoner there. In that capacity he excited the sympathy of the whole Catholic world, and was able to cause endless difficulties to the Italian state and monarchy. For to a large section of Christianity he represented the greatest moral force in the world.

The Pope's situation was a peculiar one. He was the Vicar of Christ and as such the earthly head of the Roman Catholic Church. Before 1870 he was also the sovereign prince of the Papal States, though the Romagna and the Legations had already been incorporated in the Kingdom of Italy. In October 1870, after Victor Emmanuel had entered Rome, the subjects that remained to the Pope voted by a plebiscite for incorporation in the temporal kingdom of Italy. The voice of the people decided the fate of the Pope. Victor Emmanuel's decree of October 9, 1870, declared Rome and the Roman Provinces to be an integral part of the Kingdom of Italy. The King thus evidently deprived the Pope of his power as a temporal sovereign, though leaving him in unmolested possession of the Vatican. Legal opinion asserted that the Pope's person was inviolable and his residence immune, that he had 'rights of legation'. But he enjoyed all such privileges by virtue of the law of a particular state (Italy), and not by virtue of international law. Yet later practice is not wholly consistent in this view. Bismarck recognised the Pope as an arbitrator in a territorial dispute, but The Hague Conference refused to admit his representatives in 1899 and the League of Nations declined to accept him as a member.

The position of the Pope was unique, transcending all rules, and there was a great increase of his prestige during and after the War of 1914–18. His appeals for peace were considered seriously by the various belligerents. After the war, France found it expedient to resume diplomatic relations with the Pope; and, in addition, Great Britain sent diplomatic envoys and in 1928 established a regular legation to the Holy See. It is obvious that he thus possessed or acquired an international status. Further, by the Concordat concluded with Mussolini in 1929, Italy recognised the Vatican as a State with access to the sea, and the Pontiff as an international person. Considerable rights and privileges were also granted to the Church throughout Italy, the exercise of which all Italian Governments since 1860 had previously denied. In return a solemn reconciliation between the Kingdom of Italy and the Papacy took place. This was the most important part of the agreement. The Pope conferred a lustre on the Fascist Government, and gave an authority to its continuance, in a way that no other ruler could have done. The survival of Mussolini's dictatorship for over twenty-one years was due in no small measure to his reconciliation with the line of the supreme Pontiff.

Theoretically, during the inter-war years, Italy remained a monarchy. The constitution was still based on the *Statuto fondamentale del Regno* granted by Charles Albert to his Sardinian subjects on February 8, 1848. According to this constitution, which remained in force until Italy became a republic in June 1946, the executive power of the state was vested exclusively in the Sovereign, and was exercised by him through his Ministers. In fact, during the Fascist régime, Italy was governed by the personal dictatorship of Mussolini.

There is one point of difference between Fascist Italy and Nazi Germany which is worth mentioning. The Fascists had no theory of racial purity: anti-semitism has never flourished in Italy, and Mussolini himself had on several occasions condemned any such movement. It was not until 1938, and then probably under German pressure, that a manifesto was issued, sponsored by University professors, defining the principles of a Fascist racialism. First, Starace, General Secretary of the Fascist Party, and then, on July 30, in a speech at Forli, Mussolini himself affirmed these principles. At the same time, a violent anti-Jewish campaign was waged in the press, and in August 1938 the first measures were enacted against the Jews, excluding them from the teaching profession. Other measures, mainly aimed at excluding Jews from the professions and the public services, followed in swift succession, but the active persecution of the Jews in Italy did not aim at extermination. There were no concentration camps or death chambers.

Chapter 10

INTERNATIONAL CO-OPERATION AND DOMESTIC CONFLICT. CIVIL WAR IN SPAIN, DIVISIONS IN FRANCE

Historically the League of Nations stands for the extension of the international organisation of Europe to include all the world. In the nineteenth century four, five, six Great Powers had determined what happened in much of the world. Europe was thoughtlessly referred to as the world. European opinion was called world opinion. The American participation in the War of 1914–18 began to bring to an end Europe's identification of the world with itself. 'The Congress System' of 1815–22 comprised four, and then five Powers. The concert of Europe comprised six Powers. The League of Nations (in 1932) comprised fifty-seven members each with an equal right to be heard and regarded.

Changes in technology, new communications, industrialisation, the assimilation of the problems of one Nation to those of another, meant that the scale on which things could be done had been enormously enlarged. Things once done nationally could be done internationally. The League of Nations responded to this change, not to call it revolution. Under the League's auspices the Permanent Court of International Justice was organised in 1920 and met for the first time in 1922. It obtained increasing authority and an increasing amount of business. The administration of former German colonies and of territory formerly part of Turkey (Syria, Lebanon, Palestine, Iraq and Transjordan) was pronounced to be a trust and placed under the Permanent Mandates Commission of the League. The mandatories, France, Britain, Japan, Australia, New Zealand and South Africa, were required to report to it to show that they had discharged the trust. It proved difficult for the mandatory not to regard itself as the sovereign of the mandated territory. Yet the doctrine of trusteeship, used by President Roosevelt during the War of 1939–45 to apply to conquered territory, was taken over by the United Nations and turned out to be the most effective instrument of decolonisation. So that the system of mandates was important. This enumeration of international organisations for political or legal business may end with the Commission on Disarmament. It worked out the business for an international disarmament conference. Organisations for transacting economic and social business were more numerous. The tasks of fighting disease, slavery, drug-trafficking and trafficking in women and children were entrusted to a variety of international organisations under the League. The International Labour Office, which still exists, began under the League's auspices though it later became autonomous.

In so far as the League of Nations was born out of President Wilson's Fourteen Points (see above, pp. 92–3) its purpose was to end the use of force in the settlement of international disputes. It developed an elaborate procedure for conciliation between nations in dispute. For the event of war nevertheless breaking out, it provided means to distinguish the aggressor and for action against the aggressor by other members. The second of Wilson's Fourteen Points, on the freedom of the seas, Britain succeeded in excluding from international regulation. The Fourteenth Point stated that 'a general association of nations must be formed under specific covenants for the purpose of affording mutual guarantees of political independence and territorial integrity to great and small states alike.' The crucial step was taken when the drafters of schemes—and there were many for the first League of Nations Society had been founded in England in 1916—abandoned the form of an alliance treaty and moved towards a new kind of document for which Wilson found the name of Covenant. Articles 11 to 16 of the Covenant related to war and its prevention. It was unfortunate that the Covenant was made the first section of all the Treaties signed at Paris, for this gave ground, however specious, for regarding the League as an organisation of the victors to dragoon the vanquished. It was an idea which died out in the mid twenties, but was revived by Hitler. The instruments through which the League acted were its Secretariat, its Council and its Assembly. It was served by able Secretaries: Sir Eric Drummond and the Frenchman, Joseph Avenol, acted in succession. They were permanently at the League's Headquarters in Geneva and had a good deal of initiative. Their bureaucracy built up an invaluable store of knowledge and experience. The Council first met on January 16, 1920. It was a small body on which the Great Powers were permanently represented and to which four small Powers, at first Greece, Belgium, Spain and Brazil, were elected by the Assembly. The eight members with which it began were later increased to nine and the arrangements for including the smaller Powers were changed, but the principle of a fair representation of regions and status was preserved. It met as necessary, holding ten separate sessions in the ten months which separated the coming into force of the Covenant in January 1920 and the first meeting of the Assembly in November. The Council ran the League. It was an administrative body where the members co-operated in settling the international affairs which came within its competence. It was a mediatory body for the settlement of disputes. The Assembly of the League met once a year. It had business referred to it from the Council and business which delegates to it themselves raised. Each member of the League equally had three delegates and one vote. Devices, however, were soon invented— adding expert advisers, for example—which brought very substantial delegations to Geneva. Its recommendations went back to the Governments for consideration. It was not a deciding body. It has been called 'the most original and successful organ of the League.'[1] It was a forum for international discussion. It was a true parliament of the world where views and decisions could gain the support of an extraordinarily wide public opinion. Both the Council and Assembly gained greatly in prestige during the first years of their existence. By 1924 the character and reputation of both were established. The League provided a new method for the conduct of international relations. It began to fail when Prime Ministers and Foreign Ministers began to use it as a simple adjunct to the old diplomatic machinery.

There is no need to elaborate the fact of Wilson's failure to gain the ratification of the Treaty of Versailles by the American Congress. He had campaigned strenuously up and down the country for it; it was twice voted upon (November 1919 and March 1920) and twice failed against the Republican majority in both houses; he had, unfortunately, resisted all attempts at amendment and he had the enmity of Henry Cabot Lodge. So the United States was not a member of the League and never became one.

The disputes which came before the League in its first year arose out of the disturbed conditions on the fringes of the U.S.S.R. The countries involved were Persia, Finland, Sweden, Poland, Lithuania and Armenia. The year on the whole showed the limits of the power of the Council. It was never to be stronger than the strength of its strongest member. In 1921 the League was called upon by the Supreme Council of the wartime Allies, still in session in Paris, to determine the German-Polish frontier in the rich industrial district of Upper Silesia (see above, p. 96) over which it had reached deadlock. The League grew in prestige as the result of the complicated régime it devised which remained in operation until 1937. The Germans were induced to evacuate, the industrial area, thought to be indivisible, was divided and safeguards were established where joint German-Polish enterprise was necessary. The League provided the administration of the Saar Basin for fifteen years, until the plebiscite could be taken in 1934 (it was actually taken on January 13, 1935), and it provided the Commissioner who administered the free city of Danzig as long as it existed. No other body could have done these

---

[1] F. P. Walters, *A History of the League of Nations* (1952), p. 118.

duties. The League gained further successes in 1922 by, for example, the drawing of the Albanian-Yugoslav frontier and by effecting the political and financial rescue of Austria. Its plan for Austria was operated by a League Commissioner acting in Vienna from 1922 to 1925. The Assembly, the fifth, of 1924 saw the League at the highest point of activity and importance it had yet reached. The year saw the first steps forward to the good years of 1925–29. It was irony that Woodrow Wilson should have died in February of that year.

Ramsay MacDonald, Prime Minister and Foreign Minister in Britain, Edouard Herriot, Radical-Socialist Premier in France and Gustav Stresemann, briefly Chancellor in Germany, co-operated to bring forward both European recovery and the development of the international forum the League provided. The first two attended the Assembly of 1924 in person. It was the first time a British Prime Minister had gone to Geneva. Two lines of approach to European problems were followed by Britain and France, both concerned to make the League work as an instrument of international Government. Much preparatory work had been done for a disarmament conference and from this it had become plain that no progress could be made until European security was strengthened. Britain and France, therefore, took up the idea of a general treaty of guarantee. The other line of approach was to strengthen the League by the admission of Germany and the U.S.S.R., or at least Germany, if the U.S.S.R. was not obtainable. MacDonald had renewed Britain's diplomatic relations with Russia. The first line led to a draft treaty of mutual assistance which eventually became the Geneva Protocol of August 1924. It provided that if a dispute was taken before the League and the League's decision proved unacceptable to one disputant, that disputant was no longer free, as under the Covenant, to go to war but must go to arbitration; a country which chose to go to war rather than follow this procedure would automatically become an aggressor, against whom all other members were bound to assist each other, as well as being bound to aid the victim of the aggression; the Council of the League would summon a general disarmament conference for June 1925. The Protocol was signed by seventeen states, but the new Conservative Government which succeeded MacDonald's Government in Britain refused to sign, partly at least because of the opposition of the self-governing Dominions with Canada, conscious of her unguarded frontier with America, at their head. The general guarantee had to be abandoned and the policy of regional guarantees put in its place.

Meanwhile along the other line of approach there had been some success. Stresemann, now Foreign Minister to Marx as Chancellor, announced in September that Germany would aim at entering the League at the earliest possible moment. Negotiations were begun to see that she obtained her conditions for doing so: a permanent seat on the Council and exemption, in view of Germany's disarmed condition, from the obligation of Article 16 to take, eventually, military action against an aggressor. The outcome, her admission, after a delay caused by other claims to permanent seats on the Council, in September 1926 has already been noticed (above, p. 150). Meanwhile Russia in the person of Litvinov began to appear in Geneva, making contact with various international social and economic operations of the League.

In Britain, Sir Austen Chamberlain and, in France, Aristide Briand were now in charge of Foreign Affairs. Stresemann was even more successful in establishing co-operation with them than he had been in working with MacDonald and Herriot. Together they pushed forward the policy of regional pacts after Stresemann had proposed a Rhineland Pact. The Locarno Treaties had the advantage for all those involved that they left Germany's eastern frontier unguaranteed. The series of agreements was initialled at Locarno in October 1925 and signed on December 1 at London. Of these the most important were:

(a) A treaty of mutual guarantee of the Franco-German and Franco-Belgian frontiers, signed by Germany, France, Great Britain, Italy and Belgium;

(b) A Franco-Polish and Franco-Czechoslovak treaty for mutual assistance in case of aggression by Germany.

To take the second treaties first, it is significant that Great Britain refused to sign them, though affirming that she recognised the obligations of Article 10 of the Covenant towards Poland and Czechoslovakia. Unreality showed its head here, for Britain's bond, as a result, differed as regards Covenant obligations and as regards the obligations of an ordinary treaty. In the case of treaty (a) Britain promised to defend France by arms if attacked by Germany or Germany by arms if attacked by France. This obligation was also an unreal and one-sided one. For, if Germany attacked France, Britain's small expeditionary force (say 80,000 men) might have rendered France some aid. But, if 3,000,000 well-trained and perfectly armed Frenchmen attacked some 100,000 imperfectly armed Germans, the aid given by some 80,000 British to the Germans on land would obviously have been negligible, despite the assistance of the British fleet. Britain had promised to defend Germany if attacked, but she could not really have enforced her guarantee by arms. Thus realism had been set aside, and an atmosphere of illusion began to descend on international politics. Britain never made the necessary military plans to implement her Locarno obligations. The agreement of Locarno was not useless, though it was shortsighted. It did not fulfil Austen Chamberlain's prediction that it would mark 'the real dividing point between the years of war and the years of peace.' But it did produce a temporary atmosphere of goodwill and a period of conciliation, which was of importance and might have been decisive. It was, on the other hand, unfortunate that Chamberlain was not sympathetic to the new way of conducting international relations which idealists saw in the League, and considered it rather as a new part of the old diplomatic machine.

It is obvious now, though it was less obvious in 1925, that the future depended on the League's being able to negotiate a general disarmament all round. Limitation of armaments had been promised at Versailles. The Allies had justified the disarmament of Germany and other enemy Powers by the clause that it was 'to render possible the initiation of a general limitation of the armaments of all nations.'[1] This promise was now repeated and its observance would at once have made Locarno a real treaty. For if the German and French forces were approximately equal, Britain's force, however small, could guarantee one against the other. Under the Peace Treaty Belgium had as big an army as Germany, and that state of things obviously could not continue if Germany was ever again to be a Great Power. Mussolini, though anxious for armaments, was quite willing to accept parity with France. But France seems to have been always unwilling to accept anything like parity either with Italy or with Germany. As discussion progressed, attempts were made to substitute words for swords. The United States, on the hint of Briand, first agreed to a mutual engagement with France, in which both parties renounced war as an instrument of policy. F. B. Kellogg, the American Secretary of State, negotiated this pact, and finally invited all nations to sign a treaty, renouncing aggressive war. This Kellogg Pact had been signed by all important nations, including the Soviet Union, by the year 1930. It was not really as far-reaching a pact as appeared, for nations only renounced wars of aggression. It had a real propaganda value for peace, but it was unreal in another sense. Nothing would happen if a signatory Power broke its word–there was not even provision for consultation of the signatory Powers in case of a breach.

The acid test, that is of general agreement to disarm, remained. If this could have been agreed, it seems clear that the Covenant, as subsequently interpreted by the Locarno agreement and the Kellogg Pact, would have ruled the world. It is true that in January 1921 the United States had invited Britain, France, Italy, China, Japan, Belgium, Holland and Portugal to a conference at Washington on naval disarmament and the problems of the Pacific. It had sat from November 12, 1921, to February 6, 1922. There an important treaty had been signed by the United States, Britain, France, Japan and Italy providing for a ten-year pause in naval building and the limitation

[1] Preamble to Part V (Military Clauses) of Treaty of Versailles. This was not a contractual bond, as the Germans later asserted, but was a moral obligation on the Allies.

of capital ships to give a ratio of 5:5:3 for the United States, Britain and Japan respectively, with France and Italy proportionately lower. This five-Power treaty had been accompanied by a nine-Power treaty and both had been signed in February 1922. But the central problem, how to bring armaments under international control, so that each nation would no longer be sole judge of its own needs, remained. The preparatory work for facing this problem had begun in 1925, but it was unduly and unfortunately delayed. There were some good reasons for this. One was that expenditure on armaments was tending to fall anyhow; another was that the Soviet Union was not a member of the League until 1934, though she attended the meetings of the Preparatory Commission on Disarmament. Delay proved disastrous. In October 1929 Stresemann died and, though the Rhineland was finally evacuated in 1930, that same year saw the increase of the Nazi strength in the Reichstag from 12 seats to 107. It was quite clear that in Germany, at least, those who wished to abolish the Treaty of Versailles altogether were growing stronger. So even in 1930 the chances of a satisfactory disarmament settlement were lessening.

Then in 1931 came the disaster of Manchuria. The international face of China, seen by Europe, was calm, capable and distinguished. She was a member of the Council of the League from 1920 to 1922. She was negotiating to free herself from the restrictions on her sovereignty imposed by concession-hunting Powers in the one-sided treaties of the nineteenth century. China on nearer view was seen to be in anarchy, torn to pieces by quarrelling war-lords. Yet Chang Kai-shek had established his capital at Nanking and seemed to be slowly extending his authority from there over the rest of China. The League was committed to aiding what was thought to be the Chinese recovery. From 1929 a steady stream of Secretariat officials and League experts went to China. On September 18, 1931, a foray occurred at Mukden in South Manchuria between Japanese soldiers, there to protect the Japanese-owned railway, and Chinese troops in retaliation, it was claimed, for an attack on Japanese railway guards. The province was nominally part of Chang Kai-shek's China, but really ruled by a local war-lord. The importance of Manchuria to Japan was strategically very great. Moreover, it was bordered by the Soviet Union and Japan did not wish it to be subject to Communist influences. China at once appealed to the League. Japan proceeded with her policy, on the ground that China was too disorganised to govern Manchuria, and set up a puppet state known as Manchukuo under Pu Yi, the ex-Emperor of China. The intention was to remove all the authority of the Chinese Republic and definitely to place the new state under Japanese influence. Japan completed these arrangements by officially recognising the new state on September 15, 1932. This really ended the matter, and the inability of the League to do what it wished to do, to protect China's integrity, according to Article 10 of the Covenant, became completely and painfully evident. After a full investigation of the circumstances and the publication of the valuable Lytton Report, the Assembly of the League recommended a settlement by which Manchuria would be autonomous under China (February 24, 1933). Japan entirely disregarded this recommendation, continued her control over Manchukuo, and withdrew from the League. One day after the Assembly had given its final decision, the Japanese army made a further advance into Chinese territory and severed a whole vast new province, known as Jehol, from Chinese sovereignty, thus once more flouting the authority of the League. It was the more significant that she succeeded in doing so, since Henry L. Stimson, the Secretary of State of the United States, had taken an active part in exercising diplomatic pressure.

It was difficult to interpret the Manchurian invasion at the time. Though sympathy was with China, there was no inclination at Geneva to impute guilt to Japan and there was much readiness to recognise what she had at stake in Manchuria, in the presence there of her nationals and the investment there of her capital. In retrospect, it can be seen to have been a sign that the economic depression was making it difficult for the liberally inclined Japanese Government to resist the pressure of the militarists, who were soon completely to gain the upper hand. China had appealed to the League under Article 11 of the Covenant, which declared war or the threat of war between any two members to be the concern of all, and laid down forms of conciliation procedure. It became the chief object of Britain and France to prevent any appeal to Article 16, which obliged members to regard a war on one of them as a war on all and to sever all trade and financial relations with the aggressor. The policy of Britain and France (no longer in the hands of Chamberlain and Briand) was to avoid offending Japan in the conditions of economic depression. 'The victim of aggression should not throw the responsibility for dealing with it on the other members of the Council,' said Sir John Simon in the British Cabinet.[1] He had virtually repudiated Britain's League obligations.

Manchuria was followed by Shanghai. China answered Japan's Manchurian policy by boycotting Japanese goods in Shanghai. This was so successful as to provoke an invasion of Chinese territory by Japanese forces from the International Settlement of Shanghai. China appealed to Article 15 which obliged the League to investigate to determine the aggressor. The collective opinion was against Japan and forced her evacuation. But it was the opinion of the small Powers which had made itself felt, not that of Britain and France, who again were chiefly concerned to prevent the next step: from

[1] Quoted by George Scott in *The Rise and Fall of the League of Nations* (1973), p. 216, from a minute of the cabinet meeting of November 11, 1931.

Article 15 to Article 16. In July 1937 Japan again attacked China in the hope of acquiring her five northern Provinces. But this time the Japanese miscalculated: China resisted and Japan became embroiled in a major war, which lasted eight years and became merged in world war.

Disarmament, however, remained and, though the omens were not favourable, there was just a chance of success, if it became possible to reconcile Germany's claim to equality of rights with the French demand for security. One such moment occurred at the Disarmament Conference, which met first on February 2, 1932, when Stimson, Ramsay MacDonald and Brüning, the German Chancellor, were all present. The German terms were extremely moderate,[1] but the French Premier, Tardieu, went away electioneering and the opportunity disappeared. He was succeeded by Herriot, who was anxious for agreement, but unfortunately Brüning had to give way to von Papen, who in turn was succeeded by General von Schleicher, who was speedily replaced by Hitler. The arrival of Hitler to power and the excesses committed by Nazis caused the French and British Governments to revise their terms. They felt unable to grant equality of armaments to Germany without a trial period. They accordingly proposed that, for the first four years, Germany should convert her long-service army to a short-service conscript army but that no reduction of other armies should take place. During a second period of four years, equality of rights should gradually be conceded. Germany's reply was to withdraw from the Conference and from the League. Hitler was still prepared to offer favourable terms (November 1933), though they were a good deal stiffer than those of Brüning. He asked for an army of 300,000 men with twelve months' service.[2] He was prepared to accept a good deal less than parity in the air and would have agreed to a permanent and automatic supervision for his armaments. He did not ask for any reductions in the armaments of other states for five years. Britain and Italy thought these terms ought to be accepted. But a new French Cabinet, with Louis Barthou as Foreign Minister, brusquely terminated the negotiations, and in a speech at Geneva Barthou stated that France would never agree to any German rearmament whatsoever (May 30, 1934).

From this time onward rearmament began everywhere. Germany published in 1935 a new army law for the formation of a conscript army of thirty-six divisions, defying the Treaty of Versailles. Neither

---

[1] The German terms were: A Reichswehr of 150,000 with 6 years' service instead of 12 and a small conscript force of 50,000 men with 3 months' service. The principle of the non-possession by Germany of aeroplanes and the heavier weapons forbidden by the Treaty must be rescinded, but she would be content with 'samples' only.

[2] This number was actually less by 100,000 than the figure of 400,000 proposed by the British military section as the standing army for Germany at Paris in 1919.

Britain nor France did more than protest. An Anglo-German Naval Pact arranged for a limitation on German naval construction equal to about one-third of the strength of the British fleet. It was, of course, indirectly a full acquiescence in German rearmament. With the collapse of the disarmament proposals everything became estimated in terms of force. Germany hastened to arm, France to ally with the Soviet Union; Hitler accepted naval inferiority from Britain in order to detach her from the Franco-Russian group. The old game of the Balance of Power was thus being played out.

As force was beginning to be the law in Europe, the League was beginning to recognise that moral persuasion or, at least pacific blockade, was the limit of its activities. On May 2, 1935, a compact was signed between France and the Soviet Union. The Treaty conformed in principle to the idea of mutual guarantee and was within the framework of the Covenant, but it was really a thinly disguised military alliance. It caused great uneasiness both to Italy and to Germany and so also did the entry of the Soviet Union into the League in 1934. For Britain, who was reviewing her resources, this was a relaxation of pressure (particularly on the Indian frontier) of which she was much in need. The review of her resources had shown her that navally she was not strong enough to confront even one Power— Japan or Germany—with the hope of defeating it, if the other were hostile, let alone to take on a third—Italy—if these two were hostile. She adopted a new naval standard, so as to be able to deal with the first eventuality, but during 1936 and 1937 was unable to build to it. She had also to postpone the implementation of a decision taken in the same year to equip an expeditionary force of twelve divisions for the Continent. She gave priority to rearming in the air. But from 1936 steady rearmament was her policy.

The review of her naval resources was particularly important, because 1935 was the year of Italy's invasion of Ethiopia. Since collective action always depended upon the strength of the strongest Power, League action would ultimately depend, in this geographic area, on what Britain was prepared to do together with France. An incident took place in December 1934 at Wal-Wal, an oasis which Mussolini claimed for Italian Eritrea. The Emperor of Ethiopia, Haile Selassie, appealed to the League, bringing the dispute before it under Article 11 (conciliation procedure). The Italians accepted arbitration, though objecting to the arbitrators chosen by the Emperor. They dragged out the conciliation procedure until the season was suitable for invasion. Britain was intent on maintaining friendship with Italy. Sir Eric Drummond, now Ambassador in Rome, seemed unperturbed that no settlement was in sight. Britain proposed concessions by Ethiopia in return for a cession of British territory on the Red Sea coast. During the whole of the summer Britain and France circumvented League action by direct negotiations with Mussolini, whose claims on Ethiopia were constantly enlarged as they offered him more. There was no disputing by the late summer of 1935 that if war broke out Italy would be the aggressor. Nor was there any disputing the British and French intention to 'get round' their obligation under Article 16 (whenever action under this article should be required), though Britain did mobilise the Mediterranean Fleet. On October 3, 1935, Italy invaded at last. She was at once named 'an aggressor nation' by more than fifty nations assembled at Geneva, and economic sanctions were put into force against her in the shape of an embargo on imports and measures to deprive her of rubber, tin and other metals. Nothing was said of coal, steel or oil. This very decision of the League revealed its weakness (which was really the weakness of Britain and France), for Article 16 of the Covenant prescribed an immediate 'severance of all trade and financial relations' with an aggressor. Moreover, this 'severance' was meant, in fact, to be merely the preliminary to military action by all the members of the League. Not only were the economic sanctions imposed far short of a 'severance of all trade and financial relations,' but they were not meant as the preliminary to military action, being carefully chosen to stop at the point where they might cause it, by provoking Italy. Moreover, a limited policy of 'sanctions' could only operate on Italy slowly, while half-armed Ethiopians were immediately exposed to the full weight of the attack of a first-class Power, armed with tanks, aeroplanes and poison gas. Nor could Britain and France advance, as a justification of their policy, the public attitude. When in mid December the British Foreign Secretary, now Sir Samuel Hoare, and the French Foreign Minister, Pierre Laval, tried once again the policy of buying off Mussolini with a plan for carving up Ethiopia, a shocked public opinion expressed its outrage, all the greater because Hoare had just made an impressive speech to the League Assembly, proclaiming Britain's intention to stand by the Covenant. Public opinion triumphed and Hoare had to resign. But the oil sanction was never imposed. By April 1936 Addis Ababa had fallen and the campaign was over. Mussolini had crushed Ethiopia and defied more than fifty nations. The League acknowledged its defeat. All it could do was to decline to recognise Italy's conquest. Haile Selassie went into exile in Britain until he recovered his Empire during the War of 1939–45.

Hitler, who had of course sympathised with Italy, and supported her against the League while it was busy outside Europe, secured, at this point, a victory inside Europe, On March 7, 1936, he announced in a speech that he proposed to reoccupy the Rhineland (hitherto a demilitarised zone under the Versailles Treaty) with German troops. They entered the zone that night. He was following a policy of 'risks', as one of his lieutenants explained, but the 'risks' had been carefully calculated, and he won. His advance was not an armed threat to France's safety, for in numbers (36,500) his troops were, at first, not very menacing. But it was a tearing up of the Versailles Treaty by force, and a repudiation of the whole Locarno settlement. The last was the more serious, for Hitler had hitherto maintained that Germany was not bound by the Treaty of Versailles which had been forced upon her, but was bound by Locarno and similar agreements which she had 'freely signed.' He now threw both on the scrap-heap. His argument that the French Pact with the Soviet Union had violated the Locarno Pact, and thus justified his coup, was inadmissible. For, three weeks after the Franco-Soviet Pact was signed (May 2, 1935), Hitler himself had reaffirmed the obligations of Locarno. On the remilitarisation of the Rhineland, as on German rearmament, Britain held back the French, but they were probably not sorry to be able to blame the British for their joint failure to do more than remonstrate. Britain and France kept both matters for direct negotiation with Germany and out of the hands of the League. But Britain was also pursuing the bankrupt policy of bringing Germany back to Geneva and was tempted by Hitler's offer in his speech to re-enter the League, if the Covenant was separated from the Treaty and Germany's colonial claims discussed. Also the League was distracted by the struggle with Italy. Unanimity in condemning Germany would not have been secured there. In the end nothing was done, but something came of Hitler's action. On March 26, 1936, Sir Anthony Eden, as British Foreign Secretary, made it quite clear in a speech that Britain would defend either France or Belgium, or both together, if Germany attacked their territory or independence. For the first time in British history the guarantee of defending Belgium and France against attack was made clear and absolute and independent of circumstances.

The remilitarisation of the Rhineland had also a profound effect on the position of Belgium, which had ceased *de facto* to be a neutralised state in 1919. The German action now exposed her again to the threat of sudden attack from the east, in the face of which the Locarno guarantees were inadequate. At the end of 1936 the Belgian Government, therefore, determined to pursue a policy 'exclusively and completely Belgian,' and requested Britain and France to release them from the obligations of Locarno. Britain and France acceded to the Belgian request in April 1937, but maintained their guarantees of Belgian security under the Locarno Agreement, since the Belgian Government had expressed its intention to defend the country against aggression or invasion.

The year 1936 marks a definite stage in the descent into the abyss. The League had been discredited by its inability to intervene effectively either in the attack of Japan on Manchuria or in that of Italy on Ethiopia. It demonstrated its weakness to all the world by its failure to intervene over the Rhineland. And in the summer of this year, four months after Hitler's flouting of the League, another event took place which was to provide yet a further instance of the League's powerlessness.

This new event was the outbreak on July 18, 1936, of the Spanish Civil War. A sort of revolution from the Left had been attempted in Spain after the end of the military dictatorship of Primo de Rivera in 1930 and the fall of the Monarchy in April 1931. The new Republic had introduced a constitution in August 1931 which disestablished the Catholic Church. It followed this up by abolishing the state subsidy to the clergy, expelling the Jesuit Order and closing Catholic schools. It built schools on its own account and financed education well, in a drive against illiteracy. It introduced in March 1932 a complex piece of land legislation in an attempt to deal with Spain's most serious problem. A redistribution of the land was overdue. At one extreme there were too many large estates with too little capital invested in them, under-farmed and maintaining a large number of landless labourers, living in great poverty. At the other extreme, there were too many tiny farms, which intensified poverty even when they were owned by peasant proprietors. But tenancy agreements and property conditions varied from province to province and made successful land legislation by any single law virtually impossible. Certainly the first Governments of the liberally inclined Republic effected no social revolution. Next the CEDA, led by Gil Robles, came to power. The CEDA, or Confederation of Autonomous Rightist Parties, reversed the policies of 1931–32 and attempted a revolution from the Right. Its policy was Catholic and it believed in the corporative state. As we have seen Mussolini established corporations uniting employers and employed in Italy systematically after 1929 and, as we shall see, Hitler obliged every German to belong to the German Workers' Front (DAF) or to a professional Chamber, according to his occupation. But the CEDA failed to fulfil its programme. It, too, had attempted revolution and failed. Some argue that Gil Robles was debarred from extreme measures by his respect for the law. Others argue that he was an unprincipled man intent only on gaining power. In any event there was no Rightist revolution but, in October 1934, there occurred a rising of the Asturian miners—the culmination of a succession of strikes—which was viciously suppressed. The rising was defeated but the Socialists registered the real victory. The CEDA fell and a Popular Front Government, based on an alliance between the Socialists and Communists, came to power after the Elections of February 16, 1936. The two black years, 1933–34 and 1934–35, had been years of disintegration and polarisation, when both Left and Right learned to despair of the parliamentary process as the means to obtain their objective: social justice on the Left and public order and individual security on the Right. Two equally strong sides both bent on revolutionary change, but in opposite directions, meant civil war. From February to July 1936 the army plotted against the Republic. On July 18 there were military risings all over Spain and General Franco crossed with the Nationalist troops from Spanish Morocco to the mainland.

There were places of intense, desperate and ruthless fighting, but the fighting was concentrated. The Republic after all was fighting as a responsible Government, while the Nationalists relied on a war of attrition, hoping to limit destruction and to reconstruct as they widened the area under their control. The vicious fighting was in Madrid, Barcelona, and the Santander-Bilbao area and, generally, on the frontier of the area controlled by the Nationalists when the last phase of the fighting began in March 1937. The best remembered single incident, the bombing of Guernica from the air, was ascribed to the Germans, fighting on the Nationalist side.

Both sides received foreign aid from the first. The causes of the Civil War were essentially Spanish. But the war was internationalised. Nevertheless, it was not a rehearsal for the European fighting of 1941–45, because what was at stake was also essentially Spanish. The conditions in which international Communism or international Catholicism—one hesitates to describe Fascism as international, or even to describe the Spanish Nationalists as Fascist—offered solutions to Spain's social and economic problems, were also essentially Spanish. One should bear in mind that Spain was a thinly-populated, rural country. Only eight million out of her twenty-four million may have belonged to an industrial working class and half a million to an artisan class. Working-class problems were caused by the concentration of the workers in a few cities and industrial centres. There were Anarchists (deriving their ideas from Bakunin), Syndicalists (trade unionists with Anarchist ideas), and Marxists among them, but they found it difficult to unite into a disciplined movement. The Nationalists, drawing their strength from Church, army and landowners, found it easier to unite, but they were not dependent for unity upon those factors which united Fascists in Italy or Nazis in Germany. The chief reason why the Civil War was not a rehearsal for the drama of 1941–45 was that neither the Germans nor the Soviet Union succeeded in taking over the side which they supported.

The amount of assistance furnished by the U.S.S.R. to the Republic and by the Italians and Germans to the Nationalists is known.[1] But the quantity of assistance was less important than the quality and the timing. Foreign intervention was important, but it is not 'satisfactory simply to add up' what each outsider gave or sold. Franco on July 19 asked Mussolini for 12 bomber and 3 fighter aircraft. There arrived late—on July 30—12 aircraft of which 9 only were effective.

---

[1] There are tables in Hugh Thomas, *The Spanish Civil War* (3rd edn, 1977), p. 985. His Appendix Seven discusses foreign intervention.

During the interval, Franco asked Hitler for 10 transport planes. Hitler promptly sent 20 Junker-52 transport planes. Their arrival was decisive, for it enabled Franco to carry by air-lift the Army of Africa across the Straits of Gibraltar and with it to make a salient on the mainland, soon linked to the area held by the Nationalists further north. Had this help not come when it did, the Nationalists would still have won, but the war would have taken a different course. This help was more important than the simultaneous purchase by the Republic of aircraft from France. The Communists set up an International Fund to help the Republic and organised an International Corps of 5000 men. Other International Brigades were formed of men of various views, Socialist, Marxist, Anarchist, or of no views at all, except a generalised idealism. Some 35,000 men are estimated to have been in the International Brigades fighting for the Republic. In addition the Soviet Union sold some 1000 aircraft and numbers of tanks and artillery pieces to the Republic. Aid to the Republic had a decisive effect, when Russian *matériel* and the arrival of the International Brigades enabled it to save Madrid in November 1936. 'The critical time was the start of November when the Soviet Heavy T-26 tanks and the Mosca and Chato fighters dominated the battlefield.' Russian technical advisers were also said to be important. The *matériel* sent by Mussolini and Hitler was important in keeping up the morale of the Nationalist Generals after they had failed to take Madrid. Messerschmitt fighters and Heinkel bombers and the Italian Savoia-79 'won the air' for the Nationalists. Moreover, in 1937 the Condor (Air) Legion, as it was called, already in full strength by December 1936 and autonomous under its own German Commander, was an important asset for the Nationalists all the time. On the other hand, an Italian force, acting independently, was defeated in the battle of Guadalajara, with heavy losses, by the Republic. Yet just as the Republic was never controlled from Moscow, so Franco took what the Germans or Italians gave and sold, without submitting to their control. The most that Germany gained in *concrete* advantage were mining rights of no great importance.

Franco's success in the Civil War was a military victory. By the time the war ended in 1939, foreign aid was drying up on both sides. The Nationalists' economic position was good and Franco's régime was recognised by Britain and France as well as Germany and Italy as the legitimate Government of Spain.

Theoretically the Spanish Civil War, as a wholly domestic conflict, was not the concern of the League of Nations. Only limited use was made of the League's machinery by the Powers in their efforts to prevent the Spanish conflict from developing into a general European war. The Blum Government in France, alarmed by the dangerously conflicting reactions of the French to the war, soon forbade the sending of *matérial* to either side. With British support, it then proposed an international agreement to observe the principle of non-intervention. By the end of August all European states had adhered to the Non-Intervention Agreement. On September 9, 1936, an international committee was set up in London called the Non-Intervention Committee. Its original function was to exchange information on the ways in which the different members—they included Russia, Germany and Italy—intended to fulfil their pledges. It soon found that its main business was to hear complaints of their having been broken. This committee was unconnected with the League. The Spanish Republic continued to raise at Geneva its legitimate complaint against the presence of foreign armies and air forces on Spanish soil. The Governments which sent them were by definition aggressors, but the League was powerless.

There was one instance of apparently effective international co-operation during the Spanish Civil War. Even this was illusory. During the first half of 1937, acts of piracy in the Mediterranean increased alarmingly: neutral shipping and even four British warships were attacked by aircraft and submarines, which were undoubtedly of Italian origin in the service of the Spanish Nationalists. Early in September 1937, Britain and France took the initiative in summoning a conference of the Black Sea and Mediterranean Powers to concert measures against this threat to neutral trade. Germany and Italy refused to attend the Conference which met at Nyon, and, on September 14, 1937, agreed on measures to be taken for the defence of shipping routes and the destruction of piratical submarines, surface craft and aircraft in the Mediterranean. The Italians had withdrawn their submarines before the Conference met.

In dealing with the situation created by the intervention of other Powers in the Spanish Civil War, the members of the League failed to formulate a policy which they were prepared to put into effect. The complaint of the Spanish representative at Geneva that the only effective non-intervention applied to Spain was the non-intervention of the League of Nations was clearly justified. The embarrassment of the League was reflected in the vote of the Council, in May 1938, on the Spanish Government's resolution that members of the League should consider ending the 'legal monstrosity of the formula of "Non-Intervention," which the open intervention of Germany and Italy rendered a mockery.' The resolution was rejected by four negative to two affirmative votes, but there were nine abstentions.

It seemed as if the Spanish Foreign Minister, Álvarez del Vayo, were justified in his declaration before the League Assembly, on September 19, 1938, that there had grown up at Geneva 'a strange theory according to which the best method of serving the League was to remove from its purview all questions relating to peace, and the application of the Covenant.' And the events of the autumn, discussed in the next chapter, were left to provide the answer to his question as to whether the great western democracies, before acting within the framework of the League, intended to wait until half the European nations represented at Geneva had been paralysed by discouragement, panic or the fact that they had ceased to exist as independent states.

The Spanish Civil War ended with the surrender of Madrid on March 30, 1939, and on April 20, 1939, the Non-Intervention Committee in London was formally dissolved.

As has been seen, much depended for the success or failure of the League, when European Powers were involved in disputes, upon the action of Britain and France. Since in all the instances of such disputes—Germany's repudiation of the Treaty of Versailles by rearming and remilitarising the Rhineland; Italy's invasion of Ethiopia; German, Italian and Russian intervention in Spain—the Powers concerned were neighbours of France, her action or inaction was crucial. But France was already paralysed by domestic divisions. In chapter 24 of Volume One it was said of France that she was a country with the appearance of great instability, but with important sources of real stability. Short-lived administrations, Ministries constantly changing, gave this appearance of instability. But the Chamber of Deputies itself, the army, the civil service and the Prefects gave her real stability. Central, executive government in France was weak, but her parliament was strong. Government was weak because the Chamber could thwart the action of Ministries in several ways. Parties could bring Ministries down by uniting to criticise and censure, but this occasioned no appeal to the nation, because elections were held automatically and only every four years. The last President to dissolve the Chamber before its four-year term ran out and appeal for a new majority for the Ministry to the electorate had been MacMahon in 1877. No President tried such an appeal after him. So parties united to thwart a Government, not in order to replace it with an alternative Government. Finally parliamentary commissions with the same area of competence as individual Ministers, and therefore their rivals, long interpellations and single Deputy's bills were indicated in that chapter as other means at the disposal of the Chamber for thwarting Governments and reducing them to immobility. It was also noticed in that chapter that there were writers, some with powerful minds, others mere restless agitators, who stood at the head of a kind of intellectual alienation from the Republic. These characteristics, Ministries instable and weak in action and the public's readiness to criticise the whole system by which the French state lived, marked France just before the War of 1914–18. They were equally features of the inter-war years. But the material, so to speak, on which they worked was different, so that their consequences in confusion of mind, deep political divisions and ultimate inaction were much more serious.

The twenties were, nevertheless, good years for France. The effect of the destruction and devastation in the north and east was to promote economic activity. Work and money were put into reconstruction and modernisation. During the first decade after the War of 1914–18 France recuperated to an extraordinary degree. Despite heavy war losses in men, extensive material damage to her agriculture and industry, and a heavy war debt, France became prosperous and reconstruction of the devastated northern and eastern regions was accomplished with rapidity and thoroughness.

There was a falling away of prosperity in the mid twenties, but the end of the twenties were boom years. The effect of the Wall Street crash and the slump which struck Germany first and then, in 1931, Britain, was delayed for France. Moreover, its effect gradually accumulated and so passed at first unobserved. At the beginning of 1934 it was as if France suddenly became aware of economic recession and the reaction of Frenchmen was extreme. It was as if at a stroke the effort put into recovery had become pointless.

Nor was this all. Two things happened at once. On February 2, 1932, after long years of preparation—a Preparatory Commission had sat from May 1926 to January 1931—the Disarmament Conference at last met. France attached very great importance to this. She was herself disarming as part of the budgetary deflationary policy adopted by all French Governments between 1932 and 1936 to deal with the economic difficulties. It became all the more important to reduce all armies for national purposes to the smallest size possible, while setting up an international army to which all should contribute. The Disarmament Conference was greater than the League of Nations, for it included the U.S.A. and the U.S.S.R. which the League did not. One other thing gave importance to the Conference. Even before the advent of Hitler, France was alarmed by rumours of German rearmament. The greatest alarm was caused by von Schleicher's 'Plan for the Reorganisation of the Army' announced on July 26, 1932. So the reduction of national armies and the establishment of the international army became capitally important. But the Conference, as has been seen, failed. First, on September 16, 1932, Germany withdrew. France continued her struggle. Herriot produced a new plan; MacDonald made proposals; Roosevelt made fresh proposals. Daladier, as we have seen, came forward with the idea of a four-year trial period before Germany attained equality of treatment. This in itself was a confession of failure. It was 1934 and the Conference ended. So the second thing that happened early in 1934, after a gradual approach, was a sudden understanding in·France that she must look to her own, old methods of preserving her safety. Hopes vested in a new method had been vested in an illusion.

Somewhere about 1932 an intellectual movement had become observable among the young, especially those from conservative, bourgeois backgrounds, and those in the military academies. It had expressed itself with vigour and force. It is possible to list some eight journals to which men with the most diverse careers in front of them, some to be Ministers under Pétain, others to be leaders of the Resistance, contributed articles or editorial services.[1] The future of this movement would have been different had it had a single enemy, but its enemy was confusingly uncertain. It seemed to have one, clear enemy, namely liberal individualism. But as its attacks developed, the alternatives it indicated were order and discipline as opposed to capitalist disorder and, on the other side, the interests of society as opposed to those of the individual. Was the enemy, then, fascist authoritarianism or communist anti-capitalism? France had become confused and intensely divided, because it was impossible to fight both enemies at once and, worse, the ally with whom she might be associated in fighting either enemy was intensely distasteful. This had lain in the future in 1932. Those who sought renewal by greater order and discipline were strong in the army and in the various associations of ex-servicemen. They were dangerously strong in the army, for there they had made a number of secret networks. The *Croix de Feu* was the oldest of these organisations. It grew from 15,000 members in 1930 to 60,000 in 1933. The anti-Communist activities of the army's underground networks attained considerable importance. Three of these networks became notorious: the *Corvignolles*, the *Cagoule* and the MSAR (*mouvement social d'action révolutionnaire*). Next, between 1933 and 1934 a convergence happened between the Leagues and Societies of the extreme Right, to which army officers, landowners and professional people tended to belong, and the veteran associations, to which the petty bourgeois and, sometimes, peasants belonged. Two of these last, the *Union nationale de Combatants* and the *Union Fédérale*, had each about 900,000 members in that year.

The climax came in the events of February 6, 1934. There was a sudden unanimity of hostility to 'the system' and a major riot in Paris. According to one description the Right denounced the Government in the Chamber of Deputies, the *Croix de Feu* assembled on the Esplanade des Invalides, *Action Française* militants in the Boulevard St. Michel, the *Jeuns Patriots* at the Hôtel de Ville, the *Union nationale de Combatants* on the Champs-Elysées. There was shooting. The Government fell. But on February 7 the militants could persuade no one to complete the revolution and it was all over.

In 1934, then, France acquired a Government of the Right under Doumergue. Louis Barthou, the last representative of the great political generation which had governed France from the beginning

---

[1] P. M. de la Gorce, *The French Army* (1963), translated from the French, pp. 216 ff.

of the twentieth century, was Minister for Foreign Affairs. Doumergue attempted to revise the constitution by conferring on the
President the power to dissolve the Chamber and appeal to the
nation. But Doumergue failed. In order to reunite France it became
supremely important to have a foreign policy that was not ideological. It was also important to return to the old ways of safeguarding
her security. Louis Barthou led France into the policy of making an
alliance with Soviet Russia. This was signed in May 1935, but not
ratified until February 1936. An important change of opinion happened between those two dates. At the same time, Barthou led
France towards a *rapprochement* with Italy. She had several causes
of dispute with Italy. They were rivals for naval supremacy in the
Mediterranean and, their overseas possessions being adjacent, they
had colonial rivalries. The outcome was the useless and short-lived
Stresa Front of France, Italy and Britain. The Stresa Declaration of
April 1935 committed its signatories to oppose by any suitable means
the unilateral repudiation of treaties.

Before these events were completed, Barthou, together with King
Alexander of Yugosalvia, on an official visit to France, was assassinated at Marseilles in October 1934. So the Barthou period ended
and that of Pierre Laval began. Pierre Laval took the French movement towards Italy to such an extreme that he was repudiated by the
nation. His foreign policy was far from avoiding the taint of ideology.
It was the time of the Ethiopian crisis and Laval was the source itself
of compromise with Mussolini and the undermining of League action,
such as it was. He was the author of the Hoare-Laval plan (see page
181) and he was the strongest opponent of 'the oil sanction.' The
attempt to compromise with Italy caused the Radicals to desert the
Ministry and Laval had to resign (January 22, 1936).

Laval offended in yet another way. The French constitution
allowed the Government to rule by decree instead of formal legislation in times of emergency. During the War of 1914–18 the
President had freely exercised his *pouvoir réglementaire* to make
règlements de nécessité. The practice was continued during the inter-
war years and was extended by the willingness of the French Chamber to confer on a Ministry plenary powers to deal with a particular
situation. The abuse of this authority by Laval's Ministry, when some
500 decrees were issued, led to a revulsion against such authoritarian
methods.

The importance of Pierre Laval is that he caused to come into the
open what the statesmanship of Barthou had held suppressed. Laval
aligned France with the Right: he wanted an understanding with
Germany; he cultivated the friendship of Italy; and he thought he
could draw Britain into the same alignment. The Ethiopian War
occurred between the signing of the Franco-Soviet Pact and its ratification. It changed the French attitude to that Pact. It no longer

seemed evidence of a foreign policy free from ideological prejudices; for the policy of Laval over the Ethiopian War divided France as she had not so far been divided over foreign policy. The two Frances confronted one another. The pronounced move towards the Right in foreign policy had caused the Left to coalesce. In 1935 the two trade union movements (the CGTU and the CGT) united. To fight the Elections of 1936 the Communists, the Socialists, the Socialist Republican Union and the Radical Party united. They were joined by other small Left-wing groups, such as the *Ligue des Droits de l'Homme*. They formed together the Popular Front. The aims of the Popular Front, as stated in the Programme of January 11, 1936, ranged from 'the cleansing of public life' to serious economic reforms and social legislation. The Popular Front won the Elections and Léon Blum formed a Popular Front Government with a policy of economic and social reform. In reform Blum made some headway until he, too, was reduced to inaction by the obstruction of the Chamber. In foreign policy he took good care to dispel the notion that the Government was following an ideological line. But then, in the summer of 1936, came the Spanish Civil War. This immediately deepened the abyss between the two Frances. Blum was under pressure from both sides. He found it impossible to reunite the nation. From now on France in diplomacy was reduced to passivity. Public opinion was confused. Those who yielded to 'the temptation of fascism' found it difficult to be patriotic, for patriotism was normally a matter of defence against Germany. Those who turned Leftwards found it difficult to be patriotic too. Communism and Socialism were internationally inclined. The moderate as well as the extreme Left found it increasingly difficult to think of security in terms of alliance with the Soviet Union, which between 1936 and 1939 looked unlikely to act with Liberal Europe. If the U.S.S.R. meant what it said when it disclaimed an ideological policy and it intended to work with Liberal Europe, what was it doing in Spain? The Munich Agreement of 1938 to which we shall come in the next chapter only confirmed French confusion. It divided France into Munichers and anti-Munichers and the arguments between them were most bitter. The division of France into Resisters and Collaborators was already implicit in the failure of the Governments from 1936 onwards to reunite her. But between 1936 and 1938 there was still much fluctuation and many changed sides, sometimes more than once. France was confused as well as divided. A bold and decided foreign policy was impossible for her.

Chapter 11

THE THIRD REICH, 1933–39

National Socialism was a sort of philosophy formulated by Hitler in his speeches and in *Mein Kampf* (1924). Unlike Fascist Italy, the Third Reich had its doctrines from the beginning and did not invent them to suit the situation that the struggle for power had made. This 'philosophy' was nationalist in the sense that Hitler and his followers asserted their conviction in the political supremacy of Germany and in her future of supreme human, cultural and political achievement. Most Nazis were without the educational qualifications to know from the inside the philosophic, literary and musical heritage which was theirs by right. Hitler as a young man was a voracious reader, but not of the German classics. His reading was sporadic and tended to the pamphlet rather than the long work: he read to confirm dogmatic ideas he already had formed. The Nazi 'philosophy' was a social philosophy in the sense that its doctrines were about group activity and not about the individual. Hitler and his followers commended the activities of the group, the party or the masses. They mistrusted individual independence of thought and dignity of behaviour. Their militarism was the militarism of massed armies and not the heroism of individual courage. The most important characteristic of this 'philosophy' was that it was racist (*völkisch*). The racial theory on which Nazi anti-Semitism was based was popular in Austria in the last years of the Dual Monarchy. Hitler, who was Austrian, may have picked it up in Vienna between 1908 and 1913 when he lived there in some obscurity in a men's hostel. Anti-Jewish prejudice was not necessarily racist. It would not be felt against a Jew who was baptised or was assimilated by education and way of life into the society in which he lived. It was made racist through the influence of two otherwise unimportant books. A French nobleman, Arthur de Gobineau, published just after the middle of the nineteenth century a book called *The Inequality of Human Races*. He was himself descended from Norman stock and the thesis of his book was the immense superiority of the northern or Nordic races over all others in character and intelligence. He regarded them as the foremost representatives of the Aryan stock and as innately superior to all other races, especially to the Arab and Semitic races. Thus a Frenchman exalted the historic mission of the Germans. And an Englishman, the son of an English admiral, took up the same theme and carried it to considerable notoriety. This was Houston Stewart Chamberlain, who settled in Germany, assumed German citizenship, and identified himself wholly with the German state and race. His strange book is called *The Foundations of the Nineteenth Century*. It was received with much applause in Germany and was specially praised by William II and through his influence was widely circulated among the influential classes of the country. It is a survey and interpretation of universal history, full of digressions and not without inconsistencies. It regards history as embodying a conflict between the Teutonic and Semitic races. The writer recognises a certain greatness in the Jews and speaks with reverence of Christ; but ends with a fierce indictment of them as incapable of what is greatest in humanity and as guilty of intolerance and cruelty. Contrasted with the Jews stands the Teutonic race, which Chamberlain interpreted in the widest sense, so as to include not only the Germans but also the Celts, the Scandinavians, and the English; but the highest representatives of the Teutonic race are to be found in Germany. France he regards as decadent. She rejected the Reformation which was an assertion of Teutonic characacteristics against the Latin races and has fallen under the influence of the Jews. The future of mankind lies with the Germans, when they have found a religion worthy of them and have grown conscious of their destiny. Hitler drew many of his convictions from this book, probably directly. He might have drawn them indirectly because, although the anti-Semitic current in Germany developed out of a dislike for the Jews' spiritual and economic power, the promotion of genuinely racist hatred during the years before the War of 1914–18 was the work of Richard Wagner, the Younger, whose son-in-law Chamberlain was. Hitler may well have read articles or pamphlets emanating from the Bayreuth Group.

Connected with the hatred of Jews was the hatred of Marxists and of Marxism with whom and with which they were wrongly identified. It would be easy to cite a number of Jews, such as Rathenau and Ballin, who opposed revolution in Germany, and it is probable that the majority of Jews were anti-Marxist. But these facts made no difference to the ideas suggested by Hitler for the education of the masses. These were that Judaism and Marxism were equally dangerous, that they were inseparably united, and therefore that they must be jointly destroyed. A crusade against one should also be a crusade against the other. The most effective means of fighting them was obviously the cultivation of a strenuous German nationalism and of the old military virtues of loyalty and obedience. Thus National

Socialism arose as it were from rejection of Marxism and antagonism to the Jews.

Finally, the adaptation of Darwin's evolutionary theories to social and political purposes strengthened the conviction of German racial superiority. It also produced another characteristic doctrine of the National Socialist kind of philosophy: the doctrine of permanent struggle, reflected in the title of Hitler's book, and used to justify not only the persecution of the Jews, but admiration for the strong, cruelty to the weak, biological experiments and, in the end, even the extermination of the Jews. In a speech of June 22, 1944, Hitler said: 'Nature is always teaching us that she is governed by the principle of selection. Victory always goes to the strong. Nature does not see in weakness any extenuating circumstance. . . . War is therefore the unalterable law of the whole of life. . . . Struggle has been the very essence of existence.'[1]

Germany under the Third Reich was an autocracy acting through a chaos of overlapping institutions. 'The leading politicians were not a Government but a Court.' Göring, Ribbentrop, Goebbels, Himmler, Hess, Bormann had importance not because of the positions they held in Government, but because of their relationship to Hitler. Hitler had no administrative sense. Institutions served not an administrative purpose of his, but a power-political one. They helped to make him the essential arbiter in the constant struggle for power. He used one institution against the other to prevent either from acquiring too much power and both from acquiring power at his expense. Confusion was also the result of Hitler's dislike of desk work, of his giving oral decisions, which contradicted each other, and of his essential political skill. Much of this last depended on his isolation.

No attempt can be made here systematically to set out the multiplicity of organisations performing overlapping functions. Some indications can, however, be given. First, the institutions of the state were matched by parallel Party activities rather than taken over by the Party. Next, duties of different men within the Party overlapped. Thus after December 1932 Robert Ley was head of the political organisation, but Rudolf Hess and Martin Bormann ran the Party Chancery. In 1933 Ley was put at the head of the trade unions, reorganised as the German Labour Front (DAF) to which all German workers were to belong. DAF soon developed a gigantic apparatus over which the Party had no authority. The Party and DAF were rivals. Thirdly, the institutions of the state duplicated one another, so that there was a Chancellery for the Reich President and another for the Reich Chancellor. Hitler's habit was to deal with Ministers

---

[1] Helmut Krausnick, Hans Buchheim, Martin Broszat and Hans-Adolph Jacobsen, *Anatomy of the S.S. State* (1968), p. 13, quotes this speech. The book is a set of studies prepared for the Frankfurt trial of 1963, translated into English.

separately. The Ministers met together at ever-widening intervals, so there was nothing like Cabinet decision or a Ministry's policy or even any way of sorting out separate areas of competence. Moreover, it was Hitler's constant practice to make new appointments of men with full powers to do work already assigned to a Ministry. Ley's work as head of DAF thus overlapped with the business of the existing Minister of Labour. Göring was appointed in 1936 to direct the Four-Year Plan, when the Ministry of Economics already had the direction of economic planning. The Ministry of War under Blomberg found itself at odds with the Army Command under Fritsch; the Ministry of Economics under Hugenberg was at odds with Dr. Schmitt and Hjalmar Schacht, Head of the Reichsbank, representing the business interests upon which Hitler relied. When they, one after the other, in turn succeeded Hugenberg, they battled against the Ministry of the Interior and the SS (see above, p. 153) over the persecution of the Jews, which they thought endangered the economy. The Ministry of Justice was retained despite the arbitrary death sentences and sentences of imprisonment inflicted by the SS and the secret police (Gestapo). The Ministry of the Interior overlapped with the SS, its section in charge of citizenship being drawn into the Jewish question. Indeed, the Ministry of the Interior was a veritable centre of battles, battling for the central authority against Bormann's efforts to capture local government for the Party, and battling for the law against the SS and the secret police. The Ministry of Foreign Affairs was traversed by Hitler's own intrusions into foreign affairs and by the activities of his personal agents. It was, however, within the two essentially political Ministries, that of Propaganda and Science and that of Education and Popular Enlightenment, that most confusion of functions occurred. Goebbels was put at the head of the Ministry of Propaganda when it was set up in March 1933. When a Ministry of Education was set up in May 1934 this was already to make an overlap, for school policy properly speaking belonged to the states so that the new Minister, Alfred Rosenberg, was interested not in this but in some of the business already being done by Goebbels. Rosenberg was to battle with him as well as with the Reich Youth leaders, Max Amann and Baldur von Schirach, not to mention the Churches. Goebbels's field of competence was overlapped from the beginning by that of the Party's Press Department, headed by Dr. Otto Dietrich with a hierarchy of agents under him. Max Amann, in so far as he was in charge of the *Völkischer Beobachter* and then of all the Party's publishing, was another potential rival. The Foreign Organisation of the Party under Hess overlapped from another side. There was also at the beginning a Reich Government Press Chief, Walther Funk. Funk eventually became Minister of Economics and Dietrich became Reich Press Chief, Funk's title being dropped and Dietrich building a rival empire to that of Goebbels from his new position.

The question almost asks itself: how could a régime resting on administrative chaos survive, let alone fight and nearly win a war fought on an unprecedented scale. The Führer principle is the answer. The Leader at all levels of central and local government ensured action and results or, to use a favourite Nazi word, 'dynamism.' The principle that the Leader's command was law and was to be instantly obeyed was characteristic of the National Socialist Party from its beginning, but it was not fully effective until Hitler established his supremacy over a reorganised Party after the end of his period in prison, following the failure of the Munich *putsch* (see above, p. 147). According to the record of a conversation with Otto Strasser—the Strasser brothers were to be pushed aside, and Gregor shot, as possible competitors—in 1924 Hitler said: '. . . you would give every Party member the right to decide on the idea—even to decide whether the leader is true to the so-called idea or not. This is democracy at its worst, and there is no place for such a view with us. With us the Leader and the Idea are one, and every Party member has to do what the Leader orders. The Leader incorporates the Idea and alone knows its ultimate goal.'[1] The leadership principle was exercised chiefly through the Party. A hundred thousand had joined the Party before 1930, a few hundred thousand between 1930 and 1933, and several million in May 1933. By the mid thirties membership had become the condition of a successful career, and compulsory for even minor posts in the public service. The Nazis simply did not have enough capable men to fill the top posts in the public service, and could only impose conditions on new entrants or aspirants to entry. Yet Party membership was large enough for the leadership principle to be effective, if exercised through it. There was a chain of command from the Führer and Party Chancery to the Gauleiter (generally the Leader of a state), from him to the district Leader, then down to the group Leader and so down to the Leader in a block of flats or in a small village. The local government officials, Landräte, in each state, were not all Party men. There were about forty of the all-important Gauleiter. They were Party men loyal to Hitler and to no one else, and their loyalty to him was unreserved, for they had no legal power except that which they derived from him. They built up independent empires of their own, some even being strong enough to exclude Himmler and the SS and the Gestapo from their principalities. But the idea of the Leader whose word was law meant unpredictability. There was always an element of arbitrariness in this personal power. The principle was a major factor leading to a disregard of the law and, indeed, to *anti*-constitutional measures. It worked as long as the régime continued to be successful. This

[1] Quoted by Alan Bullock in *Hitler. A Study in Tyranny* (1952), p. 140.

depended in turn upon the continued hold of Hitler; for his dictatorship, like that of Mussolini, was a personal dictatorship. This is best illustrated by the oath which all soldiers took after August 2, 1934. They swore unconditional obedience 'to Adolf Hitler, Führer, Supreme Commander of the *Wehrmacht.*' It was an oath to him by name. By the law concerning the Head of State, August 1, 1934 (President Hindenburg died on August 2), the offices of President and Chancellor were united. Hitler adopted as his title 'Führer and Reich Chancellor' and thereby made it clear that his authority was personal as well as derived from his office. The position was summed up by E. R. Huber, 'The Führer combines in his own person the entire supreme authority of the Reich; all public authority both in the State and the Movement stems from that of the Führer.' He was the executant of the united will of the people. The authority of the Führer was total and all-embracing. The political philosopher Thomas Hobbes wrote at the time of the English Civil War of the total sovereign power of the state. He postulated that it was embodied in what he called the sovereign representative, whether one man or an assembly of men. The sovereign representative—and it was one man in Hitler's instance—reduced the multitude of wills belonging to the individual members of the state to the one will of the whole state. Another time of strife, in another country, had produced, if not the theory, the practice of *Leviathan*.

The Nazis, however, neither seized power nor ever commanded more than 37 per cent of the votes in a free election. Even in the Election of March 1933 (which was not free) they only polled 43 per cent. On the night of February 27 the Reichstag building had mysteriously caught fire and was burned to the ground. It is now known that a group of SA men, under orders, set it alight. But then, it occasioned rumours of a Communist conspiracy against the State and the Election had taken place under the impression of that fear. Yet even that had not given the Nazis a majority of votes. There was, then, always a body of indifferent or hostile opinion.

The most uncompromising opposition came from the Protestant Pastors, for at first the Roman Catholic bishops were not disinclined to support Hitler in his fight against Marxism. Both Churches, however, stood firm against Nazi attempts to coerce them into approving the new racial theories, as defined in the 'Nuremberg laws' of September 1935. The struggle between the Protestant Church and the State reached a climax in 1937 when the Church was deprived of the control of its finances, and all action on the part of the Protestant opposition was forbidden, and participation in Church affairs became illegal. Some answer must then be offered to the question of how did the Nazis deal with the latent or overt opposition of more than half the nation.

The answer to this question was the rule of force and organised or indiscriminate terror. The instruments of terror were the SA, the SS and the Gestapo. The SA (Sturmabteilungen, Storm Troopers) was founded in 1920 and fully organised in 1921 with the help of Major von Röhm, who was on the staff of the Army Commander in Bavaria. Röhm became its head. It was recruited from ex-officers and ex-Freikorps men and numbered between two and three million by the end of 1933. It was from the beginning an organisation of armed squads for intimidating, injuring, or killing opponents. When Röhm gained dangerous power from the SA he, with a hundred others, was killed (June 30, 1934). The SS (Schutzstaffeln), the notorious Blackshirts, was a hand-picked élite, sworn to absolute obedience, specially trained and highly disciplined. It was used to guard the concentration camps and Death's Head Squads were chosen from it to carry out the extermination work. It began as part of the SA, but after the Röhm purge it became independent, was put under the direct orders of Hitler and the immediate command of Heinrich Himmler as Reichsführer SS. The Gestapo or secret police were organised by Göring as police for special duties in Prussia. Göring, as well as head of the Air Force, was Prussian Minister President and Minister of the Interior. The Gestapo was also put under Himmler. When special tribunals with arbitrary judicial powers were set up, the structure of the police state was complete.

The legal basis of Hitler's dictatorship was one law, the Enabling Act, passed by the Reichstag (with only the Social Democrat minority voting against it) after the Elections of March 1933. But by then the Communists had largely been arrested and held in protective custody. The emergency decree after the Reichstag fire introduced this idea. Dated February 28, 1933, it abolished Article 114 of the Weimar Constitution—under which Germany was nominally to continue to live throughout the Third Reich—and so destroyed individual freedom. Arbitrary police arrest with no prospect of a trial thus became possible. The decree also allowed the Reich to take over the police powers which had up to now belonged to the individual states. Within a few weeks all police were controlled by SA or SS leaders, political leaders of the Party or other 'reliable' Party supporters. After the Elections there was a second wave of arrests in March and April. By July 31, 1933, a total of 26,789 persons was in protective custody. By then the Nazi Party was the only legal party. In the winter of 1936–37 the total reached its lowest figure: it was then 7,500. The first of the concentration camps, where these people were held, was established at Dachau near Munich in March 1933, a fortnight after the Elections and less than two months after Hitler became Chancellor. Between August 1937 and July 1938 there were four concentration camps on Reich territory. During this summer of 1937 large numbers of Protestant Pastors were arrested and sent to concentration camps. Prominent among them was Pastor Niemöller, once famous as a U-boat commander. Between 1941 and 1945 there were some seventeen concentration camps on Reich and Polish territory. This was their 'last catastrophic phase.' By then they were not only used in the extermination of the Jews, but were serving military purposes, in the increase of armaments production, and economic purposes in a building programme to counteract bomb damage. They were used to break resistance; for there was no redress, no appeal, no known term to imprisonment, no public knowledge. Secrecy was part of the technique of terror.

The persecution of the Jews was outside the power-political purpose for which terror had been improvised. It was the application of the anti-Semitic ideas of the National Socialists by the machinery of the state as well as by that of the Party. It was in itself an education in the acceptance of the methods of terror. On April 1, 1933, a boycott of Jewish shops, Jewish goods, doctors and lawyers was instituted. It was followed by the Act of April 7, 1933, and a host of executive orders and initiatives by private and public bodies. The result was that the Jews had lost their freedom to chose their occupation, their freedom of movement and their social position. They had been excluded from all parts of public life with the object of inducing as many as possible to emigrate. On September 15, 1935, the Nuremberg Laws introduced a fresh phase of persecution. The Reich Citizen Act and the Blood Protection Act were the two main Laws. They deprived the Jews of the civil rights of citizens, forbade them to marry Aryans and isolated them in their own communities. The pogrom of November 9–10, 1938, finally destroyed their economic existence. On *Kristallnacht*, the night of broken glass, some 7000 Jewish businesses were destroyed, nearly a hundred Jews killed and thousands terrorised. The pretext for this highly organised pogrom was the murder by a Polish Jew in Paris of a German diplomat. For this the Jews were ordered to pay a collective fine of one billion Reichsmarks, in addition to the cost of damage to their own property. The decree eliminating Jews from German economic life followed. Something of what was going on in Germany was now understood abroad. The American Ambassador was withdrawn from Berlin and the British Press expressed for the first time a true sense of outrage. The worst was still to come. In conversation with the Czech Foreign Minister, in a speech and in the Memorandum of January 25, 1939, Hitler expressed his intention of destroying the Jews, not of Germany, but of Europe. In 1941, he adopted 'the final solution,' or decided on the complete extermination of the Jews. Terrible camps were set up with 'extermination facilities.' Himmler could say in addressing the SS whose task it was to provide the squads for this purpose: 'Most of you know what it means when a hundred corpses are lying side by side, or five hundred or one thousand.' Such was his attitude to the suffering of a people and the death of some six and a half million.

The persecution could not have been effective without the participation of ordinary German men and women in it. This is to be explained in part, at least, by the deadening of ordinary human sympathies by Nazi propaganda. Hitler from the beginning understood all too well how to address himself to the masses, how to arouse mass emotion and how to bewilder men and women out of their common sense. Hitler's genius as a politician lay in his use of propaganda. He wrote: 'No great idea ... can be realised in practice without the effective power which resides in the popular masses.' 'Whoever wishes to win over the masses must know the key which will open the door to their hearts.' This he certainly knew and similarly wrote of in *Mein Kampf.* 'All effective propaganda must be confined to a few bare necessities and then must be expressed in a few stereotyped formulas.' 'Only constant repetition will finally succeed in imprinting an idea on the memory of a crowd.' He would not change the stuff of his constant speeches, but repeated again and again a handful of familiar dogmas. The more impudent and larger the untruth, the more likely it was to be remembered and mistaken for truth. Vehemence, passion, fanaticism were the qualities in which he trained himself, and used to cast his spell over the crowd. With them went the dramatic stage effects, produced by marching men, uniforms, the massed scarlet banners, with the swastika, black on a circle of white, in the middle, and above all, dramatic lighting. The audiences in the Berlin Sportpalast or at Nuremberg, where the Annual Party Rallies were held, were enormous and Hitler held them in his hand. He was more ruthless in breaking the resistance of reason than Mussolini.

Even so, propaganda cannot be the only explanation of Hitler's hold. There were many Germans whom it did not reach, even by broadcasting, which was, of course, available in the thirties, and others whom it did not affect. Another explanation lies in the advantages Hitler offered. The advent of the Nazis produced immediate benefits and they went on increasing in an ever-widening area. The most important social evil, if one must single one out, which had produced the situation that allowed them to come to power was unemployment. Persecution for some made work for others; economic autarky, Party positions and positions in the police apparatus and the expenditure of public money on public works and rearmament all made work. The expenditure on public works began at once, care being taken to see that the projects begun should be useful to the armed forces as well as provide work. Thus a beginning was made with the great motorways for which Germany became famous (*Autobahnen*). Other building projects followed: the Chancellery was rebuilt, Government offices and private houses for Party leaders were built. Hitler, whose ambition to become an architect had been thwarted, gave his personal attention to vast building schemes, including an appropriate setting for the annual Nuremberg Rallies. By 1934 rearmament had begun and quickly restored full production in the German economy. It was the most important single cause of the disappearance of unemployment by 1936. Economic autarky meant the effort to make Germany independent of imports of food and raw materials. Darré as Minister for Agriculture was not entirely successful in implementing the Nazi belief in the soil by enacting that farms should be entailed from father to son, but the general policy of stimulating production by subventions and credits was more successful. Most attention was given to the raw materials of industry. Large amounts were spent in financing the costly production of substitutes for rubber, oil, coal and valuable metals of which Germany had no supply herself. These projects, for which no private firm had the resources to engage in because profit would not accrue except in the long term, had to be state financed. In 1936 the Four-Year Plan was developed as a means of controlling production. The effort spent in this field went on increasing as the planners chased after an ever receding objective.

Not only work but a place in the community was found for every German acceptable to the régime. According to his occupation every man was a member of a professional chamber, an architects' chamber, a doctors' chamber, for example, or of a section in DAF already described. Boys belonged to the Hitler Youth, girls to the League of German Girls. Although the adult women's place was in the home and family, there were various Women's Associations provided by the Party for them too. In January 1934 an organisation for leisure was set up. Known as Strength Through Joy it provided holidays, excursions, and every kind of organised activity. Fritz Todt, who eventually became Minister for Armaments and Munitions, built up from early days a vast organisation which exploited the conscripted labour available after the introduction of conscription in 1934. Labour service (*Arbeitsdienst*) was performed by young men in camps, which Hitler knew how to deck out with symbols and practices that made them spuriously attractive. A dynamic force was built up by all this activity for which an outlet had to be found if it was to survive; for which, too, a constantly renewed supply of resources was needed. A system which depends on terror, propaganda and benefits cannot demand sacrifices. It *must* succeed.

Foreign policy and then war provide an answer to the question: where was this outlet to be found, where were these resources to be discovered. The National Socialist foreign programme was a simple one of three points. All Germans must be brought into the Reich; the Treaty of Versailles must be ended; Germany must expand into new living-space. This is pretty well what happened. The repudiation of the Treaty of Versailles in the introduction of military conscription and the remilitarisation of the Rhineland, and Europe's acceptance of these things, have already been noticed. The remilitarisation of the Rhineland had meant the repudiation of the Locarno Treaties. Not only had the League of Nations been ignored, but the whole work of the treaties had been undone. Germany's intervention in the Spanish Civil War in 1936 and 1937 was an unimportant way of exercising her airmen and their machines. It was politically more important. Before Hitler embarked on eastward expansion or conquering world power, if that was the final stage in a step-by-step policy, he must make sure of his continental base. He had helped the Nationalist side to victory and might hope to have founded a relationship with the Spain of the future, which would help assure this base.

France, in the mid thirties under a Popular Front Government, worried about Italian expansion (Italy was to invade Albania in the spring of 1939), worried lest she should have to fulfil her commitments to Yugoslavia, Czechoslovakia or Poland, and indifferently secured by her pact with Russia, refrained from initiatives of her own and followed the lead of Britain. The U.S.S.R., having established its position at Geneva as one of the peace-keeping Powers, was content to wait. Italy, with whom Hitler had shown sympathy over Ethiopia, had ceased to be available for any counterpoise to Germany. The main burden then of meeting German moves in foreign policy fell upon Britain. From May 1937 Neville Chamberlain was Prime Minister with Anthony Eden as Foreign Secretary. They were associated with a policy of conciliation in the expectation that German claims were not indefinitely expandable. Beyond that point they were not agreed, but that is another story. Up to that point, their policy chimed well with that of Hitler. He hoped to achieve his first two aims, and, perhaps, continental ascendancy, in alliance with Britain.

Britain was not much inclined to provide economic assistance for Germany. Under Schacht's influence in this year (1937) economic assistance was one of the subjects under discussion with Britain; for the policy of economic self-sufficiency had cut Germany's trade, her exports were not sufficient to pay for her imports, while rearmament and public works' expenditure continued to drain her resources. Britain was not prepared to help with a loan, but she had made a Trade Treaty in 1933 and a Payments Agreement in 1934. In 1936 more serious consideration was given by Britain to the return to Germany of the colonies she had lost during the War of 1914–18. Hitler demanded their return as part of the policy of ending the Treaty of Versailles. Moreover, and again under Schacht's influence, Germany claimed that she needed the raw materials which equatorial Africa could supply. By the end of the year, however, this line of advance had been closed. Britain refused to surrender either colonial territory she owned, or anything mandated to her; the French refused to return the French mandates of Togoland and the Cameroons; and schemes for German access to equatorial raw materials, under some international guarantee, proved impractical. This was not surprising. Again it chimed with Hitler's policy. For the ending of the Versailles Treaty it was enough that Britain should have shown herself ready to discuss the colonial question. For the recovery of her position as a world Power colonies were necessary, but Hitler in his step-by-step plan conceived of world power as belonging to a stage of expansion, and to the second phase of that, after expansion eastwards. Colonies for him, though not for Schacht, had been the instrument rather of bringing about an alliance with Britain than of immediate substantive importance.

By 1937 the revision of the Versailles settlement, in relation to Austria and Czechoslovakia, was more and more clearly indicated as alone likely to afford a basis of settlement; particularly because Germany made it clear that she would not guarantee the frontiers in eastern and central Europe as part of a general settlement. Any settlement with Germany to be effective must be European. At the end of the year Lord Halifax, a Cabinet Minister, who was to succeed Eden in 1938 as Foreign Secretary, was sent to pay an informal visit to Hitler. Halifax was prepared for a 'peaceful evolution—rather liberally interpreted' of German claims on Austria and Czechoslovakia, which had recently been raised with the British Ambassador in Berlin. 'If reasonable settlements could be reached with the free assent and goodwill of those primarily concerned,' Halifax had told Hitler, Britain had no desire to stand in the way. Such was British encouragement to Hitler to proceed! He had, however, no intention patiently to negotiate, or to refrain from forcing his claims on the two countries. Just a fortnight (November 5, 1937) before Halifax's visit, Hitler had addressed the three Heads of the three Armed Services together with General von Fritsch and the Foreign Minister, von Neurath. The substance of what he said was recorded in a document known from the writer as the Hossbach Memorandum. Hitler spoke of the stage in the development of his policy, when Germany would expand eastwards to find living-space. This would be thoroughly Germanised and the Slavs, as an inferior race, would be evicted or enslaved. He recognised that the alliance of Britain, which he had hoped would have given him a free hand in the east, was not to be had. He would have to reckon with British hostility to the policy of expansion eastwards, though he might count on her not resisting his Austrian and Czech policy.

During the year 1936–37, German relations with Italy improved. The two dictators were pursuing parallel policies in Spain and had reached agreement on a number of matters, including a common front against Communism, by October 1936. It was after this agreement that Mussolini used the metaphor of the Rome–Berlin axis. The friendship was consolidated by diplomatic co-operation during 1937. In September, Mussolini visited Hitler and, in November, signed the German-Japanese Anti-Comintern Pact of 1936. Mussolini let it be known that he was tired of standing guard over Austria, so from Italy, too, Hitler had encouragement. The defensive military alliance between Germany and Italy, which was Hitler's basis for war, was not signed until January 1939.

On March 12, 1938, German troops marched into Austria; within a fortnight she was fully incorporated into the German Reich. Austria was a member of the League, but the League was totally disregarded. Since July 1936, or perhaps even since the murder of Chancellor Dollfuss in 1934, Hitler had used the Austrian Nazis to erode the power of the Austrian Chancellor. The signal for the invasion was an attempt by the Austrian Chancellor to demonstrate the support of the Austrian people, by a national referendum, for himself and for independence. Yet the coup took Europe by surprise. The reaction of Britain and France was to acquiesce in the substance of the so-called *Anschluss* while objecting to the use of force. Above all, however, they were acutely sensitive to the consequent vulnerability of Czechoslovakia. The policy of bringing all Germans into the Reich would lead next to pressure upon that country, over her treatment of her German minority.

Hitler could afford to defy Britain and France. He rightly judged that neither would take armed action to defend Czechoslovakia. Yet France had promised to assist her, if her territorial integrity was threatened, and Britain, though refraining from giving France an assurance that she would stand by her if she acted on this obligation, warned Hitler (March 24, 1938) that legal obligations were not alone involved, and if war broke out 'it would be unlikely to be confined to those who have assumed such an obligation.' During the summer of 1938 Hitler steadily, through Henlein, ran up a bill against Czechoslovakia. Henlein was the leader of the Germans who lived in the Sudetenland; he was encouraged to make demands on their behalf to the Czech Government, which no Government could be expected to satisfy, and to manufacture an increasing list of 'atrocities' to protest against. By the autumn it was virtually accepted that some separation of 'German' territory from Czechoslovakia would take place. The question by September was rather How? and When? than Whether? Britain and France acted to prevent the use of force, not to maintain Czech integrity or independence. The warning of March 24 was three times repeated, so effectively on May 21 that Hitler, who intended to move then, postponed action. In September 1938 armed invasion was only prevented by the journey of the British Prime Minister to Hitler at Berchtesgaden, his mountain retreat.

Chamberlain carried back Hitler's terms which, he had indicated, he would try to persuade the Czechs to accept, if his Cabinet and the French agreed. Chamberlain's action on September 15 was as much to restrain the French as to restrain Hitler. Daladier, now French Prime Minister, had announced that France would march, if German troops crossed the Czech border. Though the French nerve broke a few days later there was always a danger that France might precipitate a general war. After conversations with Daladier and Bonnet, the French Foreign Minister, Chamberlain returned to Germany to meet Hitler at Bad Godesberg on the Rhine, only to find that Hitler had now enlarged the territory he demanded (September 23–4). He took the new demands back to the French. At the Munich Conference (September 29–30), where he took care to see that the French and Italians were also present, these terms were accepted and Germany agreed to a phased military occupation. The terms were then accepted by the Czechs. They might have had a better chance to save themselves, had they been allowed to resist an armed invasion.

Chamberlain had sanctioned a substantial cession of Czech territory in return for an international guarantee of the frontiers of what was left of Czechoslovakia. He had carried the French with him. Chamberlain also obtained a worthless piece of paper, which he thought justified his claim to have assured 'peace in our time.' It was the note of an Anglo-German Agreement to use 'the method of consultation to deal with any other questions that may concern our two countries,' and to continue their efforts to remove possible sources of differences between them. In the light of the Hossbach Memorandum its worthlessness is evident.

Before the spring of the following year was over, Hitler had torn up the Munich Agreement. In May–June 1939 he annexed the rest of the Czech part of Czechoslovakia and turned the Slovak part into a satellite state. After a war scare during the winter of 1938–39 in which Rumania, Holland and Switzerland were all rumoured as objects of German aggression, serious concern was concentrated on Poland. Hitler's policy of gathering all Germans into the Reich was now directed to Danzig and, in the likely event of Polish resistance to German demands, Poland would be invaded. Britain gave the guarantee to Poland, to implement which she went to war. The Prime Minister announced in the House of Commons on March 31, 1939, that if the Poles resisted a threat to their independence, Britain and France 'would at once lend them all the support in their power.' It was embodied in a treaty in August. The seriousness of Britain's intention to assist the Poles was attested by her opening negotiations with the U.S.S.R. for a pact of mutual assistance and a military alliance. The negotiations were protracted, for Chamberlain was not willing for them to succeed and Stalin had another option. The negotiators had, however, cleared the substantial difficulties away when there was announced (August 23) a German-Soviet Pact of non-aggression, followed shortly afterwards by a military alliance.

Britain and France had not gained peace but had gained time to rearm. They had begun in 1936 and accelerated their pace in 1939. Britain had also ensured that she went into war as a united country. Opinion was not united against Germany before May 1939. It was strange that Britain should go to war for Poland. The truth, of course, was that the object of the war for Britain was to save the Continent from German hegemony, and to save France rather than Poland. The German invasion of Poland on September 1, 1939, brought the guarantee to Poland into operation and Britain and France declared war upon Germany on September 3. Hitler had accomplished two-thirds of his programme: all Germans had been gathered into the Reich: if any remained outside, victory would bring them in—such was Hitler's confidence in his mission that belief in victory never wavered even in 1945—and the Treaty of Versailles was ended. Hitler had said to Chamberlain at Godesberg that Germany would never attack France; if Britain and France went to war with Germany to assist another country they would have to invade Germany. In 1939 neither Britain nor France was prepared to launch a full-scale invasion of Germany. So Poland was destroyed and partitioned between the two allies, Germany and Soviet Russia, who had invaded from the east when Germany went in from the west.

Expansion in the east Hitler intended to be at the expense of the Russian as well as the Polish Slav. This was made clear in *Mein Kampf* and in the so-called Second Book written in 1928. In the memorandum which he had written in August 1936 for the Four-Year Plan he had stipulated that militarily and economically Germany should be ready for expansion in the east in 1943–45. In the Hossbach Memorandum the same dates are set for eastwards expansion. This expansion was still to come. The advance upon Poland, together with Russia, was the result as much of Stalin's policy as it was of Hitler's. When Litvinov was Russian Foreign Minister, Stalin pursued the policy of establishing Soviet Russia as part of the peace-keeping forces of Europe. After Munich he changed course. His appointment of Molotov, on May 11, 1938, to replace Litvinov was a sign of the change. He was ready to pursue an expansionist policy and he allied with Hitler to be a restraint as well as an accomplice. Munich had made two things plain to him. First, since Britain and France had invited Italy but not Russia to Munich, it was clear that the U.S.S.R. was not accepted as part of the peace-keeping establishment and membership of the League was politically no advantage, when it was ignored over Czechoslovakia as over Austria. Second, Britain and France were so averse to military action that they were unlikely to interfere to preserve the frontiers of eastern Europe. Stalin took a risk with the Soviet-German Pact, but the odds were short and when Poland was not saved he was justified.

Hitler had in fact to fight in order to achieve continental hegemony. The war of 1940 with its lightning thrusts into Scandinavia, Holland, Belgium and France completed his mastery of the Continent. The decision of 1941 to break with and invade Soviet Russia, to implement the plan, known as Barbarossa, was the implementation of the plan to win living-space in the east from the base of continental supremacy which he had won. Hitler had consolidated uncontested ascendancy in Germany by an enormous expenditure of economic resources. They could only be made good by continued conquest, continued looting, continued enrolment of slave labour to supply the manpower Germany needed to preserve her racial superiority. He had generated a dynamic power which consumed all before it until there was nothing left—and then it consumed itself.

Chapter 12

THE WAR OF 1939–45

Until 1940 or thereabouts it was customary to refer to the War of 1914–18 as the Great War. The phrase went out of use. The Second World War was on a greater scale, demanded more endurance, greater and more varied effort and involved much larger numbers. The shape of the War was one of outward movement from three centres successively: from Germany in September 1939, April–May 1940 and July 1941; from Italy in June–October 1940; from Japan in December 1941. These outward movements, especially the Japanese, which was largely by sea and air, covered vast distances. The Japanese theatre of war covered a third of the earth's surface. The first offensives were so far successful as to leave only one enemy in the field, while a new political order was imposed on the Continent of Europe. Britain fought alone from June 1940 to December 1941. Then these outward movements were reversed. The countries of the Atlantic world closed in upon the heart of Europe from its western, its eastern and its southern borders. The countries of the Pacific world closed in upon Japan. The United States of America took part in, not to say directed, both reverse movements. The hinge turned in November 1942. There were great movements of armies but also great movements of civilians, fleeing from the bombed cities, moved by Germany applying racist theories, moved by Soviet Russia, shifting of their own accord when national frontiers were redrawn. The account which follows will not say enough of human beings suffering and enduring. It will only place in their chronological order the main events which took place within this shape.

1939–40

The first phase of the War lasted from September 1, 1939, when Germany invaded Poland, to be followed by Russia on September

17, until April 9, 1940, when Germany began her offensive against Denmark and Norway. It was *la drôle de guerre* for France, the 'twilight war' for Britain. France and Britain, who were at war with Germany since September 3, thought defensively and waited to be attacked; Germany thought offensively and attacked. A good illustration is that Britain developed radar, a protective device: Germany developed direction finding beams to put her planes on target, a device to ensure an economical offensive. In this period Germany and Russia were allied. They partitioned Poland between themselves. Russia also waged war against Finland whose possession of the Karelian isthmus put the keys of the fortress of Leningrad in Finland's hands. Russia was determined to wrest them from her. The Finns checked the Russian advance in December and defeated them in battle in January 1940. But Soviet Russia recovered and bringing greater strength forward forced the Finns to capitulate on March 12, 1940.

The French had made a small advance from Saargemines across the German frontier with their fourth army on September 8, thus bringing it in contact with the advance posts of the German Siegfried Line. The French had their own defensive fortified line: the Maginot Line. It covered the frontier of Lorraine to the Ardennes, but it did not reach from the Ardennes to the sea. The French waited, although they outnumbered the Germans: so deep was their distaste for war. They had in position 35 divisions, increased by 10 British divisions (the BEF or British Expeditionary Force) and were to bring up 51 more. The Germans had 43 on that frontier. After the Polish war was over they would increase them to 157. The French and Germans were roughly equal in the quality of their tanks, but the Germans had a skill in their use which the French at this stage did not understand. For the Germans they were to be a sword, for the French a shield. For Britain, by sea, this was no time of waiting. She suffered heavy casualties in the war by sea which the Germans fought with submarines and, already in 1939, by laying magnetic mines. She lost 150 dry cargo ships in the first nine months of the war, that is, during this phase. The Cunard liner *Athenia* was sunk by torpedo on September 8 with the loss of 112 lives. The battleship *Royal Oak* was torpedoed and sunk inside Scapa Flow on October 14. The aircraft carrier *Courageous* was sunk and on December 14 the Battle of the River Plate was fought. Three British cruisers chased the German pocket battleship *Graf Spee* (built small to comply with the restrictions of the Versailles Treaty) across the Atlantic. She was cornered in Montevideo Roads and scuttled herself rather than surrender. Britain hoped to strangle Germany by blockade rather than fight her. Alternatively she might succeed in overthrowing Hitler's dictatorship by encouraging revolt. Her planes dropped leaflets and not bombs. Both hopes were illusory.

Three things Britain and France might have learnt from the Polish campaign and planned accordingly, but they did not learn them or, if they did, they did not or could not plan to counter them. The German tactics of *Blitzkrieg*, of dive-bombing and of terrorism, were practised against Poland, yet Britain and France were not prepared for any one of them, when practised against themselves. The *Blitzkrieg* or lightning thrust aimed at achieving the objective of the campaign so quickly that the enemy had no time to deploy defences. The German action in Poland was over by mid October. Poland had 40 divisions which should have allowed her to meet the Germans, though they had 63 divisions engaged. The Germans advanced so speedily that only 20 of the Polish divisions were mobilised, and their airfields were overrun before they could use them. Poland could not have defeated the Germans, but the extreme mobility of the Germans hardly gave her a chance even to fight. The new technique of dive-bombing destroyed her communications and foiled her troop movements. When applied in France it broke the nerve of exhausted troops. The sustained bombing of Warsaw on September 25 was a terrorist method against a capital already under siege.

In April the Germans occupied and took possession of Denmark and Norway. The Norwegian King and Government went into exile in London. In Norway Vidkun Quisling became Prime Minister. He gave his name to all those ready, for whatever motive, to collaborate with Germany in the attachment of their countries to the German system. King Christian remained in Copenhagen, a rallying point of Danish resistance, passive though it had to be. The incorporation of Denmark and Norway was a strategic necessity and not part of the policy of winning living-space for Germans. Germany needed Swedish iron ore which came to her more conveniently through the Norwegian port of Narvik than by the Baltic route. Norwegian and Danish ports and bases might be used by Britain (she had effected landings in Norway, though she subsequently withdrew) in her plan of sea and air warfare to reduce Germany to submission.

1940–41

The events of the second phase of the War were the defeat and fall of France, the Battle of Britain and the duel in North Africa between Britain and first, Italy, and then Germany.

The German plan for the offensive, which she opened on May 10, was a massive thrust by her Army Group A starting roughly from the Moselle, that is, from a position in the middle between Army Group B, poised to go into Holland from the lower Rhine, and Army

Group C, placed on the upper Rhine towards Baden. Army Group A would attack at the weak point where the Maginot Line ended and the front held by the mobile forces of the Allies began. Having broken through, it would swing westwards towards the mouth of the Somme and the coast. This bold plan would bring the German armies behind the Allies' forces which would then easily be encircled. The Allies had not foreseen any such movement; they expected the main attack to be made either simultaneously on Holland and Belgium or on one or the other first. In any event the offensive would be taken, they believed, north-east of the French frontier and not through the difficult Ardennes route. This offensive they proposed to go forward to meet. Thus they placed their armies in an even better position than the Germans expected for the success of their encircling movement. General Guderian exactly followed the plan, went through Luxembourg and the Ardennes and broke through the French front at Sedan, swung westwards and took Amiens on May 20 and continued towards Abbeville. The whole of the Allies' forces to the north–the Belgian army, 9 British divisions and 13 French divisions –were cut off from the rest of the French and British armies. It was a heavy defeat.

To the north Holland had fallen. The invasion began on May 10 with a simultaneous Declaration of War. On May 13 resistance was so far overwhelmed that the Queen and Government left The Hague and embarked at Rotterdam on a British destroyer. On May 14 Rotterdam was bombed and the centre of the city went up in flames, over 1000 lives were lost and over 23,000 houses were destroyed. On May 15 the Dutch laid down their arms. The Germans had used parachutes to drop German soldiers in Dutch uniforms and other disguises. The Government in exile, the Dutch merchant navy and the Dutch East Indies remained undefeated. In Belgium, on May 10, German airmen, specially rehearsed for the task on a model, landed from gliders to disable the guns of the fort of Eben Emaël. When the Germans then captured it, they had taken the main defence of the Albert Canal along which the Belgian army was deployed. By May 12 the Belgians had abandoned their position. The following day battle was joined at Gembloux and while it continued the Germans renewed their attack on Louvain. On May 15 the Allies disengaged because of the threat which the breakthrough at Sedan constituted.

The Allies' attempt to break out of encirclement southwards to meet a French thrust northwards was the only possible plan, and it was adopted but carried out confusedly. Some of the confusion was caused by a change in command from General Gamelin to General Weygand who, as we have seen, had been Foch's assistant in the War of 1914–18. He was now aged seventy-four. The British had already begun (May 20) to find the small craft which were to help the Navy in the evacuation of their army. Five days later General Gort withdrew the BEF. On May 28 King Leopold and the Belgian army surrendered. The evacuation through Dunkirk and from the beaches had already begun on May 26. In all 330,000 men reached Britain—200,000 British and 130,000 French—before the operation ended on June 4. France fought on. She was defeated a second time between June 5 and June 10. Her roads in the war zone were filled with refugees as well as troops which the Germans dive-bombed. The French Prime Minister was Paul Reynaud and he had broadened his Government to include the Socialists on the Left and Marshal Pétain and Georges Mandel, Clemenceau's right-hand man, on the Right. A British proposal that Britain and France should become one country was a gallant gesture from Churchill, said to have originated with a group of Frenchmen in London. Pétain succeeded Reynaud on June 16 and on June 22 he signed the armistice Convention of Rethondes with the Germans. The policy of collaboration had begun.

The causes of the fall of France have been written about in such a way as to throw a searching light upon the whole history of the Third Republic. Suffice it here to draw attention to the military defeat and the political defeat suffered by France and to notice at shorter length the moral defeat. The main cause of the military defeat was that France was fighting at the speed of infantry. Germany had fought at the speed of aircraft, fast cars and light and medium tanks. France thought of modern weapons as auxiliaries. Germany thought of them as determining the character of the campaign. The Germans had the advantage of initiative, of implementing a plan without meeting unpredictable responses—such as she met in the War of 1914–18—from the enemy. She had unity. The Allies acted as three independent forces. The Belgians and French, though they had the advantage of a common language, co-ordinated their plans not at all and their movements badly. One ally, Britain, had committed all the army divisions she had available, but made only a limited commitment of her air strength: she had to think of the next stage, the defence of her own shores.

The political defeat was caused by France having a Government which could not hold a divided country together. The division between Left and Right had perhaps become too great for any Government to do so. The last 'strong' Government of France had been that of Doumergue and Louis Barthou. It had ended with Barthou's murder in 1934. From June 1936 to June 1937 she had a Popular Front Government under Léon Blum. This was Blum's attempt to unite the nation on a Leftist basis. By stretching a point one might consider all five Governments between 1936 and 1940 Popular Front Governments. Blum was followed by the Radical, Camille Chautemps, who headed two successive Governments, Blum was then in office a second time, followed by Édouard Daladier (until March 1940). All five Governments were supported by the Communists at their investment by the Chamber. But the Communists were members of none. The alliance with the Communists did not break until after Daladier had taken office. It failed, however, to give France the two things which might have united her: a stable economy and a unifying foreign policy. Blum came near success. He was committed to reform, but in the end he had no coherent economic and monetary policy to check the flight of French capital abroad. Nor would he ask parliament for emergency powers. So his Government and those which followed lacked the economic strength to embark on necessary reforms. The Left felt itself frustrated and unsupported over foreign policy on which Radicals and Socialists diverged. The Right, the party of order, can be simplified to look like the Nationalists of the Spanish Civil War. But they were loyal to the Republic. They were to that extent, however, frustrated as much as the Radicals and Socialists. There was no political leader with sufficient impetus and drive to carry the nation forward in unity. The direction to go forward which any leader chose was always second best.

The moral defeat has been variously described. Pétain summed it up in the simplest terms: 'Our defeat has its roots in the laxity of our conduct.' It was not so simple. One historian has written of the decline of *l'élan vital*. The loss of life in the War of 1914–18, the low birth-rate, especially during the thirties, the industrial recession after the boom of 1929, the increase of political strife following the economic crisis of 1931, the decline in her ability to make rapid adjustments in the use of her resources to meet new situations, all added up to a loss of national confidence. This in turn was reflected in the timidity and hesitations of her Governments, which then caused further self-mistrust among Frenchmen. It is remarkable that both her military commander and her new political leader in 1940 should have been old men. Pétain was eighty-four. The younger men who were to restore France had yet to come to the fore. General Charles de Gaulle, who was to lead them, was already in London.

Britain now awaited invasion. She cleared her eastern coastal areas, built concrete defence posts and gun emplacements, trained Local Defence Volunteers (later called the Home Guard) and evacuated her cities. Children, schools and colleges had been sent to 'safe' areas in the autumn of 1939, for Britain expected the 'knock-out blow', that is a completely disabling air bombardment. She had prepared an emergency hospital service for casualties with thirty times more hospital beds than she was to need. The knock-out blow had not come. Now under Churchill's superb leadership—he had come to power on May 10—she awaited invasion and Hitler prepared Operation Sea-Lion to carry it out. Meanwhile Britain made sure of the French fleet. The armistice had provided that the ships of the fleet should repair to their home ports and there be disarmed. Britain simply seized those in her own ports, arranged for the peaceful disarming of those at Alexandria and attacked the bulk of the French fleet anchored at Mers el-Kébir (July 3). Only one French battleship escaped and over a thousand French sailors were killed. The Anglo-French alliance ended, but the Germans had been deprived of an important weapon of war, and the alliance would be renewed with other Frenchmen.

Preparations for Operation Sea-Lion went ahead until Hitler's military advisers refused to implement it, unless Germany first obtained command of the air. So the Battle of Britain, which was an air battle, was fought. It lasted from July 10 to October 31. During the first two months the battle was for the air space over south-east England, especially Kent. Then, after September 1, for two months London was subjected during the day and by night to heavy bombing, particularly heavy on her docks. Finally in November, when the Battle of Britain was officially over, Germany bombed industrial centres, beginning with Coventry and continuing until May 1941. The battle was won by Britain and the invasion never took place. Britain did not outnumber Germany, but she out-fought her; her direction of the battle and the spirit behind it was both more coherent and more flexible than was that of Germany; her machines may have been better and had been put later into mass production; her concentration in 1938–39 on building fighters rather than bombers was vindicated; most important, she had developed radar. Radar and 'ultra' gave the British airmen foreknowledge, at first only by sound but later by an image on a screen, of German movements. The Germans on their side were flying in on to their targets by direction-finding beams which intersected over the target. By June 20 British scientists had discovered the German secret. By September they were able to jam the beams and even to use them to deflect the German planes from their targets to less important areas. Germany, on her side, acquired radar. The battle of the scientists continued.[1]

Finally in this phase came the beginning of the North African battle. There was a long prelude to it beginning with the Italian Declaration of War on June 10, 1940. Italy fought on the Alpine borders of France without defeating her. Nevertheless she annexed Nice and part of Savoy and kept them until the liberation of France. The Italians also bombed Malta causing the British Fleet to evacuate it and divide itself between Gilbraltar and Alexandria. On November 11 the British sought out the Italian Fleet in Taranto harbour, disabled two cruisers and seriously damaged three out of the six battleships anchored there. The British now had naval supremacy in the Mediterranean. They returned to Malta and, using it as a kind of aircraft carrier, attacked Italian shipping from it with devastating effect, until the German air force came to Italy's aid. Meanwhile the

[1] R. V. Jones, *Most Secret War* (1978),is the most vivid account.

Italian entry into the War had enabled Britain to occupy the Italian colonies of Eritrea and Somaliland and to restore Emperor Haile Selassie to Ethiopia. That task was completed by May 1941. Egypt, however, was much the most important of Britain's strongholds: important alike to her naval supremacy in the Mediterranean and to her position in Africa. There under General Wavell she built up an army of British, Australian, New Zealand and Indian troops: 150,000 men by Jaunary 1941. Upon this stronghold General Balbo with an army of 215,000 had been ordered to advance from the Italian colony of Libya, but his forces under General Graziani proceeded cautiously and slowly. He took Sollum and Sidi Barrani and then stopped. In December Wavell, not yet reinforced, counterattacked with a small motorised army. It was highly effective. It advanced 450 miles along the coast of Cyrenaica, the eastern province of Libya. It took Bardia, Tobruk (January 21) and reached the frontier of Tripolitania, the western province of Libya (February 1941). Rommel and the Afrikakorps came to Italy's aid and an Anglo-German duel began.

Meanwhile on October 28, 1940, the Italians had invaded Greece. They were not successful here either, but their action was of great importance. The Germans went to the help of the Italians and this enabled them to establish their power in Yugoslavia as well as Greece. But Hitler's preoccupation with the Balkan Peninsula where he also established control over Rumania, King Carol abdicating in favour of his son Michael who set up a Fascist régime, and over Bulgaria, was to have a disastrous affect upon his war with Soviet Russia in the next phase. Britain, however, had suffered a setback, when she was compelled to evacuate Greece and then the island of Crete where she had hoped to make a stronghold. Before passing to the third phase we should notice that Britain had been buying war material from the United States on a cash and carry basis since the autumn of 1939. In September 1940 Britain obtained fifty reconditioned American destroyers from the War of 1914–18 and, in return, leased air and sea bases in the Caribbean and Newfoundland to the United States. In December 1940 Churchill appealed to President Roosevelt for material on some new basis, because Britain's dollar reserves were running out. Roosevelt persuaded Congress to enact the lend-lease legislation which allowed Britain to defer payment for supplies. The British dependence on America had begun.

1941–42

The third phase of the War began in June 1941 and lasted until November 1942. The chief events were the German war against

Soviet Russia, the Japanese war against the United States and all the western democracies and Operation Torch, the code name for Allied landings in Morocco and Algiers. The submarine war in the Atlantic continued and an underground war began as resistance movements developed in the German-occupied countries.

The cause of the German war with Soviet Russia was Hitler's vision of eastward expansion, of colonisation by German farmers and German entrepreneurs, and their exploitation of vast Russian resources. They would use for their own purposes the enslaved, illiterate, unhealthy, sub-human Slav. This nonsensical vision shimmered through *Mein Kampf*, the Second Book, the Memorandum for the Four-Year Plan and the Hossbach Memorandum (above, p. 203). The Soviet alliance and the Polish War had not deflected Hitler from his grand design. Hitler took the decision for the break with Soviet Russia in June 1940. Plans for the war were prepared between July 22 and December 5, 1940. Detailed plans with an invasion date of May 15, 1941, and the code name Barbarossa were next made. The invasion, postponed to enable Hitler to quell the resistance of Yugoslavia and Greece, in fact began on June 22. The Russians, despite the postponement, were, even so, taken largely by surprise.

Hitler was now Commander-in-Chief. He was also Head of State, Prime Minister and War Minister. It was Hitler and Hitler alone who was responsible for the conduct of the war. He showed an extraordinary capacity for finding unusual solutions to the problems it presented and for being right. His knowledge, memory, powers of persuasion and will-power were all out of the ordinary and help to account for his success. In the end he lost the power to think he might be wrong, which is another way of saying that he could no longer assess his opponents and the situations which faced him correctly.

His success was won by the now well-tried tactics of *Blitzkrieg*. They were used even on this enormous front, divided into three commands, two with three armies and the third with four. Very large forces either overran enemy resistance or showed up the enemy's weak points. Armoured columns and air force, acting in combination, then effected a breakthrough at the weakest point. The breakthrough was then enlarged until it was possible to begin the encirclement of the scattered armies into which the enemy forces had been broken. Within eighteen days the Germans had advanced 280 miles. Latvia, Lithuania, Byelorussia and much of the Ukraine had been conquered. During the summer they marched and drove on and on. It was possible to bring Leningrad under siege by September and to begin the vital battle for Moscow in October. But the first snows fell on October 6 and by December the Russians were able to go over to the offensive and the Germans withdrew. They never reached

Moscow. In the south they were well beyond Kharkov on December 15, a little short of the river Don.

In the late spring of 1942 Germany resumed her offensive. But the enormous front line was now too long for an offensive to be taken over more than part of it. It was to be the southern part and the objective was vital oil. If her plan for 1942 succeeded Germany would have the industrial resources of the Donetz Basin, the grain of the Ukraine and the oil of the Caucasus. The keys to the great encircling movement which she planned were Voronezh on the Don and the fortress of Sebastopol in the Crimea. The Russians held back the German advance. But in July Germany occupied the Don along its whole length and Sebastopol fell. July was too late in the short campaigning season to allow Hitler to take the next step. But Hitler, intoxicated with success, lost his sense of what was possible. His directive no. 45 of July 15, 1942, gave orders for a simultaneous advance to Stalingrad (now Volgograd) on the Volga and for the crossing of the Caucasus, further south. The Germans had initial successes but exhausted by the immense distances, with their supply lines over-lengthened and worn down by the unbroken resistance of civilians as well as soldiers, they neither permanently captured Stalingrad nor crossed the Caucasus. Stalingrad was the scene of barbarous fighting for over five months in the autumn and winter: from August 23, 1942, until January 31, 1943. The Germans had achieved the military objective of cutting the Volga, but they clung to Stalingrad, fighting house by house and floor by floor with bayonet and hand-grenade. What remained of the German army was encircled by the Russians and destroyed by February 1943. The defeat of Stalingrad was decisive. Meanwhile the German advance in the Caucasus had been held. The oil wells remained out of reach.

The Japanese-American war was, like the German-Soviet, a war of movement from strong point to strong point, that is from island to island, covering enormous distances. Japan, as we have seen, had been at war with China since 1937. It would be more accurate to say she had been at war with Chiang Kai-shek and his steadily disintegrating system. By 1941 she was in possession of Chinese ports, industrial centres, main lines of communication and the puppet state of Manchukuo. Another China was already taking shape under Mao Tse-tung and Chou En-lai, with its capital in Yenan, independent, in its mountain stronghold, of outside aid. But it would not influence events during the War. In 1940 Japan planned the Greater East Asian Co-Prosperity Sphere. As well as China and Manchukuo it would include the Pacific islands, French Indo-China, Thailand, British Burma, Dutch Indonesia and perhaps India. Such were the opportunities that the fall of France and the isolation of Britain gave to Japan. In preparation for her vast imperialist drive she let relations

217

with Germany cool, signed a non-aggression pact with Soviet Russia (April 1941) and opened negotiations with the United States. These did not prosper. Indeed, when in July 1941 Japan found pretexts for going into French Indo-China, the United States told Japan that negotiations were 'pointless', froze Japanese assets in the United States, imposed an oil embargo and appointed General MacArthur to a new operational theatre: the Far East. Nevertheless, she was wholly surprised when the Japanese, using aircraft carriers and bombers, destroyed her fleet at anchor in Pearl Harbour in the Hawaian Islands (December 7, 1941). The operation had already begun when the Japanese handed in their Declaration of War at Washington. There was no Declaration of War on Britain before hostilities began. The United States and Britain declared war on Japan on December 8. The United States, Britain, the Dutch East Indies, Australia and New Zealand united to set up a unified command (ABDA) but their interests were too divergent to make a united offensive possible. The initiative lay with Japan. On December 11 the United States exchanged Declarations of War with Germany and Italy.

The Japanese offensive opened with most skilfully combined operations. By the middle of December they had taken Guam and Wake Islands from the United States, the Gilbert Islands and Hong Kong from Britain. On February 15, 1942, Singapore, with a garrison of over 60,000 men, fell. Britain had failed to supply this fortress adequately with aircraft, but its surrender was still a shock. The Japanese conquered Malaya and Burma—Rangoon, the Burmese capital, was in their hands by March—and proceeded up the Irrawaddy, pushing back the British and the Chinese. The British with great difficulty and much heroism evacuated their Burmese forces to India. And both Britain and America surrendered extra-territorial rights in China in order to strengthen this ally. The Japanese had meanwhile replaced the Dutch in Java, Sumatra, Timor, the whole of the Dutch East Indies. By May 1942 they had replaced the United States in the Philippines. China and India were outside the great Japanese empire and like Australia, New Zealand and the western coast of America, virtually isolated by sea from the rest of the world.

But before the end of 1942 the Japanese were halted and a balance of forces established in the Pacific. The victory of the United States in the naval battle at Midway, a coral island some 2000 miles from Tokyo and something over 1000 miles from Hawaii, fought on June 4–5, made the naval balance. In July 1942 the Japanese landed on Guadalcanal, nearer the Australian coast, with the object of using it as an air-base for an advance on New Caledonia, whence they would attack Port Moresby off the Australian coast itself. A series of air and naval battles took place between August and October as the Japanese fought to keep their supply lines open. The climax was another great naval victory for the Americans (November 12–15) which allowed the Australians to retake Guadalcanal and establish a balance of military power. Meanwhile Islam and Communism, both forces which the Japanese did not understand, stimulated local resistance to the Japanese. In 1943 the Independent Front in French Indo-China became the Vietminh, led by a young scholar who became Ho Chi-minh.

Operation Torch was the culmination of the North African War. Rommel and his Afrikakorps had exactly reversed the gains won by Wavell between December 1940 and February 1941. In March 1941 it was he who occupied a tenable line in Cyrenaica: from Bardia to Sollum to Halfiya Pass on the Egyptian frontier. But because his Italian ally was weak, because German troops were locked up in Yugoslavia and Greece, so that he could not expect the reinforcements he needed, and because his supply lines were being attacked by air and sea till he was running short, Rommel was vulnerable. The British, now under Auchinleck, attacked Rommel and drove him out of Cyrenaica. It was now the British turn to be troubled with supply problems and Auchinleck had not reached as far east as Wavell. Rommel recovered. Between January and June 1942 he made a remarkable bid for Egypt which nearly succeeded. He was within forty miles of Alexandria before it was clear that he had planned beyond his petrol, his supplies and the human stamina of his men. His advance came to a halt at El Alamein. The Allies regrouped. Churchill dismissed Auchinleck. Though he was a scapegoat and his dismissal unfair, it cannot be regretted since it enabled General Montgomery to be put in command of the Eighth Army under General Alexander, who replaced Auchinleck as Commander-in-Chief. Montgomery brought a new strategy to the war in North Africa. He answered the lightning boldness of Rommel not in kind, but with caution and such pains in planning that his success had an air of inevitability. Montgomery attacked on the night of October 23–24, 1942 and after the victory at El Alamein (the battle begun on October 24 was decided by November 2) and a series of successes, brought the Eighth Army out of Cyrenaica, through Tripoli, so out of Libya, to the borders of Tunisia. He was out of Cyrenaica by December 1942 and on the Tunisian frontier by January 1943 during the next phase of the war.

The victory of El Alamein was the same sort of turning-point as the Russian victory of Stalingrad. It was decisive because it enabled the American and British armies to effect landings at Casablanca, Oran and Algiers on French territory. Steps had been taken to avoid fighting such of the inhabitants as were known to be loyal to Marshal Pétain, but the conspiracy failed and fighting in fact occurred. General Noguès resisted the American landing at Casablanca (November 8); General Juin resisted at Algiers. The Americans brought in General Giraud to govern in the name of Free France and act both in a military and a political capacity, ignoring General de Gaulle, who had by now organised the Free French forces. But Giraud was not an easy man to fit into a prearranged and limited role and the real direction of freed French territory fell naturally into the hands of de Gaulle. Giraud, however, ruled for six months until de Gaulle arrived on May 30, 1943. The French National Liberation Committee was set up under their joint Chairmanship, but Giraud soon ceased to play any political rôle as de Gaulle established ascendancy. Operation Torch was an amateurish operation of inexperienced armies, but it made possible the elimination of risks and defective techniques from the plans for the greater landings in Europe in 1944.

Stalingrad, Guadalcanal, El Alamein justify the strong sense one has of November 1942 as the turning-point of the war. Meanwhile a resistance movement developed in Norway, Denmark (though to a lesser extent), Holland, Belgium and France. It began passively among small groups of relatives and friends. It began with the sheltering of shot-down Allied airmen or of people needing protection from the occupying forces. It developed into sabotage activity by organised groups. Its first importance lay in the networks it could provide along which information or persons could be passed. Radio played its part in making possible resistance activities. But groups tended to be small and unstable. Only in unoccupied France were large and effective organisations possible. Here three were especially important: *Franc-Tireur*, *Libération Sud*, organised by d'Astier de la Vigerie, and *Combat*, organised by Henri Frenay. The structure of underground resistance included a secret army, propaganda by a secret press, intelligence, false papers, shelter, parachute drops, help for those who needed to escape, aid of every sort to sabotage. Resistance in Yugoslavia was so far successful as to make another theatre of operations. The legacy of resistance to the modern world had been too widespread a knowledge of how to make and use bombs for most countries nowadays to be free from interruptions of the public peace. Resistance was nourished by the increasingly harsh techniques of occupation which the Germans developed. The Convention of Rethondes had established a demarcation line between France, occupied by German troops with headquarters in Paris, and unoccupied France under the full authority of the French Government under Pétain with its capital at Vichy. The line ran just south of Dijon, Bourges and Tours then turned south to leave the whole of the coast in the occupied zone. Germany had means of pressure upon the Vichy Government. At the least sign of opposition the Germans closed the demarcation line, threatened the fate of the million French prisoners of war still in German hands or used their subsidised press to campaign against the Government. The Germans used a technique of running their conquests through the existing authorities because it was inexpensive and unburdensome. They had begun by paying for what they took. But in course of time, payments in worthless currency, exactions, confiscations, plain looting became the marks of occupation. Then the taking and shooting of hostages and the deportation of labour roused unquenchable hatred. Both occupiers and collaborators became isloated and by the winter of 1942–43 underground war was the rule. The distinction between occupied and unoccupied France was abolished in November 1942. The whole of France was to become a prison.

1942–44

The fourth phase of the War, which has now been reached, was a phase of preparation for the final repulse of Germany, Italy and Japan. The three Allies, America, Britain and Russia, came together. The Battle for Tunisia was followed by those for Sicily and Italy. Germany was bombed by British and American forces from Britain. She was defeated in Russia. The phase closed, as it had begun with the Allies manifesting their unity. Churchill, Roosevelt and Stalin met at Teheran.

It is, indeed, remarkable that leadership in the War was personal. It was personal in five countries; only Japan had a collective leadership. It was also civilian leadership. Stalin only became Marshal Stalin during the War. It was, then, important that Roosevelt and Churchill should confer. In August 1941 they had met off the shore of Newfoundland. They had summed up the results of their conversation in a press release on August 12. This has since become known as the Atlantic Charter. Britain and Russia had signed an alliance for the duration of the War on July 12, 1941. Stalin had accepted the principles of the Atlantic Charter and, then, in May 26, 1942, had signed with Churchill a further alliance. This provided for co-operation for twenty years, arranged safeguards against a separate peace with Germany and pledged Britain and Russia to co-operation to maintain peace after the War. Each disclaimed interference with the internal affairs of the other.

The principles of the Atlantic Charter were important for the future. The Allies disclaimed all territorial aggrandisement and said they would recognise no territorial changes which did not conform to the wishes, freely expressed, of the peoples concerned. They declared it was the right of all peoples to choose the form of government under which they wished to live, and asserted their intention to restore sovereign rights and independence to those who had been deprived of them. They proclaimed free access of all to world trade and resources, so that each individual might end his days free from fear and want. Finally they declared their intention to set up a world organisation for the preservation of peace among the nations. At the beginning of this phase of the war, at the end of 1942, the military and economic structure was built up which would enable the three Allies, while fighting their separate wars, to combine in order to realise these ultimate ideals. The dependence of Britain on American resources was further underlined, while Roosevelt began to find some sympathy in Stalin for his distaste towards the British Empire.

It was clear after Montgomery had driven Rommel to the border of Tunis and the Allies had landed in Casablanca, Oran and Algiers, that Tunis would be the next battlefield. The Germans dropped parachute forces there and forestalled the entry of the Allies. These together with Rommel's Afrikakorps formed an army under General von Arnim. Rommel himself had left Africa in March, believing deadlock had been reached. But Montgomery and the Eighth Army came in from the east and the Americans from the west, while the French army under General Barré withdrew into the mountains, taking care not to assist the Germans. General Anderson with the British forces was now able to extricate himself from the deadlock and on May 9, 1943, one German army laid down its arms to the Americans and, on May 13, the Afrikakorps and the Italians surrendered to the British and French.

Effective bombing preceded the next campaign. It caused the garrison in the island of Pantelleria to surrender on June 12, 1943. This island lay between Tunisia and Sicily and its surrender meant that the straits could be safely crossed. On the night of July 9–10 Allied forces crossed and landed in Sicily. The American forces took Palermo (July 22), the British Syracuse (July 12) and, with some difficulty, Catania (August 5), and the Americans Messina (August 16). The Allies had fought a battle of destruction, but the German forces escaped. They were evacuated to the mainland during the first week of August and the last had left by August 17. It thus came about that Italy became the theatre of operations in the Anglo-American war against Germany and the scene of an Italian civil war.

On July 19, 1943, the Allies bombed Rome. The day of this outrage was also the day when Mussolini met Hitler at Feltre. He had little satisfaction from his ally. He became ill, apathetic and seemed henceforward a detached spectator of his own downfall. The King, Court and disaffected Fascists (Ciano and Grandi) manoeuvred to bring a new Government into being under Badoglio; the Fascist Grand Council met and, in his presence, disowned Mussolini by 19 votes to 8 with one abstention (July 25, 1943). The King summoned Mussolini, dismissed him and had him taken into custody. Meanwhile the British under Montgomery crossed from Sicily to the toe of Italy, landing at Reggio and Taranto. They marched or drove northwards. The Americans by an amphibious operation landed on the beaches of Salerno and joined the northward drive. The King signed an armistice in September, but the Germans still remained to be defeated and the Allies proceeded against them slowly, for it was to their advantage to tie down as many German forces as possible in Italy. So the Germans were able to rescue Mussolini and to use him to set up a puppet Fascist Government in North Italy. It was now that Italian civil war developed. The Liberals with the prestige that the presence of Benedetto Croce gave them, the Christian Democrats under Alcide de Gasperi and the Socialists had the strength of wide-spread support. The Communists were, however, the backbone of the anti-fascist side in north Italy, as elsewhere in Europe. This period set the pattern for Italy's political development after the War, but did not have much immediate affect. The King's Government remained a primarily military one and he called no one from the parties to join it.

The Allied contribution to the defeat of Germany in 1943 was as much by bombing her cities as by fighting in Italy. Strategic bombing had never been well adjusted to its targets. There was too little information, let alone accurate information, about the siting of key industrial, aeronautical, and scientific centres, even if they had all been accessible, to make the most economical choice of targets possible. Raids were so costly that the first method of daylight raiding had to be given up. A technique was then discovered of dropping silver foil to confuse German radar and raids became less costly. Another kind of raid, that against communications, was also given up as pointless, except as part of a military operation. This was the state of affairs when radar direction-finding was perfected and American Flying Fortresses—heavy long-range bombers, able to depend on themselves without fighter escort—came into use for raids from Britain. Strategic bombing now became a less wasteful operation. The pin-pointing of single targets was still not, however, achieved, so that it became a matter of reducing whole cities to rubble. Berlin was bombed to pieces but the climax was the bombing of Dresden, not a military target, on February 13, 1945. In fourteen hours, some 135,000 people were killed. But this properly belongs to the final phase of the story.

In 1943–44 the Germans were defeated in Russia. The causes of their defeat are interesting. Already before 1940 the Russians laid plans for the evacuation of their war industries eastwards. These plans were executed with great efficiency. The Russians, therefore, surpassed the Germans in resources. The Russians outnumbered the Germans, not by much in men under arms of whom they had some 6 million to the German 5 million, but largely in reserves. Thirdly, the

Russians matched the Germans in tanks and artillery and outdid them in the air where their machines were more up-to-date. The Germans had been manufacturing too many types and had cut down (on Hitler's orders) research and the trial of new types. Their production had fallen off and, in short, they allowed themselves to be outclassed. Finally the Russians had the advantage of controlled partisan activity in the Germans' rear and outclassed them in strategy. The German strategy of breakthrough on a narrow front was not a possible answer to the Russian strategy of continuous offensive over an enormous length of front. Their artillery, tank and infantry actions were co-ordinated within each offensive and their several interlocking offensives co-ordinated with wonderful accuracy. The German strategy was sensible, not as an answer, but as a gambit when they had the initiative. But their initiative planned for May 1943, against the Russian salient thrusting westwards in the front at Kursk, began too late and then failed. They lost the initiative and had no answer to the Russian offensives which followed, one after the other, in a continuous tide. The offensive in the front at Kursk set off offensives to the north and south and then put the whole front, from Smolensk to Kherson, in motion. One incident was memorable before the German offensive failed. A great tank engagement, with more than 1,000 tanks engaged on each side, but no infantry and no planes, took place at Petrokhorovka (July 9, 1943). It was unique in the War. Though it is outside this phase of the story, it may be said in conclusion that by November 1944 the Russians had pushed their whole front between 190 and 250 miles nearer to Germany.

The meeting between Roosevelt, Churchill and Stalin at Teheran from November 28 to December 1, 1943, preceded by a meeting of Foreign Ministers in Moscow and talks in Cairo between Roosevelt, Churchill and Chiang Kai-shek, was decisive for the post-war future. It was dominated by Stalin and the interests of Russia. From the point of view of Britain the decision taken there to make a landing on the French coast in May 1944 was the most important. (Operation Overlord eventually took place in June.) Britain would have preferred a Mediterranean landing. But Stalin and Roosevelt prevailed. From the Russian point of view the most important decision related to Poland. Poland was to be pushed westwards. Thus Germany would lose East Prussia with its capital Königsberg, the birthplace of Kant and the home of a great German University, and a strip of territory which included the Silesian coalfield, that had not long been German, as well as terrirtory hers from time immemorial. On her eastern frontier Poland would lose definitively the territory taken from her by Russia in 1939. Of uncertain importance was the interest which Stalin showed in the Balkan Peninsula, for it was shared by Churchill. That rivalry was not resolved.

The last phase of the fighting has now been reached. It is the phase when eastern and central Europe fell under Soviet sway but Greece and Yugoslavia retained their independence; when France was liberated; the Battle of the Rhine was won; the settlement of Potsdam achieved; and Japan was forced to surrender.

As Germany's fortune declined, her satellites one by one tried to detach themselves from her. First, King Michael of Rumania dismissed his 'Fascist' Government and appointed a Ministry including Communists. He made overtures to the Allies who demanded unconditional surrender. He tried to make terms but gave in after Ploesti and Bucharest were bombed. By September 1944 Russian armies had entered Bucharest and Rumania enjoyed the benefits of an armistice. Bulgaria, where King Boris had died, was forced to change sides by an underground resistance movement. The 'Fatherland Front', composed of Communists, Socialists and the People's Agrarian Union, drew away whole units from the army, organised demonstrations and strikes and finally took over in September 1944. The Russian armies marched into Sofia on September 18, 1944. Bulgaria then declared war on Germany and sent an army to fight side by side with the Red Army. In 1943 Hungary also made overtures to the Allies, but she was premature. Germany tightened her controls and compelled Admiral Horthy to submit to levies of commodities and labour. In 1944 Horthy played for time hoping to make peace with the British and Americans, but the Russians in Rumania were too near and in October he too signed an armistice with Soviet Russia. In Czechoslovakia, the Slovaks had revolted on a grand scale in July 1944 and in the following month Communist resisters joined them and both joined the Russians advancing through the Pripet marshes. The Polish resistance had burst into the open too soon. The Polish rising of July 29, 1944, was a terrible disaster. Between July and the final crushing of the rising in October 50,000 inhabitants of Warsaw had been killed, wounded or taken prisoner, 350,000 were deported to Germany. The Germans systematically destroyed what was left of the city. British and American assistance, dropped from the air, arrived too late. Stalin played hot and cold, for he was aiming at handing over a Poland, weakened beyond recovery, to the so-called Lublin Committee, a body sponsored by Moscow, rather than see a liberated Poland recall her exiled Government from London. It was what he achieved.

In October 1944 Churchill went to Moscow and reached agreement with Stalin. This was the notorious partition of the Balkan, eastern and central European countries: Rumania to Russia, Greece to Britain,

Yugoslavia and Hungary to Russia and Britain in equal shares.

Meanwhile the Allied armies had slogged all the way up the boot of Italy. They were checked by the Germans' fortified defence line, the Gustav Line, south of Rome, but outflanked it by the American landing on the beach of Anzio. They were next checked by the Gothic Line, built from Pisa to Rimini. They were now joined by the Free French Army. Liberation Committees were active in German-occupied Italy and in touch with a new Government in Rome. This was headed by Bonomi, a Liberal, and was appointed by Prince Umberto who, with the title of Regent, had replaced his father, King Victor Emmanuel. Bonomi obtained an armistice in December 1944.

Operation Overlord had been successful. Final victory in the Battle of the Atlantic had allowed vast quantities of ships, men and equipment to cross from the United States. Britain had become the springboard for the final attack upon the fortress of Europe by an operation, planned on a vast scale but with the minutest detail exactly arranged, with great scientific skill and inventiveness (which prefabricated harbours well illustrated) and involving the controlled deployment of forces, far outnumbering the German, and fully supported from the air. The landings in Normandy, which took the Germans by surprise, began on June 6. The battle for Normandy was won by July 31. The Americans then went into Brittany, swinging west and then north to Paris; the British went eastwards from Normandy, developed two offensives and linked up with the French resistance. The various resistance groups were united as the French Forces of the Interior (FFI) under General Koenig, who acted in the name of the Provisional Government of France that had been set up in Algeria after the success of Operation Torch. General de Gaulle's Free French army had not been allowed to take part in the landings, but was on French soil by August. Paris, like Warsaw, rose prematurely, recovered and was finally liberated in August, authorities being installed who recognised the Provisional Government of France under de Gaulle. Meanwhile, and before the liberation of Paris, landings had been made in Provence. This was Operation Anvil. Even in this 'small' operation the Allied forces numbered 500,000 men, were transported in 450 freightships and 230 warships and supported by 1,000 aircraft. The FFI co-operated with planned sabotage and Free French forces participated, being withdrawn from Italy to do so. The Germans were surprised and retreated up the Rhone valley. Forces from Overlord and Anvil joined together in Burgundy where the Germans stood and fought (September 3–13). They were defeated and again in retreat. By November 1944 the liberation of France had been completed. The national uprising had enabled France to take her place among the Allies, who had at last recognised de Gaulle's Provisional Government as the Government of France. Fifty-four divisions were now in place for the invasion of

Germany. A group of British and Canadian armies were under Montgomery north of the Ardennes. Next, to their north, came General Bradley's group of American armies. South of the Eifel, General Denvers had a group of French and American armies.

In Germany Hitler's régime kept its hold: there was no alternative. It is true there were isolated pockets of opponents. There were Communists and former trade unionists who had avoided imprisonment. There was at least one students' organisation: the White Rose of Hans and Sophie Scholl. There was the Kreisau Circle led by Helmuth von Moltke. There were individual Catholics and Lutherans at the head of groups or alone. There was a group of generals in the army, but the strength of the opposition in the army lay with the colonels. It was Colonel von Stauffenberg who placed the bomb in a room of Hitler's Headquarters, where he was holding a working conference, on July 20, 1944. Hitler was protected by a table from the worst effects of the explosion. The conspiracy came sufficiently out into the open (Stauffenberg thought the bomb had killed Hitler and went on to carry out the next step of seizing key buildings in Berlin) for Hitler to wreak a ghastly revenge. The régime fought on. Nazi leaders took over army commands and injected fanaticism where there had only been courage. Hitler's hopes were fixed on the V1 and V2 pilotless aircraft which fell on London during the summer of 1944. The letter V stood for *Vergeltungswaffe* or instrument of reprisal. There was also a brief revival of submarine warfare as new submarines fitted with snorkels came into use. Finally, in December 1944, Germany made one last offensive. This was in the Ardennes and took a month to defeat. By January 1945 it was over.

The Yalta conference took place in the Crimea between Stalin, Roosevelt and Churchill in February 1945. Roosevelt, who had been re-elected President in November 1944, was already ill and would die in the following April, leaving his Vice-President, Harry Truman, to replace him. It was, then, the last of the meetings between the three men. By the time it took place Russian armies were on the Oder, forty-five miles from Berlin, and in the south eighty miles from Vienna. The British and Americans had not yet crossed the Rhine. It is not then surprising that Russian interests were well satisfied at Yalta, as, indeed, were American interests; for a certain sympathy existed between Roosevelt and Stalin in which Churchill did not share. Churchill was anxious to limit Russian influence in Europe, but Roosevelt did not share this aim. As to Germany, the three statesmen decided that she was to be militarily occupied and outlined the occupation zones. The French at this stage were not included, but were allowed a zone later, cut out of the British and American zones. Germany was to be dismembered and divided again into states held together by some form of federal bond. She was to pay reparation totalling 20,000 million dollars of which half was to go to

Russia. She was to be demilitarised, the concentration of her industries reduced and she was to be re-educated out of Nazism. Stalin laid claim to the occupation of Austria, but encountered Churchill's opposition. The Russian occupation of Vienna was subsequently agreed to by General Eisenhower as a military decision, Churchill's view that it was a political matter being disregarded. Stalin again obtained his aims over Poland. Her frontiers were to be the so-called Curzon line of 1920 on the east and the Oder-Neisse line (it turned out to mean the western Neisse) on the west. Her Government was to be that of the Lublin Committee rather than that of the exiled Government in London. Stalin was committed to the war against Japan and to membership of the United Nations Organisation to be founded in accordance with the Atlantic Charter. This was something gained for American and British interests. It could not, however, be denied that at Yalta the world was partitioned between two super-Powers and that the small states were ignored. At least the Allies still co-operated in trust.

The Battle for the Rhine was the last to be fought in Europe. The Allies now fought under General Eisenhower's command. Britain had hoped that Montgomery might have had the command of the ground forces under Eisenhower, but he retained it for himself. The battle was prefaced by an immense air-borne landing at Arnhem. This was not a well-managed operation, so that the force had to hold on from September 17, 1944, when it was dropped, until Antwerp had been liberated in November. Yet it had served its purpose in enabling the Allies to leap over all the obstacles from the French frontier to the Rhine, liberating Belgium on the way. The main battle was opened by the French in January in the south, taken up by the Americans in the centre and the British and Canadians in the north, the Americans crossing the Rhine first, by the good luck of the undestroyed Remagen Bridge (March 8). By April 1 the Battle for the Rhine was over and Eisenhower's victory complete. The Allies swept on eastwards, but they did not win the race for Berlin. It was taken by the Russians on April 29. On April 30 Hitler, now ruling only over the few square yards of an underground bunker, shot himself and Eva Braun. Goebbels, who with his family had also lived in the bunker, took the lives of his wife and children and his own. Admiral Doenitz, to whom Hitler had assigned the succession, took over, but never established his authority.

The Potsdam Conference now took place (July 17–August 2). Truman was there instead of Roosevelt, and Clement Attlee, soon to be Labour Prime Minister, was by Churchill's side. When once Britain had been used as the springboard for the attack on Europe, her part in the War was over. Neither she nor France could alter the pattern of continental power. Russian power extended from Finland, through the Baltic states, over Poland, East Germany, Czechoslovakia, Hungary, Rumania and Bulgaria. In Austria the Russians had set up Karl Renner, the Socialist Prime Minister of Austria in 1918, but he was a puppet. On May 12, 1945, Churchill had already given the world the phrase that summed up the situation: 'an iron curtain has fallen on the Russian front.' The Potsdam Conference did no more than register the accomplished facts. On the day the Conference opened Truman learnt that the atom bomb was ready for use. Truman might have employed this information as a means of pressure on Russia to limit her power in Europe, but he saw no American interest in doing so. He gave the information to Stalin that the Americans were in possession of a bomb more powerful than any so far used in a casual way, so that Stalin did not understand the significance of what he was told.

In the war with Japan which was still continuing the Americans had broken the perimeter of the Japanese empire at Rabaul. They had then made a series of leaps forward, conquering bases, each desperately fought for, until they were in a position to make a landing on Honshu. They now brought the war to an end by dropping the atom bomb. In fact they dropped three bombs in all. One was dropped as a test in New Mexico on July 16, the second and third on Japan: on Hiroshima on August 6 (71,000 out of 250,000 inhabitants were killed and an unknown number died subsequently) and on Nagasaki on August 9, 1945 (40,000 are estimated to have been killed and the number of subsequent deaths is unknown). The Japanese did not and could not know that the third was the last one the Americans had. On August 14, 1945, the Japanese accepted the Allies' terms and surrendered unconditionally.

It seemed at the time that this surrender was caused by the dropping of the atom bomb. If that is true, it is so in a way that is not fully expressed in one simple sentence. Had the bomb been used at a different time in the War it might not have caused surrender. When it was dropped, Japan was already 'a spent force, unable to project her strength beyond her boundaries.' The outward movement of 1941–42 had already been completely reversed. With some exaggeration the dropping of the bomb has been likened to administering poison to a man on his deathbed. If that goes too far, it is nevertheless true that Japan had been defeated. She fought on after defeat because she hoped to make the Americans, by losses during the invasion they were about to make, give up their war aim of destroying the essential Japan as embodied in the Emperor and his constitutional system. The Americans called it Japanese militarism or imperialism. She abandoned this hope under the influence of shock. Shock threw the political and military leaders off balance, because they had no answer to what had happened. But the disaster which caused the shock was only partly the disaster of the bomb. In the four days beginning on August 6 the Japanese had more than that to suffer.

The atomic bomb

They had hoped apparently right up until August 9 for the mediation of the U.S.S.R. to gain conditions of surrender and more favourable terms than unconditional surrender. But on August 9 the Russians entered Manchuria. By August 20 they had taken Port Arthur; in September they took the Kurile Islands. The unexpected entry of the U.S.S.R. in the war was as much part of the shock as the dropping of the bomb. The argument that the bombs were unnecessary because the Russians could have brought the War to an end by conventional weapons may also be valid. The Americans, however, had had enough and were not prepared to face further uncertainties. Moreover calculations had been made of the relative disasters from dropping the bomb or from continuing the War by invasion and indicated that the bomb would prove the less destructive.

Chapter 13

THE BALANCE SHEET. AFTER THE WAR

The scale of the War was immense and it changed the whole world. Casualties are impossible to know precisely. Estimates vary between the limits of 40 and 50 million people.[1] About half these may have been civilians, including many women and children. A number that is unknown died in concentration camps without their deaths having any direct relation to the needs of the War. They included some six and a half million Jews. The scale on which the War was fought and the destruction wrought was greatest in the German-Soviet war and a large part of Russian territory suffered grievously at the hands of the S.S. It is still surprising that Russian losses were estimated at 20 million dead. Poland's losses proportionately to her population were higher at 6 million, of whom only 600,000 died in battle. The civil war in Yugoslavia and Greece made the losses of civilians there especially heavy. For Yugoslavia the figures are 1,200,000 civilians and 300,000 armed men; for Greece 140,000 civilians and 20,000 armed men. Belgium, Holland and Norway lost a few tens of thousands mostly in Nazi concentration camps. France estimated her loss as 400,000 civilians missing (deportees as well as air-raid victims) and 200,000 armed men killed. Britain estimated her loss as 62,000 civilians killed in air-raids and 326,000 armed men killed. The United States estimated her loss at 300,000 military casualties divided equally between Europe and Asia. On the other side, Italy had relatively small losses, estimated at 310,000 dead of whom about half were civilians. Germany lost over 4 million of whom 1 million were civilians killed in air-raids. China's losses were estimated at between 6 and 8 million and Japan's at 3 million, including 600,000 civilians.

The War caused enormous movements of people, beginning with the movement of population from and in the countries Germany invaded in 1939–40 and continuing with the movement of people

---

[1] Figures are taken from H. Michel, *The Second World War* (1975), pp. 781 ff. and M. Balfour, *West Germany* (1968), p. 141.

from the French, German and Russian battle areas. To these must be added the movements deliberately made by Hitler and Stalin. Hitler 'brought home' German minorities from the South Tyrol, the Baltic states, the Bukovina and the Dobrudja. Hitler tried to move Germans into the Ardennes, drove out Poles, Slovenes and Czechs from their homes and tried to replace them with Germans. Stalin moved Poles, Lithuanians, Estonians into Russia, Rumanians out of Bessarabia, Magyars out of Transylvania. There were various transplantations after the settlement of frontiers at Yalta and Potsdam. Germans flooded westwards from all the places to which the Russians came: from Poland, Silesia and the Baltic states and from the Russian zone of occupation in Germany. Vast camps for displaced persons took years to empty. The number of Germans, completely without resources, seeking asylum in the British and American zones of occupation was said to be greater than German losses during the War. The movement in the fifties and sixties of West Indians, Pakistanis, and Indians and others to Britain seems in retrospect only a late manifestation of the same phenomenon.

The material and moral havoc caused by the War was on a similarly vast scale. It is impossible to quantify. Yet reparation commissions were set to work in all countries and some attempt made to add up the harbours destroyed, miles of railway line damaged, railway bridges, tunnels, road bridges and roads destroyed and damaged, buildings destroyed, coal and ore stocks exhausted, industrial output lost, agricultural crops lost or reduced and so on. But they could not take account of such things as working hours lost or production rate falling through air-raids and exhaustion; nor, indeed, the speed with which losses were sometimes made good. The factor in the War that caused the greatest moral damage was the mistrust, suspicion, hatred and thirst for revenge arising from the existence in so many countries of resisters on one side and collaborators on the other; not to mention the consequences of the barbarous habit of taking hostages. Something of the desire for revenge was run into slightly healthier channels by the Nuremberg Trial of War Criminals which opened on November 20, 1945, and the special court set up in France which tried Pétain and Pierre Laval among others.

The economic consequences may be broadly stated. The United States, Canada, the South American countries, Sweden and Switzerland had been much enriched by the War. They would have to find their way back to a slower pace of economic growth. The rest of the world had been much impoverished. Other countries were in debt, their budgets in deficit, their currencies threatened and inflation already there or kept off, as in Britain, by heavy taxation, and to begin in a few years' time. After the War regulations on economic and social subjects, made during the War, were retained. Indeed, some were greatly extended. Measures of industrial nationalisation and various systems of social security, family allowances and national health services were set up and state-aided higher education became the rule in the western democracies. Controlled economies became the pattern the world over.

The political consequences were greatest in Germany. The German state disappeared. There was no German Government with which to sign a peace treaty. Even Government officials went into hiding or were arrested by the occupying forces. Germany's industrial, railway and road system disintegrated. Everywhere men, women and familes were on the move and possessions were being burnt for fuel or bartered for food and cigarettes. The military Commands of the occupying Powers were at first the only authorities. They worked in zones whose boundaries, as we have seen, had already been agreed on at Yalta among themselves. Russia had East Germany and most of Austria, the United States had the zone west of the Russian in the south with Bavaria and Württemberg, Britain next to her in the north with Schleswig-Holstein and Rhineland-Westphalia and France had parts of each of the zones originally assigned to Britain and the United States, that is the Palatinate, Lorraine and Baden. Berlin, two-thirds of the way into the Russian zone, was nevertheless occupied by four Powers. Because the Russians had a different idea of the future of Germany from that of the United States and Britain, and because the three Powers kept France out of their Conferences at Yalta and Potsdam, the zonal administrations had hardened before the Four Power Control Council, the only body which had competence for the whole of Germany, set to work in August. Each Power behaved in its own way in its own zone and zonal boundaries came to have a political importance which they were not originally intended to have. The shape of the eventual division of Germany into the German Democratic Republic and the German Federal Republic (see pp. 261 and 298 below) appeared even before the Potsdam Conference of July 1945. The Control Council, known when it began to work as the Control Commission, dealt with the arrest of war criminals, denazification, re-education, food distribution and the admission of various relief organisations. But the political and economic functions which it was originally intended it should discharge for all Germany, were not performed by it. This was partly because the dismemberment of Germany provided for at Yalta proved too dangerous a subject to raise, since the different ideas of Britain, who had had second thoughts, and France, who wanted extreme fragmentation, and of the U.S.S.R. and the United States whose strategic interests made them think along yet other channels, threatened to break up the alliance. Even demilitarisation and reparation were, in the interest of Allied agreement, better left to be handled empirically in the course of time. Economic principles laid down at Yalta, that German production should be cut to an 'authorised figure' and 'excessive' business concentration prevented, were not implemented. They had been left too vague to be applied.

Among general political consequences, the most interesting was the move to the Left in the western democracies after the War. As for Britain, the General Election of July 1945 gave her a Labour Government under Clement Attlee with Ernest Bevin, a great trade unionist and Minister of Labour during the War, as Foreign Secretary. In France, Italy and Belgium, Communist Ministers served in the first post-war Governments. The share of the Communists in the resistance during the War had raised their standing and national importance in all the countries of western Europe. But another interesting phenomenon in these countries was the Christian Democratic Movement. Members of the Roman Catholic Church were prominent in this movement, but it arose spontaneously and separately in each country. The *Mouvement Républicain Populaire* (MRP) in France, the Christian Democratic Union (CDU) in West Germany and the Christian Democratic Party in Italy were already as strong or stronger than the Socialist-Communist Parties in those countries in 1945.

The most striking of the political consequences was the change in the balance of power, both within Europe and in the world, if the two can be considered apart, which is doubtful. Of the four great western European Powers of 1939, Britain, Germany, France and Italy, only Britain retained any strength. But it was much diminished. Britain had had a triumphant victory for which she paid with the loss of her political, economic and financial strength. Politically she was no longer equal to the United States in world influence. Economically, while her food production had increased, her industrial production, particularly in textiles, had fallen off. The industries which had provided her exports before the War were producing less than half of what they produced in 1939. It has been calculated that her merchant navy, which had surpassed that of the United States in 1939, was less than a third of it in tonnage in 1945. Even had she had the goods to export, she had lost the means to ship them. She had already lost, as a result of the War of 1914–18, her nineteenth-century financial primacy. After the War of 1939–45 she was without even the financial means to provide for reconstruction, for the release of men and women from the armed forces and from war industries into which they had been directed and for their employment in civilian work. She was heavily in debt to the United States, the Commonwealth countries, India and Egypt. She had, in fact, overseas debts amounting to a total of £3,355 million.

France was about to renew her strength and consolidate it within a diminished field, but it was with difficulty that she established her claim to equality with Britain in international relations. The difficulty was increased by de Gaulle's resignation on January 20, 1946. She can hardly be said to have established it until the second parliament of the Fourth Republic (1951–56) and, given the Indo-Chinese and the Algerian Wars, perhaps not even then. Italy came out of the War a Republic (1946), with no overseas colonies, impoverished, but able gradually to recover economically, in dispute with Yugoslavia over Trieste, and politically unstable. In Belgium there was a political crisis. While the King was in German hands his brother, commissioned by parliament, acted as Regent. But in 1951 Leopold abdicated in favour of his son, Prince Baudoin. Belgium has not become a Republic. In Holland the crisis was economic, partly consequent upon her loss of her Indonesian resources. She only recovered her overseas empire in order to negotiate its independence (recognised in 1949). The Customs Union, known as Benelux and including Luxembourg as well as Belgium and Holland, was agreed on in London in September 1944. It was a pointer to the future. Eventually the Common Market would prove to be Europe's solution to the problem of organising her economy on a larger scale and European Union an ideal for her political future in a world in which power had shifted away from western Europe to the United States on one side and to the U.S.S.R. on the other. The Arab world between was in ferment. New nations, Syria, Lebanon, Jordan, Palestine, Egypt and the North African and South Arabian states would eventually emerge there, but as a consequence of post-war developments. It is appropriate to notice the agitation here, but its purely Arab consequences are outside the scope of a history of Europe.

The United States had determined the course of the War in its last phases: since, in fact, the turning-point of November 1942. She had fought with machines rather than men and her losses had not been in proportion to her population. She had not suffered civilian casualties from air-raids. Her losses had in fact been insignificant except in human terms. Her political and economic strength was enormous. She led the way in nuclear strength. Her economic output in coal, crude oil, steel and aluminium has been calculated to have been something under or something over half the world's output. Her merchant navy gave her two-thirds of the total world shipping. Her fleet of transoceanic aircraft was unmatched and in 1945 she virtually had a monopoly of intercontinental air transport, though she was not to retain it for long. Her gold reserves, balance of trade, and balance of payments were such as to enable her to fix unilaterally the prices on world markets. The Latin American states and Canada owed much of their favourable economic position to their relations with the United States. It turned out that no country in Europe could achieve reconstruction without American aid. The so-called Marshall Plan of 1947 provided this and will occupy us briefly later on. This dependence of Europe upon the United States gave her great political influence. Her policy was empirical and liberal and has aroused no great opposition.

The U.S.S.R. emerged from the war territorially much enlarged. She kept all the territory acquired during the period of the German-Soviet pact: Karelia, the Baltic countries (Estonia, Latvia, Lithuania), Polish White Russia, Bessarabia and the northern Bukovina. In Asia she added, during the war with Japan, the Kurile Islands, South Sakhalin, Dairen and Port Arthur. Her armies in 1945 still occupied North Korea and Manchuria. In Europe she added, during the War, East Prussia and Ruthenia while her armies occupied East Germany and part of Berlin, Austria, Poland, Hungary, Czechoslovakia, Rumania and Bulgaria. She made good her claims against Turkey and might hope to dominate Yugoslavia and Albania. The question: how much of this power was she able to retain and develop will occupy us in chapter 15. At this point in the story it is only appropriate to notice the wide hearing Communist Russia had obtained from the resistance movements in all countries where they existed. She had gained admiration from her Allies for the stamina, endurance and military skill which she had shown during the War. She had gained all that the autocracy had hoped in vain to gain out of the War of 1914–18. She had, moreover, become to some extent intelligible to the west. Her power after the War did not diminish; for she did not demobilise her army and she too acquired nuclear capability. Indeed, she is apparently equal and may be superior to the United States in this element of strength. Economically she had weaknesses, but also sources of strength. The war areas were devastated, depopulated and impoverished beyond recovery except under a 'command economy.' Yet the dispersal of industrial production, by moving enterprises eastwards, had saved much of it. Coal, oil and steel production and electricity generating were stimulated by the war and boomed after it. They were sources of strength. It was impossible to tell what the economic potential of the U.S.S.R. was, nor how much of it she would be able to make politically effective.

From the failure of the League and the embroilment of the whole world in a war for the second time in a generation, grew the determination of the Allied Powers to make an international organisation capable of taking effective action in the face of a threat to peace. The Atlantic Charter of August 12, 1941, published by Churchill and Roosevelt after their first meeting, had promised it. The United Nations Declaration of January 1942 committed the Powers at war with Germany, Italy and Japan to remain united after the War. Britain, Russia and the United States decided, in October 1943, not to wait until the War was over, but to start at once to build up such an organisation. Draft proposals were drawn up by the representatives of Britain, Russia, America and China at conferences held at Dumbarton Oaks, Washington, between August and October 1944. From these proposals the United Nations Charter was drawn up by the delegates of fifty states who met at San Francisco from April to June 1945.[1] The Charter set up the United Nations Organisation, to maintain international peace and security, to develop friendly relations among nations and to achieve international co-operation in solving international problems of an economic, social, cultural or humanitarian character. Six principal organs were established to carry into effect these objectives. The General Assembly, composed of all the members of the United Nations, has the right of discussing all matters within the scope of the Charter and making recommendations on them. Eleven members of the United Nations form the Security Council, on which five of the seats are permanently allotted to the U.S.A., France, Britain, the U.S.S.R. and China, whilst the remaining six places are held for two years by members of the United Nations elected by the General Assembly. The Security Council is primarily responsible for the maintenance of peace and security: its functions are more specific than those of the Council of the League of Nations and it is given the means of enforcing its decisions relating to the pacific settlement of disputes and the prevention of aggression. Decisions in the Security Council on all matters, other than those of procedure, require an affirmative vote of seven members, including all the permanent members. This in effect gives the permanent members, or any one of them, the right of veto. It is the real voice of the Organisation. The Economic and Social Council of eighteen members, elected by the General Assembly, is to promote 'respect for, and observance of, human rights and fundamental freedoms for all.' The Trusteeship Council replaces the Permanent Mandates Commission of the League, but the territories within its competence are not named. The International Court of Justice is based on the Permanent Court of International Justice set up by the League, and its statute follows very closely that of its precursor. Finally, a Secretariat completes the organisation, supervised by a Secretary-General appointed by the General Assembly on the recommendation of the Security Council. Two other organs, set up later, the United Nations Relief and Rehabilitation Administration (UNRRA) and the United Nations Educational Scientific and Cultural Organisation (UNESCO) have been important within their respective areas.

The United Nations was devised in the light of the experience of the League of Nations, and an attempt was therefore made to avoid the errors inherent in the constitution of the League. The Charter is thus a much longer and more explicit document than the Covenant, and the powers and functions of the United Nations are considerably more extensive than those of the League. Moreover, the Covenant

[1] P. A. Reynolds and E. Hughes, *The Historian as Diplomat. Sir Charles Kingsley Webster and the United Nations* (1976), has interesting detail on the making of the Organisation.

237

formed an integral part of the Treaty of Versailles, and was drawn up in the aftermath of war. The Charter of the United Nations, on the other hand, was drafted before the conclusion of hostilities, and signed, ratified and in operation before the conclusion of peace treaties. The membership of the United Nations is also more representative of all continents than that of its precursor, and its members include all the Great Powers which emerged from the war. On the other hand, although the Governments represented in the General Assembly were at first only those, forty-nine in number, which had declared war on Germany, Italy or Japan, in course of time nation after nation has been admitted. When new nations, as a result of decolonisation, came into existence, they too have been admitted. The consequence is that it has become too big for effective action. It has lost, rather than gained in power as its membership has increased.

There are, too, differences in the machinery of the United Nations which reflect the failures of the League. It was, for example, hoped that the powers vested in the Security Council would provide adequate machinery for countering aggression at its early stages. Nevertheless, the organisation of the United Nations owes much to the League of Nations, and the origins of its aims and basic principles are to be found even further back, in the thought and ideas of the nineteenth century.

It has not been found possible to keep the peace in the modern world, and the United States has been engaged in war in Korea (1950–53) and in Vietnam (1964–74) in an effort to preserve settlements thought to have been achieved in those countries. The extent of Soviet involvement in the same countries is difficult to establish, but it has not been on the same side as that of the United States. Nevertheless, as will be seen, the United Nations has sent its own forces both into Africa and into the Middle East, which have contained conflict that might have spread into general war. But hopes for it were from the beginning restrained and less optimistic than they were for the League. 'It was never contemplated at San Francisco,' wrote Trygve Lie, first Secretary-General of the United Nations,

> that the United Nations would or could abolish differences of interest and ideology such as we see in the world to-day. It was not believed that the great Powers would always act in unity and brotherhood together. What the founders of the United Nations did believe was that the United Nations would make it possible to keep disputes between both great and small Powers within peaceful bounds, and that without the United Nations this could not be done. Finally, they rejected the idea of an irreconcilable conflict that could be settled only on the field of battle, and proclaimed on the contrary the principle that all conflicts, no matter how fundamental, should and could be settled by peaceful means . . . The United Nations has not been able to resolve great

Power differences, but the conflict has been kept within peaceful bounds and the way prepared for further progress towards a settlement.[1]

The real cause of a change in the way the United Nations may be expected to work is the effect on the likelihood of War—or perhaps its impossibility—of the possession of nuclear capability by the United States, the U.S.S.R., China, Britain and France.

[1] Introduction to the Annual Report of the Secretary-General on the work of the Organisation, July 1, 1948–June 30, 1949. Printed in *International Conciliation* (New York), September 1949, p. 589.

Chapter 14

EUROPE ALONE: HOW COLONIAL DEPENDENCIES BECAME INDEPENDENT COUNTRIES

The countries of Europe after the War rapidly shed their non-European territories. Both the speed and the air of inevitability with which this happened were astonishing. The causes of the dissolving of empires were already manifest at the beginning of the century. The indictment of late nineteenth-century imperialism was worked out by thinkers from Hobson (*Imperialism: A Study* (1902) is the best-known of his books on this subject) to Lenin (*Imperialism, the Last Stage of Capitalism* was published in 1916). It was difficult to argue against this indictment without such detailed knowledge of what had actually happened as few either by personal experience possessed or by historical reading acquired. Nor had many in the egalitarian atmosphere after the War the wish, if they had the power, to discriminate between some imperialist activity which Lenin's analysis might fit and other activity which need not be arraigned as greedy exploitation from which only a few capitalists benefited. Soviet Russia, of course, had her own policy of colonisation, though it was applied internally and not overseas, and it was not thought of as exploitation. Communist Russia was still part of the alliance of nations that had fought the War and was to remain so until 1947; there were Communist Ministers in the Governments of France, Italy and Belgium; there was generally a more open attitude in the western democracies to Communisim, the self-styled opposite of Imperialism. Nor did everyone distinguish between condemned Nazi plans for 'colonising' areas of eastern Europe 'with Germans of pure Aryan blood' and the colonial plantations of the British and French overseas. The notion of colonial settlement was permanently muddled with imperialism and loosely associated in the public consciousness with exploitation and enslavement. In Britain Churchill, in a speech after the British and American landings in North Africa, said 'We mean to hold our own. I have not become the King's First Minister in order to preside over the liquidation of the British Empire' (November 10, 1942). But Clement Attlee, who became Prime

Minister in 1945 and remained so until 1951, had said in the Cabinet two months before, 'that in the view of the Labour Party the British electorate would not be content to go on bearing a financial burden in respect of Colonies from which the advantage mainly accrued to a capitalist group' (September 10, 1942).[1]

As a result of their experience during the War the 'emergent nations', as it became fashionable to call them, no longer found the superiority of the skills of the colonising Power unquestionable. Not only had they seen Europeans defeated, but they themselves had acquired some of their technical skills when they fought side by side. The old superiority of the white man with his administrative, medical, agricultural and manufacturing techniques was displaced by the possibility of equality with the white man whose technology was perhaps not beyond their reach. Some had acquired new standards of living as well as new skills, during the fighting in North Africa, Indo-China or the Pacific Islands. Moreover in Communism, or a sort of Communism, they had a revolutionary doctrine which gave confidence and guidance to the oppressed for the overthrow of their masters. In Soviet experience they could find a model for the future and could, moreover, learn from it that the French or Dutch or British had no monopoly of the art of providing settled government. The revival of Islam has been due to the discovery in it, or rediscovery in it, of yet another alternative to the settled government which those rulers had once had the advantage of providing. From many people's standpoint it was not Europe that shed its colonies, but movements for liberty which at last triumphed.

The United States made by far the largest contribution to bringing an end to empires. It is true they did not always distinguish between Americans' aims in their War of Independence in 1776 and the aspirations which 'emergent nations' had, or ought to have had, in 1946, but their pressure upon Britain during and after the War was none the less effective for that. Nor did they appreciate the effects of the British Colonial Development Act of 1929 and Colonial Development and Welfare Acts of 1940 and 1945. All three had set money aside for economic help and the last two reflected the new concept of the social responsibilities of the State. The last had set £120 million over ten years aside for economic and social development in the dependencies.[2] Roosevelt was more impressed by the low wages of the workman in, for example, Gambia than by British policy. The Atlantic Charter stated that an aim of the War was the restoration 'of sovereign rights and self-government to those who

---

[1] Quoted in R. W. Louis, *Imperialism at Bay* (1977),p. 193.

[2] It has recently been argued that, since the British Government was never able to meet these commitments, the British Empire might be said to have disintegrated from within before it was dismantled. See D. K. Fieldhouse, *English Historical Review* (1982), p. 389, reviewing *The Official History of Colonial Development*.

have been forcibly deprived of them.' But it had not read that way in Roosevelt's original version. Churchill had added 'sovereign rights' so that the sentence might not be interpreted as applying to non-European dependencies. He failed, however, to prevent the application. Roosevelt never gave up an attitude of mind which justified the British Government in thinking that one of the American war aims was to bring the British Empire to an end. In the discussions between American and British Ministers during the War three subjects furnished the stuff of constant argument. The first was the future status of dependencies: should they have independence or self-government? America thought independence was the desirable goal. Britain had a tradition of granting self-government to her dependencies—it was how the Dominions had acquired their status—and regarded independence, which at one stroke might bring fifty new nations into existence, as disruptive of all international order. The second subject of argument related to international control. The Americans would have liked all colonies to be brought under international control. Britain considered that only the former mandates should be internationally controlled. She had no intention of putting her colonies under international supervision and never did so. The third subject of argument related to regional co-operation. The idea of regional commissions was canvassed. They might control, say, defence in a particular area. The question was whether they should comprise representatives only of those concerned or whether they should comprise representatives of a range of states, large and small, and should act as bodies to which the rulers of colonies should be accountable. Britain accepted the principle of regional co-operation between the states concerned, but would go no further. She was ready for the new international organisation arranged for in the Atlantic Charter to incorporate the principle of trusteeship and apply it through a Trusteeship Council, much as the Permanent Mandates Commission of the League of Nations had applied the same principle, to the former mandates but she stubbornly resisted any more intrusive, cumbersome machinery. She was more open to the idea of 'partnership' with her dependencies as a way of implementing regional co-operation. It was the idea that the Dutch Queen in December 1942 had proclaimed as the basis for the reconstruction of the Dutch empire in Indonesia after the war.

The British Empire was not, on the whole, dependent on American military power for its survival, and Roosevelt was committed to a Dutch restoration in Indonesia and to a French restoration in Indo-China. He was determined at least to evade the latter commitment. 'The French,' he discovered, 'have been there for nearly one hundred years and have done absolutely nothing for the place to improve the lot of the people.' He was to agree with Stalin at Teheran that the French ought not to recover Indo-China, but Churchill prevented the formulation of any decision. And, as he had done at the Cairo meeting, which preceded the meeting at Teheran with Stalin, he stated Britain's intention neither to increase nor to submit to any diminution of her Empire. The result of Churchill's firmness was that the press release for the Cairo discussions with Roosevelt and Chiang Kai-shek, issued on December 1, 1943, after the Teheran meeting, and known as the Cairo Declaration, formulated no general principles about the treatment of dependent territories, but kept to partticulars about the Far East. Japan was to lose Manchuria, Formosa and the Pescadores which she was to restore to the Republic of China. Korea 'in due course' was to become free and independent. 'Japan will also be expelled from all other territories which she has taken by violence and greed.' In that negative way the restoration of the Dutch, French and British Empires in the Far East was ensured. During 1944 Britain tried to obtain the abolition of the mandates set up after the War of 1914–18 and to prevent the formulation of the principle of trusteeship altogether. But she found two of the Dominions, New Zealand and Australia, who in January 1944 made an agreement with each other, opposed to her. When the organisation of the prospective new world order, to be known as the United Nations Organisation, was discussed at Dumbarton Oaks, a Washington mansion, the subject of trusteeship was successfully avoided. Britain was guided afterwards by a State Paper, dated December 16, 1944, which affirmed the desirability of ending the mandates and limiting international activity in relation to dependencies to regional commissions, confined to the countries directly concerned, and functional agencies dealing with such matters as health and labour. But Britain failed. At Yalta, in February 1945, Roosevelt working with Stalin and using the need to have some way of dealing with the former Italian colonies and the Japanese mandates, imposed the principle of trusteeship upon Churchill. Churchill at his most formidable declared that he would tolerate 'no suggestion that the British Empire is to be put into the dock'; he would never 'consent to forty or fifty nations thrusting interfering fingers into the life's existence of the British Empire.' He was given an assurance that the principle would not apply to the British Empire. But it was uncertain exactly what was meant and it *was* certain that the old confident rule over the Empire could no longer be asserted in the world. When the United Nations Charter was drawn up at the San Francisco Conference in June 1945 and published on June 26, it was clear that Britain had not prevented a general declaration on colonial policy, which she had steadily opposed ever since Roosevelt first mooted it. Chapter XI of the Charter was the Declaration on Non-Self-Governing Territories. It obliged those who ruled them 'to develop self-government, to take account of the political aspirations of the peoples, and to assist them in the progressive development of their free political institutions, according to the particular circumstances of each territory and its peoples and their varying stages of advancement.' Nor had she been able to prevent the formulation of the principle of international trusteeship for these territories. Chapter XII was concerned with it. The object of the trust was declared to be the 'progressive development towards independence.' A clause provided for countries voluntarily to put the non-self-governing territories which they ruled under the trust. Chapter XIII provided for the composition, functions and powers of a Trusteeship Council which replaced the Permanent Mandates Commission of the League of Nations, with a crucial change. The membership of the League organisation had been expert; that of the new organisation was political: its members were, that is, representatives of Governments, not economists or agriculturalists. Britain had not gained, then, the abolition of the mandate system set up after the War of 1914–18, but its modification. She *had* gained the possible application of the trusteeship principle only to former mandates or new acquisitions, such as the United States' acquisition of islands in the Pacific, to be administered like the old mandates. The United States hoped that Britain would place her colonies under the Trusteeship Council, but she refused to do so. Former mandates she did place under it. She had also gained that in Chapter XI the term self-government was used and (except in Chapter XII in relation to trusteeship which she intended should apply only to the mandates, new or old) the word 'independence' avoided. To that extent the Chapters were in line with the British tradition. She was not to succeed, however, in ultimately keeping all 'decolonised'territories in the Commonwealth. As for regional commissions, an Anglo-American Commission had been set up for the Caribbean in March 1942 and one was now set up for the South Pacific on which Australia and New Zealand worked successfully with the United States. There were in the end only eleven Trust Territories comprising one former Italian colony (Somaliland), former Japanese mandates and new acquisitions of the United Sates, administered like the old mandates. They obtained independence between 1960 and 1961, except Nauru Island which obtained it in 1968 and New Guinea which obtained it in 1975. The United States continued to administer Micronesia as a Trust Territory. Of the other former Italian colonies: Eritrea was absorbed by Ethiopia in 1954, but has since revolted and its future is still uncertain; Libya was a subject of contention in the Security Council and was handed over to the General Assembly for decision, becoming as a result independent in 1951. It was the first of the non-self-governing territories to be made independent through the United Nations. It may be said to have begun the process of African decolonisation.

The story of the dismantling of the British Empire needs now no more than facts and dates to tell it, for the principles involved have all been indicated. India had been destined for change already in 1929 when it was promised Dominion status: legislation of 1947, effective on August 15, conferred Dominion status on each of two parts of a divided country. Of the two India became a Republic in 1950 and Pakistan in 1956. Both remained within the Commonwealth of which they recognised the Queen as Head. India and Pakistan have not been able to pull together and have quarrelled over Kashmir. On this issue Britain and the United States stood with Pakistan, their ally in SEATO (South-East Asia Treaty Organisation, 1954), and in the Baghdad Pact, and India looked for support to the U.S.S.R. Kashmir remains part of India. India in 1962 was at war with China over their common border; while she looked for aid to the United States, Pakistan increasingly looked to the U.S.S.R. But the incident ended without resolving any problems.

For Burma an act, to come into effect on January 4, 1948, provided independence. A similar act, to come into effect on February 4, 1948, provided independence for Ceylon (Sri Lanka),which, unlike Burma, remained within the Commonwealth. In February 1948 a Federation of Malaya was formed out of nine states with a Federal Executive Council, nominated by Britain after consultation with the political parties, and an elective Federal Legislative Assembly. Singapore was similarly but separately endowed with a nominated Executive Council and an elective Legislative Assembly. Malaya became independent in 1957, remaining within the Commonwealth. A plan was then made for a new sovereign state, to be called Malaysia, comprising the Federation of Malaya, Singapore, the former British colonies of Sarawak and North Borneo and the former British Protectorate of Brunei, to be proclaimed in August 1963. But postwar federations have not been successful. Brunei revolted (1962) and Singapore seceded (1965). Malaysia, Singapore and Brunei are three separate states.

A West Indian Federation of twelve islands had a troubled existence from 1958 to 1961. It was formally dissolved in April 1962. Jamaica and Trinidad-Tobago then obtained independence and sovereign status, leaving the other nine islands a British colonial responsibility.

In Africa the Gold Coast, together with the British Trust Territory of Togo, became independent Ghana, under Nkrumah, in 1957. Nigeria, organised by Britain as a Federation in 1954, as such became independent in 1960, but endured civil war in 1967–70. The failure of the attempt by Biafra to secede from the unitary state proclaimed by a military government, set up by Colonel Gowon, only confirmed Gowon's power. Nigeria remains a unitary state. Sierra Leone became independent in 1961 and the Gambia in 1964. Kenya became independent with greater difficulty. There the Africans had been safeguarded against the wealthy European settlers by the doctrine of

African paramountcy, enunciated by the then Colonial Secretary in 1923. The Mau-Mau rebellion and its suppression nevertheless marred the transition to independence. It lasted from 1952 to 1956. Independence was achieved in 1963. Uganda had achieved it in 1962 and the Trust Territory of Tanganyika, as Tanzania, in 1961. Britain's view that the proliferation of small states was unwise had led her to seek to federate these three, i.e. Kenya, Uganda and Tanzania. Lengthy discussions between the three Heads of State led to a treaty setting up an East African Community (1967) but not a federation. The three remain independent of each other. Britain had been attempting already in 1949 to establish a Central African Federation of North and South Rhodesia and Nyasaland. It came into existence at last in 1953, but also failed and was dissolved in 1963. Nyasaland, as Malawi, became independent in July 1964 and Northern Rhodesia, as Zambia, in October 1964, both remaining within the Commonwealth. The wish not to abandon white settlers, mostly British, to the ascendancy of a black African majority and the patent dissensions among warring Africans made special difficulties in Southern Rhodesia. They were not resolved until in 1980 the independent Republic of Zimbabwe was established, after the struggle of the white settlers to preserve their ascendancy had caused more than fourteen years of illegal independence and international ostracism.

By 1970 categories of thought had changed. The category of 'the British Commonwealth' is now little used in thought about the world. There is still a special relationship between Britain and Canada, Australia and New Zealand and perhaps between Britain and South Africa. But South African apartheid has seriously eroded the latter. The attempt to include Black African states, such as Uganda, in the same community as South Africa, practising such discrimination against Black races, has little reality. It is more appropriate to the modern situation to think of (i) South Africa, (ii) Africa, and to put North Africa into (iii) the Arab world or sometimes into the Mediterranean world. A new category of states is (iv) South East Asia, and India and Pakistan belong to (v) the category Asia. The Commonwealth is now a reality in, for example, the common parliamentary tradition of the states belonging to it, but not as a unit of power among the super-Powers of the world.

No less troubled than the history of Rhodesia/Zimbabwe was that of the Belgian Congo. Belgium agreed at a conference with its political leaders in January 1960 that it should be independent by the middle of that year. She had failed, however, to agree with them on the form of its constitution. When independence was achieved in July 1960, under President Joseph Kasavubu, the federal structure embodied in a compromise constitution was still unacceptable to the Prime Minister, Patrice Lumumba, who wanted a unitary state, and Moise Tshombe, who led the Province of Katanga, rich in copper and other mineral resources, who wanted Katangan independence. Then there was a mutiny of the African soldiers of the *Force Publique* against their Belgian officers, followed by anti-European atrocities, ruthless civil and tribal war, and the flight of Europeans upon whom the economic life of the country depended. There was danger of intervention by other African states and, grounded or not, fear in the western democracies of Soviet intervention. The United Nations, under the skilful direction of its second Secretary General, Dag Hammarskjöld, organised a United Nations armed intervention. This was rather a holding operation, holding back a European conflict over the Congo, than an attempt to impose a settlement. It was not until December 1961 that a cease-fire was achieved between Tshombe and Cyrille Adoula, by now Prime Minister instead of Lumumba. By then there had been dreadful loss of life, including Hammarskjöld himself, killed in an air 'accident' within four miles of the airstrip, where he was to have landed on his way to one of the innumerable abortive attempts at negotiation. A fresh United Nations intervention was needed, first to help in the revision of the constitution towards a looser kind of federation, and then to bring Tshombe to accept what was an arrangement essentially safeguarding Katanga's autonomy, on one side, and the need of the whole Congo to benefit to some extent from Katanga's wealth on the other. A precarious peace was achieved in 1963, though a United Nations force remained in the Congolese Republic (Zaire) until 1964.

The Dutch Empire had been dismantled much earlier. After the Japanese evacuation of Java and Sumatra, a so-called Republic of Indonesia controlled those two islands. The Dutch offer in 1942 (see above, p. 242) of 'partnership' was simply disregarded. The Government of the Netherlands sent in military forces in July 1947 and again in December 1948 with the object of controlling a disorderly situation until a negotiated settlement could be achieved. American pressure, exercised partly directly and partly through the United Nations, was much to the fore here. In 1949 the Dutch withdrew after negotiating an agreement which transferred complete sovereign rights to the new Republic of Indonesia.

The dismantling of the French Empire has been left to the last in order to widen the scope of the narrative here, for it is as much part of the internal history of France as it is of European decolonisation. It had a decisive influence on events in France in the period under the Provisional Government (1944–46), under the Fourth Republic (1946–58) and under the Fifth Republic (from 1958). Just as Churchill had said 'We mean to hold our own' so de Gaulle had said the French Empire was 'intangible.' Yet it too was to go. It consisted in 1945 of: (i) Algeria and the four old colonies of Guinea, Guadeloupe, Martinique, St. Pierre and Miquelon. They were organised as departments of France and sent Deputies to the French parliament. Algeria made five departments. (ii) The African colonies, Senegal, Ivory Coast, Soudan, Mauritania, Dahomey, Niger and Upper Volta, and Madagascar made a second group. (iii) Vietnam (Cochin-China, Annam and Tonkin), Laos and Cambodia making up French Indo-China, and Tunis and Morocco were dependencies under some form of protectorate. (iv) Togoland and Cameroon were French mandates after the War of 1914–18, re-entrusted to her after the War of 1939–45. These Trust Territories became independent in 1960 and Cameroon was reunited with the former British Cameroons in 1961. The second group achieved independence between 1958 and 1960. Guinea became independent in 1958 and the seven states which had formed the Federation of West Africa became seven independent states, Soudan as Mali in 1960. Liberation did not come to the first and third groups without long wars, costly in money and lives and with significant effects on the way Frenchmen thought of the state to which they belonged.

The French at the time of de Gaulle's Provisional Government attempted to set up a framework in which French dependencies might live together in a loose association with each other and with France. It was hoped that this would be a way of both modernising and safe-guarding the empire. In February 1944 de Gaulle convened a conference of the leaders of the French African dependencies at Brazzaville. Here the idea of the French Community was inaugurated. In the Constitutions of both the Fourth (1946) and the Fifth Republic (1958) this was called L'Union Française and it was laid down that the President of the Republic should also be President of the Union into which the French dependencies were to be assembled. The Union did not come into being until 1958 and then lasted only until March 1960. The pressure of anti-imperialism was too great for any mere rearrangement to preserve any empire.

During the War Pétain had given Japan the use of air and naval bases in Vietnam, but during 1941 the Japanese occupied the whole of Indo-China. Nguyen Tat Thanh, also known as Nguyen Ai Quoc (Nguyen the Patriot) and later as Ho Chi-minh, had organised Communists and nationalist émigrés from southern China and Vietminh to drive out 'Fascists,' whether French or Japanese. In 1945 de Gaulle's forces were in Vietnam fighting the Japanese, but Vietminh guerrillas were bent on setting up an independent Republic and were virtually in control of all Vietnam by the time the Japanese were defeated. The Emperor, Bao-Dai, who had tried, while conciliating the Japanese, to prevent them from taking Vietnam over entirely, recognised the new Republic and abdicated. Ho Chi-minh now set up a Provisional Government at Hanoi in which he retained the Emperor as Supreme Counsellor, and proclaimed the Democratic Republic of Vietnam on September 2, 1945, and independence on September 7. Bao-Dai had appealed to the French to come to terms with Ho Chi-minh and accept independence, but the French missed this opportunity. De Gaulle, who was both President and Prime Minister at this time, affirmed France's intention to maintain her predominance in Indo-China and sent Admiral d'Argenlieu as High Commissioner as well as an army under General Leclerc. But China and Britain were also involved. The Potsdam Agreement made China responsible for disarming the Japanese in north Vietnam and the British for doing the same in south Vietnam. Vietnam was divided at the sixteenth parallel for this purpose. Meanwhile on January 20, 1946, de Gaulle had resigned, leaving a Constituent Assembly and a Provisional Government under Felix Gouin to become a prey to party conflict. France was preoccupied with her constitution-making and disparaged both Bao-Dai and the Communist guerrilla leaders too easily. Gouin's Government at least recognised the independence of Vietnam on March 6, 1946. With Laos and Cambodia it was to be a member of an Indo-Chinese Federation, which in turn was to be a member of the French Union. It remained to negotiate the conditions of membership of the French Union which everyone at that time wanted. For this purpose a Conference met at Fontainebleau. By the time it began France had rejected in a referendum the constitution just made and elected (June 2, 1946) a new Constituent Assembly. In the elections the Communists had lost and the MRP (*Mouvement Républicain Populaire*, a Catholic Centre party) and Radicals had gained support, for the mood of France had changed. As a result of these happenings Ho Chi-minh was treated in a dilatory, unserious fashion at the Conference and it ended in September 1946 in an unsatisfactory *modus vivendi* instead of a treaty. Meanwhile the French had recognised the formal independence of Laos and Cambodia from which China had withdrawn, while retaining control of important affairs. And in the south (Cochin-China) Admiral D'Argenlieu recognised a separate independent republic. The year 1946 ended in disaster. Clashes between the French and Vietminh guerrillas had already occurred and when the French sought to gain control of the Haiphong customs, war was unleashed. On November 23, 1946, the French bombarded Haiphong, the port of the Vietnamese capital, Hanoi. On December 19 Vietminh retaliated with a massacre of Frenchmen in Hanoi. This was the beginning of an eight-year war. Only three days earlier a new Government had taken office in Paris. The Constitution was approved by referendum in November and Léon Blum formed a Socialist Government. It was an interim Government, replaced after a month by the first Government of the Fourth Republic under Paul Ramadier. The Fourth Republic waged the war without ever supplying the military command with sufficient forces to win it. By the spring of 1947 France had another opportunity to make peace: Leclerc had stabilised the military situation and President Auriol and Paul Ramadier, at the head of a Socialist and Communist-supported Government, were ready to negotiate. But they negotiated with the wrong person and aimed at the wrong agreement. They negotiated with Bao-Dai who, in fact, never went back to Vietnam, and sought a treaty to make a united, not a federal, Vietnam, associated with Laos and Cambodia and a member of the French Union as before. By now Ho Chi-minh was too powerful to be disregarded, but the fear of Communism in France—Ramadier had shed the Communists from his Government in May 1947 and each of the two Governments which succeeded his were further to the right—was driving her into a mistaken belief that no agreement was possible with him. These negotiations, in which France seemed ready to grant Bao-Dai better terms than those she had refused to Ho Chi-minh, lasted until 1950. Meanwhile both Mao Tse-tung of China and the U.S.S.R. had recognised the Democratic Republic of Vietnam under Ho Chi-minh and China was sending military aid. This enabled him to enlarge the scale of his military effort: he was no longer by 1951 fighting a guerrilla war. France continued to keep her army short of men, refused to send the conscript levy and recruited unreliable Vietnamese auxiliaries. She had, however, sent out in December 1950, as both Commander-in-chief and High Commissioner, General Delattre de Tassigny. He made it quite clear that he was out for a military victory first, but Vietnamese independence afterwards. He died in January 1952 but he had virtually completed the restoration of the French position in the south. Under his successor the military position in the north rapidly deteriorated. While it did so Churchill, who had come back to power in Britain in October 1951, was quickening the pace of international negotiation. The Bermuda Conference of December 1953 of French, British and American Ministers led on to the meeting at Berlin (January 1954) of French, British, American and Soviet Ministers and an attempt to draw the U.S.S.R. back into the European group. The Berlin meeting brought France to consent to hammer out a settlement at an international meeting at Geneva between April and July 1954. The prospect of this conference had the effect of bringing the war to a climax. For Ho Chi-minh it was essential to win a victory in the field in order to gain as much as possible at the conference table; for the new French Commander, General Navarre, and for the Laniel Government in France, it was essential not to seem to abandon Laos and Cambodia to their fate. Navarre staked all on holding the position at Dien Bien Phu in North Vietnam to which Ho Chi-minh now laid siege. It was not a good position from the military point of view because the French superiority in planes and tanks could not be exploited there. Navarre chose it for reasons of military honour rather than military strategy. And it fell. Algeria was to reap the harvest of the shock to the French army's pride which the fall of Dien Bien Phu on May 7, 1954, administered. At Geneva, settlement was achieved on the basis of the division of Vietnam, as before along the 16th parallel, to make a Vietminh state to the north, which France now evacuated, and leaving South Vietnam, Laos and Cambodia independent to the west and south. The American war (1964–74) in Vietnam, in aid of South Vietnam against Vietminh aided by the U.S.S.R., is outside the scope of this book. Suffice it to say that even after the American withdrawal (1974) the situation has not remained stable and Communist forces have fought for power in Laos, South Vietnam and Cambodia.

No sooner was the war in Indo-China over than France was waging war in Algeria. In May 1945 there had already been a revolt there at Sétif. It had been crushed by the police. But it was a foretaste of what was to come, for there were Muslim reprisals, cruel punitive measures and panic among the *colons* or French settlers. But the future looked hopeful when the Ramadier Government in September 1947 gave Algeria a Statute. It now had an elective National Assembly of its own. The one million European inhabitants were to provide one list of electors, predominantly European, electing half the 120 members, and the 8–9 million Muslim inhabitants were to provide another list of electors, predominantly Muslim, to elect the other half. Executive power was still to belong to the Governor General, whose approval was necessary before any decision of the Assembly could become effective, and to his nominated Council. Moreover, certain matters were still reserved for the French parliament. Thus the powers of the Legislative Assembly were very limited. Other progressive measures were provided for: the separation of the Muslim religion from the State, the use of Arabic in the schools and greater Muslim participation in the administration. But during 1948 and 1949 nothing was done to implement these provisions.

So the national movement grew, unsatisfied and unchecked. It coincided with national movements in Morocco and Tunisia. Though described with the same word as the national movements of the nineteenth century in Germany, Italy and the Balkan Peninsula, these movements were quite different, because they grew within another movement, on a greater scale than anything the nineteenth century knew. This was the renaissance of Islam. It had been encouraged by Britain in its early stages. She had supported Syria and Lebanon in their movement for independence in order to gain their evacuation by the French. Then in 1945 she had made the Arab League, comprising Egypt, Saudi Arabia, Iraq and Jordan. In 1950, however, British influence began to ebb throughout the Middle East. A serious cause of this was that Iran nationalised the Anglo-Iranian Oil Company and compelled a protesting Britain totally to evacuate her nationals from Abadan in humiliating circumstances. Another cause was that a Government hostile to Britain came to power in Egypt and repudiated the Anglo-Egyptian Treaty of 1936. An independent

Egypt now replaced Britain as leader of the Islamic movement. King Farouk was overthrown by General Neguib. General Abdul Nasser in 1952 took power from Neguib. Nasser was a most able man. He consolidated Egyptian leadership by a number of striking successes. First, he successfully negotiated the independence of the Anglo-Egyptian Sudan from both Britain and his own country. Next, he won a success over the Suez Canal, defying the United States, Britain and France. In 1955–56 Egypt nationalised the Canal and drove out the European Company which had controlled it. It is true that the Baghdad Pact (February 1955) was signed by Muslim countries (Turkey, Iraq and later Pakistan) under the patronage of Britain and the United States and depended on them for its continued validity. But in the Mediterranean Egyptian leadership was uncontested. The Arab national movements which Egypt chiefly stimulated were those of Tunisia and Morocco.

The Tunisian movement was led by Bourguiba. Already in 1934 he had founded the Néo-Destour Party as the voice of Arab feeling. The local French administration after the War had sought to come to terms with this party, but had been disavowed by the Paris Government. Bourguiba then (1948) founded the Committee for the Liberation of Arabian Maghreb, a more aggressive organisation.

In Morocco, where there were fewer inhabitants of French origin and old traditions of tribal loyalities prevailed among the Berber feudatories of the interior, Sultan ben Yussif himself took the lead of the national movement. He had once preserved a precarious equilibrium between his Berber feudatories, the French Resident General and the Istiqlal, a national Arab movement which existed in Palestine before 1936. But in 1947 he changed his policy. He broke with the feudatories, the Glaouri, made a speech (April 10, 1947) directed to the Arabs of the towns, where the Istiqlal and his own power were both strongest, and claimed eventual independence. He then addressed a memorandum to President Auriol, urging a revision of the relationship with France and an end to the Protectorate established in 1912.

It was unfortunate that French policy in relation to these movements was subject to constant reversals. Short Ministries, brought down by a temporary coalescence of the Communists and the extreme Right, were a characteristic of the Fourth Republic and a consequence of its Constitution, which allowed for no appeal to the electorate when a Ministry fell. (Each of the three parliaments of the Fourth Republic completed its legal four-year term.) So toughness and conciliation alternated. Indeed, they alternated in Tunisia and Morocco too. Toughness in Paris often co-incided with conciliation in Tunisia or Morocco and contrariwise.

In 1950 Paris promised self-government to Tunisia and the Resident General made a Ministry headed by Mohammed Chenik and supported by the Néo-Destour. Thereupon the national movement raised its claims and the Bey (or ruler) rallied to it. He demanded a homogeneous Ministry, made from the majority party in an elective Assembly to which it should be responsible. In 1951 Paris abandoned conciliation and sent out a new Resident General to strengthen the bonds with France. The Bey, at the instance of Bourguiba, appealed to the United Nations. Jean de Hautcloque, the new Resident General, at once arrested Bourguiba, Mohammed Chenik and four other Ministers. In Paris Antoine Pinay was now Prime Minister and he reversed policy again, replaced Hautcloque, released Chenik and promulgated plans of reform. By now all groups were outraged: the French residents, the Tunisian nationalists and the peasants in the countryside. By 1954 there was terrorism in the towns and the countryside was dominated by armed bands of peasants.

Much the same alternation had much the same result in exacerbating feeling in Morocco. In 1950 Marshal Juin was Resident General. He proclaimed that his task was to lead Morocco to self-government, but at the same time he set about destroying the Istiqlal, threatened Mohammed ben Yussif with deposition, unless he broke with them, and enforced his threats by rousing the Glaouri against him. Marshal Juin's successor relaxed this tough policy. In 1952 Mohammed ben Yussif accordingly addressed a further note to President Auriol in which he called for a parliamentary constitution and again a revision of the relationship with France. This in turn produced another phase of toughness from Paris. In 1953 the Glaouri rose against the Sultan and with the Resident General's acquiescence deposed him. He was sent to Corsica. His elderly successor was without authority, so terrorism in 1954 was let loose in Morocco as in Tunisia.

It was now the Ministry of Pierre Mendès-France in Paris: a famous one like that of Antoine Pinay, two years before. Mendès-France was famous for his activity. Government, he said, was decision. He began with a demonstrative journey to Tunis accompanied by Marshal Juin (July 30, 1954). In a celebrated speech at Carthage he proclaimed self-government for Tunisia. This, as we have seen, had been promised before. But Mendès-France had agreed with the Néo-Destour and Bourguiba beforehand and afterwards continued negotiations with Bourguiba in Paris. On November 20 the armed nationalist and peasant forces surrendered 'with all honours of war.' This raised Bourguiba and the Arab national movement to a new status, even though they did not achieve success until the Agreement of June 3, 1955, under Faure's Government, and the proclaimation of independence under Guy Mollet on March 6, 1956. To Morocco Mendès-France sent a new Resident General, who failed because he continued to work with the Glaouri, did not restore Mohammed ben Yussif and, through him, agree with the nationalists. This policy was finally adopted and a settlement reached that way in 1956, after the Sultan had been restored and signed the Declaration of Celle Saint Cloud.

The war in Algeria began in 1954 in the year of Dien Bien Phu and of terrorism in both Tunisia and Morocco: the worst year before the steps towards settlement began. But Algeria was an old colony and part of France as Tunisia and Morocco were not. Its special position was discussed in chapter 22 of Volume One. Here only the most recent causes of conflict should be indicated. The young Muslims wanted equal citizenship. The Statute had said that 'all inhabitants of French nationality in the Department of Algeria enjoy, without distinction of origin, race, language or religion, the rights attached to French citizenship and are subject to the same obligations.' But in practice the Muslim majority remained subordinate to a minority of French citizens: the *colons*. To young Muslims it no longer seemed natural, if it ever had, that they were treated as inferiors. Secondly, the War of 1939–45 had brought young Muslims into contact with urban wealth and urban living standards and had begun to break up the old family and tribal communities and to destroy satisfaction with them. The Algerian War itself was to further this process. To realise an independent national identity meant, or was thought to mean, a higher standard of living. Thirdly, the attitude of the *colons*, however intelligible, was a barrier both to accommodation with Algerian nationalism within Algeria and to agreement between Paris and Algeria. They felt their superiority justified by superior education and superior skill, and by the work and capital they had put into the land. Algeria was their country as much as that of the Muslims. They did not wish to return to France; they did not wish to abandon their farms or professions; they did not wish to lose their privileged position within Algeria. In fact they were afraid of change and had an interest in its not happening. Fourthly, the shortcomings of French rule in Algeria distinguished it from Tunisia and Morocco. Administration was lax; capital, credit and government assistance were deficient. French administration was from Paris, centralised and remote, and it had no place for Muslims in its civil service. Representation in the French parliament and the doctrine of assimilation stood in the way of the gradual preparation of Algerians for self-government and independence. The short-lived Ministries in Paris evolved no coherent policy for Algeria any more than for Tunisia and Morocco. Finally the French army, as we have seen, had been humiliated. It would seek to redress in Algeria, by a military success, the humiliation it had suffered in Vietnam.

The Algerian War began with the rebellion in the Aurès mountains in the autumn of 1954. This was one of the poorest districts of Algeria. Europeans were murdered in a number of incidents. The leaders proclaimed their purpose to be 'the restoration of a sovereign

Algerian State within the framework of Islamic principles'
(November 1, 1954). They recruited an army of national liberation
and declared their adherence to the National Liberation Front (FLN)
centred in Cairo under Ben Bella. During the winter of 1954–55 the
War gathered momentum and, in Paris, it brought down the Government of Mendès-France. But his policy of activity left its legacy in
the shape of a Governor General, Jacques Soustelle, determined on
action. Soustelle renewed the policy of reform of 1947, at the same
time dissolving the Legislative Assembly and proclaiming the integration of Algeria in France and obtaining from Paris the men and
money to enforce it. He had made tension worse and atrocities
continued. But in 1955–56 moderate leaders, such as Ferhat Abbas
at this time was, were to the fore in Algeria. They obtained a resolution from an assembly of all the Muslims, who had sat in the
Legislative Assembly or in elective municipal councils, that the time
for integration was passed and that the majority of Algerians adhered
to the idea of a separate Algerian nationality. They also appealed to
the United Nations and the future of Algeria was included in the
agenda of the Security Council. France was able to veto its discussion, but it was a success for the national movement as, indeed, were
the achievement of independence by Tunisia and Morocco.

Meanwhile, in Paris the second parliament of the Fourth Republic
had reached its legal term; fresh elections had strengthened the
Socialist-Radical alliance but, because of the development of the
Poujade movement (see below, p. 290), not sufficiently for it to
govern confidently. Guy Mollet was Prime Minister with Mendès-
France as Foreign Minister, so the policy of action would go on.
Unfortunately it was action in the opposite direction from Soustelle's.
General Catroux was now Governor General. He promised elections
for the Legislative Assembly at the earliest time and abandoned
integration. As Soustelle had alienated the Algerian Muslims, so
Catroux alienated the *colons*. He was, therefore, replaced by Lacoste
who renewed the policy of reform, promising economic develop-
ment, social betterment, measures to prepare Algerians for self-
government and equality between Muslims and Europeans. At the
same time he insisted on the indissolubility of union with France.
This reversion to Soustelle's policy made the moderation of the
Algerian leaders impossible. Ferhat Abbas now made clear his adhe-
sion to the FLN, and acquired a fighting organisation in the National
Council of Algerian Revolution (CNRA) within a Provisional
Government. He headed this Government in exile in Tunis. The
period ended dramatically with the arrest of Ben Bella on October
22, 1956.

In this year, 1956, Egypt's repulse of the Powers, France, Britain
and the United States, over the Suez Canal, and its nationalisation,
was not only a foretaste of what might be expected from Arab soli-

darity, but a considerable encouragement to the Algerian nationalists. Terror increased as the war intensified. General Massu was given increased powers and more troops. He adopted the dangerous course, euphemistically called *regroupement*, of trying to keep Muslims and Europeans apart in what were virtually concentration camps. Terror and retaliatory terror increased. The army began to take a stand of its own. The effect of the war on domestic politics increased, because its costs became heavier and pushed inflation up beyond what industrial or agricultural production could bear. The new Government of May 1957 made a fresh attempt to extend self-government in Algeria by the *Loi-Cadre*, but could not get it through the Assembly. The next Government succeeded in passing it, too much altered to have any useful effect in Algeria. It alienated the army in Algeria and strengthened it in its own individual position. Then on February 8, 1958, came the turning-point: the aerial bombing of Sakhiet, a village in Tunisia. It was the army's retaliation for the killing of French soldiers by the FLN, but any incident might have occasioned the same irreversible hardening of attitudes which was now plain.

The army in Algiers on May 13, 1958, rebelled against the French State. The army officers attacked the Government of Algeria as their immediate objective, setting up Committees of Public Safety in the revolutionary tradition. They landed an expedition on Corsica on May 16 and planned a landing from there on metropolitan France. They intended to force the suppression of the Algerian 'revolt' and the retention of Algeria as part of France upon the French Government. There were demonstrations in forty-eight departments in France and a massive demonstration in Paris; there were strikes among army officers, police and officials. A new Prime Minister, Pflimlin, was on the point of taking office but had not done so on May 13. So there was no authority in Paris and it seemed as if the State itself would dissolve. General de Gaulle made three public statements, while he negotiated behind the scenes. The first was a tentative offer to return, the second a firmer one and in the last statement on May 27 he said 'he had set in motion the procedure necessary for the establishment of a Republican Government capable of ensuring the unity and independence of the country.' The Algerian revolt had brought about the fall of the Fourth Republic.

France had called de Gaulle back to power to settle the multi-sided Algerian conflict. He had one advantage: an extraordinary capacity to wait; to wait until the implications of speech and action made themselves evident; to wait until the significant elements in a situation had distinguished themselves; to wait until the moment for action was right. He made men confident in his fair-mindedness. He imposed his views, when arrived at after consultations, with authority.

On June 1, 1958, he took office under the forms of the Constitution of the Fourth Republic as Prime Minister. Next day he was given for six months special powers to govern by decree and to draw up a new constitution and special powers to solve the Algerian problem. He completed both missions. He founded the Fifth Republic with the constitution approved by referendum (September 28) and became its first President (December). He brought the Algerian war to an end and made, in 1962, a settlement with an independent Algeria.

By 1958 Ferhat Abbas's Provisional Government of Algeria, in exile, had been recognised by all the Arab countries and by China. For de Gaulle integration had become an option closed, for he had made a speech in which his cry of 'Long Live French Algeria' had met with such a response as to convince him of its impracticability. He nominated, as Commander-in-Chief, Maurice Challe who began to use the army more successfully to impose order. He appointed as Delegate General (avoiding the old title of Governor) Paul Delouvrier who convened the Legislative Assembly, elected not by the old half-European, half-Muslim lists, but by new lists, one-third European and two-thirds Muslim. At last, after a year's wait, de Gaulle took the first step in developing his own policy. On September 16, 1959, he made a speech in which he promised Algeria self-determination. At the same time he outlined three possible choices: complete Frenchifying which he elaborated to show the impossibility of integration; complete separation from France of which he showed the disastrous economic consequences; government of Algeria by the Algerians in close association with France of which he made plain the advantages. Then in June 1960 and again in July 1961 he had with FLN leaders discussions which, though they broke down, showed, at least, that the French Government was ready to make terms.

Challe's army began to realise that de Gaulle was aiming less at an out-and-out military victory than at a military situation which would allow him to make terms with the FLN. This exasperated it. The Republic had let it down. The Republic was no longer worth dying for. A Republic which could bring the Foreign Legion in Algeria to an end, which de Gaulle did, was a Republic which had no use for courage, loyalty and discipline, the virtues for which it and the army stood. The army rebelled. The revolt of the barricades of January 1960 was a small insurrection, a matter of fraternising with a group of Algerian European demonstrators, trying to compel the Government to harden its policy. It was checked by de Gaulle's reassuring broadcast and subsequent tour of military posts in Algeria. The second revolt was much more serious. It was the revolt of the Colonels, led by General Salan and General Challe himself. The latter had been retired a few months before the revolt. Rightly the army regarded de Gaulle's talks with the FLN leaders as already a tacit recognition of Ferhat Abbas's Provisional Government. Moreover, though in September 1960 de Gaulle had only spoken of Algerian Algeria, by November he spoke of an Algerian Republic. In January 1961 he took a referendum on the project of the law for Algerian self-determination. The Muslim population of Algeria voted for it as a vote of confidence in de Gaulle's whole policy. The European population replied with a massive 'no.' The insurrection, then, of April was an alignment of the army with the *colons*, who had already aligned themselves against the State, as well as against the solution of an independent Algerian Republic. The insurrection failed to rally enough support from junior officers and non-commissioned officers and collapsed. Challe and Salan and other leaders were brought to trial; some two hundred officers were relieved of their commands and there was later a purge of unreliable elements. But disturbance was not over. The next eleven months saw the organisation of the secret army (OAS) and its terrorist activities both in metropolitan France and North Africa. This was the period of the *plastiqueurs* and their plastic bombs. It was a last despairing attempt of the *colons*, destined to come to nothing. The worst part of the Algerian war was the fear it raised: fear in the Arab of his fellow Arabs, if he did not join the national movement, or of the *colons*, if he did; fear in the *colons* both of Algerians and French officials; now, fear in the general public of sporadic bombs. De Gaulle's realism was a corrective. He had the courage, after waiting for the OAS to show how little power it really had, to proclaim a unilateral cease-fire. Talks were then able to proceed with Ferhat Abbas's Provisional Government with the approval of the CNRA and led to the signature of an armistice on March 18, 1962. Shortly afterwards the final agreement was signed at Évian. It consisted of a compromise on the interim authorities to govern while the process of self-determination went forward and of provisions for the maintenance of order during the same period, avoiding both the army and the FLN, and of eight principles. The declaration of eight principles was an ingenious device, because it left questions sufficiently open for the Algerians to feel that they had a real choice in relation to their future, while providing certain basic safeguards for the Europeans and for the strategic interests of France.

Algerian independence was proclaimed on July 6, 1962. Civil war then broke out. But the Republic survived. This in itself was a kind of success. The Democratic and People's Republic of Algeria was proclaimed on September 25 and on October 8 Algeria was admitted to the United Nations. Algeria had acquired a more or less homogeneous Arab population. The *colons* emigrated—mostly to France—in their thousands. The OAS disappeared as suddenly as it arose. The attempt to make a French Community—a counterpart to the British Commonwealth—with which the story of the dismantling of the French empire opened was abandoned.

Chapter 15

EUROPE DIVIDED: THE COUNTRIES OF THE EASTERN BLOC, 1945–68

During the wartime conferences of the three leaders, Roosevelt and Stalin had pulled together, sometimes to isolate Churchill, sometimes even to overrule him. The alignment of the U.S.A. with the U.S.S.R. had continued into 1945 after Roosevelt's death and was responsible, among other things, for Eisenhower's restraint upon the Allies' march eastwards and the U.S.S.R.'s consequent penetration into Austria and Czechoslovakia and as far into Germany as they reached. How then did it happen that by 1947 the antagonism between the U.S.A. and the U.S.S.R. was so deep as chiefly to cause the Cold War which characterised the post-war decade? The beginning of the Cold War is sometimes dated quite precisely from June 5, 1947. On that day, through her Secretary of State, General George Marshall, the United States offered economic aid to Europe. The idea of Marshall Aid was that it should be given after the European states had concerted a programme of needs. Ernest Bevin, then British Foreign Secretary, took the lead in concerting this programme. He worked with France, Holland, Belgium and Luxembourg (the Benelux countries), approached Italy, with whom a peace treaty had been signed on February 10, 1947, and saw to it that the programme should include Greece, though she was still in civil war. It was at this date also to include the U.S.S.R. But at Paris, where Molotov had arrived to take part in the planning, the U.S.S.R. announced through him a separate view. The Soviet Union insisted that each state to benefit from Marshall Aid should prepare a separate programme of needs. The other participating states opposed this view. At the end of June Molotov walked out of the Paris meeting. A week later the Molotov plan for economic aid to eastern Europe was announced.

But this precise date is misleading because it does not do justice to the many ways in which the breach had been prepared. One of these was the enunciation of the so-called Truman doctrine on March 12, 1947. President Truman said, 'It must be the policy of the United States to support free peoples who are resisting attempted subjugation by armed minorities or by outside pressures.' The particular conflict to which the doctrine related was that going on in Greece against the wartime communist party organisation (EAM) and army (ELAS) by the National Unity Government of Giorgios Papandhreou, assisted by a British army under General Scobie. It will be recalled that at the Moscow Conference of October 1944 (above, p. 225) Greece had been allotted to Britain in an agreement between Stalin and Churchill. British forces were, indeed, to remain in Greece until 1950. The U.S.S.R. was suspected of aiding ELAS though it seems to have done no more than to urge Yugoslavia and Albania to do so. It was the generalised phrasing of the Truman doctrine which, on the one hand, was acutely offensive to the U.S.S.R., and on the other reflected a rising surge of hatred for communism in the U.S.A. and fear of its expansion.

Nor does the precise dating of the division of Europe to June 5, 1947, do justice to the antagonism which soon developed wherever the United States and the Soviet Union were nominally acting together as, for example, in Korea or, in Europe, in Austria. In Korea the Soviet Union was accepting the surrender of the Japanese north of the 38th parallel and the United States south of it, according to the agreement between Roosevelt and Stalin at Yalta in February 1945. At Moscow a four-Power trusteeship for five years over Korea had been decided on, and a Joint Commission of the Soviet Union and the United States had been appointed to set up a single provisional government for Korea in consultation with 'Korean democratic parties and organisations.' When the Joint Commission met in Seoul there was disagreement on the meaning of 'democratic' and it broke up in May 1946 to leave the Russians and the Americans proceeding separately in north and south. As for Austria, throughout the year 1945 to 1946 relations between the Soviet Union and the other three occupying powers had been growing tense and little progress as a consequence could be made towards a peace treaty with her, although she had a settled Government after the elections, held already in November 1945. The Western Powers disliked the wide interpretation being given by the Soviet Union to the 'German assets' in Austria which had been assigned to her. They had different ideas about the future internal political complexion of the country and the Soviet Union was benefiting from its continued occupation—and therefore in no hurry to conclude a peace treaty—in a way in which they were not. The signature of a peace treaty was in fact delayed until May 1955 and then only came after the change in Soviet foreign policy of that year.

Finally, the precise dating of the division of Europe and the beginning of the Cold War to June 5, 1947, does not accommodate the fact that antagonism was implicit in the Communist take-over of Bulgaria, Rumania and Poland already before the War was over and in the tight social control which the Communists established in these countries. This has been noticed in chapter 12. Control was extended to East Germany in 1945 and to Czechoslovakia and Hungary in 1948. Between 1948 and 1953 Soviet power was consolidated. After Stalin's death on March 5, 1953, there was a period of diversification in the eastern bloc and revolts against Soviet control followed in 1953, and 1956. But the eastern bloc remained under undemocratic social controls and exclusive in its policy.

To the extension of Soviet control immediately after the War we must now turn. It was extended first to East Germany. East Germany in 1945 was in complete and spectacular chaos and local Soviet Commanders put the nearest German into office in order to restore public services, to move food and to reopen communications. They used two criteria in choosing men: usefulness and a non-Nazi political past, but the latter criterion was of secondary importance. There was no worker penetration into power, because people accustomed to exercising authority were more useful then those who were not. So power remained with the old professional and official classes, and the structure of local government, the centralizing practices of which were anyhow familiar to the Russians, stayed as it was. The land reform of 1945, it is true, made change. But even that was not an application of Marxist-Leninist dogma. The big estates were broken up and the landowners deprived of their property without compensation. The land was given to two sorts of people: small farmers already in occupation; and new farmers from among the millions of Germans flooding in from the territory which had become Polish when the Polish-German frontier was redrawn along the Oder-Neisse line. It was not collectivisation of farming, but an empirical response to the situation. What happened to the landowners no one enquired: their homes only attracted public interest again when holidays in them became the prize for party or state service in the early fifties. In June 1945 the Soviet Military Administration set up what were to become the five *Länder* of the German Democratic Republic. But they followed the boundaries of the old states, as Saxony and Brandenburg, or were made, as Saxony-Anhalt, Thuringia and Mecklenburg-Pomerania, by putting two or three of the old states together. Law No. 46 of the Control Commission, which, of course, included the U.S.S.R. as long as the four Allies still worked together, declared Prussia, as the source of German militarism, abolished. Moreover, politics of a kind familiar to the western democracies were not at first discouraged. When the three other occupying Powers recognised political parties, two, the Free Democrats and the Christian Democrats, received permission to extend into the Soviet zone. Of the pre-war parties, the Communists (KPD) and Socialists (SPD) survived and, where Soviet influence prevailed, they were forcibly merged to form the Socialist Unity Party (SED). On October 21, 1946, elections took place for the parliaments of the five *Länder*. These five parties provided the candidates and, when the parliaments had been elected, the Prime Minister in each *Land* was appointed from the party which had won a majority. Other Ministries were then allotted roughly in proportion to the number of seats each party had won. In Berlin, still under four-Power administration, the election was fought throughout the city and won by the SPD. Both the KPD and the SED had run candidates, but they were defeated.

The primary object of the U.S.S.R. at this stage was to obtain reparations. The Russians removed industrial plant, took a proportion of current production and used German labour. Their zone of occupation was to be used to enable them to make good the terrible destruction of the War in western Russia. The secondary object of the U.S.S.R. was strategic security. The extension of the Socialist community and the rule of the proletariat came a poor third.

Real change only began after 1947. On March 23, 1948, the Russians withdrew from the Allied Control Commission. After the three other occupying Powers had reformed the currency throughout West Germany the Russians (June 23) had introduced the Ostmark both into their zone and into Berlin. They then severed communications between West and East Germany (June 26). They also attempted to extrude the three other Powers from the occupation of Berlin by blockading Berlin and cutting off its communications with the West. This they could, of course, effectively do because Berlin lay inside their zone of occupation. The British and Americans foiled this attempt by instituting an air-lift. Begun as a stop-gap response to the Soviet action, it proved during the winter an effective demonstration of the Berliners' determination to keep in touch with the West and the self-confidence of the Western Powers. By the spring the tonnage of supplies daily brought in reached 8000 metric tons, the amount ordinarily brought in by rail and water. Planes at the peak period were landing and taking off at 30-second intervals. But the Iron Curtain had truly descended in 1948. On October 7, 1949, the status of East Germany was changed from a zone in Soviet occupation to a sovereign State, the German Democratic Republic. Berlin, as a result of the blockade, had two Governments, one in West Berlin and one in East Berlin. In East Berlin the victory of the SPD in 1946 was cancelled. The U.S.S.R. saw to it that the new Mayor in East Berlin belonged to the SED and that elections for his City Council were also won by the SED. The constitution of the German Democratic Republic had been approved by a People's Council, elected by a People's Congress which itself had been elected in May 1949 on a single-party list. So western-type politics were over. When the Soviet Military Administration ended and the new State came into being its first Prime Minister was Otto Grotewohl. He had led the SPD when it joined the KPD in the new Socialist Unity Party and might be thought of as a statesman-like figure ready to bring the old traditions into East Germany's Communist future. Wilhelm Pieck, as ally of Rosa Luxemburg and Liebknecht in 1919, was Chairman of the Communist Party and Walter Ulbricht its Deputy Chairman. Ulbricht had led a group of ten German Communists who returned from Moscow to Germany in May 1945. Thus the structure of a Communist state took shape.

By October 1944, when Stalin and Churchill reached their agreement in Moscow, in Bulgaria the Fatherland Front had taken power by a *coup d' état*, the Russian army was in Sofia and a Bulgarian army stood by its side, against Germany. In other words, Bulgarian Communists imposed the Communist régime upon their own country. At first they preserved the Regency for the boy-King Simeon (Boris had died suddenly early in 1944), but from the key Ministries of Justice and the Interior, eventually organised a reign of terror. Some 2138 death sentences and 1940 long-term prison sentences were admitted by the régime.[1] By September 1946 the Communists felt their hold incontestable. So they arranged a plebiscite on the monarchy and, the vote being in favour of abolition, proclaimed a People's Republic in September 1946. The Sobranje was elected freely for the last time in October and it drafted a new constitution on the Soviet model. A native Communist Party was in control in a mood of hero-worship for the U.S.S.R. and actual Russian intervention was slight.

By October 1944 Rumania was under a Government into which King Michael had introduced Communist Ministers and under an armistice. The Communist Party in Rumania was, however, small, even in the fifties having fewer than 2000 members.[2] It did not have the advantage of the Bulgarian Party of being popular with at least part of the country. But it had several other advantages: first, that of good leadership. Its leaders were Gheorghiu-Dej, a railway worker with a long history of clandestine activity and imprisonment in Rumania, and a group of Rumanian Communist exiles trained in Moscow, Ana Pauker, Vasile Luca and Emil Bodnaras. A second advantage was that Rumania owed to the U.S.S.R. her acquisition of part of Transylvania and she hoped for economic aid from her. The Communists' main advantage was that they had the protection of the Soviet army. And the Soviet army was in Bucharest. The Party gradually intruded Communists into central and local government and, using various 'front' organisations, pushed the Party among professional men and the peasants. They also organised a militia. In March 1945 under Soviet pressure the King appointed a Ministry of Soviet nominees headed by Peter Groza. He remained Prime Minister until 1952. On November 19, 1946, elections were held

[1] J. F. Brown, *Bulgaria under Communist Rule* (1970), p. 10.
[2] Robert Lea Wolff, *The Balkans in our Time* (1956), p. 279.

from which this Government emerged victorious. There is no reason to suppose that they were free. Communist pressure continued. In December 1947 the King at last abdicated. Groza then held another election. The Communists obtained 405 out of 414 parliamentary seats and in the new parliament made a new constitution on the Soviet model. In April 1948 the People's Republic of Rumania was proclaimed. It was a different take-over from that in Bulgaria: more gradual, effected by manoeuvre and pressure. It was equally irresistible, unless the western democracies had been prepared to intervene by force.

Poland had no quarter from which to find liberators. Those underground resisters to Germany who had survived found themselves in 1944–45 victims of the U.S.S.R.'s ruthless elimination of all those with any claim to independence or even education. Poland was weak: over six million Polish citizens had perished as a result of German attack or occupation, one and a half million had been deported to Russia and never returned, 15,000 Army officers had been killed by the Russians at Katyn and elsewhere, thousands were prisoners of war or exiles. The Soviet army occupying Poland took from the Resistance or the Polish Government-in-exile any centres they controlled. They set up the authority of the Committee of National Liberation whose members belonged to the Communist Workers' Party. This Committee had established itself at Lublin, south-east of Warsaw, when the Germans withdrew. It was recognised as the Provisional Government of Poland by the U.S.S.R. and Czechoslovakia. The western democracies refused to recognise it until four non-Communist Ministers, including Stanislaw Mikolajczyk from the Government-in-exile, had been included and free elections promised. At this stage the U.S.S.R. had to submit, for they were treating Poland as an enemy country from which they could exact reparation. A new Provisional Government headed by the Lublin premier, with Mikolajczyk and Wladyslaw Gomulka as deputy premiers, sixteen Lubliners and five non-Communists in all, was achieved, and recognised in July 1945 by the western democracies.

The situation began to change when the U.S.S.R. found Poland an unprofitable source of reparation and the pre-war (then illegal) Polish Communist Party began to gather new support throughout Poland. Wladyslaw Gomulka (1905–82), its leader, had been made Secretary General in 1943 during the War and as an official of the Chemical Workers' Union was a trade unionist with a claim to workers' support. As the Communist Party revived it attracted the support both of pre-war Socialists and of those who sought a party on which hopes for economic recovery and patriotic loyalty (the new frontier, owed to the U.S.S.R., roused patriotic feeling) could focus. Soviet police and the Soviet army repressed any expression of support for Mikolajczyk and his position became impossible. His flight from

Poland in October 1947 after the controlled elections in January of that year had defeated the Peasant Party which he led, signalised the end of formal political opposition. A Socialist economy took shape in 1948, when large landowners were expropriated and the land given to existing tenants or new proprietors; the production of coal, oil, electricity, gas, synthetic fuels and sugar was nationalised, together with parts of the metallurgical industries and flour-milling, and a three-year plan for economic reconstruction imposed. But farming was not collectivised and many private enterprises continued to exist. Hatred for the Russians and the strength of the Catholic Church were to ensure that Poland would continue to go her own way under her own version of Communism.

Yugoslavia and Albania stand apart from the rest of the Balkan Peninsular States in their greater independence from the U.S.S.R. The personalities of their leaders and the character of the countries account for this. Josip Broz (Tito) had shaped the fortunes of the Yugoslav Communist Party from 1937, when it was little more than a foreign-supported conspiracy in a peasant country, to 1945, when it became the supreme power in a country liberated by its own Communist guerrilla armies, largely independent of foreign man-power, though not of foreign arms. He continued to rule until his death in 1980. But he ruled an independent sovereign State, bent on industrialisation. He kept it independent politically and organised economically in its own way. After 1950 its factories were run by workers' councils and not by a centralised bureaucracy. Tito owed his supremacy to his military skill, his intelligence and to the revolutionary *élan* which he and a small group of loyal allies had generated in his country. It was an advantage to be a Croat, as Tito was, in a fivefold federation that feared Serb domination. Tito's independence led to a clash with Stalin. Stalin's ways were roundabout. He organised in September 1947, at a secret meeting of representatives from the U.S.S.R., Bulgaria, Rumania, Poland, Yugoslavia, France, Italy, Czechoslovakia and Hungary, the Communist Information Bureau (Cominform). It replaced the old International as a single Communist Church. From this body Yugoslavia was formally expelled. The argument between Stalin and Tito was nominally about collectivisation and Tito's attitude to the nationalities, but actually it was about power in Yugoslavia. Tito's position, to Stalin's surprise, was not shaken by expulsion from the Cominform and, as between himself and Stalin, the victory was his. He had defied all Stalin's particular instructions, but preserved intact a fanatical loyalty to Marxism-Leninism and a tranquil but unshakeable faith in the doctrine of Soviet primacy.

Albania was under the rule of Enver Hoxha. He had been Secretary of the Albanian Communist Party before the War. He had been well educated and for some time in the civil service. He and his

Party came to the fore because they led the guerrilla fighting against the Italians and Germans. There was no place for a Communist industrial structure in his country, where the peasants were Muslim and mostly illiterate, but the large landowners were dispossessed without compensation, as elsewhere in eastern Europe, in favour of previous tenant farmers or new proprietors. Albania lived under the protection of Yugoslavia as she had once lived in the shadow of Turkey or of Italy. A Treaty of Mutual Assistance and Friendship, July 9, 1946, and a Treaty on Co-ordination of Economic Plans, Customs Union and Equalisation of Currency, November 27, 1946, were signed with Yugoslavia. Industrial enterprise in railways, electricity, oil and metals made some progress, but there could be no attempt at wholesale industrialisation.

Czechoslovakia and Hungary stood apart, because they were successor states to the old Austro-Hungarian monarchy and they were slow to lose the marks of that old and sophisticated political body. The Czechoslovak Republic was restored in 1945 as a parliamentary democracy with Eduard Beneš once again President and the separate Slovak State, made by the Nazis, reabsorbed. Sudeten Germans were ruthlessly and rapidly deprived of property and encouraged to move away. But the standing of pre-war leaders, tainted with Munich, was low, the prestige of the U.S.S.R. was high and the Communist Party found it could realise its aims through the normal political process. There was, for example, large-scale nationalisation affecting the banks and insurance companies as well as industry. When in the free elections of 1946 it won 38 per cent of the vote, Beneš called its leader, Klement Gottwald, to form a Ministry. He formed a coalition Government of Socialists, Czech Populists and Slovak Democrats as well as Communists. During the next year the Communists established control over the police, army and workers' militia. The Communists finally took over by a coup in February-March 1948. The coup happened in this way: the Government had nominated eight Communists to be police superintendents in Prague; the twelve members of the Government from the Populist and Democrat Parties had thereupon resigned. The Government's fate, therefore, lay in the hands of its Socialist members. When the workers raised an insurrection in Prague with the cry 'Government without reactionaries,' the Socialist Ministers sided with the Communists. After five days Beneš gave way, dismissed the Government and allowed Gottwald to form a new Communist and Socialist Government. The elections which followed were held on a single-party list and Gottwald became President as well as Prime Minister. The Communist take-over was complete.

Hungary, of course, did not share the Czech experience of restoration. Her pre-war institutions came through the War unscathed.

Nor was she as egalitarian or as industrially advanced. Another barrier to Communist ascendancy was her hatred of the Russians, with whom, like the Poles, she shared a frontier. In the free elections of November 1945 the Communists, who had returned to Hungary in the wake of the Red Armies, only gained 17 per cent of the vote while the Peasants' Party gained 57 per cent. The peasants were satisfied and not anxious to support revolutionary Communism, for the land reform of the spring of 1945 had given them the land they wanted. As in East Germany and Poland big landowners had been dispossessed without compensation and their estates had been divided between existing tenant farmers and peasants who already had small freehold farms. The Communists had to come to power by using the normal political process. They joined with the Socialists and the left wing of the Peasants' Party to undermine the position of the Prime Minister, who was a member of the Peasants' Party, and eventually forced his resignation. They then so manoeuvred that the new Peasant Party Prime Minister was induced to change the electoral law. In 1948 in the elections under the new law they won 60 per cent of the vote. The Communist leader Mátyás Rákosi became Prime Minister. There was no move towards industrialisation or nationalisation or even constitutional change.

By 1948 the position in the eastern bloc was relatively stable. The framework of Soviet power stood further from or closer to the several Governments according to the need of the Soviet State. The paramountcy of Soviet need was supported by the doctrine which Stalin had first developed as a weapon against Trotsky. It was the doctrine that whenever Soviet national interests clashed with the demands of international revolution, Soviet national interests should prevail. World Communism could only be achieved by the truimph of Soviet national interests.

Between 1949 and 1952 there was a series of trials or public affirmations of guilt, and purges in the several countries of the eastern bloc. In Bulgaria the power struggle was marked by trials and executions which brought Vulko Chervenkov to power by 1950. He was Prime Minister and Secretary General of the Communist Party and represented Muscovite influence as against the 'home' Communists of 1945–50. Soviet influence, originally slight, became more marked. In Rumania a new constitution, as we saw, had been proclaimed, but everything had still to be done to make a characteristic Communist State. A beginning was made by setting up Peoples' councils, elected on a single-party list. Local and central administration was reorganised. As the programme developed police supervision, deportations, concentration camps and a people's militia appeared. The Communist machinery for the rigid control of the citizen was thus set up. The Rumanian economy was reorganised on the basis of national-

267

isation, planning and the service of Soviet needs. This was the background to constant purges and trials of alleged agents of the western democracies, spies, saboteurs and reactionaries. This kind of long-drawn-out terror culminated in a power struggle in 1952 in which, as in Bulgaria, some Communists who took part in the initial take-over were eliminated.

In Poland Gomulka fell. He was placed under house arrest in July 1948. Gomulka would have withstood Soviet pressure as Tito withstood it. But Soviet power was too close to Poland for opposition to be easy and he could not rely on the cohesion of his colleagues as Tito could. Gomulka remained Secretary-General of the Party until November 1949; for his influence in Poland made him still necessary to the U.S.S.R. After that his fall was complete and he was for some time imprisoned (1951–54). In Poland as in Bulgaria and Rumania the U.S.S.R. could afford to tighten its control and dispense with those whose influence, knowledge and political skill had been necessary to win power in the first instance.

In Hungary the symptom of the tightening of Soviet power was the trial of Laszlo Rajk. He and a group of accomplices were accused of Titoism. He had been Minister of the Interior and so in charge of the police system and a key figure in Communist control. But his personal standing was too strong for the pretensions of the U.S.S.R. to be realised. Though he had been interned during some of the War years he was a hero of the Hungarian resistance. The U.S.S.R. preferred to work through Mátyás Rákosi, Ernö Gerö (who was a figure in international Communism and notable in Spain during the Civil War) and Mihály Farkas. Rajk then had to go. In Czechoslovakia there was an even more striking victim of Soviet pressure. This was Rudolf Slánský, tried and executed in November 1952. He had been Secretary General of the Czechoslovak Communist Party. He was an extremely powerful figure and Gottwald had not dared to proceed against him until he had consulted Stalin. He was arrested in November 1951 as the climax to a series of purges and trials. It then took a year for the Government to prepare his trial. Slánský and a group of eleven others, who were defendants with him, were sentenced to death and executed.

On March 5, 1953, Stalin died. His death altered the future for all the states of the eastern bloc. It was followed by a struggle for power within the Soviet leadership, which necessarily became more 'collegiate' or collective, since there was no single figure of Stalin's stature to replace him. In the U.S.S.R. Molotov, Khrushchev and Malenkov proved eventually to be dominant personalities. They represented three different attitudes to the future. Molotov, supported by Kaganovich, wished to retain both the economic and foreign policy of Stalin. Khrushchev wished to change foreign policy, but would be content to retain Stalin's economic policy. Malenkov, supported by

Beria, wished radically to alter both economic and foreign policy. Khrushchev was relieved of other functions in order to allow him to concentrate on his work in the Party Secretariat and he was not at first as important as Beria. In April the leadership in the state was collective in the hands of Molotov, vice-chairman of the Council of Ministers and in charge of foreign policy, Malenkov, chairman of the Council of Ministers and concerned with economic policy, and Beria, also a vice-chairman of the Council of Ministers and, as Minister for the Interior, head of the security police. In June Beria fell. He was dismissed from his offices and arrested. In December 1953 he with certain associates was executed after a secret trial. The collective leadership was now firmly in the hands of Molotov, Khrushchev and Malenkov. There were amnesties, price reductions and some relaxation of political pressure. Public propaganda began to notice the error of the personality cult. In March 1955 Khrushchev dismissed Malenkov and replaced him with Bulganin. By the twentieth Party Congress he had emerged as the real Soviet leader, though he did not become Prime Minister as well as Party Secretary until 1958 when he succeeded Bulganin. But the Congress which met from February 17–24, 1956, is a turning-point for another reason. It began the public process known in the West as de-Stalinisation. Khrushchev delivered a speech denouncing the 'personality cult'. At a secret session on the last day he made a famous report on the crimes of Stalin. It was gradually made known to different levels of the Party and it leaked out to the West.

The question almost asks itself: why should Khrushchev have chosen to deliver this shock to the Communist world when by doing so he was patently inviting a drop in the authority of Communism, of the U.S.S.R. and of himself? No short answer is a real answer, but it may, at least, be said that Khrushchev's method of rule was not Stalin's and that he had to establish the distinction between himself and Stalin in order to rule at all. The repudiation of the reign of terror was part of this need. But it should also be said that de-Stalinisation was a continuous process which had begun already in 1953. We may be in a better position to understand Khrushchev's action after we have considered what de-Stalinisation meant.

It meant first some change in Soviet economic policy. This was 'the Malenkov new course'. Malenkov drastically reduced the number of ministries and departments concerned with economic affairs. The attempt to rationalise the central planning system was sensible. But the varied requirements of different regions and the particular problems of specific industries, techniques and economic units soon reintroduced divisions and sub-divisions. Malenkov's real achievements, which justify historians in writing of the Malenkov new course, were different. He caused an expansion of the output of the consumer goods industries, on the assumption that the U.S.S.R. now had a powerful heavy industry and could afford to change her economic emphasis. He increased the prices paid for agricultural procurements (see above, p. 132) from the peasants and lowered tax levels for them. He made a general retail price cut of some 10 per cent. The eventual economic results of these measures were not always good, but their immediate result was to make life easier for the Soviet citizen.

When Khrushchev had emerged as the dominant figure, he continued Malenkov's policy and developed an agricultural policy of his own. This resulted in a number of small measures which eased life on the collective farms and relaxed central control over them. The managements of collective farms, for example, were allowed to decide their own work requirements and, in course of time, to make the decisions on most matters. In addition, Khrushchev initiated a colossal drive to take new land into cultivation. It was strikingly successful in Siberia and Kazakhstan. Khrushchev, like Malenkov, made an attempt to cut down the bureaucracy and streamline the economic administration. Thus a regional structure for the control of the industrial economy under the central planning agency (Gosplan) enabled him to get rid of several ministries involved in the control of industrial planning. The whole wage-structure was revised, greater mobility of labour allowed and control over it relaxed; forced labour camps were scaled down; trade unions were more active and more successful in defending workers' interests; trade with the West was expanded and new trade links established. A system in which nothing could be done unless stimulated from the centre and as part of a central plan was bound to cause actions with unforseeable and unintended consequences. It was inevitable that it should seem at times as if the central planners did not know what they were doing. Their actions made confusion, their reversals of policy to rectify mistakes made confusion within confusion. An attempt to loosen the system only worsened these tendencies. Considered merely as economic policy, there is no need to think of Khrushchev's policy as successful. It may have contributed to his fall in 1964. He was dismissed nominally, at least, for his mistakes in economic policy.

De-Stalinisation meant a complete change in foreign policy. The Cold War, which had begun in 1947, ended when an armistice was achieved between North and South Korea in the summer of 1953. The Korean War had begun when the Democratic People's Republic, proclaimed by the Russians in North Korea, invaded the Republic of Korea, under Syngman Rhee with its capital at Seoul and backed by the United Nations as the legal Government of all Korea. War began on June 25, 1950. Though, after the armistice, ground for irritation lingered in the North Korean delay in repatriating prisoners of war, the danger of a general war developing out of the war between North Korea assisted by the U.S.S.R. and China, and South

Korea, assisted by the United States supported by fifteen other states, including Britain, was over. Peace in Korea was an event which lit up the policy of détente with the western democracies for which Khrushchev was to stand. Eisenhower had taken office as President in 1953 and was open to overtures from the U.S.S.R. Churchill had returned to power in Britain in 1951 and made renewal of co-operation with the U.S.S.R. his capital aim. On May 11, 1953, he delivered a speech calling for some accommodation with the U.S.S.R. It amounted to a proposal for a three-Power meeting: Britain, the United States and the U.S.S.R. Churchill's determination to bring this about became stronger with increasing certainty that the U.S.S.R. was capable of nuclear war. She had exploded her first atom bomb in 1949. In August 1953 she exploded her first hydrogen bomb. She invested heavily in nuclear and space experiments and produced her first intercontinental ballistic missile in 1957 and the first Sputnik at the turn of the year, 1957–58. Churchill had good ground for seeking reconciliation. On November 27, 1953, the Soviet Government at last accepted Britain's proposal for what had, now, with the inclusion of France, become a four-Power conference. The U.S.S.R. had given way on her counter-proposal to include China as well as France. The conference was to consist of Foreign Ministers and to meet at Berlin on January 25, 1954. The conference itself was a failure. It reached deadlock on Austria, Germany and disarmament. The U.S.S.R., however, was unwilling to allow the threads to drop and a further meeting took place in April 1954 at which China was also represented. This conference, which met in Geneva and lasted until July, was an important success for Khrushchev: both in the presence of China and in its achievement of a settlement in Indo-China (see above, p. 250). The success of the Geneva conference did not end the project of a summit meeting. Churchill, who had visited Washington while the meeting at Geneva continued, next proposed himself to Molotov for a visit 'as a reconnoitring patrol.' Molotov in an identical note addressed to China, France, the United States and Britain (July 24, 1954) had meanwhile himself proposed a meeting. Nothing came of these somewhat disingenuous overtures but they testify to the reluctance of both East and West to lose contact. Even a plan for German reunification was fruitlessly discussed until February 1953. In May 1955 the Austrian Peace Treaty was at last signed. This was the first fruit of détente. Austria became a neutral state and the Soviet occupation forces were withdrawn. In July 1955, also at Geneva, the summit meeting at last took place. By now Eden had replaced Churchill as Prime Minister, and Macmillan, Eden, as Foreign Secretary. The results were not concrete, unless the visit of Khrushchev and Bulganin to Britain may be deemed a concrete result. But something was achieved by the discussion of European security and German reunification. This was a change of ideas: paradoxically, away from the contemplation of nuclear war and towards the consideration of nuclear weapons as deterrent of war; away from the reunification of Germany and towards an acceptance of the Soviet control of eastern Europe and East Germany and of European division. Moreover, the division of Europe was further stabilised when the U.S.S.R. signed the Treaty of Warsaw with her seven client States (Poland, German Democratic Republic, Czechoslovakia, Hungary, Rumania, Bulgaria and Albania) in May 1955. It was the counterpart for the East to the North Atlantic Treaty Organisation (see below, p. 300) for the West. Thus it legalised the presence of Soviet troops in the countries of the East.

De-Stalinisation meant, in the third place, internal diversification among the states of the eastern bloc and the development of what was known as revisionism. The German Democratic Republic was the first country where a crisis occurred. It was early and sharp and caused the least enduring effects. It was precipitated by the last bout of Stalinism which had taken the form of a movement to end artisan and craft enterprises and to intensify collectivisation in the countryside. There was an economic crisis and the Government appealed to the U.S.S.R., who made it plain that economic aid could not be expected. Whereupon the Government confessed its mistakes and adopted the Malenkov new course of lowering investment in heavy industry and offering inducements to worker and farmer to increase output. De-Stalinisation showed itself in the workers' answer to the pressure on him to increase output. Far from meeting it with the old apathetic submission, they rebelled. On June 16, 1953, strikes began in Berlin. The workers demanded the cancellation of a new increase in work quotas, called for the resignation of the Government and, most surprising of all, for free elections. The uprising became general. It was ruthlessly suppressed by Soviet military action. There are said to have been 42 executions and some 25,000 arrests. The Ulbricht-Grotewohl régime was confirmed. Nevertheless something was gained. More consumer goods were produced and living standards began to rise. Police pressure was relaxed; the U.S.S.R. stopped the flow of reparation exactions eastwards and disengaged the Soviet element from joint Soviet-German enterprises. The German Democratic Republic became more prosperous, but with the steady growth of collectivised agriculture, more socialised and more closely aligned with Russia.

In Czechoslovakia de-Stalinisation showed itself only in the establishment of a collective leadership instead of the single leadership of Gottwald. It was easily done for Gottwald had died on March 15, 1953, on his way back to Prague from Stalin's funeral. Antonín Zápotocký became President of the Republic and head of the Government, while Antonín Novotný succeeded Gottwald as Secretary of the Party. The Czechs like the East Germans suffered in 1953 from economic difficulties. But the Government responded differently. By the monetary reform, effective on June 1, it altered the value of the crown in relation to the rouble. There were disturbances, as in the German Democratic Republic, but they were less serious and without political overtones. They were repressed without Soviet intervention. There was no relaxation of economic or police pressure, no liberalisation, no observable change. Czechoslovakia, the most industrialised and egalitarian of the eastern States, seemed at this time to fit most comfortably into the Soviet system.

In Rumania, as in Czechoslovakia, power in the leadership was dispersed under de-Stalinisation. Gheorghe Apostol was appointed to lead the Party and Gheorghiu-Dej continued as Prime Minister. Like the G.D.R., Rumania relaxed its emphasis on heavy industry and began to produce more consumer goods. There was little other sign of de-Stalinisation. In Rumania, as in the G.D.R. and Czechoslovakia, industrialisation was on the whole an appropriate and successful policy. In Bulgaria the dispersal of power in the leadership meant that Chervenkov was replaced as Secretary General of the Party by Todor Zhivkov (with the title of *first* Secretary to emphasise the collective character of even that position) and retained only the position of Prime Minister. Personal leadership was eventually reestablished here, Zhivkov ousting Chervenkov and then, eventually, Yugov. There was more relaxation of police and economic pressure than in any of the countries we have so far considered, despite the strikes in the Plovdiv tobacco works in May 1953. Political prisoners were amnestied. In the towns there were price reductions and gains for the workers, clerks, private traders and artisans. There were easier credit terms for the collectives and a reduction of compulsory deliveries from them. Nearly 40 per cent of the land was still cultivated by private farmers and pressure on them to collectivise stopped. There was no change in Albania, except in separating the positions of Prime Minister and Party Secretary. Enver Hoxha, with more political insight than Chervenkov, gave up the position of Prime Minister – to an old friend – and held on to that of Secretary of the Party.

It was in Poland and Hungary that de-Stalinisation meant revolution, though not at once. Even the establishment of a collective leadership was slow in Poland. But in March 1954 Bierut, who had replaced Gomulka in 1948, received a new title as first Secretary of the Party and Zawadzki was appointed Chairman of the State Council, or Prime Minister. From the end of 1954 thousands of political prisoners were set free and several people in the police service were dismissed. By 1956 there had been slackening in the pace of industrialisation since 1953, but there was no change in the standard of living. As in the German Democratic Republic, de-Stalinisation showed itself in the people's response to their condition, not in any change in their condition. Any attempt to exact more work fanned smouldering resentment at living conditions into a flame. At the ZIS-PO armament works in Poznań, employing a labour force of 15,000, increased work schedules caused protest. When the workers marched in an orderly manner to present their grievances at the town hall, a crowd seemed to gather from nowhere and suddenly there was a formidable demonstration against the régime. By the evening of the same day (June 28, 1956) the rising had been suppressed by the Polish armed forces at the cost of 54 deaths, hundreds wounded and 300 arrests. It was important that the suppression was by the Poles themselves, for it was the source of the Soviet confidence that the Poles could be safely left to solve their own problems. During July and August there were negotiations with the U.S.S.R. from which the Polish Government gained a large new credit, an increase in the price which the U.S.S.R. paid for Polish coal and the repatriation of thousands of Poles, held since the War. There was next strife within the Central Committee of the Party between hardliners and reformers of which the unpredicted outcome was the recall to power of Gomulka, as the one man who might restore the crumbling authority of Party and Government. He had already been rehabilitated in April, having been released from prison in 1954, after Stalin's death. He now made his own terms. He demanded and obtained (October 19) a new Politburo with himself as Secretary General of the Party and Edward Gierek a member. He offered reforms: the release of peasants from the collective farms and the ultimate 'socialisation' of the countryside by consent; religious freedom and the release from prison of Cardinal Wyszynski; and a relaxation of police control. He made it clear that his rule would be no threat to the alliance with the U.S.S.R., nor to its strategic interests and the presence of Soviet troops on Polish soil as long as the Warsaw Pact organisation needed it. Meanwhile, there had been an enquiry into the Poznań rising and a trial of the rebels conducted in public and in a liberal manner. It increased the political and intellectual ferment of that summer. Gomulka had made his terms with the Russians already in Warsaw when on October 19 a second crisis occurred. The workers of Warsaw had taken to the streets; Soviet troop movements had occurred; a powerful Soviet delegation consisting of Khrushchev himself, Mikoyan, Molotov and Kaganovich had arrived in Warsaw. They left the following morning, October 20, reassured that Gomulka and his colleagues, now in office, were in control and, from the point of view of Soviet national interests, safely so. Indeed 1967–70 saw a slow and long retreat from October. Poland however remained a more liberal country, more in touch with its past traditions and with a more open and vigorous intellectual life than that of any other country of the eastern bloc. Elections took place in January 1957. They represented a show of real and not coerced support for Gomulka and his régime. Thereafter the régime, especially after 1968, became more rigid and out of touch with the country. In 1970 Gomulka had one more success in the Treaty with West Germany. But in that year power passed to Edward Gierek who succeeded Gomulka as Party Secretary. Gomulka lived on in retirement in Warsaw until his death in 1982. Gierek was powerful in industrial Silesia, was a good organiser and a technocrat, but not a popular leader as Gomulka had been in 1956–57.

In Hungary, there had also been difficulty in making the leadership collective. But in 1953 Imre Nagy was imposed, as Prime Minister, upon Rákosi by the U.S.S.R. Rákosi remained Secretary of the Party. Nagy stood for a different economic policy. He stood for abating industrialisation in favour of food production. Though there were peasant demonstrations against the excessive grain exactions. Rákosi resisted any change. He was summoned to Moscow, but resisted pressure to adopt the Malenkov new course with which Nagy sympathised. Pressure from the Kremlin continued and Rákosi was again summoned to the Soviet capital, this time with Ernö Gerö and Mihály Farkas. There was a stay in industrialisation and peasants were no longer restrained from leaving the collective farms, so that there was a considerable rise in the amount of land privately farmed. Rákosi continued his resistance, undermining Nagy and his policy from inside the régime. In October 1955 he got rid of both. But the Nagy period was important, for it had fostered the idea that an alternative economic and political method was possible within the existing system. When Rákosi resumed sole power, he could not wipe out this idea which became the more popular the more firmly the alternative was withheld. The members of the writers' union and the members of the so-called Petöfi Circle, or discussion group, elaborated this idea and stimulated arguments among students and workers with whom they made contact. The arguments about the collectivisation of the countryside and the unrealities of the Stalinist policy of industrialisation continued, and people took sides for Nagy or Rákosi. The U.S.S.R. apparently feared a repetition of Poznań in Hungary and, in July 1956, induced the Party to replace Rákosi with Ernö Gerö. But though Gerö visited the Kremlin in October, he and his colleagues could not put forward a policy to deal with an increasingly dynamic situation except the stale one of relying on the police, army and Soviet occupying forces. Nagy increasingly became the rallying point of opposition, but he had no answer any more than Gerö, except to insist on loyalty to the Party which was not enough. The rehabilitation of Rajk, tried and executed in 1949, and events in Poland precipitated revolt. On October 23 Budapest rose. Nagy was recalled and became Prime Minister, Gerö two days later was replaced as Secretary of the Party by Kádàr. The situation was confused for it was not clear whom the revolution was against. Nagy was no enemy, but he was no revolutionary leader either. Soviet troops were called in by Kàdàr and the Party leadership. They controlled the situation and on October 27 Nagy reconstituted his Government to include non-Communists. On October 28, he negotiated a cease-fire and the Soviet troops left Budapest next day. On October 30, Nagy announced that he intended to revive the pre-Stalinist Peasant and Social Democratic Parties. He was convinced that a system of several political parties was not incompatible with a Communist economy, Nagy had too little authority to institute such a profound change. On the same day, Mikoyan and Suslov, who represented the Kremlin in Budapest, issued a declaration on 'Friendship and Co-operation between the Soviet Union and other Socialist States'. It was an answer to the threat which Nagy seemed now to pose to the ideological solidarity of the eastern bloc. Khrushchev for his part was negotiating international support for Soviet armed intervention. He was in touch with Tito, Mao, and with the Czechs, East Germans, Bulgarians and Rumanians. Nagy had no outside support. On November 4, Soviet artillery fire marked the Soviet determination to prevent the establishment of a neutral, democratic—in the western sense of the word—Government in Hungary. The Soviet intervention on this second occasion was by tanks. The barricades erected and manned by all ranks of the population could not withstand a tank action. Nagy fell, for he had failed where Gomulka succeeded: he could not convince the Soviet Government that he could make a national Communist Hungary, still satisfactorily suiting the strategic and economic needs of the U.S.S.R. He took refuge in the Yugoslav Embassy until Kádár encouraged him to leave. He was then deported to Rumania. In June 1958 he was tried and executed as a political measure instigated by the U.S.S.R. Nevertheless Kádár's Hungary, which now lost by emigration, death and imprisonment those who had survived from the old upper and middle classes, became a more open country with the pace of industrialisation slowed down and police pressure relaxed. The standard of living remained low, intellectual life, except in music, stagnated.

The Polish and Hungarian risings were two dissimilar events despite their common origin. The Polish movement was so controlled by the Poles themselves as to leave the Polish Communist state still largely independent of Soviet Russia. Poland continued to exemplify national Communism. Gomulka, who controlled the movement, had a base in the factories and the U.S.S.R. knew that he could speak for the workers and that what he undertook in their name would be performed. His counterpart in Hungary, Imre Nagy, had no such base in workers' support and consequently no such control of what happened. Secondly, Poland, which had lost its educated middle and upper classes during the War, was a workers' society as Hungary was not, as well as being strategically the most important state in the eastern bloc. In Hungary a more diversified society gave opportunity to the members of the pre-war upper and middle classes, or their sons—for the barricades were manned by young boys as well as students and workers—to strike for freedom and a return to the old days. Imre Nagy by reviving the non-Communist political parties seemed to encourage them, though for him it was probably a manoeuvre in the power struggle. Finally, in Hungary there was a much more coherent philosophy of revisionism. In both countries revisionist writers and intellectuals set the movement going, but there was nothing in Poland quite like the Petöfi Circle of Budapest and the discussions which it stimulated. Revisionists, who had fully thought out their position, rejected the notion of the dictatorship of the proletariat, because they had seen that, in practice, not the workers ruled in its name, but the Party bureaucracy. They questioned the whole idea of a proletarian society because they saw inequality constantly recurring. Moreover, it was clear to them that the workers could never dispense with the intellectuals. They would protest at the inequality of the relationship with the Soviet Union. True internationalism entailed equality between all Communist states. They would protest at the stultifying rigidity of centralised planning and call for wider sharing at the grass-roots in policy-making. They rejected, finally and most characteristically, the whole notion of censorship and the repression of freedom of thought and the direction of artistic endeavour. It was unfortunate that their philosophic position was clearer than their programme. They knew better where they stood than what to do.

De-Stalinisation meant, less tragic but equally dramatic, change in the intrusion of China into European affairs. The year 1949 had seen the victory of the Communists and the establishment of the People's Republic of China under Mao Tse-tung. In February 1950 Stalin had signed a thirty-year Treaty of Alliance, Friendship and Mutual Aid with Mao. Three years of co-operation in the war in Korea had consolidated the common interests of the two States. The character of this alliance changed. As long as Stalin was alive the U.S.S.R. was the senior partner. After his death partnership was equal and Soviet services to China greater. In October 1954 Khrushchev, Bulganin and Mikoyan made a celebrated visit to Peking. A new Agreement was signed. The U.S.S.R. now withdrew from Port Arthur and from several joint Sino-Soviet enterprises, allowing, for example, the Chinese a monopoly of the exploitation of uranium deposits in Sinkiang. Moreover, the U.S.S.R. increased her military and economic aid to China. It is clear that Mao had gained important advantages that he would not have gained from Stalin. Another gain was that the U.S.S.R. began to act as the bridge which China used to bring herself on to the western as well as eastern international stage. She appeared there, as already noticed, in 1954 at Geneva. The People's Republic of China received diplomatic recognition from Britain in May 1956. Furthermore, her influence was strengthened in all the states of the eastern bloc after the Polish and Hungarian risings. It was as if these revolts had temporarily destroyed the authority of Soviet Russia and China stepped into the vacant place. In November 1957 a meeting of representatives from sixty-eight of the seventy-five existing Communist Parties took place in Moscow in celebration of the fortieth anniversary of the Soviet Revolution. A session of the representatives of the Parties actually in power (November 14–16) issued a Declaration of Principle, which Yugoslavia did not sign, and a full session issued a Peace Manifesto, which Yugoslavia did sign. On both documents Chinese influence was decisive. It was especially interesting in the first document, for Mao insisted on a wording of the Declaration, where it defined proletarian internationalism, which made the primacy of the U.S.S.R. indisputable. Yet in practice China and the U.S.S.R. were by now sharing the leadership of the eastern bloc. Mao was also responsible for the wording of the text on the subject of new Communist attitudes. It took a middle position condemning both dogmatism and revisionism as departures from Marxism-Leninism. Yet although China appeared in western as well as eastern negotiations, her influence served on the whole to harden division between eastern and western blocs, because she put so much emphasis on loyalty to the true word of Marxism-Leninism.

In 1958 Chinese influence was responsible for a revival of attacks on Yugoslavia as the great deviator. The signal was given in Peking for a flood of abuse from Sofia, Tirana and Prague and, under Chinese pressure, Khrushchev did not make the large loan to Yugoslavia that had been negotiated. It was the year of China's great leap forward to industrialisation, of her establishment of people's communes with their attached industrial enterprises. Peking rather than Moscow had become the source of the spirit 'of continuous agitation, stormy progress and permanent revolution.'[1] She was copied in Hungary by a revival of collectivisation. Between 1959 and 1961 there was a great increase in the number of collective farms produced by a mixture of persuasion and pressure. She was imitated in the G.D.R. with the same result. The figure given is 80 per cent collective farming by 1960. Poland remained outside the movement with 87 per cent of her land still cultivated privately. Bulgaria, on the other hand, was a most vigorous imitator, adopting even the Chinese phrase of a 'great leap forward,' and adopting China's practices, such as her compulsory spell of manual work for Party and Government officials. The targets she set herself, however, for industrial and agricultural production were unattainable. So that her great leap forward was more important as a sign of Chinese influence, and for the ferment it

[1] F. Fejtö. *A History of the People's Democracies since Stalin* (1965), p. 96.

caused, than for its effects on economic growth. Albania outdid even Bulgaria in imitation of China, for she saw that Chinese practices might solve some of her similar problems and, most important, China might help her to throw off the Yugoslav yoke which by 1960 was becoming irksome.

Finally, de-Stalinisation meant reconciliation between the U.S.S.R. and Yugoslavia. It was a mistrustful reconciliation; the purpose of the U.S.S.R. was to strengthen its international position, not to gain Yugoslav friendship for its own sake. Reconciliation began in October 1954 and from May 27 to June 2, 1955, Khrushchev and Bulganin were in Belgrade. The meeting had been carefully prepared by a correspondence with Tito in which the form of the Soviet 'apology' for the 'error' of 1948 was carefully negotiated. It is true that Khrushchev departed from the text in making his apology immediately on arrival, in order to emphasise ideological solidarity, but it had no effect. Tito and the Yugoslav Government were determined to keep their ideological positions, as well as their freedom to manoeuvre between East and West. They were not prepared to go beyond an improvement in relations between the two States. A Declaration was issued after the meeting which clearly reflected this limitation. Yugoslavia gained new credits from the U.S.S.R. and compensation for broken contracts for the delivery of commodities in 1948. Khrushchev had gained what he set out to gain: a success in foreign policy or a strengthening of his position in international relations. It was all he gained and he was obliged to accept the Yugoslav doctrine that there were different roads to Socialism. Tito was not to be persuaded to sign the Warsaw Pact nor to join the Warsaw Pact Organisation, made during the same month that the visit to Belgrade took place. He was determined to keep his uncommitted position. Yet his ability to do so depended upon acceptance both in his own country and in the U.S.S.R. of a delicate distinction between 'more than one path to socialism', which he believed was true, and 'the multi-party state' of Imre Nagy which he believed was a deviation from Marxism-Leninism. When the fresh break came in 1958, most members of the Party in Yugoslavia are said to have felt that Yugoslavia had escaped unscathed from a risky adventure. From the Soviet point of view the break was necessary, after it was clear that Khrushchev had failed to persuade Yugoslavia to abandon her non-committed position. If she would not submit to the exclusiveness of the eastern bloc she was a threat to its solidarity and to the Sino-Soviet leadership of it. So in 1958 Yugoslavia paid the price of her independence in a fresh break.

By 1961–62 a fresh break between the U.S.S.R. and China had also occurred. The Twenty-second Congress of the Party in October 1961 witnessed a Chinese challenge to the authority of the U.S.S.R. which masked Sino-Soviet schism. The new break entailed a break also with the Chinese-influenced Albania, with which relations were broken off in November 1961. So Khrushchev's foreign policy had in the end failed too. This failure may also have contributed to his fall. He was dismissed, as has already been noticed, in 1964. Nevertheless by 1964 the eastern bloc was a different, more diversified, open group than it was in 1953. More important, the members of it were more humane and liberal societies and more in touch with their past traditions. And with the West a policy of co-existence prevailed, though world revolution remained the ultimate goal.

After this lengthy examination of de-Stalinisation we can return to the question asked about Khrushchev: why should he have invited such a shock to Communism as his denunciation of Stalin's crimes in 1956 was? The answer will now suggest itself that he really had no alternative. Stalin's great personal power was already under strain. Khrushchev could not have maintained Stalin's refusal to allow diversity within the eastern bloc. Khrushchev, in order himself to rule, had to fit the situation which existed and repudiate Stalin's personal power.

Khrushchev's action in 1956 should therefore be seen as a genuine rejection of the great personal power which Stalin had accumulated. It did not, as we have seen, initiate a tenure of power that was an all-round success. Khrushchev was dismissed for failures both in economic and foreign policy. But in the longer perspective, because he had adjusted the situation inside the Soviet Union, and in its relations with the eastern-bloc countries and in the U.S.S.R.'s position in world politics to a less concentrated kind of rule and one less ready to *impose* its decisions at whatever cost, including the cost of lives, success may be ascribed to him. During the War three great Powers, personalised in Churchill, Roosevelt and Stalin, had shared the leadership of the world. After the War power had polarised. Khrushchev inherited from Stalin rule over a super-Power in a world where there were only two. It is sometimes said that he left to his successors less power than he inherited in a world in which there were again three rivals for international leadership, the U.S.S.R., the U.S.A. and the P.R.C.[1]

The Brezhnev-Kosygin-Gromyko régime which followed that of Khrushchev—Kosygin was Prime Minister, Gromyko Foreign Minister—tilted Russian policy towards closer concern with the affairs of South East Asia where the Vietnam War had begun and was the focal point of Russian relations with China and the United States. Pressure on the eastern bloc was to that extent relieved.

In 1968 Czechoslovakia in a remarkable movement for reform, led by a most courageous man, a Slovak, Alexander Dubćek, seemed to rediscover her own past. She was a country, as we have already

[1] See G. Segal, *The Great Power Triangle* (1982).

noticed, with an egalitarian society, a high standard of education and a humane as well as democratic tradition. It will be recalled that before the coup of 1948 the Communists had moved near power by the normal political process. It was characteristic of a politically sophisticated and humane people that this should be so. During the fifties Czechoslovakia had flourished. Her standard of living was relatively good; she was highly industrialised; the state procurement system worked satisfactorily taking agricultural products from state farms, collective farms and a minority of independent farms. In 1961 Czechoslovakia was declared to have achieved socialism and was considered ready to work for the next stage: complete communism. She was the only country of the eastern bloc to have won this distinction.

Then everything began to go wrong. The Third Five-Year Plan, adopted in January 1961, proved to be impossible to fulfil and was abandoned. Industrial output failed to reach the level expected; agricultural production fell off; a fifth of Czech imports was of food; she suddenly had an adverse balance of payments. In 1963 her economic position was disastrous: the planned rate of growth could be no more than one per cent, contrasting sharply with a rate of 11 per cent actually *achieved* in 1958–60.[1] Agricultural production showed a rate of decline and food queues appeared in the cities. The shock felt by a people with a high standard of living need not be stressed. Czech trade fell off more and more noticeably, with a drop in the quality of goods offered and a falling away of selling techniques.

It is not suggested that economic strain was the cause of the movement for reform. But it provoked a widespread discussion of economic problems and some criticism of Party and state officials. This discussion and criticism made a situation in which a more open airing of ideas was generally possible. It was this which was important. Nor did open discussion cause an anti-Communist movement. The Czech reform movement, like the Polish of 1956, but unlike the Hungarian of the same year, was a movement within the Communist Party, not against it. It was a movement to find a more effective role for the Party within society and within a particularly Czechoslovak society, the same kind of humane, open society that the Slovak section of it especially believed it had always been. One root of the reform movement was certainly the Slovak sense of the particular Slovak contribution Slovakia could make to the Czechoslovak State.

The Czechoslovak reform movement, moreover, began with change at the top. It did not begin with strikes, manifestations of popular discontent, nor demands from workers. Nor was it a movement of protest. Revisionism was an important cause of the movement as it was of Hungary's rising in 1956. Its leaders had, however,

[1] G. Golan, *The Czechoslovak Reform Movement. Communism in Crisis, 1962–68* (1971), pp. 11–12.

a much clearer idea of the direction reform should take than the Hungarians had had. The movement began with the economists (men such as Ota Sik), the writers and the students in so far as revisionism began it. But before they made their contribution, change had begun at the top with the education reforms applied in the school year of 1965–66 to the schools and in 1966 to the Universities. These emanated from the Ministry of Education. Their tendency was to relax Party control, to give greater importance to substantive achievement in knowledge and less to good Party behaviour and to allow greater independence to the Universities.

In the same years, 1965 and 1966, the economy was reformed. A working party of economists had drawn up in 1964 a set of basic principles as a starting-point. They were now applied. The result may be summed up in greater attention to costs of production, to material incentives, to wage rates, to worker participation in management and to the satisfaction of the consumers' wants. A drive was made to increase foreign trade, to raise the quality of Czech goods and to make trade agreements with the West. A new labour code was adopted. Historians notice the achievement of Czech theatre, cinema and television in 1965 and 1966 as especially lively, innovative and, in its comments on the passing scene, satirical with a new openness towards the West.

So we come to the fall of Novotný and his replacement by Alexander Dubček. The meeting of the Central Committee of the Party on October 30–31, 1967, was the scene of criticism, charges and counter-charges between two sides, the one headed by Novotný and the other by Dubček. The struggle continued during November. On December 8, Brezhnev arrived in Prague from Moscow to try to settle the dispute, but he left without doing anything, under the impression that the Party was in control and that, if there was a change in personnel, it would not matter. Novotný offered his resignation after extensive criticism at another full meeting of the Central Committee on December 19–21 and further meetings of the Praesidium and Central Committee at which he had fought unavailingly for his position. At last, on January 5, 1968, Novotný resigned the Party leadership and Dubček took his place. Other changes of personnel followed. There were no trials, no purges, no punishments. This in itself was an achievement.

It is impossible here to describe in detail the political reforms now introduced. So first the general principles of reform will be noticed and then something said of the reasons why the U.S.S.R. eventually found it necessary to invade Czechoslovakia and to put an end to the Dubček régime.

The first principle of reform related to the Communist Party's position. Its leadership was not to be abolished, but it was to be obliged to justify its right to lead. It was to lose its right to impose its leadership by command. It must patently provide the correct solution to a problem, be seen to do so and be able to persuade dissentients that it did so. There was to be every opportunity for discussion and the right to attempt to make one's view prevail. Freedom of association was, therefore, granted and censorship was relaxed. The question then was, how far might one go in expressing one's view, *after* the Party had taken a decision. The limit was set by the continued ban on 'factionalism'. The Party was still to provide the goals, the guidelines, the important decisions. There were also many reforms within the Party, as, for example, introduction of rotation of offices, of the right to resign and of the right to be present at proceedings against oneself.

The second principle of reform weakened the idea of the one-Party state. Electoral reform allowed some choice. Elective organs, including the National Assembly, met more frequently, for longer sessions and had more power. The National Assembly, though it still only debated bills coming from the Government, now began to cause them to be amended, revised and improved. It had ceased to be a rubber stamp and it was possible to believe that opposition might perform a useful function.

The third principle of reform related to the economy. Large concerns were broken down and individual enterprises assured of some independence. Enterprise councils were set up, on which the workers were represented, for the management of individual enterprises. Enterprises were grouped and groups of enterprises became the instruments of central control. A new Party programme, issued in April 1968, and known as the Action Programme, described the new system. The general result of much piecemeal change was less Government interference in the several branches of the economy and more influence upon it of the market. But the Government repeated, time and again, that Czechoslovakia was completely loyal to the Council for Mutual Economic Aid (CMEA), which was the name of the organisation which supervised the economic arrangements of the eastern bloc.

Fourthly the reformers, men such as Josef Špaček and Josef Smrkovský as well as Dubček, affirmed the importance of means being provided for the expression of different social interests. These were bound to arise from differences in age, qualifications, intellectual ability and work and should be expressed through appropriate institutions. The trade unions, regarded as one such institution, were given a new statute in June 1968 and acquired new life and importance. The new Party programme also referred to this principle of reform. New security and new life appeared in all sorts of group organisations, such as student groups, the circle of independent writers, KAN or the club of committed non-Party members, religious groups and K-231, that is a group of persons found guilty in the

Stalin era of illegal political activity under article 231 of the penal code.

Finally a declaration known as the 2000 words was published in various journals, on June 27, 1968. Signed by a selected list of workers, writers, artists, scientists, farmers, sportsmen and engineers, it asserted that reform had reached a critical stage and called upon the people to assert their rights. Thousands signed copies that were displayed in the streets. Its meaning was not clear and the Party Praesidium condemned it, for fear that it might be interpreted as revolution from below.

To turn now to the reasons for Soviet intervention: the first pressure upon Czechoslovakia from other members of the eastern bloc was prompted by supposedly dangerous internal relaxation. A meeting of eastern bloc leaders at Dresden on March 23, 1968, called the Czechs to account. But this pressure was lifted when Dubček gave assurances of Czech loyalty to the Warsaw Pact and insisted that the Czech reforms constituted no threat to Socialism. Some five weeks later pressure began from the U.S.S.R. On May 4 Dubček had talks in Moscow with Brezhnev at which he insisted that the Czechs should be left to manage their own affairs. Soviet pressure on Czechoslovakia, both military and political, continued through the summer. The political pressure culminated in the letter sent from Warsaw to the Czechoslovak Party Central Committee on July 15 by the Soviet, Bulgarian, G.D.R., Hungarian and Polish Parties. It enunciated what became known as the Brezhnev doctrine: that is, that internal developments in a 'fraternal' country were the legitimate concern of the whole 'Socialist Commonwealth'. Military pressure took the form of Warsaw Pact manoeuvres inside Czechoslovakia from which the troops did not disperse and troop concentrations on Czechslovakia's frontiers. Meetings finally took place at Cierna-nad-Tisou on the Czechslovak-Soviet border (July 29–August 1) and Bratislavia (August 3) at which agreement seemed to have been reached. But accusations that the Czechs had not been loyal to the agreements arrived at there provided the pretext for the Soviet invasion of Czechoslovakia. This took place, with the support of the G.D.R., Poland, Bulgaria and Hungary, on August 20–21, 1968. The Czechoslovak people, offered resourceful passive resistance and the U.S.S.R. could not form an alternative puppet Government.

There had been rumours of a concentration of troops preparatory to invasion ever since Dubček left Moscow. The Soviet restraint is said to have been due to fear of the effect of forceful action upon the international Communist movement. The final decision to invade was due, it is thought, not to fear for strategical interests nor for the close alliance with the G.D.R. (no troops were sent to the Czech-West German border) but to fear for the solidarity in ideas of the eastern bloc. The Russians were not afraid that reforms might lead the

Czechs out of the bloc. They *were* afraid that a particular Czech way to Socialism threatened Socialism, as they conceived it. The U.S.S.R.'s concept of power could not accommodate a notion of a Communist state without a Communist Party which commanded. The Russians invaded in order to restore the Czechoslovak Party to absolute power.

Chapter 16

EUROPE UNITED: FRANCE, WEST GERMANY AND THE WESTERN BLOC, 1945–70

In France these were the years of Charles de Gaulle. Whether he was Head of State (1944–46 and 1958–69) or waiting in withdrawal for tendencies alien to himself to work themselves out (1946–58, during the Fourth Republic) his was the greatest single influence on affairs. He had great strength of character, reinforced by an accumulation of success. He had clear and sharply outlined ideas and penetration to basic causal principles. He had the unusual ability not only to take decisions but to take them all so much along the grain of the wood that their very coherence, in themselves and with the situation, made them carry conviction. He was able to identify himself with France and to attach loyalty from both Right and Left to a common patriotism. He was not a dictator, but a politician in the sense that he knew how to gain power, how to keep it and how to use it, as well as how to pay the price—in responsibility—which it exacted.

During the period of the Provisional Government, while continuing to organise France's contribution to the war effort, his main task was to establish its authority, in the name of the French state, over France and especially over the several resistance committees which had usurped authority in the localities. The hierarchy of Prefects, sub-Prefects and Mayors and their elective councils in Departments and Communes was restored. It was important to bring to an end the summary 'justice' being administered all over France, when resisters took the law into their own hands against alleged or actual collaborators. If 'justice' was to be done, it must be done in the name of the state. The regular courts were in operation by October 1944 and on November 18, 1944, the decree was issued which set up a High Court of five judges and twenty-four jurymen, chosen by a complicated system combining chance with reputation, to deal with those upon whom the desire for revenge was principally focused. The trials did not finally peter out until 1949. But with the execution of Joseph Darnand, who had hunted down resisters, and of Pierre Laval and the trial of Marshal Pétain (then aged eighty-nine, he spent six years in prison, dying in 1951) the worst was over. Meanwhile political life revived. The Communists, still under their pre-war leader, Maurice Thorez, and the Socialists under Léon Blum, released from detention, were strong from their part in the resistance. Edouard Herriot, freed from German hands by the Russians, revived the old Radical Party, declining office under de Gaulle to do so. It was a small opposition party. Georges Bidault, who had been at the head of the National Council of Resistance from 1943 to 1944, when it was replaced by the Provisional Government, led the *Mouvement Républicain Populaire* (MRP), a Catholic middle-of-the-road party corresponding to the Christian Democratic Parties of Germany, Italy and Belgium. It was a strong party, gaining 23 per cent of the vote and 151 seats in the Election for the Constituent Assembly which took place in the autumn. The MRP, the Communists with 150 seats and the Socialists with 139 were the three Government parties in the years of 'tripartism' immediately after the War. France, by means of a referendum, gave authority to this Assembly to make a new constitution. It was one of de Gaulle's achievements that he guided France to break with the Third Republic, without breaking political continuity altogether. The Assembly when it met unanimously elected de Gaulle President of the Government of the Republic and he appointed a Ministry which included Maurice Thorez. In foreign affairs de Gaulle's service to France was to give her a position among the Powers which she had not had at the Potsdam Conference of July 1945. She was not represented there, but she *was* included among the occupying Powers of Germany and Berlin and among the permanent members of the Security Council of the United Nations. She was to make good her claim to equality with Britain. De Gaulle obtained what he believed was due to France. Similarly he made good her right to belong to the nuclear Powers. In 1945 he established her atomic energy commission and saw to it that money was set aside for research and development. A start was made in characteristic European policies of the post-war period by de Gaulle's Ministers. The public ownership of coal, electricity, gas, credit and insurance was quietly introduced. The increase of family allowances, the establishment of old-age pensions, of industrial unemployment allowances and sickness payments was also quietly begun. De Gaulle's Socialist Minister for Agriculture, who continued Minister until 1947, dissolved the co-operative system for agriculture introduced under Pétain, but quietly retained and developed provision for the co-operative purchase and use of expensive farm machinery (such as tractors), provision for marketing agencies and the protection of tenant rights. He did not succeed in reducing the number of small farms or imposing a national agricultural plan.

De Gaulle resigned on January 20, 1946, and the constitution was not made under his guidance. Indeed, the first version with a single-chamber parliament was rejected by France when a referendum was taken in June 1946. It was not, therefore, until November 1946 that the constitution of the Fourth Republic was completed and accepted by the nation after a further referendum. De Gaulle believed a tendency was re-establishing itself in France towards power for parliament, what he called the régime of the parties, instead of power for the Government. He resigned because the permanent threat, which had hung over the men who were Ministers under the Third Republic, of losing their parliamentary support with the consequent chronic state of crisis, the trafficking with party leaders outside and of intrigue inside the Council of Ministers, was likely to be renewed under the constitution then being made.[1] Félix Gouin formed a stop-gap Ministry.

The constitution of the Fourth Republic, which came into effect in November 1946, departed from the Socialist doctrine of the single chamber. Parliament was composed of a Chamber of Deputies, elected by universal suffrage of men and women, and a so-called Council of the Republic. The latter was, as its name implies, a counselling body without power to decide. It would propose amendments to legislation without being able to insist on them. It was chosen by an elaborate system involving the members of the Chamber, members of the Departmental Councils and so-called 'Great Electors,' themselves elected by universal suffrage. The Chamber was elected for four years. This fixed period between General Elections has been blamed for the most unsatisfactory characteristic of the Fourth Republic: a new Ministry every few months. But the same provision in the constitution of the German Federal Republic did not result in the same ministerial instability. This was because in Germany the President, at the request of the Chancellor, if he asked for a vote of confidence and failed to obtain it, could dissolve the parliament. In France no provision had been made for an appeal to the electorate in this way. Fallen Governments were simply replaced by new Governments, supported by much the same coalition as before, and as vulnerable as before to displacement. There was another reason, also, for this ministerial instability. The parties behaved in the same way that they had behaved under the Third Republic, uniting to defeat a Ministry but dividing again as soon as its defeat was accomplished. Those who caused the fall of a Ministry felt no obligation to replace it. Party practice in this respect was exaggerated under the Fourth Republic after tripartism had broken down and after de Gaulle had formed the *Rassemblement du Peuple Français* (RPF). Tripartism broke down when, on May 5, 1947, the Communists left the Ramadier Government, prompted thereto by the split between

[1] Charles de Gaulle, *Mémoires de Guerre, Le Salut 1944–1946* (1959), p. 264.

East and West in Europe, the development of the war in Indo-China, an insurrection in Madagascar (March 29) and a strike in the national-ised Renault motor works. The RPF worked in parliament as the opposite extreme to the Communists. It proved constantly possible for these two extremes to unite to cause a Ministry suddenly to lose its majority. But, of course, since they disagreed on everything except dissatisfaction with the Ministry, they could not stay united to make an alternative Government.

Under the new constitution the President was elected by the Members of the Chamber and of the Council meeting in joint session. It was the practice under the Fourth Republic, though the constitution did not provide for this, for the President to take soundings among men likely to be able to make an adequate coalition of supporters and so to find a possible First Minister. If, after a speech outlining his intentions, he proved acceptable, he was invested by the Chamber, made his Government and presented it to the Chamber for its approval. It was a cumbersome procedure and resulted, because the making of Ministries became more and more difficult towards 1958, in there being intervals as long as five weeks between Governments. Nevertheless the Fourth Republic survived through three parliaments, 1946–51, 1951–56, 1956–58, two Presidents, Vincent Auriol (who had entered politics in 1914) (1946–54), and René Coty (1954–58) and twenty-one Governments.

The period of tripartism was followed by the period of the so-called Third Force. It was a misnomer, for the union of the Socialists, MRP and Radicals, to which it was applied, was anything but dynamic. The moderates stood together in immobility, it was said, because they could not agree on policies. The Communist and Gaullist extremes stayed in opposition.

Some sound work was done by legislation quietly promoted by individual Ministers in the nationalisation, social security and peasants' co-operative enterprises outlined above, but the first parliament of the Fourth Republic sought its successes chiefly in dealing with inflation and industrial unrest, and it did not find them. The strike in the Renault works was followed by others. They were particularly serious from June 4, 1947, when the railway strike began, to November 28, 1948, when the general miners' strike ended, for they were accompanied by sporadic insurrection and riot. The pattern was always the same: a trade union demanded an increase in wages, the Government refused, the union organised a strike, the Government settled at a figure higher than the first demand. Prices continued to rise and supplies continued to fall. Then Robert Schuman, who was Prime Minister after Ramadier, had success. He attacked at least one of the roots of inflation by limiting the money supply with a levy on incomes, and devaluing the franc. The effect of these measures did not last. Schuman fell and after a few months of André Marie, Henri

Queuille was Prime Minister. He was in fact head of three different Governments before the parliament ended in 1951. It was he who was especially associated with what was called immobility.

Marshall Aid promised in 1947 and the supplies which began to come from America under the Marshall Plan brought a sort of recovery. Yet France 'though it appeared convalescent was really under an anaesthetic.' It was only during the second parliament, when there was increased public spending—on rearmament—that economic recovery began. This was the period of Pinay's miracle. Antoine Pinay was Prime Minister from March to December 1952. He seemed even to have checked Third Force politics, for he attached to himself a piece of the extremist opposition in the shape of twenty-seven Gaullist members. The miracle was the arrest of inflation. Pinay roused confidence with economies, an amnesty designed to bring back illegally exported capital, fresh borrowing, bans on certain price increases and appeals for voluntary restraint. During the whole year the rate of inflation declined month by month. But his Government fell. A second period of confidence occurred under Mendès-France, Prime Minister from June 1954 to February 1955, but again it did not last. When inflation fell, unemployment and recession followed. By now the régime itself was under attack from at least one section of the community and that a section not usually articulate. This was the section of owners of small businesses and workshops. They were organised by Pierre Poujade in the Union for the Defence of Shop-keepers (Commerçants) and Artisans: the UDCA. In the General Election of 1956 it obtained 2.5 million votes and gained fifty-three seats. But its leaders were incompetent and, though it expressed a widespread dissatisfaction, it proposed no constructive alternatives to what it disliked. It was anti-parliament, anti-industrialisation, anti-Big Business, anti-Paris, anti-taxes. But when these things did not disappear by merely being shouted down, it did not know what to do next and by 1958 it had begun to peter out. It was only important as an indication of the way in which the Fourth Republic was a political failure.

Meanwhile in the economy there was again improvement. Guy Mollet's planning and measures to assist economic expansion seemed at last to bring some stability. Peace and equilibrium was, however, restricted to the cities and industrial centres. In the countryside the last years of the second parliament of the Fourth Republic, 1954 and 1955, were years of falling profits, increasing overproduction of wine, of pig and dairy produce, even of grain, and armed demonstrations. The Government had recourse to price support for wine, meat and milk, aid in marketing surpluses and aid in reducing acreage devoted to certain crops. These measures and natural causes gradually took effect. By 1956 agriculture was relatively prosperous. By 1958 France was economically quite well placed. The crisis of May 13 which brought down the Fourth Republic was not economic. France like other European countries had adopted central economic planning. The Commission for planning had been established already in August 1946. Jean Monnet was put at its head. His first plan ran from 1947 to 1950 and was limited in scope. It was concerned mainly with the modernisation of industrial equipment and methods. Nor was its target in production achieved. The second plan of 1954 to 1957 shifted the emphasis from capital investment to consumer goods and achieved its targets. The measures taken by Gaillard, the Finance Minister, in the last year of the Fourth Republic, were succeeding in stabilising the franc. Nevertheless prices and wages were again chasing goods and inflation still existed when, in 1958, the Fourth Republic ended.

As we have seen, the crisis of May 13 which brought de Gaulle back to power by May 27 was precipitated by the Algerian War. Nevertheless, had France found any satisfaction in the Fourth Republic she would not have responded to de Gaulle's offer on May 15 to assume the powers of the Republic. He made this offer in a public statement which he confirmed in a Press Conference on May 19, when he also made it clear that he would not take power unless it was delegated to him by the Republic. In other words, he would not take it only to be bound by the constitution of 1946. To recall de Gaulle meant to change the constitution. As we have seen, he took office as Prime Minister under the forms of the constitution of 1946, but was at once given for six months powers to rule by decree and to draw up a new constitution.

De Gaulle set to work aided by a small committee, much influenced by his close associate Michel Debré. The constitution they devised was accepted by the nation in the referendum of September 28, 1958, with an exceptionally high poll. The balance of the new constitution favoured the President and gave him a special relationship with the electorate. He was not, however, elected by universal suffrage (until the change in the constitution made in 1962), but by an electoral college of some 80,000 political notabilities. De Gaulle was elected first President of the Fifth Republic on December 21, 1958. His constitutional powers were large. He was Head of State, its spokesman in its relations with other states, the signatory of its treaties and its embodiment on all ceremonial occasions. He was, more significantly, the actual head of its Government and the shaper of its policy; for he was the harmoniser of group interests and the guardian of the national interest. He chose the Prime Minister, with both stability and parliamentary support in mind, and changed him when necessary. But since this constitution is still the constitution of France it is appropriate to continue to describe it in the present tense. The President presides over cabinet meetings. He is the country's most prominent politician, defends the Government's policy before parliament and the nation (by the media), influences the parties in order to keep his Government in office and, most important, chooses the time for and manner of conducting a General Election. He is the fount of patronage; political, civil service, military, naval and judicial appointments all depend on him.

Yet the French state is two-headed, for the Prime Minister, though in form subordinate, in that he is chosen by the President and may be removed by him, is in practice an independent power in large areas of government activity, simply because there is too much business for even the most active and widely interested President to do. De Gaulle himself concentrated on foreign policy and his successive Prime Ministers, Michel Debré and Georges Pompidou, upon domestic and economic policy. In economic policy the Finance Minister is another force to be reckoned with.

The power of parliament was deliberately diminished. It remains a two-chamber body: the two chambers are now called the Senate and National Assembly. It can only meet twice a year for periods each of a stated length: eighty days from October 2 for the budget and ninety days from April 1 for legislation (five and a half months in all: as in so many respects a reminder of the Napoleonic Constitution, see Volume One, p. 176). Secondly, ministerial office and membership of the Assembly are declared by the constitution to be incompatible, in order to eliminate the ambition of rival members of the Assembly, thought to cause ministerial instability. A system of substitutes allows a member on becoming a Minister to continue to cultivate his constituency. Thirdly, since the constitution defines the scope of the Assembly's activity no one can any longer claim sovereignty for parliament. Some subjects are declared outside its legislative competence; on some it supplies guidance, on others fundamental principles, delegating to the Government the power to fill in details. Fourthly, it does not have control of its own timetable. The Government controls parliamentary time, presents its own version of a law to be passed and can impose the budget, if it is not passed within seventy days. Finally a motion of censure is the only way the constitution provides for bringing down a Government. Such a motion can only be voted on forty-eight hours after its introduction, that is, after a pause. It needs ten movers, who can then not move another such motion for a period, and has to be passed by a majority of the whole Assembly, so that absentees and abstainers are assumed to be for the Government.

The effect has been to bring a tendency forward towards polarisation between Government supporters, on one side, and an opposition on the other. The parties remain as before, loosely organised and ill-defined, except for the Communists and the Socialists. The CDS or Christian Democrats have succeeded the old MRP. Thus the National Assembly, though not all-powerful, must not be disparaged.

It has offered important amendments to legislation and succeeded in gaining them.

The constitution added a Constitutional Council of nine members to safeguard the constitution itself and the constitutional rights of citizens. It can only be activated by the President, the Prime Minister or members of the National Assembly. Ordinary citizens have, however, access, for a review of any decision which concerns them, to the Council of State, to which important powers are also given.

De Gaulle had made a speech at Bayeux on June 16, 1946, when the Constituent Assembly was about to produce for referendum the draft constitution which the referendum then rejected. In this speech he had already laid down the requirements of good institutions: 'It is, therefore,' he had said, 'the Head of the State, placed above parties, elected . . . in such a way as to make him President of the French Union [which was stillborn, see above, p. 248] at the same time as President of the Republic, it is from him that executive power must proceed. . . . It is his province to serve as arbitrator above political contingencies, either normally through the cabinet or otherwise, or at moments of serious confusion, by asking the country to make known its sovereign decision through elections.' These principles the constitution now embodied.

It appeared to be the Fifth Republic that finally cured France's inflation and combined an expanding economy with stability. De Gaulle left his Finance Minister to deal with economic problems in conjunction with the Prime Minister. The Finance Minister was Antoine Pinay, the author of the miracle of 1952, and he called in again Jacques Rueff, who had advised him then, as well as a committee of experts. The Third Monnet plan elaborated for 1958 had been abandoned, but an interim plan for 1960–61 was successfully applied. The 'nouveau franc' was introduced. This stabilised the franc by devaluing it by 17.5 per cent. Both taxes and social security payments were increased. An improved system for fixing agricultural subsidies was introduced and a good many controls and restrictions relaxed. The movement from agriculture to industry continued. So that by 1962 only 20 per cent as against 37 per cent in 1938 of France's working population were employed on the land. The fourth Monnet plan, for 1961–65, was introduced and nearly achieved its target of economic growth at the rate of 6 per cent a year. When inflation returned in 1962 and 1963, there was again industrial and agricultural unrest. De Gaulle dealt with it sharply. When the miners went on strike they were called up for their military service. It was the same device that Briand had used in 1910 and it was again effective. De Gaulle's popularity, however, fell sharply. Georges Pompidou was now Prime Minister and the Finance Minister was Giscard d'Estaing. They checked renewed inflation by the stabilisation plan of September 1963. The period as a whole saw a steady rise in real wages and in returns from agriculture and a widening improvement in the national standard of living. In 1965 de Gaulle stood for election as President for a second seven-year term. After 1962 and the settlement of the Algerian problem the sense of emergency had disappeared. The justification for firm government no longer existed. De Gaulle's popularity was not reinforced by the success of the economic policy for this aimed at distant satisfaction by means of immediate sacrifices. De Gaulle had tested his popularity in 1962, when the constitutional change, establishing the election of the President by universal suffrage, was submitted to a referendum. (The referendum was as characteristic of de Gaulle's style as it had been of Napoleon III's.) De Gaulle gained an overwhelming majority in 1962. In 1963 he would not have gained the same show of confidence. In 1965 he was unable to win re-election on the first ballot. There had been an attempt to put up the active and popular Mayor of Marseilles against him. The more successful opponents were François Mitterrand, the Socialist, and Jean Lecanuet, the Radical. He won in the second ballot against Mitterrand, but even then it was not an overwhelming victory.

After the declining birthrate of the nineteenth century had continued until 1940 (France in 1940 had a slightly lower population than her 40.6 million of 1900), France had at last attained a rising rate. She was a more dynamic country. In 1958 she had a population of 44.5 million. Between 1945 and 1965 her population increased more than it had done between 1830 and 1945. This carried with it a change in the structure of the population and an expansion of the 18–20-year age-group round about 1968 that was quite out of the ordinary. This put such pressure on higher education as to bring about the student unrest of that year. There was now, in 1969, a reform of the Senate and administrative reforms grouping the departments into regions for economic planning. In the fifth referendum of the Fifth Republic these were sanctioned by a small majority. De Gaulle believed he had exhausted his mission and resigned. He died in November 1970. The Fifth Republic survived his resignation and has now outlived him by a long enough period for it to seem permanent.

If this was the period of Charles de Gaulle in France it was the period of Konrad Adenauer in West Germany. As de Gaulle identified himself with France and France with himself, so Adenauer identified himself with West Germany and West Germany with himself. He was a Rhinelander from Cologne and had been chief Mayor (Oberbürgermeister) of his great city, a position which carried with it membership of the Prussian Upper House in the days of Imperial Germany. He had been a successful politician as a member of the Catholic Centre Party under the Weimar Republic. He had continued Mayor of Cologne. He had lived in forced retirement during the Nazi period and been interned in a concentration camp for some months in 1944. He, like de Gaulle, had the power of thinking consistently along the grain of the wood with a sure sense of what was possible.

To understand what Adenauer meant to Germany we must go back to the period of German reconstruction after the War. It will be recalled that in May 1945 the German state had collapsed. The four zones of occupation (agreed upon as long ago as 1943) became the one stable element in an otherwise fluid situation, the Control Council or Commission for all Germany only getting to work in the autumn. Allied decisions had to be taken quickly to deal with urgent practical problems in situations where discontinuity with the past was a deliberate aim, though it could not always be achieved. One set of problems related to food distribution, the restoration of public services and the rebuilding of communications. Another set of problems related to the care of displaced persons who included prisoners of war, people released from concentration camps and forced labour organisations, above all returning and homeless evacuees, and the ever-mounting flood of refugees from the east. Yet another set of problems related to house building, temporary or permanent, and the removal of rubble. In these problems, which were, of course, simultaneous and not successive, options of policy were hardly differentiated. Over the trial of war criminals, de-nazification and re-education, there were political options and they were differently selected in the four zones, especially different between the Soviet zone and the rest.

Political activity among Germans themselves was banned. Within a month of Germany's surrender it had, however, begun: on one side accepting discontinuity, on the other, seeking links with the Weimar Republic. Adenauer's party, the Christian Democratic Movement, accepted discontinuity and set itself, as its deliberately adopted purpose, to replace 'the materialist greed of the Third Reich by regard for the individual and his spiritual needs and by respect for life'; and to replace the Catholic character of the Centre Party of Imperial Germany and the Weimar Republic by confessional unity on a popular, mass, undogmatic basis. Informal committees arose spontaneously in Berlin, most large towns of the west, and in rural centres for wide areas. The guiding principles of the Cologne Committee were drawn up already in June; those of Frankfurt-am-Main in September. By December 1945 it was possible to convene all Christian Democratic leaders in Bad Godesberg. The outcome of their conference was the Christian Democratic Union. The word 'party' was deliberately, since it aimed at discontinuity, avoided. The Christian Socialist Union was its Bavarian counterpart. These were the origins of two political parties which still exist and still act together (CDU/CSU).

Kurt Schumacher (1895–1952) was a prominent SPD leader and journalist in Stuttgart during the Weimar Republic and an SPD member of the Reichstag from 1930 to 1933. In 1933 he was arrested and he spent most of the next ten years in Dachau concentration camp. His survival of that experience and of illness gave him an authority among Socialists that was quite out of the ordinary. He was able to grasp control of a Socialist revival which had begun spontaneously. Anti-fascist committees composed of Socialists and Communists, active before the War, set themselves up in Berlin and most large cities while political activity was still banned. Former Communists and Socialists were often given office by the military Commanders, looking for reliable men to do what needed to be done. They drew in their relatives, friends and party contacts. A network of contacts was easily revived from the Weimar Republic. Kurt Schumacher lived after his release in Hanover. From there he quickly made active his own network from his Stuttgart, his Reichstag and even his camp days. Hanover and Berlin became rival Socialist centres. We have already seen in chapter 15 how the SPD defeated the SED in the Berlin Election of 1946. In other words, Kurt Schumacher revived the pre-war Social Democratic Party. It differed in three respects from the CDU/CSU as it was to be under Konrad Adenauer. It rejected the view that all Germany's past was to be forgotten and condemned only Hitlerism and those Germans who had allowed themselves to be imposed upon. It did not recognise any particular debt to the Allies, nor any need to co-operate with them. It stood loyal to the historical German nation whose national life it wished to renew. Moreover, the Socialists returned to their pre-war close organisation—their first national congress took place on May 11, 1946—and had a leader in Schumacher whose authority was unquestioned. In April 1946, after the Berlin Election, the party was made illegal in the Soviet zone.

In their zones the British, American and French licensed the CDU/CSU, the SPD and various liberal groups which coalesced to form the Free Democrats (FDP). Various groups suspected of rightist ideas were refused licences. So three parties had spontaneously shaped themselves. The places for their debate were first provided when the *Länder* (see above, pp. 233 and 261) were organised in each zone. This was not the consequence of any single political decision, but an acceptance of German traditions as the only effective way to run the zones. Next, in a speech at Stuttgart in September 1946 the American Secretary of State proclaimed the American intention of restoring to the German people responsibility for their own affairs. As a first step the Americans set up an advisory council of leaders of the three *Länder* in their zone. In June 1946 Elections took place in the American zone for Constituent Assemblies in each of their *Länder*. In October, Elections were held for municipal and rural councils in the British zone for the British still believed, as they did in the nineteenth century, that *local* self-government was the true nursery of democracy. There followed successively, during 1946–47, Elections for the parliaments of Baden, Württemberg ar.d Bavaria (in the American zone) and for parliaments of the states in the British and French zones. Thus the arenas for political debate were made.

The Federal Republic still had to be made. The first step was the decision (June 1946) to set up a bi-zonal Economic Council; for the British and Americans had found it impossible to go on bearing the high costs of running their zones as two separate economies. The negotiations for amalgamating the three zones were difficult, because the French still cherished the hope of separating from the rest of Germany the Ruhr Basin and its industries. In January 1947 the bi-zonal Economic Council was at last achieved. A single administration of the two zones, from which the French found it increasingly difficult to hold aloof, was gradually shaped. The French were partially satisfied when the Saarland was economically associated with France, but made politically autonomous. A customs union with France remained until 1960, but the Saarland was politically reunited with Germany in 1955 after a referendum. If the bi-zonal administration was the first decisive step towards the single West German state, the second was the currency reform of 1948. This applied to all three western zones: the French had found it impossible to continue to hold aloof. We have already seen its importance. It will be recollected that it precipitated the Russian blockade of Berlin. The reform proved to be the basis of economic expansion in West Germany. Yet the greatest single cohesive factor of West Germany from 1948 to 1955 was the energy which its people universally applied to economic recovery, to the programme of social security and to making prosperity. It was not a Socialist economy which was achieved, but one stamped with the ideas of Ludwig Erhard. He was to be the first Federal Minister for Economic Affairs and later to succeed Adenauer as Chancellor. He shaped the economic policy of the CDU. His ideas, it was claimed, represented a compromise between state socialism, because some industries were nationalised, and private capitalism, because the basis of the economy was free competition between private enterprises. He called his ideal a social market economy,[1] because the State would protect the weaker members of society against economic monopolies and provide social security against poverty, unemployment and ill-health. It diverged most sharply from the Socialist ideal in there being no provision for state planning. Nearly all the Nazi controls over prices, wages and production remained abolished. The trade unions had been rendered politically neutral during the first year of the occupation and they did not re-enter politics. There was some provision for workers' participation in management and decision-making in various industries and post-

[1] G. Pridham, *Christian Democracy in Western Germany* (1977), p. 31.

war Germany was free from the strikes which were such a drag on the economy in France and Britain.

Political settlement had followed soon after the currency reform. The German Federal Republic existed from May 23, 1949, the date of the enactment of its constitution. A parliamentary council composed of delegates sent by the Governments of the eleven *Länder* had been convened and empowered to draw up a basic law for a single West German Federal Republic. It met under the Presidency of Konrad Adenauer in Bonn. The constitution which it drew up left considerable power in the hands of the States, as we may now call the *Länder*, whose interests were represented in the Federal Council (*Bundesrat*),the Upper House of a two-chamber parliament. It provided adequately, as the Bismarckian constitution had not, for a strong central financial power, central control of defence, economic and foreign policy. It strengthened the powers of the Chancellor at the expense of those of the President. The elective Chamber of the parliament (the *Bundestag*) was elected for a four-year legislative period, but if the Chancellor asked for a vote of confidence and failed to obtain it, he could ask the President for a dissolution and an appeal to the electorate. It was hoped that this provision would discourage the constant falls of Ministries which had occurred under the Weimar constitution. The Chancellor was to be the leader of the party with a majority in the Bundestag, he was to make his Ministry and to present it to the Bundestag for approval. Since this constitution is still that of West Germany, it is appropriate to continue in the present tense. Voting is in single-member constituencies, but each elector has two votes; the second vote he uses to vote for a party list, so that while avoiding complete proportional representation, which under the Weimar constitution had produced too many little parties, the Bundestag yet reflects the support for the different parties in the electorate.

On August 14, 1949, Elections took place for the first Bundestag of the Federal Republic. The electors returned a majority for the CDU. It was the largest single party in the Bundestag. It won election victories again in 1953 and 1957. It remained the governing party for two decades, though its majority fell away in the sixties. In 1966 it shared power with the Socialists and went into opposition in 1969. In 1949 Adenauer, however, negotiated a coalition cabinet after a preliminary meeting of CDU/CSU leaders at his home at Rhöndorf. He arranged to present to the Bundestag a cabinet of 13 members, 6 from the CDU, 2 from the CSU, 3 from the FDP and 2 from the German Party (right-wing). Theodor Heuss, the Chairman of the FDP, was elected President of the Republic by the Bundestag and Konrad Adenauer formally elected Chancellor on September 15, 1949. The sovereignty of the Federal Republic was a political fact and the military and punitive measures of the Allies ended. It did not become a juridical fact until May 5, 1955, after the ratification of the Paris Treaty of Peace. The state of war had ended on July 9, 1951. The revival of Germany's sovereignty was a success for Adenauer and a triumph for his policy of working with the occupying authorities and for the Christian Democratic movement which supported him.

Adenauer now also became Minister for Foreign Affairs. He continued the policy of co-operation with the western Allies and silence on the position of East Germany. He believed that Germany's hopes for the future depended on the achievement of a federated or united Europe. Only when both East and West Germany were equal members of a 'United Europe' could they find unity between themselves. It is interesting that the same line of thought made Flemings and Walloons in Belgium rest their hopes for greater recognition of their separate national identities also in 'United Europe.'

The idea of united Europe is, however, rooted in other needs than these. Three are especially important. And of these three the need for defence is the most important. Between 1945 and 1948 this was thought of in traditional terms or, in other words, in the same terms as during the War. As a result in March 1947 Britain and France made the Treaty of Dunkirk in which they promised to aid each other in the event of a revival of German aggression. On March 17, 1948, this was superseded by the Brussels Treaty Organisation. Britain, France, Belgium, Luxembourg and Holland guaranteed each other against any attack, set up a permanent consultative Council of Ambassadors and Officials and provided for periodic meetings of their Defence or Foreign Ministers. The Cold War, which began in 1947, had already made the idea of defence solely against a state in the heart of the continent, out of date. Defence came to mean defence against Soviet Russia, against a state, that is, on the perimeter instead of in the heart of Europe, one which could also be in conflict with the United States, one which was a land-minded state without a strong naval tradition and with a tendency to use its air force tactically, to aid its army, and not strategically. For nearly a century Russia had been on the defensive. She was so no longer. Her experience, in 1854–56, 1877–78, 1904–05 and after 1917, had been one of military defeat or humiliation. The Great Patriotic War of 1941–45 had broken the series. The passive hostility of the rest of the world which began in 1947 was implicit in this change and especially in the situation of 1945. When by 1948 Soviet Russia had consolidated her hold on the eastern bloc, the differences with the rest of Europe, subdued during the fight against Germany, reasserted themselves. The reassertion was encouraged by the profound distaste for Communism which appeared in the United States at about the same time. The consolidation of Soviet power in eastern Europe was more than the extension of Russian power. It was a victory for crusading Communism and there was no telling where the crusade would stop. The Berlin blockade (June 18, 1948–May 12, 1949) saw the unity of Europe in action. It was in action against the U.S.S.R. and its unity was supported by the resources of the United States. Success would have been impossible without them. When Nationalist China fell in 1949 and Communist China appeared as a possible ally of Soviet Russia, the assumption that European defence meant defence against Soviet Russia seemed to have been proved to be the correct assumption. In June 1950 Communist Korea invaded South Korea. The United States, with token support from Britain and France and other Allies and under the aegis of the United Nations, rushed to the South's defence. Under General MacArthur, the American forces regained the initiative for the South which advanced far into North Korea. China then came to the aid of the North Koreans and the United States were glad eventually to withdraw from the stalemate which ensued. With the truce of 1953 the war ended, but what had happened in the way of fastening upon Russia the role of potential aggressor and upon the United States that of Europe's permanent shield, could not be undone. The North Atlantic System had already been made and fitted neatly into this situation. The Atlantic Pact was signed on March 15, 1949, by all the Brussels Treaty states and the United States and Canada. The North Atlantic Treaty was signed on April 4, 1949, by the states of the Atlantic Pact together with Norway, Denmark, Iceland, Italy and Portugal. They constituted the North Atlantic Treaty Organisation (NATO). Greece and Turkey joined in February 1952. Within this organisation until 1960 the United States and Britain alone possessed nuclear weapons. During the Berlin blockade Britain made airfields available to American B-29 bombers and the atomic weapons they carried. When they were withdrawn, they were replaced with more up-to-date carriers. From Britain an atomic bomb could now be dropped behind the Iron Curtain. After the Warsaw Pact (above, p. 272) only Sweden, Austria, Switzerland and, possibly, Yugoslavia and Finland are neutral or non-aligned. This division of Europe faced Adenauer's Ministry from the beginning with the question not where do we stand—that was clear—but how can we stand unarmed as a member of a western alliance of which the essential bond is an obligation to consider 'an armed attack against one or more of them in Europe or America . . . [as] an attack against them all.' Adenauer, when the opportunity came, would accept rearmament.

The second root of European unity was economic. The European countries had already been drawn together into the OEEC (Organisation for European Economic Co-operation) by the treaty signed at Paris on April 16, 1948, by sixteen states for the convenient reception of Marshall Aid. George Marshall was the American Secretary of State who had offered American aid for the economic recovery of

Europe in 1947. But this was not the only economic root of European unity. There was a German as well as an American root. The control of German industry and the international authority controlling the Ruhr industry, set up after the Potsdam meeting in July 1945, must eventually decline. They had, indeed, become indefensible when once the German Federal Republic acted as a sovereign state. France and other countries saw that German industrial supremacy would be re-established and might again be turned to a military purpose unless German economic success could be absorbed into a single successful European economy. Idealism and interest combined in the persons of Jean Monnet, the inspirer, and Robert Schuman, the proposer of the European Coal and Steel Community. The idea had already been canvassed both in the consultative assembly of the Council of Europe, of which more presently, and in the economic committee for Europe of the United Nations, when Schuman sprang the proposal on a surprised press conference on May 9, 1950. 'The French Government proposed to place the total Franco-German production of coal and steel under a common authority in an organisation open to the participation of the other countries of Europe.' This was the first piece in a piece-by-piece approach to European economic unity. The difficulty of achieving even a customs union at one stroke was being simultaneously illustrated by the slow achievement of the Benelux customs union, first proposed in 1944 (see above, p. 235). Adenauer at once recognised the advantage to Germany of Schuman's proposal. It would mean the removal of the last vestige of foreign control over her basic industries; it would give her a status equal to that of other countries as a member of the authority administering the proposed community; it offered her reconciliation with France. On May 16, Adenauer in Germany's name welcomed the proposal. He had the support of the majority of parliament and nation, even though the SPD opposed the unification of Europe on a capitalist basis. So the European Coal and Steel Community came into existence as a community of the six who were the founder nations of the European Common Market in 1957: France, Germany, Belgium, Holland, Luxembourg and Italy. Britain did not join until 1973.

The third root of European unity was political. The movement for political unity had many inspirers. One thinks, however, especially of Paul-Henri Spaak, the gifted Belgian Foreign Minister of the thirties, Jean Monnet and Winston Churchill, who had referred to it in a famous broadcast speech on March 21, 1943, as well as at Fulton and Zürich in 1946. The movement, however, owed its vitality to the committees to support it which came into existence spontaneously in a number of countries at the same time. They attracted some of the greatest figures. In December 1947, after long negotiations, an international committee was set up to co-ordinate these various activities. The 'European Movement' was adopted as the name for the movement in all the countries. It organised the Congress of Europe which met at The Hague in May 1948 and brought together some eight hundred European personalities of those days. Further meetings followed at Brussels in February 1949 and Westminster in April 1949. The last, being concerned with financial and economic matters, came under the aegis of the European Organisation for Economic Co-operation which was a league of Governments. Next the Council of the Brussels Treaty Organisation, that is, the Foreign Ministers of Britain, France, Belgium, Holland and Luxembourg, acted to bring the movement effectively out of private hands. It approached the Foreign Ministers of Italy, Sweden, Norway, Denmark and Eire and, together with them, set up on January 28, 1949, the Council of Europe, which they then (May 5) endowed with a Statute. This defined its competence and divided it into two: a Committee of Ministers and a Consultative Assembly. The Assembly was at first composed of Members of Parliament of the member states. In 1951 they were chosen by the parliaments of the states; in 1979 they were elected by direct election by all the people of twenty-one countries of western Europe. Thus the inheritance of the old League of Nations seems to have been split: United Europe takes some part and the United Nations takes another part of it.

As far as Germany was concerned, Adenauer saw an opportunity here which again he was not slow to take. Again he took it without the support of the Socialists. Adenauer took the view, as he said at a Congress of the CDU in October 1950, that 'We belong to the west, not to Soviet Russia.' He accepted the division of Europe and renounced any idea of an independent initiative for Germany. The Socialist view was different. Socialists believed that militarily, economically and politically Germany should seek independence and belong neither to East nor West, but act as a bridge between the two.

Adenauer aligned the Federal Republic with the West and the West took further steps towards a common defence policy—at first over-ambitious—in 1950 to 1954. This, it will be recalled, was the time of the Korean War. The United States defended South Korea and the U.S.S.R. was sympathetic to North Korea. The United States had to take precautions lest this local war should become general. She wished to strengthen NATO. She began to press for a German contribution to it. In September 1950 the Council of Ministers of the NATO countries decided to ask Germany for a contribution. Thus the spectre of German militarism suddenly walked on to the stage. France had the strongest interest both in increasing the defences of the continent against the U.S.S.R. and in preventing the revival of a German national army and air force. Pleven, who was Prime Minister briefly between two Ministries of Henri Queuille, proposed to do both these two incompatible things. To do them he proposed a European Defence Community with a supra-national authority in command of a common European force comprising land and air forces made up of contingents from the signatory countries. Their contingents would comprise all their forces except those needed for overseas defence, so Germany, for example, would have no army outside the European Army. The Pleven scheme became the European Defence Community (EDC) of May 27, 1952. This was the date of the signature of a Treaty by France, Germany, Italy and the three Benelux countries.

The Treaty was climacteric in France, Britain and Germany. In all three it was a turning-point in thinking. The Communists and much of the Socialist Left in France, Britain and Germany were against the EDC as a matter of course. In France, de Gaulle and the RPF were the proponents of an alternative policy. They remembered that France was still allied to the Soviet Union and wished to lead Europe not against the U.S.S.R., but towards her, by a Confederation of National Armies which should include the Soviet Army. The Elections of 1951 intervened in France between the approval of the scheme and the ratification of the Treaty. The 121 RPF members in the new Assembly doomed the Pleven Ministry and its Treaty. In Britain commitments to the Commonwealth and to the United States stood in the way of agreement with the continentally-minded proponents of EDC. Nor was her new Conservative Government, which included Churchill, anxious to worsen relations with the U.S.S.R. In Germany Adenauer failed to consult both his colleagues and the CDU members of the Bundestag, either before signing the Treaty or during ratification proceedings. This may have been the natural behaviour of an autocratic man, but it probably reflected his sense that this was a forking of the ways, an irreversible step towards westward commitment and the acceptance of German division. The Treaty was in fact ratified by the Bundestag in May 1953. By contrast on August 30 the French National Assembly rejected it. Stalin had timed proposals for a reconsideration of German division to coincide with French, British and German debate about the Pleven scheme. This would seem to be further evidence of its importance to European-Soviet relations. Anyhow, EDC had now failed. In the meantime, of course, it had become less necessary, for Stalin had died in March 1953 and an armistice had been achieved in Korea in July 1953.

Adenauer in his foreign policy continued to aim at rearmament within a European framework and this he did attain. The signature on October 28, 1954, of the Treaties of Paris resulted in the inclusion of Germany, re-armed, within NATO. So Adenauer had succeeded. The first of these treaties recognised that legally the German Federal Republic was a sovereign state and exacted from her in return the maintenance of NATO forces on her soil. The second was between the G.F.R. and the Brussels Treaty Powers and prescribed the land forces which Britain, France and the G.F.R. were severally to supply for continental defence: 4 divisions from Britain, 14 from France and 12 from the G.F.R. The third Treaty was between the G.F.R. and the NATO Powers and integrated the G.F.R. into that system with a Declaration from the G.F.R. that she would not seek to bring about, by force, German reunification and a Declaration from her co-signatories that they would continue to aim at reunification. These three Treaties were duly ratified and entered into force in May 1955. The Paris Treaties represent a step towards European unity for defence, though not the long step EDC would have been, yet a practical step because they recognised the Anglo-American axis on which the machine necessarily turned as long as Britain and the United State monopolised, in the West, nuclear weapons.

The next step, indeed, related to nuclear power. A European Atomic Community of the principal users of atomic energy, of which France, but not Britain nor the G.F.R., was part was made by a Treaty of 1957. France safeguarded her right to make nuclear weapons within Euratom. She exploded her first bomb in 1960. Britian followed the line of co-operation with the United States, but did not succeed in maintaining equality with her. In October 1952 she had exploded her first atom bomb and in 1957 she exploded her first H-bomb. This was five years after America had done this. What was at stake after 1954—the year the United States lifted the MacMahon Act (1946), prohibiting the passing of nuclear information to other countries, in favour of Britain—was the use of nuclear weapons for the battlefield, the intermediate range ballistic missiles (IRBM), rockets with nuclear 'warheads' which were to be carried at first by aeroplanes but afterwards by submarines to ensure greater range. Britain planned to make the *Blue Streak* missile in 1955 which was carried by bomber, but abandoned it to buy from the United States. The sale of nuclear weapons by the United States to Britain was still proceeding in 1982. Meanwhile by another set of negotiations the banning of atomic tests was being pushed and would eventually reach a Treaty in 1963.

During the fifties European economic unity was also developing. The Council of Ministers of the European Coal and Steel Community, meeting at Messina in June 1955, took the first step on the initiative of the Benelux countries. They resolved on June 3, 1955, to set up a single economic community which would achieve, as well as a single market and a single external tariff, a harmonising of economic and social policies. A committee was accordingly set up under Paul-Henri Spaak of Belgium to work out acceptable ways and means. The report of this committee was a most able and thorough document. It formulated the philosophy of the Common Market as well as practical and comprehensive measures for achieving it. When the Council met again at Venice in May 1956 it was able to proceed to the formulation of two treaties: one for Euratom and the other for the EEC. In 1956 the Suez Canal crisis (see above, p. 252) showed how weak Europe was in face of determined opposition and gave urgency to attaining unity. At Rome on March 25, 1957, the Treaties for Euratom and the EEC were signed. They were ratified before the end of the year and came into force on January 1, 1959.

The members of the European Economic Community were the six countries: France, Italy, the Benelux countries and the G.F.R. Britain had not taken part in the negotiations. She had followed the separate policy of bringing about a free trade area within the world organisation for tariffs (GATT). GATT came under the United Nations Organisation. Britain with her American and Commonwealth commitments could not fit into the policy lines of her more continentally-minded neighbours. By the end of 1959 she had formed her own organisation of seven states: Britain, the three Scandinavian countries, Austria, Switzerland and Portugal (EFTA). Its scope was limited to removing tariffs on trade in industrial goods. This alternative to the EEC had little chance of survival after France, since 1958 again under de Gaulle, refused to join. Britain, therefore, applied to join the EEC in July 1961. Her membership was vetoed by de Gaulle, on January 14, 1963. Her second application was successful and she became part of the European Community together with Denmark and Eire in 1973. The original six became nine, in 1981 with the admission of Greece, ten, and later with the admission of Spain and Portugal, twelve.

Meanwhile Adenauer had proceeded with the German reconciliation with France. He was met half-way here by Guy Mollet. Mollet was Prime Minister of the Fourth Republic from February 2, 1956, to May 21, 1957, with a Socialist majority and a hope, at least, of stability. Reconciliation owed much to a conversation between these two men. But in 1958 de Gaulle returned to power. His return meant a return to the policy of grandeur. The greatness of France entitled her to claim the leadership of Europe and entitled her to lead Europe out of the orbit of the United States. He was eventually to resist American influence by withdrawing French forces from NATO (1966), but while the Algerian War was still weakening France he was content to find a counterpoise to the United States in the U.S.S.R. This policy made it difficult for Adenauer to continue to move towards France, for he could not afford to move away from the United States. He was now in his eighties and slower than he had been. Moreover, he had lost something of his authority in Germany when, in 1959, he first offered himself as a candidate for the Presidency and then stood down. Moreover, his foreign policy had been fiercely attacked in January and March 1958 in debates in the Bundestag. Yet Catholicism, personal admiration and a common regard for French culture, as well as a shared mistrust of Teutonic behaviour, drew Adenauer and de Gaulle together. Adenauer visited de Gaulle at Colombey-les-deux-Églises, where he lived, in September and de Gaulle came to Adenauer at Bad Kreuznach in November 1958. By the time of their second meeting, de Gaulle was identified with another difficulty. The French *rapprochement* with the Soviet Union had produced a Soviet initiative. On November 27, 1958, the U.S.S.R. proposed to end the four-Power régime in Berlin, to incorporate East Berlin in the German Democratic Republic and to establish a free, demilitarised West Berlin (the so-called Khrushchev ultimatum). The Soviet Union carried out its intentions in East Berlin—the Berlin Wall, built in 1961 resulted—but the United States, Britain and France held to their rights in West Berlin. De Gaulle had formulated the French view in a separate note. To move towards France seemed to Adenauer to involve movement towards the U.S.S.R. with unforeseeable implications in relation to German reunification.

The Berlin crisis, however, ended in Khrushchev visiting Eisenhower in Washington and Macmillan, the British Prime Minister, visiting Khrushchev in Moscow and a meeting of Heads of State in May 1959. This seemed a success for the Anglo-Saxons and a setback for de Gaulle. Then Khrushchev broke up the Summit meeting. The Russians had shot down an American military aircraft, a U-52, over Soviet territory and the United States mishandled their subsequent explanations of what it was doing there. Khrushchev had declared he could not negotiate with the United States while she continued to send espionage aeroplanes over Soviet territory and had withdrawn from the meeting. It then seemed as if de Gaulle might begin again his policy of approaching the U.S.S.R. in order to free Europe from the U.S.A. There was a further meeting between de Gaulle and Adenauer at Rambouillet between July 28 and 30, 1960.

This situation did not, however, last either. It seemed to Adenauer that he might after all have to make a choice between France and the United States. France was free of the Algerian War and no longer looked towards the U.S.S.R. as a counterpoise to the United States. In the same year, 1962, that France brought the Algerian trouble to an end, the U.S.S.R. was defeated by the United States when she tried to take advantage of a Communist takeover in Cuba to place nuclear missiles there. This further discouraged *rapprochement* with the U.S.S.R. President Kennedy who had succeeded Eisenhower seemed likely to make American influence stronger than ever in Europe. This encouraged in de Gaulle a firmer and more open opposition. If Adenauer had to choose between France and the United States, he would have to ask himself whether France could provide an adequate nuclear shield for Germany. France was building an independent nuclear force: the *force de frappe*, that is a force strong enough to strike once and strike anywhere, but not to retaliate in answer to the response. This was the period when the idea of the nuclear deterrent prevailed. The French force would be strong enough to deter any Power from making nuclear war, not strong enough to win such a war. In a nuclear war there would be no victors, so the object of possessing the *force de frappe* would be to prevent nuclear war. France made weapons accordingly under the plans of 1960–65 and 1965–70. Atomic bombs were produced to be carried by Mirage IVa aircraft of which France had sixty-two by 1967. They were capable of 2000 miles or more, but only when refuelled in the air by KC-135F tankers. These were purchased from the United States under an arrangement made by de Gaulle with President Kennedy in 1961. Solid fuel intermediate-range ballistic missiles (IRBMs) were installed in silos in Haute Provence. They had more powerful nuclear charges in their warheads than the atomic bombs. They were capable of going 1800 miles. (So that they had, in fact, a regional, rather than a global range.) It was planned to have the first squadron of nine missiles ready by 1971. Finally France planned a fleet of five nuclear-powered submarines armed with a battery of sixteen underwater IRBMs each. The *Redoutable* was launched in 1967 and the second in 1972. Two others were planned for 1976.

Whether France had the best return on the money she spent, or whether the *force de frappe* was capable of achieving its purpose, must be open to doubt. That France was refusing to join a security system which depended for success or failure upon the vagaries of the two super-Powers, and their mutual relationship, was certain. It was made more certain when she refused to sign the test-ban Treaty of 1963, to take part in the United Nations disarmament conference and to adhere to the nuclear non-proliferation Treaty and, finally, when she withdrew her forces from NATO in 1966. De Gaulle's intention was to lead a third European force in a world in which it would have the United States on one side and the U.S.S.R. on the other, both further advanced in nuclear technology than France or any other state in the proposed third force, and each with larger resources to invest in its nuclear programme.

Adenauer might well consider that there was a better alternative to following in the wake of France. Yet he kept Germany behind France until the end of his Chancellorship in 1963. Indeed, the climax of his policy, the Treaty of Friendship with France, was signed on January 22, 1963. It crowned his life's work of reconciliation. Germany's relationship with France lost the personal element when Ludwig Erhard succeeded Adenauer, and, when Kiesinger succeeded Erhard, it began to lose any political advantage it might once have had. After the Election of 1964 the SPD for the first time became a Government party. Willy Brandt became Foreign Minister and German foreign policy began to have an independent direction. De Gaulle lost the initiative which he had so far enjoyed in continental policy. Germany offered an alternative leader to European policy-makers. Germany embarked upon *Ostpolitik*, a policy of independent overtures to the eastern bloc. At the same time she sought to widen her nuclear shield with a proposal for a multilateral nuclear force. Thus de Gaulle had passed the peak of his success. This was perhaps his visit to Moscow in June 1966. It resulted in a number of agreements in the field of science and technology and perhaps some softening of the West German-Soviet antagonism. But all the gains of détente, whether initiated by de Gaulle or by Willy Brandt, were lost in the more dramatic events of the American involvement in Vietnam which began in 1964 and lasted until 1974, and the Czechoslovak rising of 1968. Germany remained during the seventies under Socialist Chancellors, but Willy Brandt lost his forward position in her affairs. Yet perhaps the most important gain for Germany, after all, was the outcome of his *Ostpolitik*: the West German-Polish Treaty of 1970. By this treaty West Germany recognised Poland's western frontier (the Oder-Neisse line) as permanent. To this extent, she achieved stability in central Europe, whatever her future relations with East Germany might be.

THREE PROBLEMS OF THE NINETEEN-EIGHTIES

It is appropriate in a volume in which so much space has been given to war and peace to take up this matter in the conclusion. It is, indeed, important to do so, since the place of war in international relations, because of the discovery of nuclear weapons, has changed.

It is easier than it used to be to engage in small wars, 'punitive actions' or precautionary occupations, even individual acts of terror ism; it is harder to use war, in the full sense, as a threat and so an instrument of policy. Nuclear weapons now exist and Europe has to live with that irreversible fact. It has, moreover, to live with two other facts: that their power of destruction is so great as to amount to a power of annihilation; that the possession of these weapons was for some time an American monopoly, that when that monopoly was broken, parity with America was obtained, not by any single western European country, but by the U.S.S.R. Thus Europe has lost, in one respect, some would say in the most critical respect, its independence. This is the chief reason why some assert that the history of Europe is now merged in global history or that events in western Europe are governed by the relationship between two (or if China is included, three) super-Powers outside western Europe, rather than by the wills of the several states which compose it. Thus consequent upon atomic power is not only the change in the meaning of war, but also a change in the status of Europe in the world. Economic and social change within the several European countries consequent upon the peaceful use of nuclear and other technology is still too ill-defined to admit of the summary discussion which is all a book concerned mainly with political history could give it.

Suffice it here, then, to indicate some of the implications of the use, or possible use, of atomic power in war. In the period 1945–49, under the impression of the dropping of the atomic bomb on two Japanese cities, it was thought that nuclear war was essentially total war, directed primarily at the heart of the state, at its cities where government and producing power resided. To bomb with atomic bombs was to bomb strategically, in the sense that the strategy of the bombing would by itself decide the outcome of the war. But during the same period the limitations upon the power to wage nuclear war came to be better understood. Bombs were tremendously costly to produce: only countries with unlimited resources and prepared to devote a large part of them to the production of atomic bombs and with the economic control and the organising ability to do so, could make atomic bombs. This became more obviously true as it came to be understood that only more than one bomb, indeed, only a stock-pile, as it was called, could assure their effective use. Large stockpiles were difficult to accumulate and not only would they be vulnerable to an enemy, but their explosion by an enemy attack would destroy the country where they had been accumulated. There were no stock-piles before 1947, when post-war production began in the United States. Secondly there was at that time no known defence against a nuclear attack. This made it difficult, when the United States should lose its monopoly, and there was no doubt that in time it would, ever to use the atomic weapon. For to trigger nuclear war, as the phrase went, by a nuclear attack was to bring destruction on oneself. This can be put another way by saying that because there was no defence the doctrine developed that the only answer to atomic attack was massive reprisal, and no country would provoke the kind of war in which attack could only be answered in that kind of way. Finally, as time went on, the carrier for delivering nuclear weapons shaped itself in men's minds as a third limitation on their use. The atomic bomb was first carried by the heavy American bomber, the B-29, with a long, but still limited, range. As long as it could not be delivered to any place in the world, or as long as it needed a springboard in Europe to be delivered to a European country, it could not be freely used.

After the immediate post-war period the basic conception of nuclear war as necessarily total war, in which the nuclear weapon must be strategically used, was gradually modified. The monopoly of the United States has not only been broken, but many states seem likely to obtain access to nuclear weapons of several kinds. Every one of the limiting conditions just listed has been disregarded or overcome. Stockpiles exist. Defences have been developed. Carriers with ever increasing range and ever lessening vulnerability are con-structed. The question asks itself whether the doctrine deduced from these conditions survives the disappearance of the conditions. The doctrine was the doctrine of deterrence. It was believed that the only use of nuclear war was to deter nuclear war, or, to write without the epigram, the only purpose of a stock of nuclear weapons was to threaten a possible attacker with nuclear reprisals and so to deter any state with nuclear weapons from provoking nuclear war. Is the pros-pect of annihilation as the consequence of nuclear war still so certain and so appalling that nuclear war can never happen?

It is difficult to treat separately the history of the interlocking subjects which it is necessary to examine in order to approach such a question. It will be best to give first the order in which countries other than the United States acquired nuclear weapons, although this will mean recapitulation, then to describe the further development of weapons and carriers, then to notice the investment of resources in defence and finally to consider what has been thought of the uses to which nuclear weapons may be put.

Already in 1947 the Russians initiated a programme of expenditure for producing nuclear weapons that could be used for purposes other than the total destruction of cities. These were at first nuclear weapons for use on the battlefield and later, in the 1950s, were rockets with nuclear warheads, which were called ballistic missiles and were of long enough range to be described as intercontinental. They proceeded at the same time with work on an atomic bomb and exploded their first two years later, in 1949. It was some years before they could be said to have a stock of any weapon. They had a vehicle similar to the American B-29 bomber for delivery and produced a medium-range bomber in 1955. By 1955–56 they were able to produce a bomber which could reach the United States at least on a one-way mission. By the fifties the United States had also initiated a programme for the production of ballistic missiles of intercontinental and intermediate range. By the mid fifties the United States had intercontinental ballistic missiles (ICBMs). Meanwhile she had also improved the range of her delivery vehicles. The B-29 had a range of 4000 miles. The B-36 which followed had a range of 8000 miles and reduced American dependence on overseas bases. It had the disadvantage of flying at very high altitudes. Next came in-flight fuelling. Fuelling in the air from air tankers would enable larger distances to be flown. The B-50, developed from the B-29 with a longer range, was preferred to the B-36 with its high altitude. But in 1955 the B-52 with the long range of the B-36, but without its high altitude, was operational. In short, from 1955 the U.S.S.R. and the U.S.A. went forward step for step with both ballistic weapons and delivery vehicles. By 1961 both had developed the nuclear powered submarine as the delivery weapon and preferred it as less vulnerable than the bomber. But by the end of the sixties both had also improved bombers, the U.S.A. now flying the B-70.

Moreover, during the same post-war period both developed a new type of bomb. The fusion or hydrogen bomb had a destructive power many times that of a fission bomb such as the first atom bomb.

In the fission bomb energy is released when heavy nuclei split. The principle of the fusion bomb is based on the energy released when the lightest atoms combine to form heavier atoms. To initiate this fusion process a considerable investment in energy is required; more than can normally be produced by artificial methods. However a sufficiently high temperature to cause fusion reactions with the heaviest isotopes of hydrogen (deuterium or tritium) can be created by the explosion of a uranium or plutonium fission bomb. There is no 'critical size' for the fusionable material; the amounts of the reacting elements included determine the size of the eventual explosion.[1]

The United States had a hydrogen bomb in 1952, the U.S.S.R. somewhat later, in 1953. But in another important area it was the U.S.S.R. which led. At the beginning of the fifties the Russians initiated a space programme. By a supreme effort and a concentration of resources, of which perhaps a totalitarian Power with a command economy is alone capable, they launched their first spaceship, the Sputnik, on October 4, 1957. The Russians thus gained the power to put a satellite in space. This was important in relation to war in that it enabled them to penetrate the offensive or the defensive system of the Unites States, to inform themselves of the sites of launching positions and stockpiles, for example, in so far at least as photography was able to supply such information. The Russians were two years before the Americans in orbiting a satellite which could take reconnaissance photographs. Both Powers had done this by early 1961.

The research which lay behind the production of the first atom bomb by the United States, as is well known, had owed as much to British as to American scientists. But Britain did not put money into the development of the atom bomb until after the return of Churchill to power in October 1951, though the decision to do so was taken by Attlee's Government. For Britain the possession of a bomb was the recognition of her scientific and technological superiority and numerical inferiority in manpower, and of the claim she still made to be a Great Power, but, above all, it was the great deterrent of nuclear attack on herself or on western Europe. Britain tested her first atomic bomb in October 1952. She had already sanctioned the stationing of delivery vehicles (American B-29s) on her territory during the Berlin crisis of 1948–49 and they were retained there until the sixties. By then they were for the delivery of intermediate-range ballistic missiles. The British development of atomic bombs increased, rather than diminished, her dependence on the United States. Indeed, it increased, rather than diminished, the dependence of NATO as a whole upon the United States. In 1958 the United States amended the MacMahon legislation, which prohibited the sharing of nuclear information, in favour of Britain. The United States thus became the senior partner in joint Anglo-Saxon devel-

---

[1] L. Freedman, *The Evolution of Nuclear Strategy* (1981), p. 65. The whole of this section is based on this book.

opment. Britain exploded her first hydrogen bomb in 1957. But the plan for the development of a ballistic missile was abandoned. Britain preferred to buy from the United States. She did not produce the ballistic missile *Blue Streak*, but in 1960 accepted the American offer to sell her *Skybolt*, an air-launched missile, instead. In return, she promised to make a base in Holy Island available for American submarines. In the end she did not purchase *Skybolt* either, since in 1962 the Americans cancelled its production, but in 1963 was purchasing *Polaris* submarine-launched missiles (*SLBMs*). This has continued, only being modified in the mid seventies by a change to the *Chevaline* warhead. In 1982, with the obsolescence of *Polaris* in view, she was committed to buy, as the basis of her nuclear system, the American SLBM Trident D-5. This missile, to be introduced in the early 1990s, is notable for its long range, its accuracy and the number of its warheads, of which it can have as many as fourteen.

France, as we have seen (above, p. 306), was led by de Gaulle into developing an independent nuclear capability as a means of lessening her dependence upon the United States. She began to develop a programme of nuclear missiles in 1958. She exploded her first atom bomb in 1960. She concentrated, however, as we have seen, on intermediate-range ballistic missiles and Mirage planes for their delivery and began at the end of the sixties a programme of submarine building with the object of developing a better carrier. In 1966 she withdrew French forces from the integrated NATO force as a means of emphasising her distaste for dependence on the United States. Yet such independence as she has is more formal than real, since her nuclear capability can, because of her limited resources, never do more than supplement that of one of the super-Powers and perhaps help to deter nuclear attack upon her own territory.

In October 1964 the Chinese detonated their first atom bomb, made second, third and fourth tests in 1965 and 1966 and in March/April 1967 exploded their first hydrogen bomb. The fourth Chinese nuclear device had, moreover, been carried by a missile. She has, therefore, entered into full nuclear competition with the U.S.S.R. and the U.S.A. There are those who think of her as the third super-Power and trace her effect on international relations in that capacity from the sixties onwards. Finally by the end of the seventies it seems likely that nuclear capability may be even more widely shared.

In noticing the order in which the several countries obtained nuclear capability most of what needs to be said of weapons and carriers has already been said. It remains to draw attention to the technological break-through which the arrival in 1955–56 of the intercontinental ballistic missile (ICBM) represented. This weapon was launched from a launching site—at first an exposed table, later a concealed table dug into the ground—and did not need a bomber to carry it, though it could be carried by one. Similarly the invention of the intermediate-range ballistic missile was a technological step, though a less considerable one. *Thor* and *Juno* had a range of 1500 miles and were deployed in Europe as the most advanced threat possible to the Soviet Union. The next step was to make the *Minuteman* ICBM which had the advantage of mobility and possible dispersal, which the first ICBMs had not had. When the next step was taken and it became possible to launch the ICBMs from submarines (1961) they became well-nigh invulnerable. It was now also possible to launch them from aircraft carriers at sea. From the 1960s until 1980 the United States kept the figure for its ICBMs at 1054 and for submarine-launched ballistic missiles (SLBMs) at 656. Missiles did not completely replace bombers and bombs, for with men in control, these last had advantages of accuracy and flexible use. Before 1969 came the next break-through with the arrival of the MIRVs. These were rockets with multiple warheads, capable of re-entry into the launching country. This weapon was first possessed by the United States, but a year or so later equally possessed by the U.S.S.R. After 1975 it became possible to make the cruise missile, a pilotless but guided aircraft with continuous propulsion. This was developed from the Germans' V-1 of the War of 1939–45, just as the ballistic missile was developed from their V-2. The cruise missile had the advantage of great accuracy, was able to operate at a variety of ranges, with either conventional or nuclear warheads, and from a variety of launching platforms, so that it had versatility as well as mobility. By the end of the seventies Russia had the cruise missile. Technology continues to add to the armouries of both super-Powers.

The search for defence against nuclear weapons began optimistically during the Truman administration in the United States on the assumption that historically every new weapon has, in the end, been countered by some new defence. But before 1961 defence was thought about in terms of possibilities such as the interception of the bombing force, its destruction before it left its base, the destruction of the stockpile of bombs, of bases and of supporting depots of fuel and other material before they could be used. But the best defence was still thought to be the power of massive retaliation, after the enemy had exhausted his nuclear capacity in his first strike. This was the situation through the whole of the Eisenhower Administration (1953–61). During the same period an anti-aircraft system was constructed. This involved a line of radar stations on sea and land to provide early warning from a distance, and a variety of guided interceptors with supporting control facilities to get them to the right place at the right time, and a national command and control machine. All this was, however, rendered out of date by the arrival of the ICBM, and was revised. The ICBMs could not be met by the interceptor missile planned for the bombers, because the trajectory of an incoming missile could not be detected and established quickly enough for them to be launched in time. At the end, then, of the Eisenhower Administration the only recourse was that of rendering one's nuclear armoury as invulnerable as possible. During McNamara's period as Secretary of State for Defence (1961–68) the United States gave some attention to the planning of fall-out shelters, that is, well-stocked shelters where people, some distance away (say, 13 miles) from the centre of a nuclear explosion, could wait days (or weeks) until any cloud of radioactive material released by the explosion had dispersed. The programme had been abandoned by 1965. Next the anti-ballistic missile (ABM) was developed in both the United States and Soviet Russia. The U.S.S.R. began to build in 1965 and the U.S.A. in 1967. But a complete ABM system was very costly and could not, in any event, provide a complete shield. It had only a limited success and was dropped in the U.S.S.R. in 1968 and by the U.S.A. after 1974. Neither *Sentinel*, directed against China, nor *Safeguard*, directed against the U.S.S.R., had proved acceptable.

These failures combined with the arms race between the super-Powers, to which technology was being applied, led to attention being more and more directed to the control of nuclear weapons by agreement. To this conclusion thinking about the use of nuclear weapons was by this time also pointing. We have said so far on this subject that the starting-point had been that the use of nuclear weapons was necessarily strategical and against civilians in cities and that the conclusion of such thinking was that the only use of nuclear weapons was to prevent nuclear war. But the starting-point does not obviously lead to the variety of ideas about nuclear war conceived today nor is the conclusion compatible with the variety of nuclear weapons now produced and deployed.

The notion of the unique destructive power of the nuclear bomb was weakened with time and reflection. It had not taken a nuclear bomb to deal out death as it had been dealt out at Dresden (above, p. 223). By 1947 those planning strategy and expenditure on nuclear weapons were planning for their use against armed forces. Counter-force use was especially prevalent in the thinking while Stalin and Eisenhower still lived. Thinking had thus returned to the position where war was fought between the armed representatives of nations and not between whole nations.

Moreover, thinking about the use of nuclear power had been rendered precise by the fixing upon the U.S.S.R. and upon the U.S.A. of the roles of predestined enemies. To remind ourselves how this happened is to understand the emotional, unquantifiable, perhaps irrational character of this predetermined hostility. It began when the U.S.S.R. withdrew from the plan for Europe's receiving economic aid from the U.S.A. through the Marshall Plan; it continued when she tried to extrude the three other Powers from Berlin (1948–49), having herself withdrawn from the *joint* occupation of Germany. At the same time there welled up in the U.S.A. a hatred and fear of Communism, exacerbated by the conviction that there was no limit to what Communists might do to extend the territory which they already controlled. In 1950–53 the United States fought a war against Communism in Korea of which the indecisive result increased her distaste. In 1958 Krushchev issued the 'ultimatum' which provoked the crisis in international relations over Berlin in 1961, when Kennedy was President in the U.S.A. The Berlin Wall was built and East Germany lost its only access to the West, but the three Powers and West Germany did not lose their access to West Berlin. In October 1962 the U.S.S.R. tried to establish launching sites for medium-range missiles (IRBMs) on Cuba, where a Communist régime had taken power and an American effort to expel it been a fiasco. The United States detected the missiles before the operation was complete and compelled the Soviet Union to withdraw them. The U.S.A. deployed B-47 bombers on civilian airfields which not only made clear her readiness to use force and eventually nuclear force, to compel the Russians to withdraw, but also put them into the position where they would have to attack civilian installations if they defied the U.S.A. to use force and would bring, by that step, total war nearer. Since the Russians failed in both their challenges to the United States under Kennedy, the doctrine of deterrence seemed to have been vindicated for the States. The Russians cannot have been assured from their side that it was vindicated for them, the more especially since under President Johnson the United States engaged in a fresh war against Communists. The war against Communists in Vietnam lasted from 1964 to 1974 and ended in an ignominious withdrawal. The Americans had not been prepared to finish it by nuclear war. The doctrine of deterrence was vindicated then for the Russians on their side too. It is not, then, surprising that thinking about nuclear war had come to be in terms of stalemate or stability.

Another thread should, however, be followed before the implications of this are indicated. Not only had the U.S.S.R. and the U.S.A. been established as the predestined enemies, but their technological competition had taken the form of an arms race between them. In this race first one and then the other had taken the lead. The United States had an uncontested lead at the start. By the mid fifties the Russians had caught up. They were soon in the lead. It was customary during 1957–62 for Americans to speak of a missile gap. By 1962 the Americans had caught up and by the end of the sixties had re-established superiority. In the early seventies there was again parity and by the mid seventies it is probable that the U.S.S.R. were again in the lead. It is not surprising that thinking about the use of nuclear weapons should change as the see-saw went up or down. In the United States, while her lead was uncontested, the fashion was to canvass the notion of the preventive strike. The United States should plan so as to be strong enough to annihilate an enemy before the enemy could destroy her. When the U.S.S.R. gained in nuclear strength the fashion changed. A pre-emptive strike was now spoken of. The United States should plan to be strong enough by a nuclear strike to control the uncertain factor. The enemy might survive such a nuclear attack, but it would be certain not to strike back. By the time the U.S.S.R. had gained parity and begun to overreach the U.S.A. the terms of discussion were those of 'first' and 'second' strike. The United States and, indeed, France too followed the line of thought that the enemy should be allowed to begin and to exhaust its strength in the 'first strike'. As long as one had strength to survive and saved it for the 'second strike', one's nuclear armament was sufficient. Before America regained parity and while the missile gap still existed, deterrence was less spoken of than the making of an equilibrium of terror. But from the idea of equilibrium in conflict came the idea of incomplete antagonism or the possibility of using the nuclear threat, not to prevent nuclear war, but to force an antagonist's compliance in a situation where neither side was ready in fact to resort to nuclear war. The threat, in other words, could be a political instrument. But this use of it raised the danger that mutual pressure exercised by the two antagonists on one another in the process of political bargaining might become so intense as in itself to precipitate nuclear war by what was called 'escalation'. The word was in general use by 1960. The flaw in thinking about nuclear war as possible to avert by preventing, through one's own dominance of choices, a kind of mechanical escalation was that it omitted the incalculable factor both in the enemy's decision and in one's own. One side or the other might take a decision *not* in accordance with sound reasoning or quantifiable information. One or other might be irrational, influenced by chance or might even prefer annihilation to giving way. This idea of escalation too went out of fashion. Throughout the later sixties the United States maintained its superiority, but the idea of the purpose of nuclear weapons was not now expressed in the word deterrence, but in the phrase 'mutually assured destruction'. This was first used in 1964 and quickly became current usage. It too was destined to go out of fashion. One was left then with all the incalculability of nuclear war, without any sure direction in planning a nuclear strategy.

The conclusion from these three trains of thought—about counterforce use, the arms race, and planning—has not in fact proved to be that the only use of nuclear war is to prevent nuclear war but, for the two super-Powers, that they should agree to limit the use of nuclear weapons and, for the less powerful members of the NATO alliance, that they should aim at a multi-lateral or perhaps a multi-national force to retain the maximum of flexibility compatible with the declining military expenditure of the sixties.

The phrase 'arms control' had become current already in the mid fifties. It was assumed that the conflict of national interest between the two super-Powers could not be removed by negotiation and yet it was thought that the method of conducting the conflict might be controlled. The word 'disarmament' with its association with the failures of the League of Nations was dropped; for it implied that nuclear weapons might be abolished and this was an idea no one in government was prepared to entertain after the forties. Outside Governments, movements to ban the bomb and the movement for nuclear disarmament were a mark of the late fifties and early sixties in both Europe and the United States, and had much public support especially in the fifties. They lost support in Europe during the sixties as expenditure on armaments declined and in the United States some of their supporters were deflected into opposition to the Vietnam War. Those who still adhered became in their desperation more extreme and extremism caused further supporters to fall away. To return to the Governments, at a point of parity about 1962 both super-Powers were ready for a negotiated agreement to control the use of nuclear arms. In 1963 they signed the partial test-ban treaty. It banned the atmospheric tests of nuclear explosives. Tests henceforward had to be underground. It was thought that the next step should be the banning of all tests, but this step was not taken. The United States proposed to the U.S.S.R. an agreement to ban the bombing of cities, but this was misinterpreted by the Russians and rejected. The Americans went forward to superiority while the Russians had difficulties with ICBMs and SLBMs. In February 1967 the United States, in a position of superiority under President Johnson, proposed to the U.S.S.R. strategic arms limitation talks (SALT). In November 1969, the U.S.A. now being under Nixon, two delegations met at Helsinki. It was not until 1972 that the first SALT treaty was signed. It made a substantial step forward. It was an interim five-year agreement. It was agreed to keep the numbers of missile launchers as they were but with an allowance for the momentum of the Soviet construction programme. Further, the United States was allowed 1054 ICBMs and 656 SLBMs—the number she had—and the Soviet Union 1409 ICBMs and 950 SLBMs, with a sub-limit of 308 'heavy' ICBMs. In other words, it had been agreed to offset Soviet superiority in numbers of missiles by American superiority in technology and bombers. Anti-ballistic missiles were limited on both sides, first to two systems each and then to one each. Negotiations for a permanent treaty then proceeded. In November 1974 President Ford and Secretary Brezhnev agreed on a framework for a new treaty. It would allow ceilings of 2400 strategic nuclear delivery vehicles

(SNDVs), that is bombers and missiles, and dealt with MIRVs by counting not warheads but MIRVed missiles for which a sub-ceiling would be set of 1320. This framework, however, was never transformed into a treaty. Two things prevented it: the Soviet Union produced a missile which disrupted the distinction between 'heavy' and 'light' ICBMs and the United States produced the cruise missile which was, at that time, a unilateral advantage with nothing to set against it on the other side. Negotiations, however, continued. In 1977, with President Carter and the Democrats in power in the U.S.A., a new framework was at last constructed. Two years of further negotiation turned this into a treaty. The second SALT treaty was still not permanent. It was to last only until 1985. It would limit SNDVs to 2250, with sub-limits on MIRVed missiles and bombers carrying air-launched cruise missiles (1320), on MIRVed missiles (1200), on MIRVed ICBMs (820) and 'heavy' MIRVed ICBMs (308). It was still necessary to put a number of unsolved problems including ground- and sea-launched cruise missiles and mobile missiles into a three-year protocol to allow time for more negotiation. By this time confidence in SALT had been much shaken. There were recriminations on both sides and SALT seemed to exacerbate East–West hostility and to stimulate the arms race rather than to relax it. It was already apparent that it would be difficult to collect the necessary two-thirds majority to ratify the treaty in the American Senate when the Soviet invasion of Afghanistan in January 1980 rendered this impossible. SALT has been abandoned and President Reagan in 1982 has made a fresh initiative with the Strategic Arms Reduction Talks (START).

Finally, to consider NATO means to go back to the early sixties when the range of missiles, of delivery vehicles and of satellite capability as it exists today had, in outline at least, been achieved. The Russians after the fall of Khrushchev were again under an ascendant military influence while the Americans were occupied in the Vietnam venture. Europe was in one of its least complacent attitudes in regard to NATO and defence. Europe was afraid of being a battlefield in a war provoked by the United States and its hostility to Communists. Such a war might well escalate from the Vietnam War and would be easier for the U.S.S.R. to fight in Europe. Europe was afraid of being deserted by the United States. If a different situation was postulated and a war arose out of some European nation's interest, unshared by America, Europe might be deserted, when it most needed American resources. Europe was conscious of an older tradition and longer experience and European nations, though none so much as the French, resented the American direction of NATO. European Governments wanted NATO to be neither completely dependent on nuclear weapons, nor completely dependent on conventional weapons, and NATO had had during its existence a bias first one way and then the other. Europe, moreover, liked none of the ways of solving the problem of forward defence, which was NATO's policy. The problem arose from NATO's undertaking to Germany, when she agreed to rearm, that no part of her territory should be surrendered to the enemy in the event of war, even if the object of such a surrender should be withdrawal to more defensible positions. In 1954 the Bonn Government had also undertaken not to manufacture in its territory any atomic weapons so that 'forward defence' had to be solved without an independent German nuclear armament, or, in other words, had to be solved through NATO. Finally, Europe, alert to the public discussion in the United States of the uses of nuclear weapons, was acutely aware, as the Americans seemed not to realise, that the success or failure of any strategic plan must ultimately depend on the political context in which it had to be implemented, when the time came. She had, therefore, little faith in planning which depended on the distinction between limited or general war, nor in the American notion of the 'firebreak', or essential pause between the use of conventional and of nuclear weapons. Such notions seemed abstruse and did nothing to encourage complacency.

The general policy of the United States by the end of the fifties had established itself as one of sharing nuclear power with NATO. At the end of 1960 in the last days of the Eisenhower Administration the United States offered to make 300 *Polaris* submarine missiles available to NATO and to put them under the control of NATO Council. Her object was to establish a NATO deterrent as the most effective answer to pressure from European countries—primarily, of course, France—for independent nuclear capability. A shared NATO nuclear force, called a multilateral force, distinct from the separate forces of the nuclear countries, was much under discussion. Its advantage was that it would spread the power to decide when to use nuclear weapons and prevent its being concentrated and centralised in the United States. It was Germany, with her undertaking not to become a nuclear country, who was most interested in schemes for a multilateral force. No scheme was, however, implemented and after about 1965 it was no longer under discussion. NATO claimed in 1967 that its strategy was one of 'a flexible and balanced range of appropriate responses, conventional and nuclear,' designed to deter aggression, but, if it occurred, 'to maintain the security of the North Atlantic Treaty area within the concept of forward defence.' But how far forward that defence was, was subject to interpretation. Moreover the NATO nuclear force of which the British *Polaris* and later *Polaris-Chevaline* missiles were a part, but the French IRBMs and Mirage delivery planes were not, was rather a multinational than a multilateral force, because Britain retained the power of deciding when her missiles should be used. The dispersal of decision-making better suited the situation of the seventies, when as the superiority of the U.S.S.R. increased and the United States fell back, it also became less certain that the U.S.S.R. was the only predestined enemy in all conditions. NATO seems better advised to rely on the psychology of uncertainty than upon the logic of certainty.

Now, at the beginning of the eighties, local wars are being fought both in Africa and Latin America in which Communist-aligned forces face non-Communists. But in Africa when Communist support had been given to one side American intervention on behalf of the other has not seemed likely. Conversely, in Latin America though the influence of the United States is exercised and intervention in a peace-keeping direction is always likely, Soviet intervention, since the Cuban missile incident of 1962, has not seemed likely. In a third area, the Middle East, there is not only war between two Muslim states, Iran and Iraq, which seems likely to remain local, but perennial war between Israelis and Arabs. Of all these conflicts it is this last which has most bearing on events in Europe. It has set up a pattern of terrorism in the Middle East which constantly extends to Europe. The Arabs have for some time looked to the U.S.S.R. and used Soviet arms whereas Israel claims some measure of American support. Israel is a state embedded in an arc of Arab states from Lebanon and Syria in the north, Jordan in the east to Eygpt in the south. The Arabs of what was once, not Israel, but Palestine, have no territory. They may be inhabitants of Israel, living among Jews whom they regard as intruders; they may be refugees living in refugee camps on the borders of Israel, in Lebanon chiefly, Syria or Jordan; they may be members of guerrilla forces organised by the Palestine Liberation Organisation with headquarters and strongholds in Lebanon or elsewhere or some other smaller organisation.

All these states were once part of the Ottoman Empire and to understand how the present situation has come about one must go back to the time when the Ottoman Empire and Persia were the political units of the Muslim Middle East. Under the influence of European ideas both became parliamentary states before the War of 1914–18. Persia, as Iran, continued after that war as a monarchy, cultivating modern ideas but expelling foreign advisers. The Ottoman Empire had disappeared, leaving a number of successor states. After the Treaty of Lausanne (1923) Turkey was a small compact Republic in Asia Minor, though with a foothold in Europe at Istanbul and some way beyond, under a single ruler. She so continued after the War of 1939–45, developing economically, but less stable internally being subject to military coups. Iran too failed to develop as a constitutional monarchy of a European type and at last (1980) deposed its monarch and yielded to a mood of religious revivalism. But to return to the successor states of the Ottoman Empire: the successor state east of Turkey was Iraq, formed out of three Ottoman provinces, Mosul, Baghdad and Basra, conquered and occupied by Britain during the War of 1914–18. It was placed by Britain under King Feisal, who had been evicted by the French from Syria. He was the third son of the Sherif Hussein of Mecca, Britain's dealings with whom are described above (p. 118). It was a centralised and, after 1925, parliamentary monarchy, ruled from Baghdad. Until 1932 it was a mandate of which Britain was the mandatory. After the mandate ended the state became the victim of military coups, the last of which, in 1941, put a pro-German régime into power. This led to British military intervention, which did not outlast the War. Iraq continued as before the War, now under the grandson of King Feisal I, until 1958. In July of that year King Feisal II, his relatives, the Prime Minister and his supporters were brutally assassinated and Iraq became a military Republic. At the opposite end of the old Ottoman Empire, its African extremity, lies the successor state of Egypt. Still nominally under Ottoman sovereignty, it passed from British occupation to a British protectorate in 1914. It became, in 1922, an independent parliamentary monarchy though defence, British imperial communications, foreign interests and the Anglo-Egyptian Soudan were still subject to British control. These matters were regulated by a fresh treaty in 1936 and, as we have seen, Egypt was the key to Allied control of North Africa during the War of 1939–45. King Farouk kept Egypt faithful to the British connection until King and parliamentary monarchy were overthrown in 1952. After a period of instability, Nasser's régime worked as a focal point of Arab nationalism in the Middle East. By a treaty of 1954 Britain gained independence for the Anglo-Egyptian Soudan but was to prove unable to safeguard any of her other former interests. The original agreement for the partition of the Ottoman Empire, the Sykes-Picot Agreement of May 1916 between Britain and France with Russia as an adherent, had not survived the making of the Turkish Republic and Iraq, let alone the Russian Revolution. But its collapse left the whole area between Egypt and Iraq difficult to settle. Saudi Arabia and Transjordan were made independent but the settlement which divided the rest of the area between two mandatories was not final. France was the mandatory of Lebanon and Syria, but in 1939 did not ratify the treaties, signed in 1936, which should have made them independent. Britain was the mandatory of Palestine and was faced here with an intractable problem. The future of Lebanon and Syria was settled by the events of 1940–45. When they passed under the régime of Vichy France, Britain, in June 1941, had ground for occupying Lebanon. A Free French contingent accompanied the invading force and Free France eventually governed Lebanon and Syria, after issuing a declaration promising complete independence at the end of the War. In 1943 Lebanon, and in 1946 Syria, became independent, both only after a clash with the French in which they were supported by the British. The future of Palestine was not, however, settled by the War and remained as intractable as ever.

The Palestine mandate had been extremely difficult to administer from the beginning. The mandatory was not obliged, as other mandatories elsewhere were obliged, to facilitate the progressive development of the country into an independent state, but instead was made 'responsible for putting into effect' the Balfour Declaration. This had taken the form of a letter to the President of the Zionist Organisation from Arthur Balfour, then British Foreign Secretary, written in November 1917. It read 'His Majesty's Government view with favour the establishment in Palestine of a National Home for the Jewish People, and will use their best endeavours to facilitate this object, it being understood that nothing shall be done which may prejudice the civil and religious rights of existing non-Jewish Communities in Palestine.' It will be readily understood that it was open to maximum and minimum interpretations. But the chief difficulty lay in adjusting the Declaration to the Letter of Sir Henry McMahon to Sherif Hussein, October 25, 1915. McMahon had replied to Hussein's claim of independence for the Arab people, defining the territory to which it applied, 'Great Britain is prepared to recognise and support the independence of the Arabs in all the regions within the limits demanded by the Sherif of Mecca' except the districts of Mersina and Alexandretta and the portion of Syria lying to the west of Damascus, Homs, Hama and Aleppo. This too was open to maximum and minimum interpretations and was claimed to exclude Palestine.

It was inevitable that Arab-speaking Muslims should resist Zionist colonisation in the British mandate of Palestine. They, early in the history of the mandate, protested and rioted against Jewish agricultural colonies. But the Arab population, as well as the Jewish, was increasing and the economic development of the country was most marked. It was British policy to keep immigration compatible with 'the economic absorptive capacity' of the country. This was a flexible phrase and, whatever it meant, British policy had to be imposed by a firm hand. The riots of 1929 (the Wailing Wall riots) were, nevertheless, serious. The agitation even so may have been an attempt to intimidate Britain into abandoning her Zionist commitment and when, on the one hand, the mandatory made it clear that it was not to be intimidated and, on the other hand, Jewish immigration fell off, it might have died down. It had had no chance to die down when the consequences of the advent of the Third Reich in Germany and of Italian aggressiveness in the Mediterranean affected the situation. Jewish immigration gained momentum rather than slackened and Britain, hard-pressed in the Mediterranean, could not afford to be so firm against the Arabs in Palestine. Arab agitation, therefore, increased and came to a head in a full-scale rebellion in 1936. A

Royal Commission under Lord Peel was set up and reported in 1937. It recommended, since the mandate was unworkable as it existed, that a small Jewish state should be set up in Palestine and the rest of Palestine joined to Transjordan. This form of partition was not acceptable as it stood. In February to March 1939 a Conference (called Round Table though Jewish and Arab delegates met separately), summoned by Britain, was in session. The importance of this was not in its achievement, for it reached no agreement, but that in seeking a basis for agreement Britain had recognised an Arab 'collectivity.' She invited to the Conference Iraq, Egypt, Saudi Arabia, Yemen and Transjordan. The White Paper of May 1939 published the resulting British proposals. These aimed at the establishment, step by step within ten years, of an independent Palestinian state, with Jewish, Arab and Mixed provinces and meanwhile limited Jewish immigration to 75,000 over the next five years. The proposals seemed to put end to all Jewish hopes just when Nazi persecution made their need greater than it had ever been. But the proposals were rejected by both sides. So the British mandate continued and after the War still continued. An Anglo-American committee appointed by President Truman and Prime Minister Attlee, agreed, at least, to the admission at once of 100,000 Jewish immigrants. By July 1946 new Anglo-American proposals held the field. These sketched out the basis for an independent Palestinian state composed of a Jewish and an Arab province, Jerusalem under independent control and the uninhabited Negev treated separately. Each province should manage its own affairs, including immigration, while a central government should be responsible for defence, foreign affairs and external trade regulation. The proposals were rejected by both Arab and Jewish organisations. It was at this point that the terrorism of the present situation began. (There had been isolated acts of terrorism before, and the Jewish so-called Stern Gang had been active during the War.) On the Jewish side there was an explosion in the King David Hotel which killed nearly 100 people. On the Arab side terrorism was less spectacular, but continued sporadically. Moreover, the Arab states imposed an effective boycott of Jewish industry and trade.

Britain appealed to the United Nations which reached a decision in favour of partition (November 19, 1947) and a commission, working to the date of May 15, 1948, was sent out to arrange it. At the same time Britain gave notice that she intended to surrender the mandate. It would be terminated not later than August 1, 1948, and British troops withdrawn. In fact, it ended in May when partition was completed. At once the Jewish National Council and the General Zionist Council declared the establishment of a Jewish state to be called Israel. Dr. Chaim Weizmann became its first President and David Ben-Gurion its first Prime Minister. It was immediately recognised by the United States (May 14) and by Soviet Russia (May 17).

When Israel was declared an independent state the United Nations proposals for partition were virtually overridden and there was no Arab province, nor, indeed, a Palestine. Israel was attacked by the surrounding Arab states. After the war between Arab and Jew in which an armistice was not achieved until May 1949, Israel was left with the frontier of the old British mandate, except for the Gaza strip and the West Bank of the river Jordan. It was only then that Britain recognised Israel. One of the terms of the truce was the incorporation of the Arab West Bank of the Jordan in Transjordan, which now changed its name to Jordan. The Gaza strip remained in the hands of Egypt.

In 1948 then Israel began its war-ridden existence. Never secure, by 1980 it had already lived through three periods of declared war, 1955–56, 1967 and 1973–78 and had in addition been responsible for continued insecurity in the Lebanon, which in 1958 and again in 1975–76 was torn by civil war. Yet there have been several attempts to control the situation. The first was by the Three-Power Declaration of May 25, 1950. Great Britain, France and the United States undertook to prevent the violation of the frontiers of Israel as they existed under the armistice of 1949. But the Arab boycott continued and Egypt built up her military strength and put military installations into the Gaza strip. The Declaration did nothing to stabilise the situation. Nor did the Baghdad Pact of 1955. This was a defence organisation arranged by Britain and the United States with Turkey, Iraq (who withdrew in 1959), Iran and Pakistan. It provided no control for the situation, because it was answered by Egypt's leading the Arab states in a nationalist movement increasingly aligned with the U.S.S.R. In September 1955 there was a flare-up in the Gaza strip, which Israel raided, destroying the Egyptian military installations but not remaining in occupation. The Gaza raid was on September 4. A few weeks later, on September 28, Egypt announced an arrangement with the U.S.S.R. whereby the Soviet Union bought part of the Egyptian cotton crop and agreed to supply, through Czechoslovakia, Russian arms in considerable amounts. Czechoslovakia also obtained Egyptian cotton and rice. The alignment of Egypt with the Communists was underlined when the United States repudiated her undertaking to finance the Aswan Dam which Egypt was committed to build.

Events now moved forward to the Suez crisis of 1956. The Egyptian seizure of the Canal, the property of an international company, caused a dispute between Egypt and the users of the Canal, represented by the British and French Governments. With this dispute as a background, Israel mobilised on October 27, 1956 and invaded the Sinai Peninsula on October 29. As in 1955 she was acting in retaliation to provocation, but the provocation was inevitable as the Arabs fought against dispossession—by 1949 there were already a million Jews in Israel—and found increasing cohesion—Syria backed the Egyptian closure of the Canal by cutting the pipeline bringing Iraqi oil to the Mediterranean—under Egyptian leadership.

The attempt by Britain and France to control the situation proved to be a spectacular demonstration of the relative loss of power by these two countries. They were unable to impose their decisions, when the United States withheld its support and was moreover supported by the Soviet Union: an unusual combination. On October 30, Britain and France issued an ultimatum calling upon both Egypt and Israel to suspend hostilities and to withdraw their forces from the Canal. They were given twelve hours in which to comply and told that, if either failed to do so, the British and French forces would occupy the key positions of Port Said, Ismailia and Suez. On October 31 Israel accepted, and Egypt rejected, the Anglo-French note. Hostilities, conducted from Cyprus, began against Egypt. Meanwhile Israel, but not Egypt, had been censured by the Security Council of the United Nations. Britain, supported by France but not by the United States, vetoed the resolution. The United States acted together with Soviet Russia, apparently, in favour of Egypt. There was a week of acute tension from November 1 to November 7. Events were dramatic. The Egyptian air-force was destroyed on November 4, British and French airborne forces landed at Port Said on November 5. There was a fresh United Nations' Resolution and on November 6 the British Cabinet decided to order British forces to cease fire unless they were attacked. The incident was over when British and French forces withdrew and their place was taken by a United Nations Emergency Force. The last British soldiers left on December 22. Before the end of the year Israeli troops were also withdrawn. They retained the Gaza strip, the Sharm el Sheikh heights and the head of the Gulf of Aqaba, where they developed the port of Eilat. Egypt, however, refused to open the Canal to British and French ships as long as Israel remained in Sinai. By March 1957 their withdrawal was completed and even the Gaza strip was clear. The United Nations Emergency Force moved in, step by step, as they withdrew. By April 1957 the Syrian pipeline and the Canal were open.

The year 1958 was the year of the Lebanon civil war. But it was a confused year with France holding aloof and Britain and the United States seeking a counterpoise to increasing Arab solidarity. On February 1, 1958, Arab solidarity was affirmed by the agreement of Egypt and Syria to form the United Arab Republic. Yemen announced a federal relationship with it. The Baghdad Pact Powers encouraged closer relations between Iraq, Jordan and Saudi Arabia as an answer. They were so far successful that Jordan and Iraq federated as the Arab Union. But after the coup of July 1958 in Iraq Britain and the United States could do no more: the Arab Union broke up, Iraq became part of the Arab bloc and next year left the

Baghdad Pact. Jordan was now dangerously exposed. She might well be absorbed in the U.A.R. So too might Lebanon. This state was now split apart by war between Christian and Muslim. Such was the effect of Arab national solidarity, for up to now Christian and Muslim had lived in harmony under President Camille Chamoun, a Christian, and his Prime Minister, a Muslim. The danger was that Lebanon would collapse as an independent state, for Egypt was stimulating the Muslims, and they were receiving Russian arms. Britain and the United States were both prepared to send military expeditions to maintain the independence of Jordan and Lebanon and, despite Russian opposition on the Security Council, they had the backing of the United Nations. The American troops landed at Beirut, Lebanon, on July 15 and were assured that a United Nations Emergency Force would take control in due course. Britain sent an expedition—flying over Israel with its assent to do so—to support King Hussein of Jordan. Israel assented to the over-flying under American pressure, but eventually failed to resist Russian pressure in the opposite sense and withdrew her assent. By then the Security Council had committed itself to a Resolution to maintain the independence of Jordan and Lebanon and American and British forces were withdrawn (October and November 1958).

The United Arab Republic had failed and Lebanon and Jordan maintained their stability for ten more years. During those years Arab terrorist organisations grew in strength, using Lebanon and Jordan as their headquarters. There were over a million Arab refugees in Lebanon, Syria, Jordan and Egypt and they provided the manpower for the PLO (Palestine Liberation Organisation) and other terrorist bands. Egyptian chauvinism exercised irresistible pressure on Jordan. So the events of 1956 were repeated in 1967. Israel again took pre-emptive action in order to preserve its freedom or to win security. The final provocation was a defence pact between Egypt and Jordan (May 1967) soon joined by Iraq (June 4). Israel launched and won the six-day war, the Yom Kippur War, in June 1967 against Egypt, Syria and Jordan. Jordan was despoiled of half its territory and Israel was again in occupation of Sinai and the Gaza strip, taken from Egypt, while from Syria it acquired the Golan Heights.

The next interval was somewhat shorter. Israel was again at war with Syria and Egypt in 1973. In 1974 there was the first disengagement agreement and Israel once more withdrew in 1975 from territory she had taken, a buffer zone being made in Sinai under United Nations supervision between Egypt and Israel and in the north between Israel and Syria. In 1976 Syria occupied bases in Lebanon and Israel invaded Lebanon. The Egyptian President and the Israeli Prime Minister signed the framework of an agreement at Camp David in the United States under the influence of the American President. This became a peace treaty on March 25, 1979. It has not,

327

however, kept the peace. Israel still fights for security and Arab organisations still recruit their strength to win back possession of a state of which they claim to have been despoiled. The interval between 1957 and 1967 was ten years, between 1967 and 1973 six years, between 1979 and 1982, when Israel has renewed war, only three years. Moreover, the involvement of the two super-Powers in what goes on has not declined, though the direct involvement of Europe may have diminished. The activity of the United Nations in each period of peace has been important. Where there is a will to peace it can clearly help, but it has not been able to prevent the renewal of war at ever-diminishing intervals.

European union within the United Nations would seem to some people to lie at the end of the road along which events have been moving since 1945. But countries are members of UNO individually as themselves and not collectively as part of united Europe. European 'unification' as distinct from 'united action' is perhaps as far away as ever it was, for there has been no real decline in national sovereignty since the War of 1939–45. Indeed in the seventies there has even been a slackening of the momentum of progress towards new areas of united European action. The period of the making of the European community ended with the sixties. It has been followed by consolidation, but without impetus. Nor is there any model for what is being aimed at. The most obvious thing observers see is a bureaucratic machine in Brussels, growing yearly more complicated. In the *Report on European Institutions* of October 1979, 6000 committee meetings are said to have taken place in one year. But this is how the business of discussion irons out differences and gradually assimilates European practices and policies, though, admittedly, many committees only prepare business for other committees. The point is that policies are put into gear with each other. They are not absorbed into a single European policy by the removal of national interests and the differences between them. This takes an enormous expenditure of effort, though perhaps not a disproportionate one. One must be clear about the limited character of what was intended to understand that, in fact, something substantial has been achieved. What is called, in the language of the community, the 'acquis', has been definitive and has been preserved.

To recapitulate then: the beginning was in a customs union. Outside the customs union other European countries made a free trade area. Next, the six members of the customs union made a common market among themselves for agricultural and industrial goods by the Treaty of Rome (1957). The free trade area did not succeed and the members of it, one after the other, have joined the common market. The Treaty of Rome and associated Treaties have been fulfilled both in their economic provisions and in those political provisions which related the economic community (EEC) to the already existing European Parliament and Council. But the Treaties left important areas of activity uncovered and these gaps, in the movement of capital and financial services, monetary policy and transport, are being filled. This is far from European unity. In relation to that meagre framework what has been done, though not supranational—that was checked by France during the period of de Gaulle—is yet a good deal of united action.

The Presidency of the European Community rotates among the member nations and is held by each for six months at a time. This determines who takes the chair at meetings of the European Council (Summit Meetings), of the Council of Ministers and of the various other Councils which are aspects of this body. The President is in a key position and determines the impetus and efficiency of the whole community while he holds office. His success in part depends on co-ordination up and down in preparation of business and follow-up of decisions, and outwards and inwards across different bodies concerned with the same topics. The President can make or mar such co-ordination. The relations of the Community's three primary institutions depend upon him, for he is the spokesman of the Council to Parliament and to the Commission. These are the three primary institutions of the European community: Council, Parliament and Commission. It is now thought to be important that the President should appear in Parliament, not only to answer questions, which he is bound to do by the Treaties, but to explain his priorities at the beginning of his term and to report on what has been done at the end of it. He is also the spokesman of the Community to the world outside it and is, therefore, especially important in political co-operation, called 'CoPo', in the Community's language. The Presidency supplies administrative resources from the country supplying the Presidency for the time being, but can also call upon the Community's resources, especially the Council's Secretariat.

The European Parliament is composed of 410 members, directly elected for the first time in June 1979 by the voters in each of twenty-one countries. Before 1979 there were 198 members nominated by the Parliaments of the European countries. Only a quarter of its members are now also members of the Parliaments of their own countries. As has been seen (above, p. 302) it antedates the European Economic Community (EEC) and represents all West European countries.[1] It meets in Strassburg for some six months in the year between July and December. It is not a legislature and does not appoint an executive. It debates and decides matters within its competence. The enactment of its decisions is the function of the Council

[1] Countries not in the EEC in 1984 but represented in the Parliament are Sweden, Norway, Iceland, Austria, Switzerland, Cyprus, Malta, Liechtenstein and Turkey. The position of Finland and Yugoslavia is indeterminate.

of Ministers. This must be so, since the Parliament relies on the Governments of the member countries to apply its decisions and these act together in the Council of Ministers. Between 1975 and 1978 the Council adopted 2481 acts. Parliament receives proposals for legislation from the Commission, whose duty it is to prepare them, through the Council. The present tendency is for Parliament to stand in a closer relationship with the Council than with the Commission, though the Rome Treaty intended that its relations with the Commission, which it can dismiss by a 2/3 majority, should be the closer. Some restriction is put on the competence of Parliament by the convention that matters of security and defence are strictly kept outside the range of the Community. The Rome Treaty (article 203) gave the European Parliament the power to reject the draft budget of the European Economic Community and to request a new budget to be drafted. It did not use this power until the Treaty amendments of 1970 and 1975 had given it control of non-obligatory expenditure and it had been directly elected. In December 1979, however, it rejected the EEC budget with the intention of deflecting expenditure from agriculture to regional, social and industrial policies and of bringing under its scrutiny EEC borrowing and lending activities and its aid to developing countries. The budget relates only to expenditure, for revenue comes automatically to the EEC from import duties and levies and from part of Value Added Tax. The revised budget was achieved. But the budget has a limited substance. It is not the budget of a federal Government. It is true a large part of expenditure is on the salaries of the bureaucracy and of the European Members of Parliament themselves. But otherwise expenditure is only on agreed policies, the bulk of it on the common agricultural policy. Individual member Governments, with their electorates in mind, tend to aim at contributing to European expenditure only in proportion to the gains they hope to derive from Europe. To put in as much only as you get out, is to leave nothing for European objects.

What used to be known as Summit Meetings have become the meetings of the European Council and been put (1974) on a regular, three-times-a-year basis. The European Council is as intimate and flexible in its behaviour as a national Cabinet. Attendance is limited to Prime Ministers and Foreign Ministers (virtually Heads of Government) of the ten member countries (twelve by 1984) of EEC together with the President of the Commission and one Vice-president and four observers (two each from the Council secretariat and the Presidency staff) for recording purposes. It is an institution not provided for in any Treaty so that it can act both within the Treaties and outside them. Though, since it is composed of Heads of Government, it is the highest organ of the Community, looked at in another way it is seen as an aspect of the Council of Ministers, which *is* provided for in the Treaty of Rome, but is also composed of

Ministers (Foreign Ministers usually), members of Governments and therefore, except in having specified functions, is much the same in authority. It has to fulfil duties entrusted to it by the Treaties, derives its power from the Treaties and has to act in accordance with procedures laid down in them. In this aspect it acts legislatively. It receives proposals from the Commission, reviews them and puts them to Parliament, receives them back accepted, amended or rejected. It then negotiates with Parliament on rejections and amendments and eventually adopts the resultant proposals which are then presumed enacted. But it also acts outside the Treaties and, since it is composed of members of the Governments of the member countries, it does a great deal of business outside the Treaties in the way of harmonising national interests. It has, however, to accommodate itself to the existence of the European Council and, now that this is on a regular basis, it is in danger of ceding business upwards to it and losing the key role which it must continue to play if the Community is not to lose impetus. It originally met as a General Council made up of Foreign Ministers, as a matter of convenience, since they were the Ministers in most countries who dealt with European business. When the Ministers are Foreign Ministers it can also meet as a Foreign Affairs Council on a level with other specialist councils. There are a number of specialist councils composed of appropriate Ministers as, for example, the Finance Council (Eco/Fin Council), the Agriculture Council and the most recent, the Energy Council. The Council of Ministers has a Secretariat which plays an important part in preserving continuity, seeing that rules are observed and business followed up.

The third member of the triangle is the European Commission. Its members are appointed by the Governments of the members of the European Economic Community. But it represents the European point of view as compared with the national points of view represented and harmonised in the Council of Ministers. 'Without the Commission the European Economic Community could never have been constructed. Without it, it could never function.' Under the Treaties it has the right of initiative. All legislative action takes place on the basis of its proposals coming up to Parliament through the Council of Ministers. It makes the proposals for the budget. It is drawn in to make revised proposals, if its original proposals for legislation, or the budget, are amended or rejected. It is the guardian of the Treaties and has the power to act on infringements of their provisions, to ban state aids, for example, which conflict with the provision on competition. According to the Treaties it is the executive arm of the EEC. It carries out through its members the enactments of the Council of Ministers. In July 1967 it absorbed the Commission of Euratom and the High Authority of the European Coal and Steel Community (the institutions antecedent to the EEC, above, p. 301) and inherited their functions. The Commission has declined from the high position and authority it had at first. As the Treaties were gradually fulfilled, the Commission had to enter new fields and here the Governments preferred to break the new ground themselves and work together initially outside the Commission. During the economic recession of the seventies and the financial and social troubles which it brought to each state, again national Governments have tended to try to harmonise national policies outside the Commission. Parliament tends, moreover, to take more notice of the Council as the enacting body, and less notice of the Commission than the Treaties intended. The Commission's standing, in short, is high or low according to whether the common European interest or the several national interests prevail. This is also reflected in the enactments coming to it for implementation from the Council of Ministers. It is likely that authority will come back to it, for the greater its authority, the better the EEC is likely to work.

The Commission, to the outside world, means the President of the Commission. He is a semi-permanent official, not a six-months presence. He is chosen personally by the Council or Ministers and attends the Meetings of the European Council as well as those of the Council of Ministers. Upon him falls the task of making the Commission a collegiate body, a true collective. He is a most important figure and it is sensible that his authority should be kept high, for he is the effective head of the whole bureaucracy of the European union. The office has been held by a succession of notable men. From 1958 to 1967 it was held by Walter Hallstein, an outstanding jurist, diplomat and linguist who left his mark upon the office. From 1976 to 1980 the office was held by Roy Jenkins. The commission can be dismissed as a whole by the Parliament on a 2/3 majority vote. When it takes office it prepares a programme and goes to Parliament to present this programme and takes part in debates, through its President or Commissioners selected by him. The President necessarily spends much time and energy managing the Commission's relations with Parliament.

In 1979, after the entry of Britain, Eire and Denmark in 1973, the Commission was a thirteen-man body, each of the thirteen having some specialist office. Nine members were appointed by each of the nine member countries and one more from each of the large states, Germany, France, Italy and Britain. It will be impossible to carry over this weighting into the new Commission after the entry of Greece, Portugal and Spain, without making it too big for each member to have a meaningful portfolio. There may well then be one from each member country and the President may be found within the number or added to it, to give twelve or thirteen members as the case may be. Each Commissioner has an appropriate office with a Director-General and staff. Examples of offices are those for industry, agriculture, monetary policy, finance and the budget, social affairs, aid to developing countries, external affairs, press and information services. All these have headquarters in Brussels.

The most important institution outside the triangle of Council, Parliament and Commission, is the Committee of Permanent Representatives (COREPER). This also works in Brussels. It is always in existence and is the instrument for preserving continuity and seeing that nothing is let slip. It has subordinate bodies and they and it take a great many decisions of a minor or routine kind. It prepares the work for the Council of Ministers. The Permanent Representatives or their deputies attend the meetings of the Council. They can also put points to it in writing, which can then be decided without debate, unless some state makes a last-minute objection. They are the pivots on which relations between the member Governments and the institutions of EEC turn. They are given instructions from their Governments which allow them to solve many problems by negotiating among themselves. Coreper routes business and distributes it appropriately among working parties and technical committees below it. There are a great many of these. Every decision in implementing some policy adopted by the Council of Ministers or the Commission, which in a single country could be the work of a single official, tends in this multiple Community to be the work of some committee. Examples are the Management Committee, Legislative Committee, Technical Progress Committee. There are in addition committees subordinate to the various specialised Councils, an agricultural committee, for example, under the Agricultural Council and several under the Eco/Fin Council.

The way the functioning of the Community is conditioned all through by its being a multiple and not a single body is well illustrated by its practice of avoiding a vote as a means of reaching a decision. United action is based on agreement, or consensus, to use the Community's language. Majority decisions are excluded from Coreper's activities and unanimity is prescribed by the Treaties in many fields. Only the most technical and unimportant things are decided by a vote. In 1967 the so-called Luxembourg Compromise—really an agreement to differ—laid it down that a member state could not be overridden on an essential national interest. Thus, by declaring something an essential national interest, a member country can bestow on itself the right of veto. In 1982 the rest of the Community has considered that Britain has used this right to the detriment of the common interest and has withheld the right of veto from her. The Luxembourg Compromise seemed to break down but has probably not been permanently lost. The principle, of which perhaps it was an extreme example, that national interests must be put in gear with each other and not overborne, is too important to be lost.

A further complicating factor in the machinery of the European Economic Community is its relationship to the undeveloped countries of the Third World. This began in a relationship to the countries of the old French colonial empire, was broadened, in 1973, to include the heritage of the British Empire and by 1979 covered all 58 countries of Africa, the Caribbean and the Pacific (ACP countries) with a population of 298.5 millions. They supply important foodstuffs and raw materials (including metals) for industry and can take machinery and manufactured goods. Relations have been governed by two conventions, signed at Lomé, capital of Togo, in 1974 and 1979.

There are a number of other institutions through which united European action can be taken. The European Court is a basic and indispensable institution. It has a close-knit, collegiate character and functions well, despite its burden of work. It acts in perfect independence from both Governments and EEC institutions. There is the Economic and Social Committee, set up by the Treaty of Rome as a consultative body, and a number of bodies which bring workers and employers together. In 1977 a Court of Auditors was set up.

The most important area of development in the history of European union as it stood at the end of the seventies is in the movement towards a European currency. It is argued that so much economic convergence has now happened as between the different member countries, that a single currency could now be introduced without unfairness. Indeed, a sort of currency exists in the 'écu' (European Currency Unit), a paper entry obtained by a kind of averaging out of the currencies. The pound sterling has a weighting, like each of the nine other currencies, in the currency credit, but Britain is not a member and the pound is not in the system. The first attempt to regulate exchange rates within some single system was prompted by France who under de Gaulle wished to escape from the control of the American dollar. But in 1968 there was a currency crisis in France with repercussions on Germany. A Franco-German initiative produced in 1969 the European Monetary Union. It was a union against the United States. But it failed when the Arab states placed an embargo on oil exports in 1973 and the price of oil rocketed. President Nixon had already taken measures which made the revision of European monetary arrangements desirable. EMU having died, a system to control the fluctuations of European currencies in terms of the dollar was set up known as 'the snake,' but when Europe entered the worst of the recession 'the snake' lost in turn the pound, the lira and the franc. In 1977 after a speech by Roy Jenkins at Florence and a new Franco-German initiative the so-called Bremen plan brought the present system into existence. This is EMS or the European Monetary System. But the single coinage, like much else, remains in 1982 a desirable objective. It, like everything else discussed in this Conclusion, raises the question whether Europe can survive as a separate community within the framework created by the super-Powers.

MAPS

1. Austria–Hungary in 1908

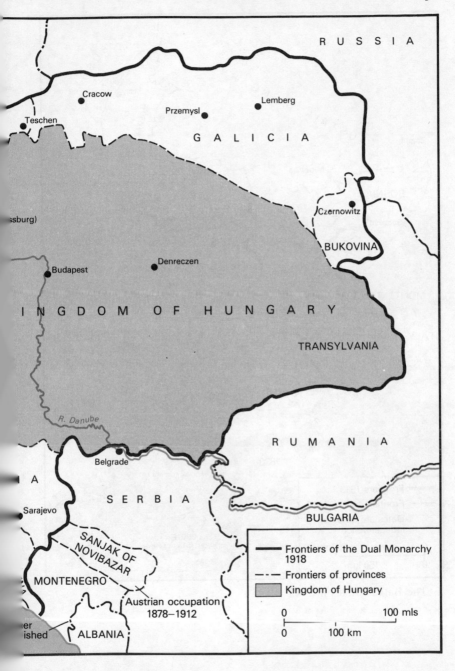

R U S S I A

Cracow

Lemberg

Teschen

Przemysl

G A L I C I A

ssburg)

Czernowitz

BUKOVINA

Budapest

Denreczen

I N G D O M   O F   H U N G A R Y

TRANSYLVANIA

R. Danube

Belgrade

R U M A N I A

A

S E R B I A

Sarajevo

BULGARIA

SANJAK OF
NOVIBAZAR

MONTENEGRO

Austrian occupation
1878–1912

er
ished

ALBANIA

Frontiers of the Dual Monarchy
1918

Frontiers of provinces

Kingdom of Hungary

0		100 mls
0	100 km	

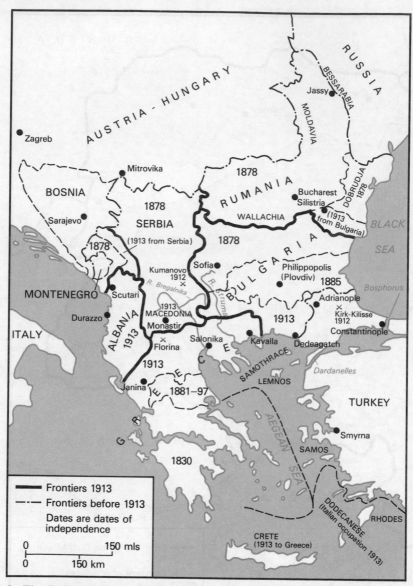

2. The Balkan States in 1913

3. The Eastern Front, 1914–16

Legend:
- Front in Winter 1914–15
- Russian losses to Germany
- Austrian losses to Russia
- Russian gains before 26 August 1914

0 — 100 mls
0 — 100 km

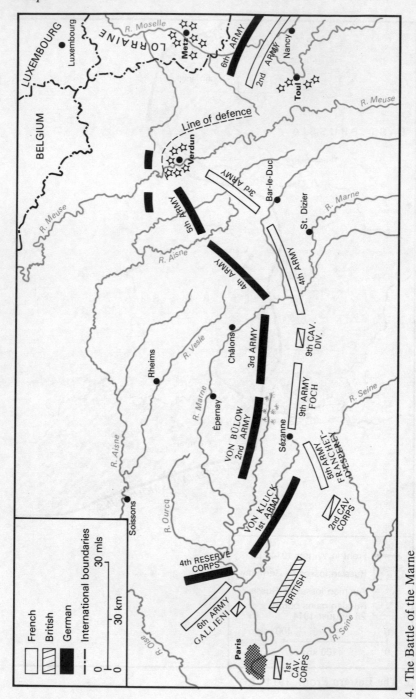

4. The Battle of the Marne

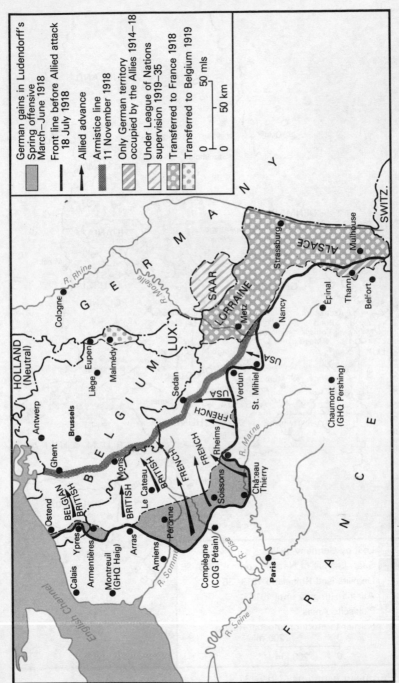

5. The Western Front, 1918, with changes of sovereignty in 1919

Legend:

German gains in Ludendorff's Spring offensive March–June 1918

Front line before Allied attack 18 July 1918

Allied advance

Armistice line 11 November 1918

Only German territory occupied by the Allies 1914–18

Under League of Nations supervision 1919–35

Transferred to France 1918

Transferred to Belgium 1919

50 km

50 mls

HOLLAND (Neutral)

GERMANY

BELGIUM

FRANCE

SWITZ.

LUX.

English Channel

R. Rhine

R. Moselle

R. Marne

R. Somme

R. Oise

R. Seine

Calais
Ostend
Ypres
Armentières
Montreuil (GHQ Haig)
Arras
Amiens
Compiègne (CQG Pétain)
Paris
Antwerp
Ghent
Brussels
Liège
Eupen
Malmédy
Mons
Le Cateau
Péronne
Soissons
Château Thierry
Rheims
Sedan
Verdun
St. Mihiel
Chaumont (GHQ Pershing)
Cologne
Nancy
Épinal
Thann
Belfort
Mulhouse
Strassburg
Metz

BELGIAN
BRITISH
BRITISH
FRENCH
FRENCH
FRENCH
USA
USA

SAAR
LORRAINE
ALSACE

Legend:
- Lost by Germany 1919
- Saar: League of Nations control 1919–35
- Demilitarised Rhineland 1919–36
- Austria-Hungary until 1918
- Plebiscite Areas
- Former territory of Imperial Russia

0   200 mls
0   200 km

6. European Frontiers, 1919–37

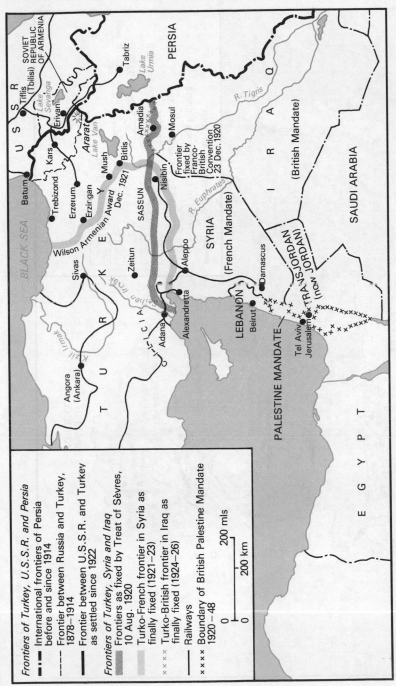

7. The Middle East. The Arab World

Legend:

Frontiers of Turkey, U.S.S.R. and Persia
— · — · International frontiers of Persia before and since 1914
— — — Frontier between Russia and Turkey, 1878–1914
———— Frontier between U.S.S.R. and Turkey as settled since 1922

Frontiers of Turkey, Syria and Iraq
Frontiers as fixed by Treaty of Sèvres, 10 Aug. 1920
Turko-French frontier in Syria as finally fixed (1921–23)
× × × × Turko-British frontier in Iraq as finally fixed (1924–26)
———— Railways
× × × × Boundary of British Palestine Mandate 1920–48

0 — 200 mls
0 — 200 km

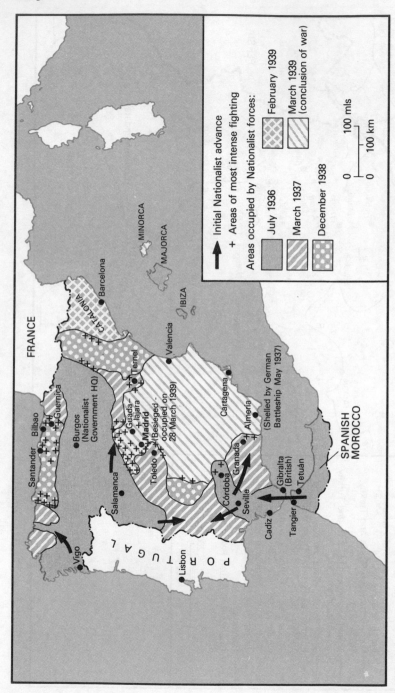

8. The Civil War in Spain

Initial Nationalist advance

+ Areas of most intense fighting

Areas occupied by Nationalist forces:

February 1939	
March 1939 (conclusion of war)	

July 1936	
March 1937	
December 1938	

100 mls

100 km

FRANCE

CATALONIA

Barcelona

MINORCA

MAJORCA

IBIZA

Valencia

Teruel

Guada-lajara

Madrid (Besieged - occupied on 28 March 1939)

Toledo

Cartagena

Almería

Granada

Córdoba

(Shelled by German Battleship May 1937)

Seville

Gibralta (British)

Tetuán

Cadiz

Tangier

SPANISH MOROCCO

Córdoba

Burgos (Nationalist Government HQ)

Guernica

Bilbao

Santander

Salamanca

Vigo

PORTUGAL

Lisbon

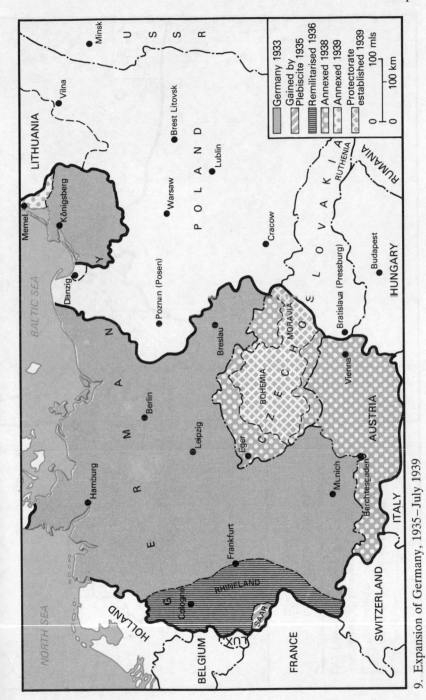

9. Expansion of Germany, 1935–July 1939

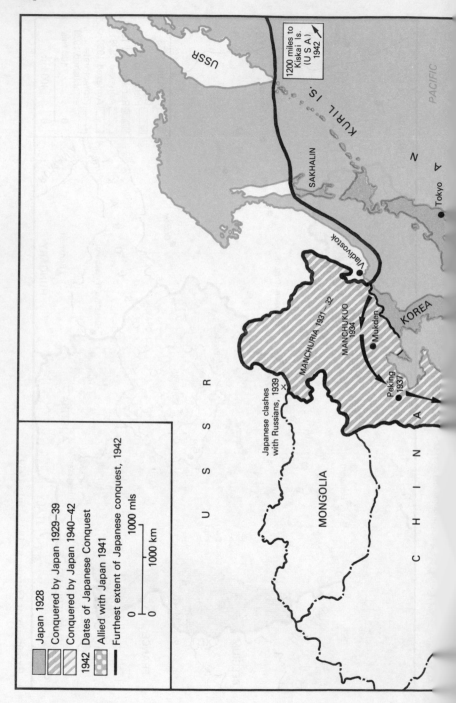

1200 miles to
Kiskai Is.
(U.S.A.)
1942

PACIFIC

USSR

KURIL IS.

SAKHALIN

N

Tokyo

Vladivostok

KOREA

MANCHURIA 1931–32

MANCHUKUO
1934

Mukden

Peking
1937

Japanese clashes
with Russians, 1939

U S S R

MONGOLIA

C H I N A

Japan 1928

Conquered by Japan 1929–39

Conquered by Japan 1940–42

Dates of Japanese Conquest

Allied with Japan 1941

Furthest extent of Japanese conquest, 1942

1942

0   1000 mls

0   1000 km

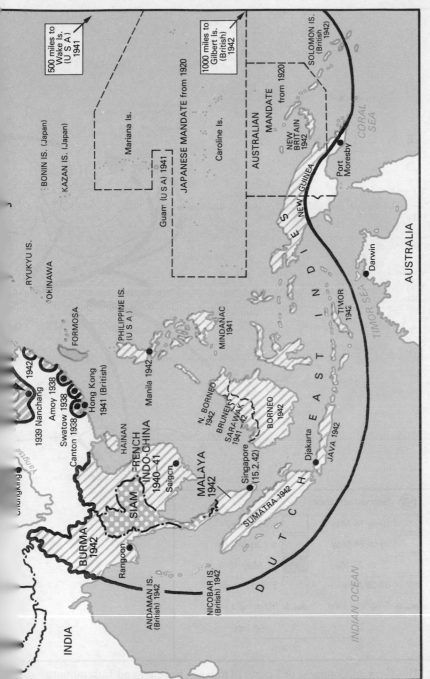

10. Expansion of Japan, 1931–42

Text labels on map:

500 miles to Wake Is. (U S A) 1941

1000 miles to Gilbert Is. (British) 1942

BONIN IS. (Japan)

KAZAN IS. (Japan)

Mariana Is.

JAPANESE MANDATE from 1920

Caroline Is.

Guam (U S A) 1941

AUSTRALIAN MANDATE from 1920

SOLOMON IS. (British) 1942

NEW BRITAIN 1942

CORAL SEA

Port Moresby

NEW GUINEA

AUSTRALIA

Darwin

TIMOR SEA

TIMOR 1942

RYUKYU IS.

OKINAWA

FORMOSA

PHILIPPINE IS. (U S A)

MINDANAO 1941

Manila 1942

1942

1939 Nanchang

Amoy 1938

Swatow 1938

Canton 1938

Hong Kong 1941 (British)

HAINAN

FRENCH INDO-CHINA 1940–41

Saigon

SIAM

BURMA 1942

MALAYA 1942

Singapore (15.2.42)

N. BORNEO 1942

BRUNEI SARAWAK 1941–42

BORNEO 1942

Djakarta

JAVA 1942

SUMATRA 1942

D U T C H   E A S T   I N D I E S

Yangtse

Chungking

Rangoon

ANDAMAN IS. (British) 1942

NICOBAR IS. (British) 1942

INDIA

INDIAN OCEAN

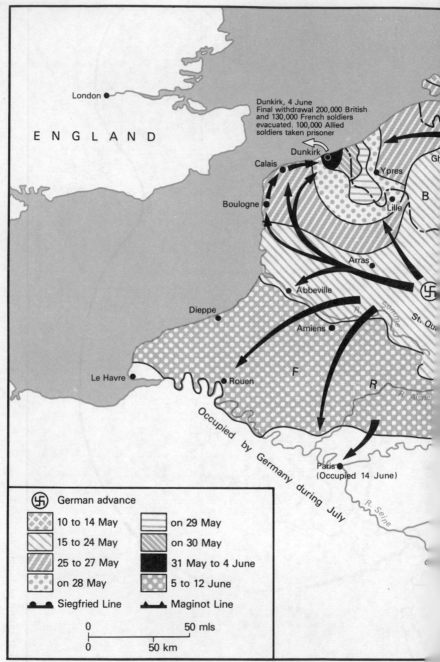

Dunkirk, 4 June
Final withdrawal 200,000 British
and 130,000 French soldiers
evacuated. 100,000 Allied
soldiers taken prisoner

ENGLAND

London

Dunkirk

Calais

Ypres

Boulogne

Lille

B

Arras

Abbeville

Dieppe

R. Somme

St. Qu

Amiens

Le Havre

Rouen

F

R

R. Aisne

Occupied by Germany during July

Paris
(Occupied 14 June)

R. Seine

German advance

10 to 14 May

on 29 May

15 to 24 May

on 30 May

25 to 27 May

31 May to 4 June

on 28 May

5 to 12 June

Siegfried Line

Maginot Line

0   50 mls

0   50 km

11. The German Conquest of France, Holland, Belgium and Luxembourg,
    1940

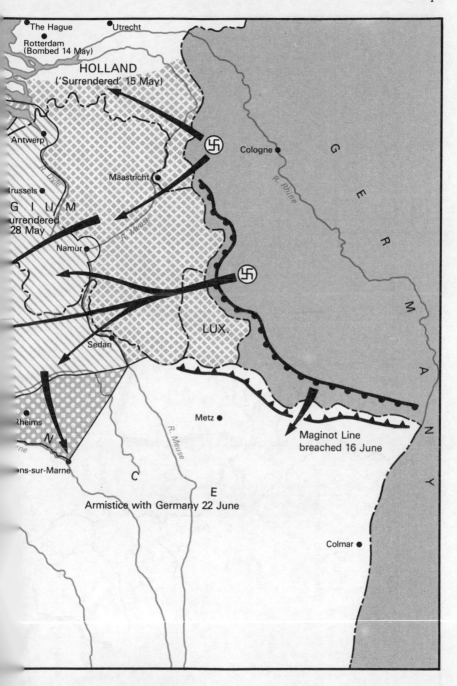

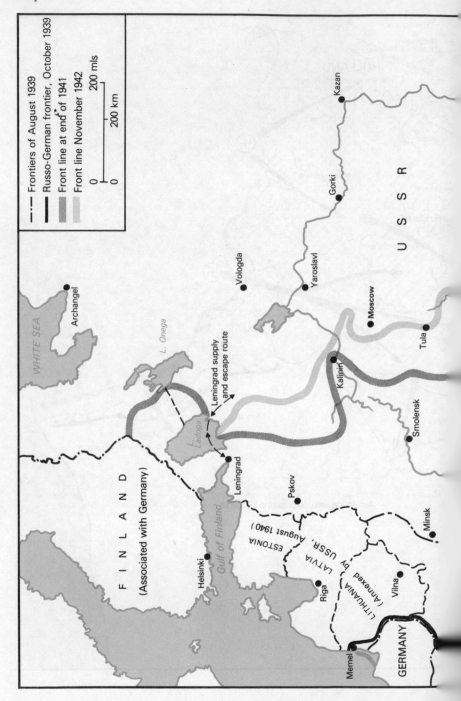

Maps

350

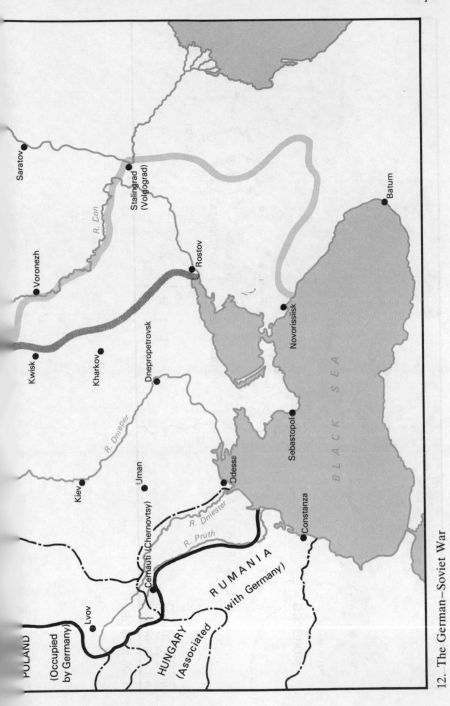

12. The German–Soviet War

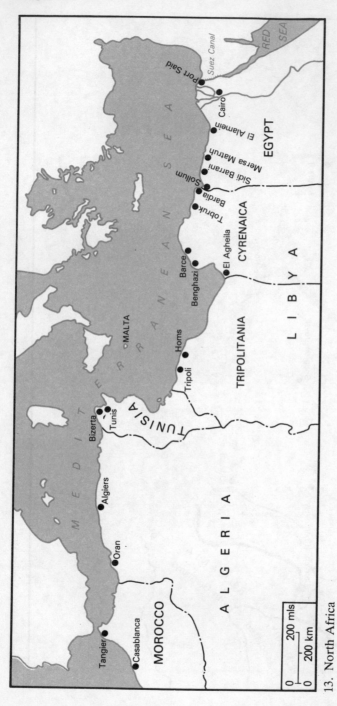

MEDITERRANEAN SEA

RED SEA

Suez Canal

Port Said

Cairo

El Alamein

Mersa Matruh

Sidi Barrani

Sollum

Bardia

Tobruk

Barce

El Agheila

Benghazi

CYRENAICA

EGYPT

LIBYA

MALTA

Homs

TRIPOLITANIA

Tripoli

Bizerta

Tunis

TUNISIA

Algiers

ALGERIA

Oran

Tangier

Casablanca

MOROCCO

0   200 mls
0   200 km

13. North Africa

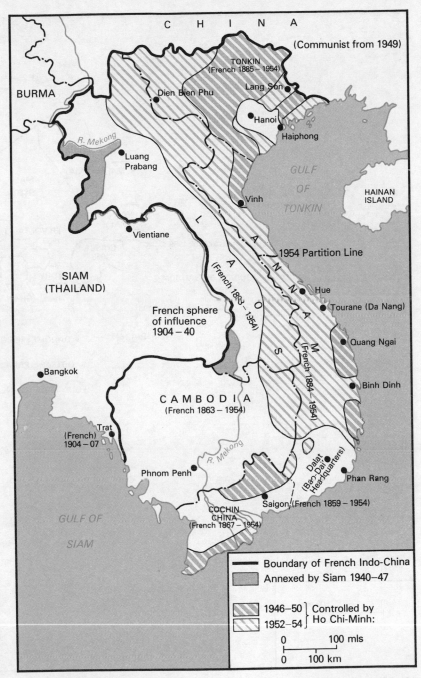

14. French Indo-China to 1954

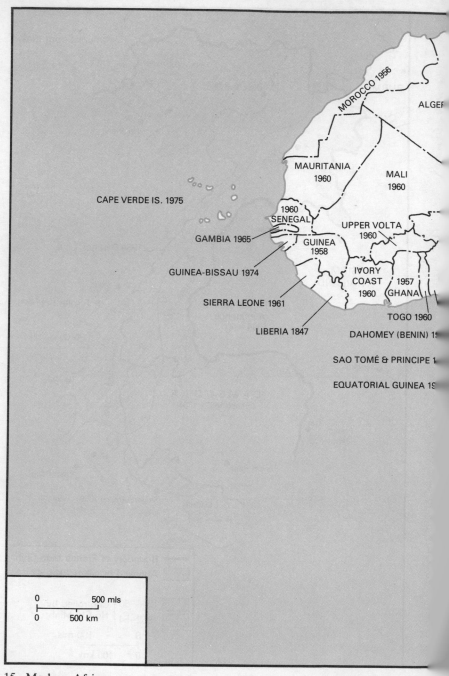

15. Modern Africa

INDEX

367

United States: at Algeciras, 19; and War of 1914–18, 78–9, 82, 86, 88, 89; and absence from the League of Nations, 93, 94, 173; and Turkish settlement, 113; and renunciation of war, 176; Washington Conference, 1921, 176–7; and Japan, 176, 177, 178; attends Disarmament Conference, 1932, 188; and German persecution of Jews, 199; and war of 1939–45, 215, 217, 222–3, 226–7, 228–9, 235; and war with Japan, 217–19, 229–30; war casualties, 231; enriched by the war, 232; German zone of occupation, 233; power of, 1945, 234, 235; nuclear capability of, 236, 309–12, 314; war in Korea and Vietnam, 238 271, 300, 308; administers Micronesia, 244; supports Pakistan over Kashmir, 245; and decolonisation, 247; and Suez Canal crisis, 252, 326; and U.S.S.R. 259–61, 306, 316–17; Europe's permanent shield, 300; NATO, 300, 302–3; and nuclear power, 304; defence against nuclear weapons, 314–15; and limitation of strategic arms (SALT), 318–19; policy towards European defence, 320–1; and Israel, 321, 324, 325; France and, 305–6

U.S.S.R. (Union of Soviet Socialist Republics), 1; constitution of the state, 129–30; under war communism, 131–2; New Economic Policy, 132–3, 134; economic planning and five-year plan, 132, 134–5; food procurements, 132, 133, 135–6; industrialisation, 133–4; achievements of by 1939, 137; supports Spartacists, 140; disturbed frontiers, 173; and League of Nations, 174, 175, 177, 180, 202; signs Kellogg Pact, 176; and Japan, 177; and intervention in Spanish Civil War, 184–6; attends Disarmament Conference, 1932, 188; and European policy, 191; negotiates with Britain and Germany, 1939, 205–6; invades Poland, 206; invaded by Germany, 1941, 207; defeats Germany, 216–17, 223–4; war against Japan, 228, 230; power in 1945, 228–9, 235, 236; German zone of occupation, 1945, 233; territorial acquisitions by 1945, 236; army not

demobilised in 1945, 236; and UNO, 237; supports India over Kashmir, 245; recognises Democratic Republic of Vietnam, 250; breach with U.S.A., 259–61, 280; and Marshall aid, 259; in Korea and Austria, 260; in East Germany, 261–3; in Poland, 263; and Yugoslavia, 265, 279; in Czechoslovakia, 266; power in Eastern bloc stable, 267–8; de-Stalinisation, 269–80; nuclear capability of, 236, 271, 309, 311–12, 314; military intervention in states of the eastern bloc, 272, 275–6, 282, 284–5; relations with China, 277–8, 279–80; assumed to be the enemy of western Powers, 299–300, 315–16; France and, 305–6; and Berlin Wall, 306, 316; and U.S. military aircraft (U-52), 306; space programme, 310; defence against nuclear weapons, 315; arms race with U.S.A., 316–17; and limitation of strategic arms (SALT), 318–19; and Arab movement, 321, 325; acts with U.S.A. over Suez Canal, 326

Venizelos, E., 40, 43 *n*, 80–1, 112–13, 114
Victor Emmanuel III, King of Italy, 1900–46, 157, 164, 165, 167, 222, 226
Vietminh, 249, 251
Vietnam, 248–51
Vietnam War, 1964–74, 238, 251, 280, 308, 316, 318
Viviani, R., 17, 52, 53

Wagner, Richard, the Younger, 193
Wallachia, 77
War, as an instrument of policy, 309
'War-guilt', 9, 101
War, nuclear, 272, 309–11, 317; counter-force, 315; defence (ABM) system, 314–15; deterrence, 310, 312, 316; equilibrium of terror, 317; escalation, 317; massive retaliation, 310, 312; mutually assured destruction, 317
War of 1914–18, 1, 212, 213, 234, 236, Chapter 3, 321; *see also* Battles and Sieges
War of 1939–45, 1; radar, 209, 214, 223; direction-finding beams, 209, 214; *Blitzkrieg*, 210, 216; dive-bombing, 210, 212; Eben Emaël taken, 211; evacuation from Dunkirk, 212;

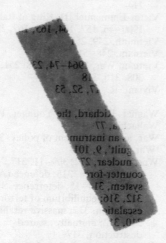